# LAND PROBLEMS AND POLICIES

# LAND PROBLEMS AND POLICIES

V. WEBSTER JOHNSON

Formerly Head of Division of Land Economics
United States Department of Agriculture

RALEIGH BARLOWE

Professor of Agricultural Economics
Michigan State College

NEW YORK    TORONTO    LONDON

McGRAW-HILL BOOK COMPANY, INC.

1954

# LAND PROBLEMS AND POLICIES

II

THE MAPLE PRESS COMPANY, YORK, PA.

**1113538**

*To*

LEWIS CECIL GRAY

A profound scholar and inspiring
leader with a crusading spirit for a land
policy vested with a social trust

# Preface

This book finds its beginnings in the work of Dr. Lewis C. Gray of the United States Department of Agriculture. While he was active in land-program work during the latter part of the 1930's, Dr. Gray outlined and started to write a book on land problems and policies. His plan called for 25 to 30 chapters, many of which were to deal with major types of land use. First drafts were prepared for a few of the chapters, and notes were assembled for others. Unfortunately, however, Dr. Gray found it necessary to forgo the completion of his original project.

During recent years, the senior author has had access to the materials that had been assembled by Dr. Gray and to a set of his papers and speeches. Dr. Gray was never able to review the use made of these materials; but his contribution to this analysis of our land problems and policies was very substantial. Indeed, without it, this book probably would not have been written. In this respect, considerable credit is due to Mrs. Gray for her help and cooperation in making these materials available.

Since the 1930's a great deal has happened in the field of land economics. The social and economic climate in which many things were said, written, and done has undergone marked change. Some of the emphasis in Dr. Gray's writings is not directly pertinent to land issues in the United States today. His concern, however, over land economics as "that field in which the focus of interest is land as an object or objects of human use, property or other relationships, and valuation considered primarily from the standpoint of social significance, with particular reference to collective or public policy" still defines the distinctive character of the field.

This book is concerned primarily with land problems and policies rather than with the theoretical framework of land economics. Attention has been given in a few chapters to brief statements of the economic principles that are involved in the analysis of particular land problems. It has not been the purpose of the authors in this volume, however, to provide a detailed discourse on the application of economic principles to the problems of land use. As a matter of fact, land economics deals largely with institutional controls and powers present in the holding and use of land, and these forces cannot be expressed in established economic principles.

Consideration is given in the first chapter to the nature and scope of our land problems and to the forces that have a significant effect upon land policies and programs. Historical perspective for many of our present land problems is provided in Chaps. 2 and 3. The first of these two chapters traces the rise of our present concept of land ownership and use rights, which were largely established during the colonial and precolonial period. Chapter 3 outlines the major public land disposal and settlement policies employed in the alienation of the public domain. Chapter 4 recognizes the turn of the present century as the breaking point in land policy, as the point in time at which the concern over land policy, which for a century had dealt almost exclusively with problems of public land disposal and land settlement, began to branch out to include the many fields now considered as aspects of land policy. These four chapters, together with the discussions of economic principles included in Chaps. 5 and 6, provide background material for the later chapters on specific land problems and policies. The particular problems treated are those of land-resource evaluation, conservation, population pressure against land resources, agricultural land requirements and production potentialities, the development and settlement of agricultural land, land tenure, the numerous institutional arrangements that have arisen from the impact of government programs on land use, land planning, and land reform.

In their presentation the authors have endeavored to set forth a balanced framework of thought and analysis, with occasional suggestions and observations, in regard to land problems and policies. No attempt has been made to find universal solutions, for such is not possible. The authors have been more concerned with the analysis of basic relationships than with descriptive detail, but they feel that the description presented is adequate to provide a framework of reference to major land-problem situations and suitable material for the discussions of these problems. It is recognized that some elaboration of these materials may be needed for class discussion purposes. It is suggested that discussion leaders, instructors, and students draw upon readily available supplementary materials, use current statistical information, and adapt their discussions to the specific problems of their local areas or regions.

The major responsibility for the planning and organization of this book and for the preparation of most of its chapters rests with the senior author. Chapters 4, 8, 10, and 11 were prepared by the junior author. Both authors, however, participated in the final review and revision of the entire manuscript. Chapters 2 and 3 are based largely upon manuscripts prepared by Dr. Gray, and extensive use has been made in a number of other chapters of materials and thoughts he developed. It is believed that this book well represents the thinking of Dr. Gray in the development of the field of land economics.

Throughout the preparation of this book, the authors have drawn freely upon the resources of the Division of Land Economics in the Bureau of Agricultural Economics, United States Department of Agriculture. Considerable use has been made of many valuable materials assembled in the Division over a period of several years. Valuable help and suggestions also have been provided by several people within the Division. For this assistance the authors express a warm sense of gratitude. Special recognition is due to Hugh H. Wooten for his joint participation in the preparation of the chapter on land requirements, for his contribution to the chapter on land settlement, and for supplying and checking the data on the present land-use situation and on the acquisition, disposition, and use of Federally owned lands. His contribution was most substantial. Special credit also is due Mark M. Regan who read and criticized several chapters; to Charles W. Loomer and John Muehlbeier for assistance on phases of public land policies; and to Miss Frances Jackson who carefully reviewed the chapters with respect to clarity of expression and presentation.

Besides the cooperation and helpful suggestions of our coworkers in the Division of Land Economics, the authors wish to acknowledge their debt of gratitude to Profs. Raymond J. Penn and Charles W. Loomer of the University of Wisconsin for the pertinent comments and suggestions they made in reviewing some of these chapters. The authors also wish to express their sincere appreciation to the many others who have helped in the preparation of this book.

V. Webster Johnson
Raleigh Barlowe

# Contents

CHAPTER 1    *Scope and Objectives*
               *of Land Problems and Policies*

Land policies, like other types of policy, necessarily reflect the economic, social, and political objectives of the nations in which they are formed. As the experience of the United States during the 1930's suggests, economic conditions may have a marked effect upon the nature of land policies and programs. Social conditions and objectives also may have an important effect, as even a simple comparison of the land policies developed under feudalism with those sponsored on the egalitarian frontier will show. Similarly, in a setting where nations are governed by a philosophy that calls for enhancement of national greatness and exaltation of power, and where the individual and his welfare are largely subordinated to these ends, the policies developed with respect to land usually will differ considerably from those in the free nations of the world.

Historically, the United States has passed the stage at which it appears desirable to employ land policies as a means of attracting immigration. In fact, our immigration policy not only definitely excludes certain immigrants, but also restricts the volume of immigration, with a view to avoiding overpopulation and surplus labor. This is a policy of significance in its influence on the character of land problems and practices in this country. It indicates that we are at a stage of relative maturity in resource development and exploitation and that free land no longer exists. We have also behind us the experience of industrial depression, as during the latter part of the 1920's and early 1930's, when a large part of the abnormal unemployment was thrown back on rural areas through the return of the unemployed to the farms. As many of the families returned to submarginal land areas, this was an additional factor in spotlighting the submarginal land problem of that period. In another area, the extent to which trade-agreement policies open up foreign markets for American farm products is of importance in determining and conditioning the character and success of adjustments in agricultural land use and tenure.

In this connection, the Marshall Plan and the International Wheat

1

Agreement are examples of political and economic weapons to foster international trade among the free nations of the world and to make for economic recovery, economic development, and rearmament in the interest of world peace and stability among nations. The present tension in the world also makes desirable the creation of agricultural stockpiles as a means of meeting possible future food shortages and exceptional demands upon our agricultural industry. These and similar conditions and programs are playing an increasing role in the evaluation of land resources and the use of land.

## Focus of Interest in Land Problems and Policies

In a discussion of land problems and policies in the United States, an understanding is necessary of certain basic concepts and the general focus of interest and its relation to the field of land economics.

*Nature of Land.* The farmer might conceive of land as the soil which he cultivates; the city dweller thinks of land in terms of factory sites or residential lots. But what of the minerals beneath the surface of the farmer's soil, the trees of his woodlot, the harbor of the city, the fish in the harbor, or the water power that turns the wheels of the factories? Economists have been inclined to employ the term "land" to include all of these. In fact, land may be defined as the resources provided by nature which are of present or potential significance for human welfare.

However, the resources provided by nature may be so changed by human action that in many respects they cease to have the character that nature gave them. The farmer's land may be seriously eroded, a building may be constructed on a city lot, a desert may be provided with water by irrigation works, and by construction of a reservoir and the installation of turbines river water may be transformed into an enormous source of power. In spite of these transformations in the resources nature has provided, the modified resources are important in the consideration of land problems and policies.

On the other hand, some natural resources may be so transformed by human action that they cease to be considered land in the sense of our definition. Thus, the fish in the harbor, after they are caught and canned, have passed beyond the realm of land problems and policies—and, likewise, the iron in an automobile or the chemical elements of the soil in our bread and meat. When natural objects have been materially changed through human action, we shall include them in the concept of land only when they continue to have an inseparable property relationship with a specific area of the earth's surface.

*Land Problems and Centers of Interest.* It would clearly be too narrow a conception to limit land problems merely to those matters that bear immediately on the physical character or condition of the land itself, as we have defined it. Thus the erosion of soil is clearly a land problem, but a workable solution to the problem usually involves much more than the development of methods of contour plowing or the construction of terraces. A great deal may depend, for instance, on whether the land is publicly or privately owned; whether it is operated by owners or by tenants, and if by tenants, on the kind of relationship between the tenant and his landlord; and whether farming is commercial or for subsistence.

On the other hand, in avoiding too narrow an attack on the problems which immediately relate to land, we may be led so far afield that we find our subject of land problems and policies comprising the entire field of economics, political science, and sociology, not to speak of the natural sciences. This would indeed be a *reductio ad absurdum*. For instance, the manner of using land and also its value are both significantly influenced by the prices of its products, and the student of land problems as such will find it necessary to take into account the influence of prices; but obviously the general subject of prices does not belong within the field of inquiry into land problems and policies. Likewise, taxation of land most assuredly affects the utilization of land and human relationships to land, but taxation as a general subject of inquiry is a different field.

Land problems are considered as those maladjustments that are a part of a confused situation in which land is a strategic factor—maladjustments which, if understood and corrected, would remove a part or the whole of the difficulty. Changes within man-to-man relationships that arise in land utilization and tenure arrangements are necessary if conflicts of interests are to be overcome or a problem is to be solved. Land economics deals largely with problems that involve policy decisions and often require some type of action. If it did not deal with this type of problem, it would be primarily descriptive in character and would represent a more or less formal type of statistical-collection process; very worth while indeed, but not too useful in the sense of searching for solutions to social conflicts or problems. "A conception of causes to be relevant in the problem and to have power in its solution must have its basic focus not upon present circumstances and their antecedents, but upon present possible courses of action and their probable consequence."[1]

The task of the land economist in studying current problems is first to isolate and clearly state problems, and then to present the best possible research results and evidence on means-consequence relationships that would be involved in alternative courses of action in problem solution, and thus to widen the basis for value judgments in regard to programs or policies for land improvement.[2]

[1] Erven J. Long, "Discussion," *Journal of Farm Economics*, Vol. 31, No. 4 (Part 2), p. 1112, November, 1949.

[2] V. Webster Johnson, "Problem Research," *Journal of Farm Economics*, Vol. 30, No. 3, p. 576, August, 1948. Also see Kenneth H. Parsons, "The Logical Foundation

Agricultural economists are particularly concerned with land economic problems that are within the agricultural sector of land economics, rather than with the urban sector of the field or such specific aspects as wildlife management in relation to land use. A brief listing of the principal problem situations or areas in the field which are of interest to rural economists should be helpful to further consideration of the nature of land problems, and also as an orientation to what is land economics—the over-all subject-matter field with which we are concerned. Specifically, some of the principal problem areas are:

1. Problems of major land uses and subclasses by use capabilities, productivity, or other purposeful groupings in relation to desirable uses, trends, and shifts in uses, *i.e.*, shifts of land from cotton production to grazing and recommended land classifications as approached or determined through economic analysis.

2. Conflicts of land utilization at the use margins, *i.e.*, with situations where relatively small changes in conditions cause rather wide change of uses, as on the forest-farm fringe, on the farm-urban fringe, and the farm-grazing fringe.

3. Considerations of the intensity of land uses and the effects of differing product price and cost conditions, varying efficiency or capacity of lands for production, and presence of scarce or limiting supplies of certain productive factors on the selection of profitable combinations of the factors of land, labor, capital, and management in the production process.

4. Problems of land development, land settlement, and land retirement programs, including consideration of needs and benefits and costs from the position of both the individual and the public.

5. Problems of land conservation considered from condition of resource base in relation to food and fiber needs, types of arrangements and inducements for achieving conservation, and particularly the social interests involved, rather than conservation as a phase of good farm management.

6. Problems in the use and control of water as an economic resource —irrigation, drainage, flood control—utilization and tenure aspects, and organizations and policies in the use and development of water resources.

7. Conflicts that arise in rights to occupy, use, and transfer land and in tenure patterns; problems in leasing land; and problem situations in regard to acquiring, maintaining, and transferring land ownership.

8. Situations in the land market and in farm real-estate rentals and relation of rents to land values; problems of land valuation, capitalization of benefit payments into land values, and economic feasibility of apprais-

of Economic Research," *Journal of Farm Economics*, Part 1, Vol. 31, No. 4, November, 1949.

ing land-improvement projects and planning activities; and studies of theory and principles of social evaluation of land resources.

9. Studies of tax burdens and tax policies and procedures in relation to land use and to local governmental structure and functions as a force conditioning land use and occupancy.

10. Problems associated with the development and control of suburban land uses—fringe areas around cities—*i.e.*, competition of uses and situations present in planning and zoning.

11. Problems associated with the selection, holding, and development of rural lands for long-term or future forest or recreational use.

12. Study of measures for affecting land uses, occupancy, and tenure that stem from custom, statutes, administrative measures, local ordinances, and public land-management practices, *i.e.*, grazing districts, soil-conservation districts, or rural zoning.

These centers of interest are not mutually exclusive nor are they all-inclusive of the field of rural land economics. Furthermore, they are problem areas in land economics to the extent that the land factor is strategic in social conflict. Specific problems lie within these areas; the areas themselves are not specific problems, but rather include different problems. For instance, in the field of land tenure, as outlined in item 7, there are many problems between landlords and tenants in the working out of equitable lease arrangements and in the passing of farms from one generation to the next as going concerns.

The field of study encompassed by the problem areas or situations presented has come to be known as rural land economics. With these problem areas in mind, let us try to generalize in regard to the nature and scope of the field and with reference to land problems and policies.

*Land Economics.* Attempts to define fields of work in the social sciences can readily result in a fruitless discussion over the meaning of words. It is well to recognize at the outset that no clear-cut lines of demarcation exist between areas of inquiry in the social sciences. Rather the several areas exist as bands of interest that overlap one another. The distinctive features of each discipline are marked by centers of interest in problems and also to a degree by research methods and procedures commonly used. One of the distinctive characteristics of land economics is its social or group aspects.

The breakdown of the social sciences into the major fields of political science, economics, sociology, anthropology, history, and psychology is now generally accepted. There is a less clearly defined division of economics into subordinate fields, and within these a still less clearly established further specialization based upon economic functions, *e.g.*, agricultural marketing economist, agricultural land economist, farm management economist, and agricultural price economist. Historically, the field of economics has been subdivided in accordance with areas where problems lie and by economic functions considered. But there is no ideal, fixed, or master logic to determine a particular way of dividing up the field of economics or of agricultural economics.

Ely and Wehrwein[3] defined land economics as "the science which deals with the utilization of the earth's surface, or space, as conditioned by property and other institutions and which includes the use of natural forces and productive powers above and below that space over which the owner has property rights." They point out that the field is concerned primarily with economic problems that arise in the relationships among men in the utilization and control of natural resources. It is particularly important to note that they stress the relationships that arise among men rather than the relationship of man to land. In a somewhat similar manner, Renne says:[4] "Land economics focuses attention on situations and problems in which the use of land is the strategic, limiting, or decisive factor . . . the problems with which land economics is concerned are those associated with the institution of property in land."

The field of scientific inquiry which has come to be referred to as "land economics" is here defined as that field which is primarily concerned with man's economic use of the surface resources of the earth and with the physical, economic, and institutional relationships that affect, condition, and control his use of these resources.

As defined, the concept of land economics is both narrower and broader than the subject of agricultural economics: narrower because agricultural economics devotes attention to other subjects as well as to the economic aspects of land; broader in the sense that land economics is concerned with legal and social aspects as well as strictly economic relationships in respect to land. For instance, because of its concern with land policies it is necessary to consider aspects of legal and social relationships to a much greater degree than in other phases of agricultural economics. It is also broader than agricultural economics in that land economics deals with land problems outside of the agricultural sector of our economy, *i.e.*, urban lands, mineral lands, and recreational lands.

The land economist, starting with an interest in land and a preoccupation with land problems, tends to get into many of the related fields out of necessity. In other words, land economics must of necessity draw heavily on geography, law, taxation, political science, and other related fields. In incorporating the subject matter of these fields into the study of land problems, however, land economics emphasizes economic and man-to-man relationships.

[3] Richard T. Ely and George S. Wehrwein, *Land Economics*, p. vi, The Macmillan Company, New York, 1940.
[4] Roland R. Renne, *Land Economics*, pp. 6–7, Harper & Brothers, New York, 1947.

Land economics is primarily concerned with those economic factors and processes that affect man in his use of land. This concern is tempered by a keen appreciation of the operation of numerous institutional arrangements that also have considerable impact upon man's use of land resources. Accordingly, the land economist places heavy emphasis on the nature and distribution of property rights in land and on social evaluations of land uses. This emphasis distinguishes the interests of land economists from the interests of other economists in land. Inasmuch as land economists are significantly concerned with relations arising between individuals and between individuals and society in the use and control of land resources, public policies and programs also are an important phase of the field. The emphasis on public policy and group action springs partially from the fact that many of the principal land problems studied involve aspects of group or government action. This interest of land economists in the importance of property concepts and in the role played by public policy and public programs applies equally to considerations of land tenure as to land-utilization problems.

*Nature of Land Policies and Programs.* A policy is generally considered as a settled or defined course of action adopted and followed by a government, a group, or even by an individual. In a loose or broader sense, a policy might include also beliefs and principles and the vaguely defined urges that are never quite expressed as a settled or defined course of action. We are here primarily concerned, however, with land policy as expressed through Federal, state, or local governments. Being a new country with abundant resources, it is not surprising that we have not had a consistent and well-developed land policy. As a matter of fact, we should speak of land "policies" rather than land "policy," since there has hardly been any single integrated "policy" in the United States.[5] The policy of Congress to establish and to make concessions for family farms comes as near as anything in our history to the pronouncement of a land policy, but even here there has been no consistent policy, and much legislation has tended to work at cross-purposes with the establishment of family farms.

Land policies continue to change, and as they were affected by many situations and factors that arose in the nation in the disposal of its public lands, it is difficult to conceive how we could have had a consistent land policy. But this is not to say that a better job might not have been done or that we are not now reaching a state of development when it should be particularly desirable to formulate more definite public land policies for such basic natural resources as soil and water, and strategic minerals such as oil. We have become a mature nation, and with the passing of a

---

[5] Benjamin H. Hibbard, *A History of the Public Land Policies*, p. 548, The Macmillan Company, New York, 1924.

substantial part of our great natural resources, it is time to take stock of the situation and more effectively plan for the use, conservation, and development of our land resources.

Land programs are the particular plans of action designed to advance or carry out land policy or land policies. Some are forward-looking; others are set up merely to correct past mistakes of man. The most recent large-scale land programs in the United States occurred during the 1930's with the submarginal land purchase program, resettlement program, conservation movement, and various similar land activities that dealt with the development and prevention of wastage of land resource and the relief of human maladjustments arising from improper land uses. Later chapters will deal at some length with problems and policies that gave rise to such programs and also briefly consider these land programs and the agencies through which they did or do operate.

### General Goals of Land Policies

In a consideration of land policies and programs, it is well to bear in mind the interrelationship between specific land policies and programs and general goals of national, social, and economic policy. In briefly discussing some of these goals, it should be noted that they are by no means mutually exclusive; many of them overlap and compete with one another. In fact, in outlining goals or objectives it is not always easy to distinguish ends from means. A means to an end may itself become an objective, and the more specific the objectives considered, the more likely they are to be means toward more highly generalized objectives.

*Military Security.* A group of objectives which may frequently be found antithetical to some of the other goals is that of military security. The exigencies of war have forced nations to sacrifice forest and other natural resources at a rate inconsistent with the principles of conservation. Military considerations have also induced certain nations to pursue a population policy that is quite inconsistent with certain goals that look more definitely in the direction of individual well-being. Likewise, avoidance of an undue or dangerous dependence on foreign sources of supply of food and raw materials has motivated agricultural and land policies that might be found quite indefensible if it were possible to pursue goals other than that of military security.

The United States is much less compelled than most of the civilized nations of the world to modify drastically the utilization of its natural resources, and particularly its agriculture, for the mere purpose of lessening its dependence on foreign sources of supply. In the realm of agricultural production, our dependence on foreign sources of supply has not been significant because of our great diversity of production and our productivity capacity; nevertheless, it is becoming a matter of increasing concern.

*Political Stability.* Scarcely less serious than military hazards are the dangers from political disturbances, especially those that take a revolutionary course rather than following established constitutional procedures. Nations do take account of such considerations, especially in regard to the greater degree of political conservatism of small landowners as compared with an urban or agricultural proletariat. Experience has shown that farm owners, except as regards policies that may threaten the integrity of their property, are inherently conservative. Political considerations have exerted a large influence on land policies in European countries since the First World War, where racial and partisan, as well as political and economic, motives have influenced the redistribution of agricultural land.

Major redistributions of land followed the First World War in Europe, and even more violent ones have taken place in Central and Eastern Europe since 1945. Drastic reforms of a revolutionary nature, accompanied by considerable bloodshed and violence, have characterized the Soviet efforts to reorient their European satellites. The Baltic States, Poland, Eastern Germany, Czechoslovakia, Rumania, Hungary, and to a lesser extent Bulgaria and (prior to 1948) Yugoslavia have all felt the iron imprint of these Soviet-inspired land reforms. Even here, however, the peasants' love of their land has forced Soviet policy into circuitous routes to its announced goal. One of the best examples is the Soviet zone of Germany, where the Soviets have broken up the large *Junker* estates into numerous small and (nominally) privately owned peasant farms. The Communist argument is that this seemingly unsocialistic measure is a necessary and wise political step in the "dialectic development of Marxian socialism."[6]

The present land-reform movement, with emphasis on improved tenure systems and solutions of related problems, to which Chapter 15 is devoted, recognizes the place of the widespread ownership of property in the growth and strengthening of democratic institutions.

*Maximum National Production.* An increase in or maintenance of a large volume of production is an important objective in national policy, for, other things equal, it is basic to the welfare of the nation. The availability of a large food supply is especially significant, not only because it permits a high average consumption of such products by the population, but also because a large surplus of food over and above the

---

[6] Philip M. Raup, *Land Reform in Post-war Germany: The Soviet Zone Experiment,"* p. 415, unpublished doctor's thesis, University of Wisconsin, Madison, Wis., 1949.

requirements of the food producers is a prerequisite to the employment
of a large percentage of the population in nonagricultural lines of production if the nation is not to depend on foreign sources of food supply.
Closely related to this is the availability of a large supply of raw materials, *e.g.*, fibers, produced within the nation. Maximum production is an
objective, however, which must be kept consistent with conservation of
natural resources, with maintenance of proper balance between employment of the nation's population in the production of food and raw materials and in other lines of production or services, and with achievement
of various objectives concerned with the welfare of those engaged in
production from the land.

At times the aim of achieving maximum production of food and raw
materials, especially with a view to independence of foreign sources, may
be carried beyond the point of economic efficiency and therefore
result in lessening the welfare of the total population or of that part of
the population engaged in the utilization of land resources. For instance,
the presence of agricultural trade barriers in Europe, partly as self-
sufficiency measures, definitely restricts the productivity of Western
Europe and its power to expand agricultural production.

*Maximum Income.* Maximum physical production may be only partly
consistent with maximum income, because the latter is affected by the
ratios at which the product is exchanged for other products. For a nation
as a whole, maximum production of certain goods for exportation may
result in some sacrifice in income if the increase in production results in
adverse ratios of exchange in the foreign market. The intricate regulations
and restrictions on foreign trade, which have been so greatly elaborated
in recent years, represent in part an effort of nations to obtain advantages
from one another in exchange relationships. Likewise, within a nation,
maximum production of land products in general, or of particular land
products, must be kept within such limits as will not adversely affect
income of the producers themselves. In so far as such products enter into
an exchange economy, it may be found necessary to sacrifice the objective
of maximum production to income considerations. Without doubt, however, a more important concern of national policy should be to make
these points consistent with one another, in so far as this can be done
without sacrificing the benefits rendered by an exchange economy, by
directing the use of human and capital resources into various lines of
productive effort in proper proportion to corresponding wants.

*Economic Security and Stability.* Maximum income is not necessarily
consistent with maximum economic security, for the latter is a function
largely of the continuity and stability of income. The sense of security
indeed may itself be regarded as an important form of income which may
justify sacrificing a certain amount of less dependable income. How

much men value security is shown by their painful striving to accumulate wealth in order to provide against future hazards that may eliminate income itself. Thus, for millions of families a significant part of the current income must be withheld from current consumption to provide for "a rainy day."

In agriculture, especially where a large proportion of the workers are small operators, instability at times has caused great personal losses and necessitated costly and wasteful readjustments in occupation and resource use. For instance, the instability that has characterized share-cropping in the South has resulted in a greater degree of mobility than was desirable for efficient use of resources or from the standpoint of human well-being.

Systems of economic organization that afford the worker a reasonable assurance of continuity of income may provide a more adequate average standard of living than more ample irregular incomes would provide. Some systems of organization which might appear most desirable from the standpoint of maximum production and efficiency, as may be true in large-scale farming, may require a large agricultural group exposed to the hazards of irregular employment. Such workers, subject to excessive rental payments and in general afflicted by a continuing sense of economic insecurity, can become the basis for political instability. Therefore it is necessary to appraise land policies in terms of their significance for security and stability as well as in terms of their significance for production and income.

*Individual Freedom.* Freedom from arbitrary restraints has been one of the most influential ideals of American democracy. It largely motivated the migration of European populations to this country. The increasing complexity of industrial civilization, however, has made it necessary to restrict individual freedom of action along many lines, even in the interest of the individuals who compose the social aggregate. In a sense, it is only a figure of speech to speak of many restrictions as an infringement on freedom, since virtually all individuals find their welfare advanced by certain types of restrictions. Institutional restrictions can represent progress in freedom although they are restrictions on one's liberty. In discussing the place of economic institutions in the present-day society, John R. Commons defines an institution as "group action in restraint, liberation and expansion of individual action."[7]

There is a zone of governmental policy, however, within which the further development of restraints may be found to produce aggregate benefits not sufficiently worth while to justify the sacrifice of freedom. Freedom itself is so worth while a good that in consideration of public

[7] John R. Commons, *Institutional Economics,* p. 73, The Macmillan Company, New York, 1934.

policy we must carefully guard against interference with individual freedom. One of the great merits of farming is that it is perhaps the last great occupation in which a considerable measure of self-direction is still possible. We should be concerned in land policy with preserving this freedom, but also with mitigating its disadvantages in so far as it is wise.

*Conservation of Human Resources.* In a sense, human welfare is the end and aim of policy. Yet we may also think of human beings as means to ends in the sense that in economic terms labor is a resource whose conservation and improvement should be a continuing matter of concern, although it may not always be possible to separate sharply measures justified because they conserve human resources from measures which seek the general welfare of the population for its own sake.

Professor T. N. Carver expresses the opinion that in many respects the character of human resources is more important than the abundance and quality of natural resources. He declares:[8]

> The most valuable resource of any country is its fund of human energy, that is, the working power, both mental and physical, of its people. It is safe to say that any capable race of men who will conserve, economize and utilize that fund will be able not only to extract a living but actually to prosper in the midst of poor natural surroundings. On the other hand, if they fail to economize their fund of energy, if they waste and dissipate it, they will certainly decay in the midst of the richest geographical and material resources.

He illustrates the point by the example of New England, where great economic progress was made in spite of an unfriendly climate, sterile soil, and absence of extensive mineral resources, attributing this progress largely to the intelligence, industry, sobriety, thrift, forethought, and cooperativeness of the "old New England stock."

These considerations point to the importance of the early environment in which the qualities of the population are formed. It is most significant that in certain areas of the United States where the natural rate of net reproduction per generation among native whites is highest, there are found the lowest per capita expenditures for education and also the smallest number of physicians, dentists, and nurses in proportion to the population.

Another serious source of waste of human resources is unemployment, particularly that which is involuntary. Involuntary idleness creates a deep resentment likely to bear fruit in unsocial activity and waste and tends to break down the morale of a population. During the latter part of the 1920's and the first half of the 1930's, an unusually large number of farm people were in this class. It should be an essential aim of social policy, and

[8] Richard T. Ely, Ralph H. Hess, Charles K. Leith, and Thomas Nixon Carver, *The Foundations of National Prosperity*, p. 275, The Macmillan Company, New York, 1917.

of land policy, not only to provide work for those who want to work for a livelihood, but also to provide conditions of work under which the workers themselves may feel that they are making an honest contribution to the general well-being. Nothing is so discouraging as a sense of futility.

*Conservation of Natural Resources.* A major objective in national policy, and one particularly significant for land policy, is the conservation of natural resources. In some respects this problem may be even more significant than the conservation of human resources; for certain natural resources are exhaustible, while human resources are continually being reproduced and sometimes appear even redundant because of over-population or the deficiencies of organized society in accomplishing full employment.

The conservation of natural resources has emerged only gradually into prominence in public policy in the United States. The conservation movement in its various aspects has awakened us none too soon to the serious extent to which our pioneer prodigality has proceeded in impairing our heritage of natural resources.

Our efforts as a nation to expand and improve our culture and to defend it against aggression will be in vain unless we succeed also in defending it against the more gradual but insidious process of land-resource destruction, for our natural resources constitute a fundamental basis of our civilization. Conservation is not merely a matter of depriving ourselves in the present in order to pass on our heritage of natural resources to remote generations. Much of the most serious destruction of resources is mere wanton waste that benefits no one, or, at most, redounds to the benefit of individual business interests without commensurate benefit to —often to the serious detriment of—the community and the nation as a whole.

## Scope of Land Problems and Policies Considered

Our very early land policies were largely determined by the aspirations of a growing nation in an era of land expansion and settlement. These policies, going back to the time when the Thirteen Colonies were autonomous and ending with the formation of the Federal Union in 1789, were much influenced by the English land-tenure system as England expanded and settled in the New World. It was not, however, until the time of the signing of the Articles of Confederation in 1781 that we as a government began to evolve land policies. The need arose to carry out promises of land that were made to Revolutionary soldiers, to resolve conflicting claims of the colonies, and to provide a source of revenue for the Federal government.

A review of the influences of the English land-tenure system on colonial land policy and of the alienation of land through sale, credit, grants, and homestead allotments—in brief, the story of early colonial land policies, of the disposal of land, and of the motivating forces in the American frontier—needs to be told before undertaking a consideration of some of our recent land problems and policies. Thus, the following two chapters are devoted to this period of our history. The remaining chapters deal with aspects of significant land problems, situations, and policies that have arisen largely in land use and tenure since the turn of the century; more specifically, with problems, policies, and programs that bear on the use of major types of land, land-resource evaluations, land conservation, tenure arrangements, land requirements, land planning, and institutional arrangements that affect or condition the use and occupancy of land. As indicated in the preceding pages, concern is with order, security, property, and liberty, as well as efficiency, in the use and occupancy of land. The approach is within an economic framework that emphasizes forces and factors that have been present in the problem situations and consideration of obstacles to be overcome, with some suggestions for a more en-lightened public land policy.

## CHAPTER 2

*Rise of Colonial Land Policies*

The policies adopted in the formative stages of our national land system were the product of a gradual evolution during the colonial period from policies and practices transplanted from England. A brief glance at these origins will serve two purposes: it will reveal the nature of the roots from which present American policies have sprung, and it will emphasize the wide difference in the adjustments with which we have been confronted and those encountered by the English in adapting land tenure and utilization to the needs of the modern age.

*The Village System*

When Jamestown and Plymouth were settled, English land tenure was in transition from the manorial system to more modern forms of tenure and attitudes toward land. The manorial system had resulted from a combination of feudal relationships with a much older form of rural organization, the "village system." It appears to have developed gradually as herding and tribal migration were superseded by settled agriculture and when protection necessitated a more or less compact, rather than a dispersed, pattern of settlement.

*Extent and Significance.* With differences in detail, the village system prevailed at one time or another in widespread parts of the world—not only in much of what is now Great Britain and Ireland, but also in most of the countries of Continental Europe, in Russia, and even in India. The Germans with whom Julius Caesar came into contact (around 56 B.C.) were still in the nomadic tribal stage, but a century and a half later Tacitus found the Germans had developed a fairly settled village life. The Anglo-Saxon invasion of Britain introduced the village system and customs in the areas overrun, and similar institutions may have prevailed in some localities among the Celtic populations.

The village system in England was essentially an agricultural, rather than an urban, unit of economic and social organization. Most of the

15

population of the village consisted of farm families producing food, fuel, and clothing mainly for family consumption, together with a sprinkling of artisans, such as carpenters, the blacksmith, and the miller. Although there were villages in England and on the Continent that consisted of scattered homes or widely separated groups of houses, the dwellings were commonly grouped fairly close together, each occupying a bit of land—an "in-lot"—sufficient for a garden and livestock runs and pens.

*The Open-Field System of the Village.* The land not attached to the dwellings was operated under the open-field, or common-field, system. The individual families did not each work a compact enclosed area, but all worked portions of land in the same field or fields. Whether situated in one large enclosed field or in several, the arable land was operated in accordance with one of two systems of rotation—the two-field system or the three-field system. Under the former the arable land was alternately cultivated or left fallow. Under the latter winter grain was followed by spring grain, and that in turn by fallow. After harvest, stock belonging to members of the village were turned in to graze on the stubble and weeds. Thus all the farm workers of the village were engaged at once in the same phase of the rotation. The woodland and other nonarable lands were used in common as a source of fuel or for pasture.

Viewed through modern eyes, the village field system appears incredibly irrational and inefficient. Since it compelled all the families of the village to plant the same crops and in the same order generation after generation, it afforded little opportunity for individual initiative or adoption of new crops and improved systems of rotation.

For many reasons, however, the medieval open-field system was not ill-adapted to the conditions under which it developed. The new type of crops that have served to diversify our agriculture were then unknown. For many centuries farming mainly provided food for the cultivator and his family; little was produced for sale until the development of the Continental market for wool. In an age when there was no wire fencing, there was a great advantage in avoiding the laborious tasks of enclosing each individual unit of land with hedges, palings, or rails. If the individual holdings were not to be enclosed anyway, it made little difference that the holdings consisted of scattered strips. The layout of the fields permitted a nicer adjustment to variations in contour and the varying requirements of drainage, and provided needed flexibility when the slow process of clearing or draining new ground added parcels bit by bit to the arable land. The scattering strips probably permitted a more flexible division of labor and adjustment to changing seasonal requirements for those engaged in cooperative plowing with the huge unwieldy plows and teams of six to ten oxen. Furthermore, it made possible a readier readjustment of labor and land resources within the community in an age when the labor resources of the individual family were subject to extreme fluctuations from disease and violence.[1]

*Influence of the Village System in the Colonies.* Not only did the village system influence later forms of tenure in Europe, but also through English land policy it influenced materially the evolution of land tenure and policy in the colonies, particularly in early New England. Here its influence was strengthened by strong religious bonds and the noncommercial character of agriculture in the early period.

The earlier New England towns were careful in the layout and distribution of their holdings. Quite frequently a town common or park and lands for the support of the church and school were reserved. The earlier distributions among individuals were generally made on the basis of need and ability to work the land. The portion assigned to each family consisted of an in-lot in the village and a farm out-lot, and usually a considerable area of common land remained undistributed and served as a source of fuel and timber and for pasture, under the regulation of the corporate town. However, about the beginning of the eighteenth century, a tendency developed for the original members of towns to claim the unallotted lands as their collective property, rather than that of the town as a corporate entity, and to insist on their right to dispose of it to newcomers for their exclusive profit.

While the village, or town, system gained its widest foothold in the New England colonies, it also took root in other parts of the colonies. In 1701 the authorities of Virginia undertook the establishment of frontier posts in which the settlers were to be given in-lots and out-lots as tenants in common. Governor Spottswood's Palatines at Germanna in Virginia, and in North Carolina, De Graffenreid's settlement at New Berne and the Moravian settlement at Wachovia were essentially European village communities. The proprietors of South Carolina proposed to establish a number of agricultural villages, with in-lots and out-lots. The ideal of the village type of agricultural organization was adopted by the Georgia trustees, and they made an earnest effort to realize their ideal. The French also established a number of agricultural villages along the Mississippi. But before following further early land developments in this country, we must return for brief consideration of other forms of land tenure in England that materially affected our early land policies.

[1] For a fuller elaboration of this line of argument, see C. S. Orwin, *The Open Fields,* pp. 1–60, Oxford University Press, New York, 1939.

*Medieval Land Tenure*

In the Middle Ages the relationship of the English cultivator to the land was largely the result of feudal concepts and conditions under which the land was held by lords. Land tenure involved much more than economic rights to the use of land; it constituted as well a complex of social, political, and military rights and obligations. The form of tenure under which one held his land largely determined, and in turn reflected, his position in society. In fact, different individuals might have various personal rights and obligations with respect to the same piece of land, all strongly fortified by custom. Thus land could not be an economic good in the modern sense, to be bought and sold or leased purely for pecuniary reasons, for the free sale of land would have profoundly altered the complex of social and political relationships associated with land tenure.

*Free and Unfree Tenure.* In the latter part of the medieval period English tenures comprised two great groups—free and unfree. The free tenures were in the main honorable and were maintainable in the king's courts. Unfree tenures, at least in theory, were subject only to the will of the lord of the manor and involved servile obligations. The principal forms of free tenure were (1) knight service (involving military obligation by the tenant), (2) frankalmoign (owing masses and prayers on account of land held), (3) sergeanty (grand and petty), (4) and socage.

Sergeanty, which means service, involved various obligations to perform services of an honorable character in the household of the king or about the person of the king, such as duties of the sword-bearer, the butler, the seneschal, and a host of minor services, some of which gradually became administrative or political.

Socage tenure deserves particular attention because, unlike the other types, it might be either a free tenure or an unfree tenure. By the close of the medieval period all freehold lands not held under knight service, sergeanty, or frankalmoign were held in free socage. This form of tenure was not subject to knight service or scutage (the payment for exemption therefrom) nor subject to wardship and marriage controls or obligations. Generally there arose an obligation for an annual payment in money or in kind, but frequently the payment was merely nominal as a recognition of fealty to the lord. While some socage tenures were subject to labor payments and the tenant was personally unfree, it became increasingly the predominant form of free tenure into which the other types of free tenure were converted; for tenure by frankalmoign was materially impaired by the Statute of Quia Emptores (1290), which prohibited any further grants of land in frankalmoign unless sanctioned by the king; and tenure by knight service was formally changed into socage tenure by the Statute of 1660. By this statute land grants were to be made exclusively in common socage.

This legislation of 1660 completed the economic task begun by the Statute Quia Emptores 370 years before, namely the shift, in the selling of fee interests in land, from stress on benefits derivable in the future from recurrent or occasional payments to be made by the tenant to a stress on a lump-sum payment at the time of sale as the capital equivalent of the asset conveyed.

In addition to the primary obligation which characterized each of the free tenures, there were a number of other obligations. Among these were homage, the oath of fealty, payment to the lord on death of the tenant (heriot, in theory a return of arms and other property loaned by the lord), payment by the heir for the right to inherit (relief), financial assistance or other help toward the lord's ransom, payments on account of the marriage of the lord's eldest son or daughter (aids), the right and obligation of the lord to exercise wardship during the minority of an heir of the tenant and to dispose of his daughter's hand in marriage (rights which came to have great pecuniary value), and the right of escheat, that is, to resume title to the land if the tenant died without heirs or if he committed a felony.[3] One reason why socage emerged as the predominant form of free tenure was its comparative lack of these personal obligations, and therefore its greater adaptability to the increasing commercialism and freedom of movement which characterized the modern period.

However, in the medieval period the majority of the cultivators were attached to a manor under unfree tenure, known as villein tenure. The villein was not personally unfree, for, subject to his customary obligations to the lord of the manor, his time was his own, and he enjoyed freedom of movement and immunity of life and limb. Nevertheless, he was born into his status and in legal theory utilized his landholding subject to the arbitrary will of his lord. Commonly, a villein holding was about 30 acres (a "virgate"), for which the villein must render to his lord 3 days' work a week in summer on the lord's demesne lands—that is, the lands operated by the lord directly through his servants—and extra labor in harvest (boon work). In addition the villein must render to his lord *gafel*, or tribute in money or kind, and various obligations due on special occasions, similar to some of the incidents of free tenures.

*Characteristics of the Manor.* The medieval manor was a self-sufficient unit of political, economic, and social organization, rigidly controlled by

[2] Richard R. Powell, *The Law of Real Property*, Vol. 1, p. 33, Matthew Bender & Company, Inc., New York, 1949.

[3] For a fuller account of these various incidents of medieval tenures, see Sir William S. Holdsworth, *An Historical Introduction to the Land Law*, pp. 29*ff.*, Oxford University Press, New York, 1927.

customs adjudicated in its own courts (courts-baron and courts-leet). It might consist of a single agricultural village or of several. In addition to the lord and his retainers and servants and the officials who aided the lord in administration, such as the steward, bailiff, and reeve, there were freemen holding their lands of the lord in free tenure; socmen whose status was intermediate between that of freemen and villeins; the villeins themselves; a class known as "bordars," whose landholdings were less than those of the villeins, though subject to similar status; cottars, or cottagers, occupying small bits of land subject to various obligations and services; co-liberti, or household servants of freemen; and at the time of Doomsday Survey, slaves, although this class virtually disappeared in about a century. There were also the clergy and the various artisans residing in the villages and incumbents of the various petty offices necessary to the collective economy of the manor, such as stock tenders, wardens of forests and fences, leaders of plow teams, leaders of the harvest, and those who had responsibility of reporting losses of stock.

The latter part of the medieval period and the early modern period witnessed a profound transformation in the rigid structure of the manors. The rise of royal power and the consequent decay of the power of the lords lessened the significance of the military and other services, weakened the authority of the lords, and correspondingly strengthened the personal rights and enlarged the freedom of the peasants. This tendency is believed to have been promoted in part by the extreme mortality during the Black Death and other epidemics, which created a notable scarcity of labor. The increase of trade and resulting greater freedom of movement, more numerous contacts with the world beyond the manor, and the more extensive use of money contributed powerfully to change the character of medieval land tenure. The rise of the wool trade, introducing a commercial element into the hitherto self-sufficing system of agriculture, the consequent consolidation through enclosure of villein holdings into the lord's demesne, and the leasing of these holdings under the so-called "stock and land leases" caused the lords to have less need for the work of the villeins. This inclined the lords to commute labor obligations into payments in money or in kind, a process which in turn was made possible by the increase in commerce.

*Rise of Copyhold Tenure.* Although there were isolated cases of villeinage until the latter part of the seventeenth century, by the close of the fifteenth century the majority of landholdings formerly characterized by villein tenure, and not consolidated into the lord's demesne, were no longer occupied by villeins. During the thirteenth and fourteenth centuries the changes which had tended to enfranchise villeins resulted also in a custom of reducing to writing on the manorial rolls and records of the manorial courts the various rights and obligations of the lord and his tenants. Thus the former villeins were gradually converted into the numerous class known as "copyholders," who owed the lord fixed annual payments in place of regular labor dues and occasional obligations which formerly characterized villein tenure. With the notable fall in the value of money following the influx of precious metals from the New World, these fixed money obligations gradually became largely nominal in effect, so that economically the copyholders were almost as well off as freeholders holding by socage tenure; furthermore, the copyholders enjoyed substantial security of tenure as leaseholds frequently extended from one to three lives.

Although theoretically the copyholder still held his land subject to the will of the lord, in the latter part of the fifteenth century the royal courts gradually extended their jurisdiction to maintenance of the rights and obligations inscribed on the manorial rolls, preventing arbitrary ejection of copyholders in the interest of enlarging the lord's demesne.

*Various Estates in Land.* The rising forms of tenure in land, which have been very briefly and sketchily reviewed, led to different estates in land, that is, forms of property in land that established rights of tenants in land and their duties and obligations.

The most comprehensive estate that arose was possession in fee simple, under which the tenant might dispose of his holdings at will, subject to the conditions of his tenure, and pass it on to his heirs either lineal or collateral. By the Statute De Donis Conditionalibus (1285) there was created the estate tail, under which a grant to a donee and the heirs of his body limited his right of alienation to his own lifetime. He might alienate the land, but only for the duration of his lifetime. This limitation was subsequently held to apply also to the subsequent heirs of the original donee. During the fifteenth century the lawyers developed a fictitious procedure under which an estate tail could be "barred" and converted into an estate in fee simple. During the latter part of the sixteenth century, however, the lawyers found a way to establish a system of unbarrable estates tail known as "settlements," which in effect again made it possible for a tenant in fee simple to determine a succession of limited interests in perpetuity; but the English courts, interested in preserving freedom of transfer, ultimately managed to develop a body of rules which in effect prevented entails for an indefinite period.[4]

Still another type of estate in possession was the estate for life, which is to be distinguished from a life lease in that it included the right of alienation for the duration of the estate. The estate in fee tail and for life resulted in two classes of estates in expectancy: the estate in reversion, under which possession might revert to an original donor in the case of a lapse in the limited estate, and an estate in remainder, under

[4] *Ibid.*, pp. 219ff.

which the remainderman had a right of expectancy on the termination of
the rights of the possessor of a limited estate. There developed also
various types of estates to secure money lent.

Thus it was of profound significance for the early evolution of land
tenure in the American colonies that by the time of early American
settlement English land tenure had reached a degree of enfranchisement
from manorial restrictions not attained in France until the French Revolution nor in Germany and most other European countries until a much
later period. The continued existence of the large class of small freeholders, copyholders, and independent leaseholders in the mother country also gave a different direction to American land tenure than it might
have taken had initial colonization occurred, say, in the middle of the
nineteenth century.

### Transplantation of European Land Tenure to American Colonies

Those who were instrumental in promoting English colonization were
naturally inclined to transplant the type of land tenure and land law
under which they had lived in the mother country. Since, however,
English land institutions were evolutionary, there was a considerable
variety of them in different parts of England, some representing earlier
and others later stages of evolution. Consequently, there was a similar
variety in the initial characteristics of land tenure in different parts of the
colonies.

For instance, the Virginia Company of London was largely dominated
by the new bourgeoisie. Naturally, therefore, it tended to adopt the less
reactionary forms of land tenure, and in founding the first permanent
English colony, established precedents of profound influence on other
colonial enterprises. The royal charters granted land to the Virginia
Company in free and common socage after the manner of that form of
tenure prevailing in the royal manor of East Greenwich and the bishopric
of Durham. In addition to the theoretical obligations of fealty evidenced
by the obligation to pay quitrent—in some cases purely nominal, such as
a peppercorn—these grants reserved to the king a percentage of the
product of gold and silver. The earlier subgrants by the colonial authorities were also in socage tenure.

In the Southern colonies and the proprietary Middle colonies subgrants were usually subject to a quitrent that was intended to be substantial. In the "corporate" New England colonies, quitrent requirements
were usually omitted, and sometimes in grants by royal governors to
friends. The difficulties of collecting fixed money payments from impecunious frontiersmen, in spite of agreements to receive payment in
kind, were perennial. For the colonists, aided by isolation, uncertain
boundaries, local public opinion, and inadequacy of administrative ma-

chinery, avoided payments and were largely successful in making quit-rents a more important source of irritation than of revenue. Until late in the colonial period, moreover, quitrents were virtually in lieu of land taxes.

*Methods of Granting Land.* In the early years of the Virginia colony there developed a peculiar system of granting land, which spread to the other Southern colonies. The person desiring to acquire land from the public domain obtained from the authorities a warrant of survey, on whatever terms and conditions prevailed at the time. The warrant called for a definite amount of land but no specific location, since, in general, land grants were made without a prior authoritative survey. The holder was entitled to select the area called for in any part of the public domain which he believed had not yet passed into private ownership. He then proceeded to have a survey made of the area selected. The tendency was to make the boundary very irregular in order to include as much good land as possible, a tendency somewhat restricted by regulations limiting the ratio of length along a stream to width of the tract. The surveys, frequently made by inexperienced surveyors, with the lines or points of reference designated by "metes and bounds," such as a mean-dering stream, a large rock, or a chestnut stump, were characterized by a high degree of inaccuracy and generally exceeded the area designated in the warrant of survey. In order to curb this tendency some of the colonies adopted the device of offering the excess to anyone who would discover and prove it. Since boundary marks might be changed, fre-quently by interested parties, the practice of "processioning" developed; that is, reliable individuals were designated from time to time to view and verify the boundary marks.

The next step in acquiring land from the public domain consisted in presenting to the land office the warrant of survey together with the newly surveyed boundaries of the land selected. Notice of the prospec-tive granting of a patent conveying title was then published as a warning to any interested persons in order that they might issue a caveat, or formal protest. If no valid protest was received within the time required by law, patent was issued.

This awkward system of granting land was strongly favored by the pioneers because it enabled them to range far and wide in locating land according to their liking without waiting for official surveys. Neverthe-less, the system was subject to serious abuses. Owing to the delay and expense of traveling a second time to the land office in order to receive a patent, many grantees omitted this step and thus subjected their hold-ings later to "claim jumpers." This tendency and the looseness of the system of survey and marking of boundaries resulted in endless litigation.

In 1774, the British government undertook to reform the system in

Virginia by requiring an official survey prior to issuance of a land warrant, to be followed by sales at auction subject to certain minimum prices graded according to quality of the land. There was strong opposition, however, by the frontiersmen, and the outbreak of war prevented effective application of the British government's land reforms.

In New England, such reforms as those proposed in Virginia had become established. There priority of survey, frequently in rectangular units, and the requirements of a more or less compact mode of settlement were more generally accepted.

*Encouraging Settlement.* The earlier colonial policies in the granting of land emphasized occupancy and improvement. However, this was secondary to the attraction of settlers, and to this end a number of methods were employed. For example, the Virginia Company of London, in order to sell its stock, proposed to grant a small amount of land to each purchaser of a share. For the purpose of attracting colonists, the company offered a share of stock, and therefore a corresponding "dividend" of land, to each individual who would venture himself in the personal hazards of the enterprise. This was the beginning of a practice of offering land to attract settlers, adopted in one form or another by virtually all the colonization enterprises.

After the termination of the Virginia Company, its then worthless stock was no longer an inducement, nor were funds available for the transport of settlers. Consequently, there developed from the original precedent the so-called "headright" policy, under which 50 acres of Virginia land was offered to each person emigrating and settling himself at his own expense or paying the expense of introducing another settler. Since tobacco production afforded the basis for commercial agriculture, persons of capital imported indentured servants, taking the land appertaining to the headrights and employing the servants, and afterwards Negro slaves, on the land thus acquired. Persons who acquired headrights but did not desire land frequently sold them, and thus a speculative market was created for these paper rights to land, just as in a later time people traded in the land scrip issued by the Federal government. In time, laxity and connivance of administrative officials resulted in the granting of headrights for fictitious persons. Such laxity was tolerated by authorities partly because many of them were financially concerned and partly because, theoretically, the more land that passed into private ownership the more quitrents would accrue.

The headright policy was followed, with variations in detail, in all Southern and Middle colonies. In some cases land was granted also to the servant after the expiration of his indenture, particularly as an inducement to settle on dangerous frontiers. In New England, also, the headright principle was widely employed, though less for the reward of capitalist importers of labor than as an inducement to actual settlers.

*Attempts to Introduce the Manorial System.* Although the manorial system in England was moribund, there were not lacking persons who cherished its aristocratic spirit and yearned to reproduce in the New World some of the manorial forms. For example, the Baltimores made many large grants of land, which were called manors, particularly to subcolonizers who undertook to import a specified number of persons for whom they were to receive a definite amount of land per person. The Maryland proprietors also reserved for themselves large tracts of land known as proprietary manors. On both classes of manors some of the manorial forms and terminology were introduced. There were demesne farms, courts-leet, and courts-baron. Lords of manors had the right of escheat and to impose alienation fines.

Likewise the plan for the proprietors of the Carolinas provided for an aristocratic hierarchy, the members of which bore resounding feudal titles. It was proposed that the large grants of proprietary land associated with the grandiose titles should be worked by hereditary leetmen. Provisions were made for courts-leet and courts-baron. Manors and certain manorial forms were also established by the favorites to whom Charles II granted the northern neck of Virginia, and in the Granville proprietorship in North Carolina. The patroonships created by the Dutch along the Hudson were also semimanorial. In the late eighteenth century extensive grants made by the English governors resulted in the establishment of a number of manors, such as Fordham and Pelham in New York.

In none of the English colonies did the manorial system attain a significant economic or political vitality through creating an inferior class of hereditary tenants. In Maryland and Virginia, it is true, there were tenants for long terms after the English fashion, but their status was essentially contractual rather than fixed in immemorial custom. It remained for indentured servitude and slavery to supply the more fortunate classes with the means of obtaining a soft-handed income and to develop a well-marked social stratification. The so-called manors either disintegrated or became plantations.

*Systems of Inheritance.* From early colonial attitudes toward land and from efforts to establish manorial estates, it is not surprising that in the earlier colonial period emphasis was on the retention of land as an enduring family patrimony. This was reflected in reluctance to alienate land, and in the prevalence of primogeniture, particularly in the South. Primogeniture was further reinforced by the practice of entailing. Nevertheless, owing to the greater abundance of land and greater freedom from tradition, these practices were less generally followed than in

England. The dividing of an estate equally among the sons, sometimes modified by giving a double portion to the eldest, was the prevalent rule of inheritance in New England, New Jersey, and Pennsylvania, as well as in parts of the Southern colonies occupied by settlers from Northern colonies. Even among some of the colonial gentry there was a tendency toward relaxation in adherence to primogeniture, and occasionally legislatures undertook to dock entails.

## Modifications in Colonial Land System

Even though earlier colonial policy contemplated a stable rural economy, with emphasis on occupancy and improvement and with occasional restrictions on alienation, gradually such measures were withdrawn or ignored. The abundance of virgin natural resources worked against such a policy.

For example, after 1725, even in New England, the policy of selling lands was more generally practiced than in the previous century. Instead of granting wild lands mainly to groups of settlers, they were more and more sold to individuals, frequently in large units, for speculation. This was true especially of New Hampshire, western Connecticut, and western New York. Indeed, until the Revolutionary War large land grants in western New York were retarding settlement. Furthermore, many colonial governors were lavish in bestowing huge grants upon friends and political supporters, and in some colonies there was extensive engrossment of land.

In this regard the progress of capitalism introduced an ever-increasing spirit of land speculation and mobility in land transfer, especially in the years just before the Revolutionary War and immediately afterward. Thus were broken down the various barriers that had been erected to ensure stability of tenure. Furthermore, the increasing tendency to look upon land as a readily exchangeable commodity led also to a disposition to employ it as a public financial asset, which in itself encouraged speculation.

In the Southern colonies extensive engrossment of land no doubt facilitated development of the plantation system and, in turn, increased the pressure for liberal sale policies. On the other hand, in the back country, even of the Southern colonies, and in areas which, because of isolation or poor soil, were not favorable to production of commercial staples, small holdings and family farming developed in spite of the ease with which land could be acquired. Precisely because of such conditions New England found it possible to adopt and maintain for a longer time conservative policies for the disposal of public land and to a greater degree to stave off speculation.

During the period of the Revolutionary War and the years immediately following there were notable changes in colonial land tenure, in the direction of further throwing off restrictions on disposition and the vestige of feudal incidents in land tenure. The severance of connection with the crown eliminated the fealty characteristics of socage tenure, except in so far as the colonial governments succeeded to the rights of the king—these governments tacitly permitted the obligation to become obsolete—or explicitly by the formal abolition of quitrents. The democratic spirit was also hostile to primogeniture and entails, which had facilitated the formation and maintenance of large estates.

## Land Policies of Various Commonwealths after the Revolution

At the close of the Revolutionary War a number of the former colonies asserted claims to extensive areas beyond the Appalachians. Many of these claims overlapped. Since they were a potential source of disagreement, the Continental Congress proposed in 1777 that the lands under dispute be placed at its disposal. Aspects of land policies of former colonies, in different parts of the country after the Revolution, might well be reviewed.

In the granting of land, New England and New York swung still further than formerly toward liberal sales policies and lavish grants. In New York and Pennsylvania the tendency toward land speculation was promoted by military bounties, frequently sold by the recipients to speculators. After restrictions were removed in 1791, huge land grants were made in western New York, and there was an orgy of land speculation, more or less duplicated in Maine. New Hampshire, Rhode Island, Delaware, New Jersey, and Maryland had no claims to Western land. The pressure of these commonwealths, however, had much to do in bringing about the later cession by the landholding commonwealths. Connecticut's conflicting claims were recognized in the so-called Western Reserve, set aside in northern Ohio as a condition of Connecticut's renunciation of her claims; but the greater part of the reservation was shortly disposed of in a single transaction for the sum of $1,200,000.

Virginia disposed of the greater portion of Kentucky, and North Carolina of a large part of Tennessee, before the cessions to the Confederation and the Federal government, respectively. Virginia, North Carolina, and South Carolina followed an extremely lavish policy in making sales and in granting soldier bonuses. Sale prices were low, lower even than the minimum prices required by the Federal government, and acquisition was further facilitated by currency depreciation and privilege of purchase on credit. There were virtually no restrictions on the area acquirable by an individual, although South Carolina tried to impose certain restrictions shortly before cession of its lands to the Federal government. Under the loose system of issuing warrants prior to survey, grants were made for much more land than was actually available. There were numerous overlapping claims, especially through occupancy and improvement by squatters of land afterward granted to others. Both Virginia and North Carolina continued after the Revolution the colonial policy of making grants on condition of settlement and recognized the prescriptive, or preemption, rights of squatters who resided a sufficient time on the land and made certain improvements.

A considerable proportion of the grants made by the two commonwealths had not gone to patent at the time of the cession of their residual claims, and the states that were formed, Kentucky and Tennessee, continued for many years to dispose of their reserved rights.

Although the Georgia claims extended to the Mississippi River, grants were confined mainly within the approximate boundaries of the present state, until cession of its remaining lands to the Federal government in 1801. During the interval Georgia's policy was far more conservative than had been the case with Virginia and the Carolinas. There was much greater emphasis on the homestead principle, recognition of preemption rights, and limitation of grants to units of family size, except to planters, who were compelled to pay a progressively higher rate in proportion to the size of area granted. The lottery system of distribution was employed in granting homesteads, persons successful in drawing being required to pay small fees graduated in accordance with quality of the land acquired.

### Influence on National Policies

Our early national policies reflected the characteristics of the later colonial period. The policies of this period emphasized the use of the public domain as a source of revenue through sale of land, and this became the central principle of the initial national policies. The policy of gratuitous distribution of land on condition of settlement and improvement, as embodied in the headright system, recognition of a prescriptive right for squatters, and similar policies had to wait many decades before adoption of the preemption principle and nearly three-quarters of a century before passage of the first Homestead Act.

Policies for surveys, grants, and patents were modeled after practices in various colonies. Use of land grants for the encouragement of education rested upon numerous colonial precedents, and later grants to encourage the making of "internal" improvements had their colonial counterpart in grants for establishment of ferries, warehouses, and mills. Military-bounty grants, so extensively employed in the national period, had been widely employed in the colonial period. The sale of land on credit, tried for a time in the early national period, had been employed by Pennsylvania before the Revolutionary War and by a number of the commonwealths immediately following the Revolution. Above all else, the later colonial period had set the precedent of liberal sale policies and the granting of land without restriction on disposition and mode of use.

*Ideological Background.* The colonial and Revolutionary period reflected the potent influence of the economic, political, social, and religious factors of England and the political philosophy of Rousseau and the economic philosophy of the physiocrats. Central in the latter were the ideas contained in the expressions *laissez faire* and *laissez passer*. In the changing point of view in regard to property rights, John Locke had a tremendous influence on the political thought of the eighteenth century. According to Locke, property rights in land arise from the relationship of the individual to nature and not of man to man. Property rights do not depend on the consent of others, but accrue to individuals because of their labor power or individual labor efforts. Nature was available to all alike, and property or usable goods were the outcome of the individual as a workman mixing his labor with raw resources. Property was a natural right, not derived from the state, but the product of individual labor that the state itself must respect and protect.

Adam Smith and the economists of the English classical school drew from and further developed this philosophy into their doctrine of the self-interest of individuals, free competition, and the labor theory of value. A central conception was that the individual is best able to direct his activities toward the realization of a maximum of welfare; interference or restrictions imposed by governments merely serve to thwart the individual. Therefore, it was held, the role of the state should be restricted to maintenance of order and protection from external violence. It was further argued that since society is an aggregate of individuals, the maximum social well-being would be realized by a policy of noninterference.

Thomas Jefferson, who had a profound influence in shaping our early land policies, was acquainted with these ideas and personally acquainted with English and French philosophers of this new era of thought. To Jefferson a wide diffusion of property interests in land was essential to the establishment of democratic institutions and democratic government. He declared that "the small landholders are the most precious part of a state" and that the power of government should be used to establish numerous freeholds.

An implication of the views held in respect to land policy was that governments possessed of a public domain should not reserve it or retain it for public use but rather should put it rapidly into individual ownership. And the people believed they found in unrestricted land ownership a guaranty of the liberties which they had come here to achieve.

CHAPTER 3 *Disposal of the Public Domain*

The history of land policy in the national period divides into four major epochs which more or less overlap. Each of them, although continuing some of the policies of the preceding epoch, is distinguished by a predominantly characteristic attitude toward the land question. They are as follows: (1) the financial period, when land policy was largely dominated by financial motives; (2) the homestead period, when agricultural-settlement objectives predominated; (3) the period of reservation and reacquisition, marked by a reversal of the policy of rapid disposition; and (4) the recent period, during which special public attention has been given to a variety of land problems ranging from land development and conservation to land credit, land tenure, and land-use planning and zoning.

The first two epochs were largely influenced by the concepts of *laissez faire,* and only the phases of land policy which belong to these epochs will be sketched and appraised in the present chapter. This phase of our history already has been well described by Hibbard, Robbins, and others.[1] This chapter is in the nature of a summary of what has been written about our early land policy. The problems and policies of the last two epochs will be considered in subsequent chapters.

*Acquisition of Public Domain*

Between 1784 and 1801 all of the former colonies that had claims to Western lands ceded their rights to the Federal government, subject to various reservations. Among the most important of the reservations was recognition of grants already patented and in some cases of warrants not yet patented, including under certain conditions squatters' rights. Because of these reservations the Federal government had at its disposal

[1] See Benjamin H. Hibbard, *A History of the Public Land Policies,* The Macmillan Company, New York, 1924; also Roy M. Robbins, *Our Landed Heritage,* Princeton University Press, Princeton, N.J., 1942.

none of Kentucky and only a small proportion of Tennessee, while in the domain ceded by Georgia there were extensive claims, including the notorious Yazoo claim, which was long the subject of litigation. A similar obligation was assumed in acquiring lands by treaty with foreign powers.

The public domain—that is, the lands to which the Federal government acquired title—consisted of the cessions made by the former colonies together with larger areas later acquired by treaty from other countries. The net area to which the Federal government acquired title was considerably smaller than the area over which it acquired political jurisdiction. Table 1 shows the sources of acquisition, acres acquired, and, where

*Table* 1. Acquisition of the Public Domain

| How acquired | Land area, acres* | Water area, acres* | Total area, acres* | Amount paid | |
|---|---|---|---|---|---|
| | | | | Total | Per acre† |
| State cessions (1781–1802)... | 262,482,560 | 3,944,960 | 266,427,520 | $ 6,200,000 | 2.3¢ |
| Louisiana Purchase (1803)... | 523,446,400 | 6,465,280 | 529,911,680 | 27,267,622 | 5.1 |
| Purchase from Spain (1819).. | 43,342,720‡ | 2,801,920 | 46,144,640 | 6,489,768 | 14.1 |
| Oregon Compromise (1846).. | 180,644,480 | 2,741,760 | 183,386,240 | | |
| Mexican Cession (1848)..... | 334,479,360 | 4,201,600 | 338,680,960 | 15,000,000 | 4.4 |
| Purchase from Texas (1850). | 78,842,880 | 83,840 | 78,926,720 | 16,000,000 | 20.3 |
| Gadsden Purchase (1853).... | 18,961,920 | 26,880 | 18,988,800 | 10,000,000 | 52.7 |
| Total in the states........ | 1,442,200,320 | 20,266,240 | 1,462,466,560 | $80,957,390 | 5.5¢ |
| Alaska Purchase (1867)..... | 365,481,600 | 9,814,400 | 375,296,600 | 7,200,000 | 1.9 |
| Grand total.............. | 1,807,681,920 | 30,080,640 | 1,837,763,160 | $88,157,390 | 4.8¢ |

* J. R. Mahoney, *Natural Resources Activity of the Federal Government*, The Library of Congress Legislative Reference Service, Public Affairs Bulletin 76, Washington, January, 1950.

† Computed.

‡ Includes 33,920 acres of water area subsequently recognized as part of the state of Texas, which is not a public-land state.

SOURCE: All areas, except that of Alaska, were computed in 1912 by a committee representing the General Land Office, the Geological Survey of the Department of the Interior, the Bureau of Statistics, and the Bureau of the Census of the Department of Commerce and Labor. The area of Alaska was recomputed in connection with the 1940 decennial census.

costs were involved, the total purchase price and the price per acre to the Federal government. In addition to a total area of approximately 1,442,200,320 acres acquired in the states, title to about 505,000,000 acres rested in individual states and their political subdivision or in private owners. In other words, valid private claims in the area of the nonpublic-land states plus reservations in Ohio amounted to approximately 505,000,-000 acres.[2]

[2] Larry A. Reuss and Orville O. McCracken, *Federal Rural Lands*, p. 2, U.S. Bureau of Agricultural Economics, June, 1947.

*Basic Policies of Disposition*

Inasmuch as Virginia in 1784 ceded its extensive claims to western lands north of the Ohio River, and New York, Massachusetts, and Connecticut followed this example during the next 3 years, it fell to the Confederation to formulate a land policy. Its Ordinances of 1784, 1785, and 1787, dealing with methods and procedures in the disposal of land, established basic precedents for the land policy of the newly forming nation. In various parts of the country, as has been indicated, socage tenure had been virtually converted to alodial tenure in fee simple through the desuetude of its feudal features, that is, through nonpayment of quitrents and the customary recognition of the owner's unrestricted right of disposition. Legislation of the Revolutionary period had in effect converted socage tenure in a number of the former colonies into alodial tenure in fee simple. Subsequently, certain of the states formally adopted alodial tenure, or the passing of land in fee simple from the government to the first purchaser. In 1787, for instance, New York abolished all extant military tenures, changing them into tenure by free and common socage, and provided that all state lands should be granted in alodial tenure.

It is true that the Ordinances of 1784, 1785, and 1787 did not specifically establish alodial tenure, but the Ordinance of 1787 did so by implication through providing that in the Northwest Territory, estates (including real estate) might be devised or bequeathed by wills in writing and that real estate might be conveyed by lease and release, or bargain and sale. In section 9 of the Ordinance of 1787 eligibility for election as a representative was made contingent on ownership of at least 200 acres within the district "in fee simple."

From the beginning of the Federal government, alodial tenure appears to have been employed in the grants of title to the Federal public domain. Moreover, the Ordinance of 1787 established an important precedent by the provision that new states created from the national domain "shall never interfere with the primary disposal of the soil by the United States nor with any regulations that the United States may find necessary for securing the title in such soil to the bona-fide purchasers." Thus alodial tenure in fee simple, so favorable to the interests both of the capitalist and of the pioneer settler, became a basic element of policy in the disposition of the public domain, though departed from on occasion, particularly in certain legislation for the disposition of mineral lands and lands reserved for the Indians.

The Ordinance of 1787 also profoundly influenced American land tenure by provisions governing inheritance in intestacy. Section 2 provided that estates of landowners dying intestate should "descend to, and be distributed among their children, and the descendants of a deceased child, in equal parts," subject to dower rights of a widow to the life use of a one-third share of the real estate. Although even the application of this provision in the Northwest Territory was subject to modification by the states subsequently created, the principle of equal partition thus established set the precedent followed with minor modifications by the various states.

The new land policies in fact granted land to private individuals on the tacit theory that the rights of ownership extend indefinitely downward and upward. It should be pointed out that this policy waived reservation of rights to minerals beneath all lands, a policy of great significance. Although the Ordinance of 1785 provided for reservation of a one-third part of all gold, silver, and lead mines, and thus the principle of a different policy for mineral lands as distinguished from agricultural lands was given recognition, nevertheless such distinct policies were applicable mainly to lands predominantly mineral as determined by official classification. For many decades only easily recognizable mineral areas, consisting mainly of significant surface deposits of copper, lead, and coal, were set aside from the application of the general land laws, and the great bulk of the land was disposed of without any reservation of vast mineral treasures that lay beneath the surface. Furthermore, trespass, plunder, and illegal entry were frequent.

The failure during the earlier decades to distinguish the uses for which different types of land were adapted and to develop distinctive policies for each major type was no less notable in the case of forest land than for mineral land. In fact, the early land laws reflected a primary emphasis on agricultural expansion, to which forests were an obstacle to be removed as rapidly as possible, although a good deal of the land disposed of to farmers was better adapted for forests than for farming.

The prevailing laissez-faire point of view left the task of selection to the individual, and there was no serious attempt during the first century of our nation's policies to assert a public responsibility for the classification of agricultural land. In the General Land Act of 1796, to be sure, land surveyors were instructed to note the quality of the lands surveyed, as well as the location of salt licks and springs, mill sites, and mines, but these instructions were obeyed only perfunctorily, if at all.

Barring provision by an act of 1817 and subsequent acts for reserving certain live oak and red cedar forests for naval use, the vast forests east of the Mississippi River were disposed of under the general land acts without distinction between agricultural and forest lands. It was not until the Timber Cutting Act and the Timber and Stone Act, both passed in 1878, that further specific measures for the disposal of timber and timberland were provided. A year later the Federal Geological Survey was established and was charged not only with continuing duties in classifying mineral lands but also with making a broader classification to distinguish such categories as arable, irrigable, timber, pasture, and swamp lands. From this time forward there was an increasing tendency toward more discrimination in legislating for the disposition of different classes of land.

The principle of prior official surveys, which the British colonial authorities had futilely tried to introduce, was incorporated in the Ordinances of 1784 and 1785. It was provided also that grants should be carefully recorded. This was facilitated by adoption of rectangular surveys, which had already been employed in New England and sporadically in other colonies. The public domain was to be laid out in strips, or "ranges," running north and south, between meridian lines 6 miles apart, and numbered east or west from the principal meridian adopted for the survey. Each range was to be subdivided into townships 6 miles square, numbered north and south from a base survey line. In spite of some opposition, this policy was retained in subsequent land legislation. In a few of the earlier large grants to companies, only exterior boundaries were officially surveyed, the companies undertaking to run interior lines. The General Land Act of 1796, however, provided for a surveyor general and a corps of assistants, and henceforward the Federal government assumed all responsibility for initial surveys.

Thus, the Southern hit-or-miss practice of warrant, private survey, caveat, and patent was rejected, and very fortunately a large portion of the nation escaped the irregular boundary lines and associated complications and disadvantages that characterize the system of "metes and bounds." But the pressure of pioneer or speculative interests tended to break down the well-meant but halfhearted attempts to prevent a too rapid dispersion of population and to require a reasonable amount of compactness in settlement. The various land laws restricted the disposition of public lands to areas officially surveyed, but the multitude of squatters paid little regard even to that requirement, and their insistent demands tended to hasten the surveys and ultimately to compel recognition of their prescriptive rights.

### Sales Policies

The early years of the new and impecunious nation were marked by emphasis on disposition of the public domain as a source of revenue. This was the keynote of the well-known plan for disposition of public lands prepared by Hamilton in 1790 at the request of Congress. Neither Hamilton nor his contemporary statesmen, however, ignored the necessity of providing in some measure for the needs of the pioneers while considering the necessities of the treasury. His no less thrifty successor, Albert Gallatin, was even more inclined to stress the importance of facilitating settlement. From the very beginning, therefore, Federal land policy had a dual orientation, but the passage of time steadily lessened the emphasis on revenue motives and increased the tendency to regard the needs of the pioneer. This was due in part to the fact that public lands proved to be a poor source of revenue.

Nevertheless, the financial interest was sufficiently powerful to prevent a return to the homestead policies of the colonial period and to confine the distribution of land among individuals primarily to sales for nearly three-quarters of a century.    **1113538**

*Methods of Sale.* Owing partly to the revenue interest and partly to the belief that sales in large blocks to colonizing companies would promote greater compactness of settlement, the Confederation entered into contracts with several colonizing companies. More than 2 million acres were granted, at $1 an acre, but payable in depreciated Confederation obligations, with allowances for lands of poor quality, and subject to deferred payments. Through nonfulfillment and for other reasons, however, a much smaller area was actually patented.

The Ordinance of 1785 provided for the sale of land at auction by townships. One-half of the township might be purchased as a block, and one-half in units as small as a section. The minimum price was $1 per acre, but payable in depreciated currency. There was a slight gesture toward promoting compact disposition by providing that all the land in a township must be sold before another township could be offered. This principle was preferred by Washington, Jefferson, and other statesmen, but even this limitation was soon discarded.

From this time until adoption of the Homestead Acts, purchase at public auction subject to a minimum price was the principal method by which lands could be acquired from the Federal government by private individuals.

The minimum price was raised to $2 an acre in 1796, partly in the hope that the comparatively high minimum might discourage speculation and too rapid settlement. Pressure of competition from colonial and state grants, however, was such that it was difficult to dispose of Federal lands during the early years of the republic. It is true, choice lands usually commanded prices far above the minimum, particularly during the boom period 1818–1819, but the average price of Federal land from 1796 to 1820 was little above minimum.

By reason of the lag in sales and the pressure of pioneer interests, the minimum price was lowered to $1.25 in 1820 and was continued at that level for several decades. There also was a gradual reduction in the minimum acreage purchasable until it was finally lowered to 40 acres.

Table 2 shows the acreage sold and the average annual receipts per acre by periods from 1800 to 1860. The general downward trend in the receipts from the sale of land indicates efforts made to obtain free land and the concessions made to settlers.

Table 2. Sales and Receipts, Public Domain, 1800 to 1860

| Period | Average annual sales, acres | Average annual receipts per acre |
|--------|-----------------------------|----------------------------------|
| 1800–1809 | 330,219 | $2.08 |
| 1810–1819 | 1,432,319 | 2.68 |
| 1820–1829 | 866,991 | 1.41 |
| 1830–1839 | 6,231,612 | 1.27 |
| 1840–1849 | 1,773,695 | 1.17 |
| 1850–1860 | 8,238,538 | 0.91 |

SOURCE: Adapted from Benjamin H. Hibbard, *A History of the Public Land Policies*, The Macmillan Company, New York, 1924.

In spite of the existence of general land acts governing conditions of purchase, such as those of 1796, 1800, 1804, and 1820, the decision to offer specific areas for sale required action by Congress. After affirmative action the lands to be offered were advertised for not less than 3 months. Each auction sale must be kept open not less than 2 weeks. If all the land offered was not sold it might be offered again. Finally, land remaining unsold was purchasable at the minimum price.

The attempt to get in on the first offer for particularly desirable tracts sometimes led to a mad scramble at the door of the land office. In time a system of registration of applicants precluded such riotous disorder, and after the sales policy came to be confined to land opened to sale in Indian or other public reservations, a lottery system for selection of purchasers was sometimes employed. Gradually, also, the convenience of the frontiersmen in acquiring land was better served by a wider distribution of land offices.

*Absence of Restrictions on Ownership, Use, or Disposition.* Until after the outbreak of the Civil War, there was no limitation on the maximum acreage purchasable by an individual except his ability to pay for it.

Even this limitation was considerably modified for a time by the credit system, begun by the Confederation and further extended by the Land Act of 1796 and successive acts. Just as in the experience of the colonies, the credit system stimulated speculative purchase, as well as acquisition by frontiersmen, who at times overestimated their ability to obtain an early money income. Following the general financial collapse of 1819, Congress was confronted with the need for a long succession of stay laws, provisions for revision of interest, settlement for only part of the land contracted for, and other adjustments, which proved necessary for a dozen years after the credit policy was abandoned in 1820. The policy had stimulated excessive land speculation and intensified the financial difficulties of the nation.

There also were proposals from time to time that purchasers of Federal land be required to improve or settle it, but no such limitations were adopted until the Civil War.

Friends of the policy to dispose of public land to encourage settlement also proposed that the sales policy be restricted to units only large enough for a single farm, but not until after the passage of the Homestead Act was there a notable tendency to impose restrictions on the amounts of land obtainable under the sales policies.

Finally, there were no restrictions as to the subsequent disposition of the land after patent had been issued, either under the sales policy or under other methods of disposing of public domain.

## The Graduation Act

A modification of the policy of selling public lands subject to the minimum price of $1.25 an acre was effected by the Graduation Act, passed in 1854. From an early period proposals had been made to adjust the price of public lands in accordance with their relative desirability. Thomas H. Benton had been the champion of this idea over a period of three decades. By the middle of the nineteenth century the process of picking over and selecting the best of the public lands had left on the government's hands large areas of scattering tracts that appeared to sell but slowly. Accordingly, a sort of bargain-counter policy was adopted under which lands were offered for sale at a minimum price range from 12½ cents to $1 an acre. The minimum price varied in accordance with length of time the land had remained unsold since first offered. Much of the land that had remained unsold was relatively inaccessible rather than inferior in quality, and with improved means of transportation this land acquired a ready demand.

## The Preemption Policies

*The Squatter Problem.* For more than a decade after formation of the Union, squatters were technically considered trespassers. They were so numerous, however, and so widely supported by local public opinion that, except for a few sporadic attempts at ejectment, they were generally tolerated. Nevertheless, they were subject to the possibility that others might purchase their land at public auction and acquire a legal basis for dispossession. In order to guard against such an eventuality, pressure of frontier sentiment resulted in passage of a number of special preemption acts.

To a large extent, it is true, the squatters protected their own rights. Long before the Federal government formally recognized them they

banded together locally to discourage bidding on lands already occupied
and improved. They often visited land auctions in large numbers, formed
a protective cordon about the door or auction block, and made it appear
difficult and hazardous to those who manifested an interest in bidding on
land already occupied. In time the squatters established formal organizations known as "claim associations." These were extralegal bodies,
but they gave expression to local customs and to an overwhelming local
public opinion that had the effect of law. Their function was not only to
protect their rights against outsiders but also to adjudicate claims of their
own members and to prevent any member from encroaching on rights of
his neighbors, even though such rights had the sanction only of local
custom and public opinion. As there was no statutory definition of the
amount of land which could be preempted by occupancy and improvement, there was much overlapping and room for dispute as to the extent
of the individual squatter rights. The claim associations organized themselves to deal judicially with these disputes as well as to regulate procedures for bidding on lands to which duly recognized claims were
established.

*Arguments for and against Preemption.* To the pioneer who endured
the initial hazards and hardships of frontier settlement, who had opened
roads, stood off the Indians, and improved his land, it seemed monstrous
that another, by taking advantage of legal technicalities, should eject him
from his home. Moreover, the Federal government's tolerance of squatterism and its occasional recognition of squatters' rights were held to have
constituted a commitment which the government was obligated to recognize. There were also the usual arguments of the frontier interest in favor
of legislation facilitating settlement: the danger that foreign governments
would obtain a foothold in the West; greater protection of frontiers
against Indians; increased value of the remaining government lands; importance of enlarging tax rolls and public revenues; and the contribution
of rapid settlement to national income, wealth, security, and greatness.

Opposition to preemption reflected the desire for maximum revenues
from public lands, but this argument was largely nullified by failure of
land sales to yield on the average any appreciable amount above the
minimum price. It was also argued that if legally recognized, squatterism
would become universal and uncontrollable and that the general privilege
of purchasing at the minimum might depress land values in already-de-
veloped areas. To some extent opposition reflected the ever-present reluctance of older-settled sections to seeing their residents enticed away.

*Adoption of a General Preemption Policy.* This complex of motives was
sufficient to postpone for several decades a general acceptance of preemption. In 1830, 1834, and 1838, respectively, general preemption acts
valid for a single year were passed. Finally, in 1841, a general preemption

act applicable to certain states was adopted. The Homestead Act of 1862 made it applicable in all states and territories. Heads of families, male citizens 21 years of age or over, and widows, and in all cases citizens of the United States or aliens who had declared intention were granted a preemption right to purchase at $1.25 per acre land they had occupied and improved, up to a maximum of 160 acres per individual, provided the preemptor did not already own more than 320 acres within the United States.

The Preemption Act of 1841 did not confer a preemption right on settlers who occupied land in advance of official survey, and foes of the policy succeeded in postponing until 1853 and 1854 extension of the privilege to unsurveyed lands and in holding it even then to only six states.

The Preemption Act of 1841 marked the end of the old conservative land policy established in 1785. As Robbins describes it:[3]

This new policy in general recognized four important principles: first, it was evident that Congress at last regarded the settlement of the public domain as more desirable than the revenue that might be obtained from it; second, that Congress intended that the domain should not fall into the hands of those who already had enough land; third, that the domain should be settled in small farms so as to extend the blessing of cheap land to the largest number; and fourth, that settlers should be protected from all intrusion and allowed a reasonable time to earn or gather together a sum sufficient to buy the land. It was at last intended that the actual settler be placed on an equal basis with the speculator in competition for land.

## Abandonment of Sales Policies

Passage of the Homestead Act of 1862 has been commonly regarded as marking virtually the end of sales as the predominant method of distributing Federal land to individuals. Unfortunately, this was not the case. For one thing, Congress did not repeal the Preemption Act at that time, and for nearly three decades it continued to be possible for individuals to acquire a quarter section by preemption purchase, in addition to the land homesteaded. Furthermore, land previously formally offered for sale at auction and remaining unsold continued to be available for purchase by private entry at the minimum price of $1.25 for cash, script, or warrant until the general sales policy was finally repealed by Congress in 1891. In fact, in 1862 there remained available for cash sale 83,919,649 acres.[4] During the 1860's and 1870's as much as 20,000,000 acres, particularly of timberland, continued to be offered for sale at auction.

Both the Desert Land Act and the Timber and Stone Act, hereafter discussed, contained the purchase principle, although they limited

[3] Robbins, *op. cit.*, p. 91.

[4] Paul Wallace Gates, "The Homestead Law in an Incongruous Land System," *American Historical Review*, Vol. 61, p. 660, 1936.

amounts available to each individual. Furthermore, by special treaties with Indian tribes large areas in Indian reservations were thrown open to sale.

In some cases these sales were not even made at auction, but the land was disposed of in large blocks to railways and speculators who brought to bear potent political influence. In some of the later sales of Indian lands a gesture was made toward the homestead principle by restricting pur- chases to 160 acres and to persons able to qualify as homesteaders. Of course, the hundreds of millions of acres granted to states and railways were also disposed of largely by sale, although not directly by the Federal government.

Gradually, however, the effects of these extensive disposals in restrict- ing the area of desirable land open to homesteading and the accompany- ing excessive speculation and political corruption aroused public opinion to demand repeal of sales policies. A first step was an act of 1866 making public lands in Alabama, Arkansas, Florida, Louisiana, and Mississippi subject to entry only under the Homestead Act. This action, however, was mainly an aftermath of the Civil War, and in 1876 pressure by Southern interests and Northern timber barons brought about its repeal. In 1868, a resolution to end land sales passed the House of Representatives but failed to become law, and for nearly a quarter of a century longer, whole- sale sales and the accompanying orgy of speculation continued to parallel the Homestead Act. Finally, in 1891, Congress repealed the policies for land sales, including also the Preemption Act, although it still continued possible from time to time to purchase Indian lands.

## Military Bounties

*Return to Colonial Bounty Policies.* In continuation of colonial policies, military bounties to induce enlistment were employed by a majority of the commonwealths during the Revolutionary War. Even the Continental Congress, in spite of the fact that it had no land, offered generous bounties to privates and officers according to rank. In 1812 and in the Mexican War land bounties were resorted to, although in the former case officers were excluded.

In order that settlements of veterans might serve as a protective screen along the frontiers, the earlier military-bounty legislation tended to re- strict selection of land to particular military reservations. In land cessions to the Federal government a number of colonies reserved designated districts for entry of their outstanding military warrants. Congress re- served a large military district in Ohio to satisfy its Revolutionary land warrants, and other reserved areas were provided to take care of the land warrants of the War of 1812. When little desirable land remained in reservation, special legislation provided for issuance of land script ex- changeable for public land elsewhere in the public domain. After 1842, however, military-bounty warrants might be located on any lands subject to sale at private entry.

*Commercialization, Abuse, and Abandonment of Bounties.* The year 1850 witnessed a marked change in Federal policies for military bounties. Earlier acts had been offers to encourage enlistment. In 1850, the policy was given an ex post facto character by an act which granted military bounties for service in previous wars since the year 1798; and acts in 1855 and 1856 granted 160 acres to any soldier or his heirs who had served as long as 14 days in any previous war, beginning with the Revolutionary War. Furthermore, in 1852 Federal military warrants were made generally transferable. This altered the essential character of the policy from one related to the homestead ideal to the principle of financial inducement or reward for military service.

The new policy greatly stimulated speculation. Soldiers quickly disposed of the transferable warrants for prices well below even the established minimum sale price for government land, and soon great quantities of military warrants were being quoted and sold on the New York stock exchange. Land speculators were enabled to acquire rights to millions of acres at as low as 50 cents an acre, subsequently reselling at advanced prices to settlers.

Fortunately, at the outbreak of the Civil War, after more than 64 million acres had been disposed of through military warrants, the abuses were clearly apparent, and the near prospect of free land under homestead legislation was sufficient to prevent use of military bounties to induce enlistment.

## Public Support for a Homestead Policy

Preoccupation with the financial possibilities of the public domain long prevented adoption of the principle of granting land free to settlers. Failure to follow the colonial precedents is all the more notable in view of the fact that a number of the commonwealths were actively employing the homestead principle. During the first decade after adoption of the Constitution, moreover, a number of petitions from frontier settlers were received, and from this period forward the idea of free land for settlers was proposed from time to time by Congressmen from Western states.

As early as 1825, Senator Thomas Hart Benton, champion of graduation and in general of liberalization of public land laws, proposed the granting of refuse lands free to settlers, a proposal supported by memorials from a number of state legislatures. The spirit of the settlers was eloquently expounded by Benton. In speaking of the freeholder, he said:[5]

[5] From a speech by Thomas Hart Benton found in his *Thirty Years' View: A History of the Working of the American Government for Thirty Years, from 1820 to 1850*, Vol. I, Chap. IV, pp. 11–12.

Tenantry is unfavorable to freedom. It lays the foundation for separate orders in society, annihilates the love of country, and weakens the spirit of independence. The farming tenant has, in fact, no country, no hearth, no domestic altar, no household god. The freeholder, on the contrary, is the natural supporter of a free government; and it should be the policy of republics to multiply their freeholders, as it is the policy of monarchies to multiply tenants. We are a republic, and we wish to continue so: then multiply the class of freeholders; pass the public lands cheaply and easily into the hands of the people; sell, for a reasonable price, to those who are able to pay; and give, without price, to those who are not. I say give, without price, to those who are not able to pay; and that which is so given, I consider as sold for the best of prices; for a price above gold and silver; a price which cannot be carried away by delinquent officers, nor lost in failing banks, nor stolen by thieves, nor squandered by an improvident and extravagant administration. It brings a price above rubies—a race of virtuous and independent laborers, the true supporters of their country, and the stock from which its best defenders must be drawn.

> What constitutes a State?
> Not high-rais'd battlements, nor labored mound,
> Thick wall, nor moated gate;
> Nor cities proud, with spires and turrets crown'd
> Nor starr'd and spangled courts,
> Where low-born baseness wafts perfume to pride:
> But MEN! high-minded men,
> Who their duties know, but know their RIGHTS,
> And, knowing, dare maintain them.

In 1828, the House Committee on Public Lands recommended granting 80-acre homesteads, but no favorable action was taken. In 1842, Congress inaugurated a series of special Homestead Acts. The first, applying exclusively to Florida, reverted to the colonial policy of granting land to settlers on dangerous frontiers. It offered in certain exposed areas to settlers capable of bearing arms 160 acres on condition of building a house, cultivating 5 acres, and residing for not less than 4 years. An act passed in 1850 rewarded settlers who had wrested Oregon from the Indians by granting a half section to each man who had settled there before 1850 and an additional amount to the wife of each settler. To those arriving between 1850 and 1853, one-half of these amounts was offered. Similar acts were passed to apply to Washington and New Mexico.

*Sectional Character of Opposition to Homesteads.* During the two decades just preceding the Civil War, the homestead idea came to be bound up with the sectional cleavage over the tariff and extension of slavery. The plantation interests emphasized the adverse relation of homesteads to political, economic, and social objectives of the South, and in the face of the aggressive slavocracy, support of a liberal land policy by the frontier portions of the South gradually gave way. In the Senate, champions of the plantation interests, aided by Eastern conservatives, were able to postpone action for a dozen years after the homestead principle had won a substantial majority in the House. A homestead bill finally was passed by both Houses in 1860 but was vetoed by President Buchanan.

The opposition was not always frank in declaring the real reasons for its antagonism but resorted to arguments that at times carried the odor of sophistry. It was argued that Congress had no constitutional right to give to individuals property that belonged to the nation; that the proposal violated state rights; that the homestead policy would favor farmers to the detriment of other citizens; that poor families were easily able to acquire land under the preemption laws; and even that the Federal government would be deprived of needed revenues. More clearly reflecting the real motives were the allegations that free homesteads would lower land prices in the older states, draw away their population, adversely affect holders of military-bounty warrants (mostly speculators), stimulate foreign immigration, promote expansion of "free" territory, and enhance the political power of antislavery forces.

## The New Homestead Philosophy

On the other hand, the homestead agitation gave rise to a new and significant philosophic attitude with respect to land, formulated and given expression by the National Reform Association, of which Horace Greeley was the prophet. To some extent it was espoused by the newly formed Free Soil party. While employing the familiar arguments of the frontier brought forward in support of preemption, the new philosophy also included points of view somewhat in advance of the public opinion of that period. For one thing, the argument was advanced that the increase of receipts from customs and other taxes resulting from a rapid expansion of population would greatly exceed the small income that could be derived from land sales.

The new philosophy, however, was not merely opposed to the sale of public land but, rather, urged that it be disposed of exclusively to those who would occupy and use it. The land reformers were willing even to support a policy of sale at higher prices than required under preemption, provided such sales were exclusively to bona fide settlers and not to speculators. Merely making land free or cheap, without proper restrictions, the reformers recognized, might only stimulate speculation.

*Restrictions on Land Acquired.* The new doctrine rested on the dogma of natural rights. Just as every man is entitled to "life, liberty, and the pursuit of happiness," so, it was held, every man has a natural right to land, the essential basis of life and welfare. This right must necessarily be restricted to the area requisite for a family's needs; otherwise, there would result the twin evils, land speculation and land monopoly. Speculation compelled the settler either to pay an excessive price for land or to range far and wide in search of free land and to settle in dispersed locations, thus making it difficult and expensive to provide schools and other facilities. Meanwhile, the speculator held the intervening lands out of use until he could profit from the progress of the community brought about by the pioneer's toil. Land monopolization tended to deprive the would-be users of land from access to it or compelled them to resort to tenancy.

A variant of this theme was the labor-and-wages argument for free land emphasized in the 1840's by George Henry Evans and other labor leaders. They held that access to free land would help to maintain the economic independence of the wage-earning class and to support the wage structure.

The reformers were urging a complete about-face in national land policy. They proposed the cessation of unrestricted sales, military bounties, and lavish grants to states and corporations for internal improvements —in short, the exclusive restriction of land grants to settlers.

Without restrictions, however, the settler himself was likely to turn speculator or to become the prey of speculators and land sharks. Therefore the reformers proposed that land not be eligible for foreclosure for debt. The homesteader might dispose of a portion of his homestead, but only to someone who, with the new acquisition, would have no more than 160 acres. Evans and his labor associates proposed that homesteads should not be alienable for money or property but only by exchange for another homestead.

### Adoption of the Homestead Policy

The full proposals of the land reformers were too radical to obtain support by public opinion, which had not advanced sufficiently to accept the idea of restrictions on alienation or even complete elimination of other methods of disposing of public domain. It is true the Homestead Act of 1862 required 5 years' residence, but this fell far short of the objective of the reformers. Moreover, the Homestead Act did further violence to their ideals by permitting commutation at the option of the homesteader, after 6 months' residence, by satisfying preemption requirements and paying $1.25 an acre (in certain canal and railway grant areas, $2.50). After 1891, 14 months' residence was required, but the entryman might wait 6 months before establishing residence, leaving a net of only 8 months' residence before commuting was allowed. In 1912, partly to meet competition of the Canadian homestead provisions and partly because of the hardships of residence during frigid winter weather,

*Table* 3. Methods of Disposal by Land Acts, 1784 to 1862

| Land act | Minimum sale price | Method of sale or disposal | Size of tract | Terms of sale |
|---|---|---|---|---|
| Ordinances of 1784 and 1785 | $1 an acre Discount of one-third to companies and acceptance of government paper | Auction | Half of townships offered entire, other half by 640-acre tracts | Cash until 1787, then one-third cash and rest in 3 months |
| Act of 1796 | $2 an acre Evidence of public debt accepted at face value | Auction | Half of tracts 5,760 acres, the rest 640 acres | One-twentieth cash, credit of 30 days on balance of first half, and a year on second half |
| Act of 1800 | $2 an acre | Auction | Minimum of 320 acres | 8 per cent discount for cash Liberal credit system inaugurated |
| Act of 1820 | $1.25 an acre | Auction | 160 acres or 80 acres | Cash |
| Act of 1841 (Preemption) | $1.25 an acre Grants to railroads and canals at $2.50 | Select and settle, then purchase at minimum price | Not more than 160 acres | Cash |
| Act of 1854 (Graduation Act) | Price graduated. For example, if on market from 10–14 years, $1 an acre; 20–24 years, 50¢; over 30 years, 12½¢ | Offered for sale at stated minimum price | | Cash |
| Act of 1862 (Homestead) Act) | Free homesteads of 160 acres Only payment was a fee ranging from $26 to $34 | Settle and "prove up" | Not to exceed 160 acres | Only a nominal fee, but other conditions had to be met |

SOURCE: Benjamin H. Hibbard, *A History of the Public Land Policies*, The Macmillan Company, New York, 1924; Roy M. Robbins, *Our Landed Heritage*, Princeton University Press, Princeton, N.J., 1942.

the residence requirement was lowered to 7 months' actual residence in each of 3 years.

From time to time, residence requirements were suspended or modified during absence on military duty, and credit on residence requirements was allowed on account of military service.

Some of the principal features of methods of disposal by land acts that have so far been considered are summarized in Table 3.

### Extension of the Homestead Policy to Dry-Land Areas

*Adjustments with Reference to Dry-Farming and Range Areas.* It gradually became clear that the limitation of area to 160 acres did not fit semiarid regions, where 160 acres proved too much for irrigation and too little for grazing or mechanized grain farming. Congress recognized these facts tardily. But in 1904, it passed the Kinkaid Act, which permitted a maximum of 640 acres in the Sand Hills region of Nebraska, an area considered adapted only to grazing. Somewhat more cautiously, the Enlarged Homestead Act of 1909 was passed. This Act was applicable to nine Western states, but soon was extended to apply to three others. It permitted homesteading of 320 acres of nonirrigable land, but required cultivation of one-fourth of the area (except in Idaho, where one-half was required as a condition of permitting the settler to reside within 20 miles of his homestead when portable water was not obtainable on the land homesteaded). This Act, however, fell so far short of meeting conditions that during the next 5 years little more than 1 per cent of the available area was entered. In 1916, therefore, Congress passed the Stock-raising Homestead Act, which permitted the homesteading of 640 acres certified by the Secretary of the Interior as nonirrigable, suitable only for grazing land and forage, without merchantable timber, and of such character that 640 acres were required to support a family.

The Department of the Interior endeavored to interpret the 640-acre provision as a responsibility to prevent homesteading where 640 acres were insufficient for a livelihood. However, local pressures were such that the Department was able to maintain a minimum requirement of only the capacity of 640 acres to carry 25 head of cattle. This measure also introduced new and significant principles into our public land policy. For the first time the nation reserved the right to coal and other minerals beneath the surface of lands granted for agricultural use. Water holes and trails leading to them were also reserved. No commutation privileges were permitted.

*The Timber Culture Acts.* Another measure to adjust the homestead principle to the special conditions of the Great Plains was the Timber Culture Act of 1873. It reflected a recognition of the special advantages of timber in the farm economy, and its potential benefits in the treeless regions of the Plains. The Act granted 160 acres to any person (later limited to a citizen or a person declaring intention) 21 years old and head of a family, who would plant 40 acres to trees 12 feet apart and cultivate the tract for 10 years. Amendments soon passed reduced the period of cultivation to 8 years, and in 1878 the area of requisite planting was reduced to 10 acres.

The Timber Culture Act accomplished little toward realization of its objective. It was employed mainly for speculation in relinquishments. It was possible to make entry and, through perfunctory compliance with requirements for improvement, hold the homestead right for about 3 years with a view to taking advantage of locally rising land values. With the aid of associates, this process could be repeated so long as there was prospect of speculative profit, until finally a genuine settler acquired the claim by purchasing the relinquishment and attempted to comply with requirements of the law. Similarly, the law was employed by large live-stock concerns to retard settlement of the range. When the Act was re-placed in 1891, only a little more than 10,000,000 acres had been pat-ented. That the Act was used merely to exclude others from acquiring title is shown by the fact that for the 4 years from 1879 to 1882, inclu-sive, 13,657,146 acres were entered under the Act, and only 23,571 acres reached final entry.[6]

*Homestead Policies for Lands Requiring Irrigation.* There were exten-sive areas where no agriculture was possible without irrigation that re-quired far more expenditure than the usual homesteader was capable of making. Frequently large aggregates of capital were needed.

To meet these conditions, special modifications of the homestead pol-icy appeared essential. In 1876, Congress through the Desert Land Act provided for granting 640 acres to each settler who would irrigate it within 3 years after filing. Payment of 25 cents an acre was required at time of filing, and $1 more at the time proof was rendered. Thus, the Act was a combination of preemption and homestead principles, the larger maximum area being intended to compensate for the extra costs of irrigation.

The shortcomings of the measure were soon apparent. The require-ments for irrigation were vague, and the intent of the Act was largely evaded by running shallow ditches and other perfunctory gestures. The Act was used, along with regular homestead measures, to acquire large areas for purposes not intended by Congress, including mineral lands, strategic water holes, and valuable timber. In fact, the policy contributed more to land speculation than to agricultural development by irrigation.

The Act gave too much land for an ordinary irrigation homestead, but

[6] Thomas Donaldson, *The Public Domain,* p. 1090, Government Printing Office, Washington, 1884.

too little to compensate for large-scale irrigation enterprises. Even when entrymen lumped their holdings, desert land before irrigation was of little capital value as a basis for borrowing.

In 1888, Congress authorized the President to withdraw from entry land suitable for reservoirs, canals, or the application of water by irrigation. For some years there was administrative failure to give substantial effect to the measure, although in course of time important reservoir sites were withdrawn. Meanwhile, the Desert Land Act of 1876 continued in force. The General Land Act of 1891 restricted to 320 acres the amount of agricultural land that could be entered under any land act. For desert-land entries the Act stipulated that the entryman must make reclamation improvements in each of 3 years, amounting to $1 an acre a year, and before proving up must make water available for the entire homestead and put one-eighth into cultivation.

In spite of these more stringent provisions, it continued to be possible to get title to large areas. The same man was permitted to make a regular homestead entry and also a desert-land entry, while both husband and wife might enter land under the Desert Land Act. Dummy corporations were formed to make entry, and various devices continued to be employed for avoiding or perfunctorily fulfilling the requirements of irrigation. On the other hand, sincere attempts by settlers to fulfill the requirements encountered difficulties, as shown by the fact that the area of final entries was only about one-fourth that of original entries. This led to a relief act in 1915, extending the time of performance and providing alternative means of acquiring the homestead in case the entryman had complied with requirements in regard to expenditures without success in getting water.

*The Carey Act.* Obvious abuse of the Desert Land Acts and increasing pressure for an effective reclamation policy led Congress to try a new tack in 1894 by passage of the Carey Act. The various states of the arid region had developed their own laws and administrative arrangements relative to water rights and regulation of concerns engaged in irrigation. This made it difficult for the Federal government to deal at long range with diverse conditions through general laws for the conditional distribution of land.

The Carey Act shifted these responsibilities to the respective states. Grants of 1 million acres each were authorized to each of 10 states, with additional amounts for certain specified states, making an aggregate authorization of 14 million acres. To obtain such grants, however, the states must cause the lands to be irrigated, occupied, and partly put into cultivation. The state might receive patents from time to time to the areas on which it had fulfilled the conditions or designate individuals to whom patent might issue, but not to exceed 160 acres per individual.

The usual method of operation was for the state to approve specific projects promoted by irrigation concerns. Thereupon the state made application to the Secretary of the Interior for withdrawal of the specified lands from entry under the general land laws. If approved by the Secretary, the land was segregated and withdrawn, provided, however, that construction must be initiated within 3 years and the land be under irrigation within 10 years. Thereupon the state authorized the promoting concern to construct the proposed irrigation works under the conditions required, the state agreeing to dispose of the land only to those who contracted to purchase water rights. Generally the land was sold by the state, at 50 cents an acre. When the land and water rights had been purchased, the concern responsible for construction was required to deed the irrigation works to the water users' association.

The Carey Act fell far short of meeting expectations. Not a few of the projects launched were ill-considered, resulting in losses to bondholders. Private-irrigation bonds acquired such an unfavorable reputation that it was difficult to float them. As late as 1931, of the 14,000,000 acres authorized, only 1,174,903 had been patented under the Carey Act.

The advocates of reclamation, therefore, turned to the Federal government and succeeded in inducing Congress to pass the Reclamation Act of 1902, which provided for Federal financing, construction, and administration of reclamation projects. The issuance of a patent to a homestead was made conditional on repayment of cost of construction, reclamation of at least half of the irrigable area of the homestead, and fulfillment of the regular homestead residence requirements.

## Special Provisions for Disposing of Timber and Timberland

Under the sales policy it was possible to buy timberland in any part of the public domain, except in the minor areas reserved for naval purposes, without limitations as to area and at prices governed by the demand, subject to the minimum specified in the general land laws. Under the lavish military-bounty policies and generous grants to states, timberlands could be purchased at prices less than the minimum. Under the auction system, combination among agents of large timber companies made it easy to avoid competition in bidding.

It was the practice for a few individuals and huge lumber companies to acquire timberlands through corruption of the preemption and homestead systems, by employing dummy entrymen or other devices, by purchase at private sale of so-called "offered" lands, or by the practice of wholesale thefts. Until near the close of the century the appropriation of timber occurred with little restraint, and for a period following, the administrative facilities available to the Land Office for protecting the public domain were wholly inadequate, nor was local public opinion an adequate safeguard, for timber was generally regarded as an obstacle to development.

*The Timber Cutting Act and the Timber and Stone Act.* Hoping to put an end to such abuses, Congress as early as 1878 passed two measures to this end. The Timber Cutting Act was designed ostensibly to remove the excuse for appropriating timber illegally, by permitting citizens of certain states and territories to cut free of charge from the public domain timber for the special requirements of agricultural settlers and miners. The Act, however, merely gave legal recognition to the excuses that had long been brought forward to justify wholesale theft. It would have been far better if Congress had frankly faced the problem and made provision for the sale of timber at officially appraised values. While this was proposed by officials of the General Land Office, Congress was not yet prepared to differentiate a forest policy from the general agricultural land policy.

In fact, the same year Congress also passed the Timber and Stone Act, which was in theory intended to give the homesteader opportunity to acquire an additional quarter section from which to provide for his needs for timber and stone. While it originally applied only to the three Pacific states and Nevada, the Act was extended in 1892 to all the public-land states. It permitted a citizen to purchase 160 acres of nonmineral land valuable mainly for timber and stone, at a minimum price of $2.50 per acre. This was also the maximum price asked by the Land Office until after Nov. 30, 1908, when timberland sold at appraised value, subject to the minimum price provided by the law.

Timber interests experienced no difficulty in taking advantage of the Act. Scores of dummy entrymen were brought in and directed to make entry for the particular quarter sections previously determined to bear the most valuable stands of timber. In spite of the required oath that the land was not obtained for speculation but for the exclusive use and benefit of the entryman, on obtaining patent he disposed of the holding to the lumber company. Under the Timber and Stone Act, therefore, the Federal government disposed of, for a price averaging little more than $3 an acre, nearly 14 million acres of land probably worth ten times the price for which it was sold.

*The Forest Homestead Act.* The Forest Homestead Act, passed in 1912, was in theory and intent akin to the other homestead legislation. In effect, however, it should be classed with the forest-disposal measures because it actually operated mainly as a means of getting valuable timber in the national forests into private possession.

The Act was passed in response to the Western argument that the wholesale reservation of lands included extensive areas suitable for farming. The measure put the burden of discovery on the homesteader, who was permitted to define the location of his land by metes and bounds, provided the tract did not extend more than a mile, thus permitting tracts of irregular shape. Subject to approval by the Federal Forest Service, the land then became subject to entry under the Homestead Act, but without the privilege of commutation.

In his study of national forest policy, Professor John Ise has presented striking statistics that illustrate how the Act was employed mainly as a means of acquiring timber. For instance,

. . . of a total of 12,330 acres in certain contested claims in the Northwest, only 47 acres were found to be under cultivation. Over 400,000 acres eliminated from the Olympic National Forest at the instance of the Washington delegation in Congress on the ground that it was agricultural land, was largely taken up under the Forest Homestead Act. Ten years later, the total area in cultivation was only 570 acres. In the case of nine townships in Idaho adjacent to the St. Joe National Forest, it was found that, of 264 homesteads patented, 208 passed to lumber companies within three years after patent was issued, and nearly all the rest were being held for speculation.[7]

### Grants of Public Land as Subventions and Subsidies

More than a quarter of the public domain available for disposition by the Federal government was granted to states or private corporations, either as subventions in encouragement of education or subsidies to stimulate development of transport facilities. For the most part, the grantees were left free to decide methods, terms, and conditions of disposition. Therefore, such grants constituted a resignation by the Federal government of its responsibility in determining the future character of tenure and utilization of the lands concerned.

*The Distribution Acts.* Congress early recognized the right of the individual states to share in the proceeds from sales of public domain within their borders. In connection with the credit system of land sales Congress stipulated on the admission of new states that public lands sold to private persons be exempt from taxation for 5 years and, in some cases also, that the states not tax nonresident purchasers higher than residents. By way of compensation Congress agreed to pay the states concerned a percentage of receipts from land sales—3 per cent to Ohio and Louisiana, and 5 per cent to states subsequently admitted, with stipulations for the use of the funds for internal improvements or education. After the repeal of the credit system, the conditions imposed on the states were gradually abandoned, but the 5 per cent grants continued.

As the financial position of the Federal government improved, there developed a demand for distribution of remaining lands or the proceeds therefrom to the states. The public-land states tended to favor distribution

---

[7] John Ise, *United States Forest Policy*, p. 259, Yale University Press, New Haven, Conn., 1920.

of the lands, and this form of the proposal received support from the Southern colonial states because it appeared consistent with the doctrine of state rights. They also favored the Federal government's getting more of its revenue from lower duties and not discouraging this source of revenue through high protective-tariff rates. However, in the period just preceding the Crisis of 1837, public revenues had become redundant, which was embarrassing to the supporters of the protective-tariff policy. To be rid of this embarrassment, the financial and industrial interests of the nation, operating through the Whig Party, supported the proposal for distributing the proceeds of the public lands, which gained many advocates also, because, in contrast to the proposal to distribute the lands to the states in which they lay, it appeared to make possible doing justice to the older, as well as to the newer, states and to avoid difficulties arising from lack of uniformity in methods of disposing of land.

After a long struggle in Congress, under the leadership of Henry Clay, a bill to distribute the proceeds was passed in 1841. Before the next year was out, however, the severe financial depression had led to so serious a fiscal deficit that Congress was compelled to suspend operation of the financial provisions, but the provision to grant each new state 500,000 acres in aid of internal improvements was retained.

*Swampland Grants.* In Louisiana, private and state enterprise began to grapple with the problem of wet lands early in the eighteenth century, and by the middle of the nineteenth had brought large areas into cultivation. This had much to do with influencing Congress in its decision to delegate to the states the responsibility for reclaiming such lands, including the responsibility of selection, though subject to Federal approval. In 1849 Congress granted to Louisiana the swamplands belonging to the public domain in that state and extended the policy to other states the following year. In 1860, the policy was applied to Oregon and Minnesota, but without the privilege of lieu selections and indemnity which had applied to the states earlier admitted. The Swamp Land Grants applied to the states bordering the Mississippi, except Tennessee and Kentucky, and to Alabama, Michigan, Ohio, Indiana, Oregon, and California.

Unfortunately, although the alleged purpose was to promote reclamation, no requirements to that effect were imposed on the states to which the land was granted, and the actual results in reclamation were negligible. Whatever was accomplished resulted from private enterprise, after title passed into private hands.

In general the states were extremely slow in exercising the privilege of selection and making application for patents. In the meantime, much of the land subsequently claimed under terms of the Swamp Land Act had been disposed of by the Federal government. These circumstances were further complicated by the fact that the states sometimes sold the same land claimed by individuals or corporations under Federal patents.[8] To remedy this thoroughly confused situation, Congress found it necessary to take action along two lines: (1) to permit lieu selections in other parts of the public domain subject to entry at $1.25 or less per acre, and (2) to indemnify the states for swamplands sold by the Federal government by transferring the proceeds to the states concerned.

The Swamp Land Grants were the occasion for widespread fraud, collusion, and speculation.[9] While for a time several states made their selections on the basis of Federal survey maps, the states usually employed their own surveyors on a fee basis, which encouraged designation of the largest possible area. Extensive areas overflowed at rare intervals, and lands merely made wet occasionally by rain or snow were included. Although the General Land Office retained power of approval, there was an extreme degree of administrative laxity.

*Subvention for Education.* The colonial policy of reservations of public land for encouragement of education was incorporated in the Ordinance of 1785 by reservation of the sixteenth section in each township for support of common schools, a policy continued in subsequent land legislation. In 1848, Congress provided for reservation for the same purpose of an additional section, number 36, in each state admitted during or after that year. Three states, New Mexico, Arizona, and Utah, received a grant of a third section, number 32. Very early the principle was established that if the designated sections had been disposed of or were within military, Indian, or other specially reserved areas, the state might make lieu selections, preferably in the same township or in an adjoining township. Beginning with 1866, it came to be customary to require lieu selections when the designated sections included mineral lands, and after 1910, similarly for valuable water-power sites. In time, lieu selections were required for areas occupied and improved by squatters.

The earlier grants carried the presumption that the lands would become a permanent source of income through renting them. Some of the states, however, found the role of landlord for such widely scattered properties difficult and costly and petitioned Congress for permission to sell the land. This privilege was granted to Ohio in 1836 and thereafter

---

[8] These difficulties were largely avoided in Oregon and Minnesota by requiring those states to make their selections within 2 years and by excluding from the grants lands already patented.

[9] Robert W. Harrison, *Swamp Land Reclamation in Louisiana, 1849–1879*, Baton Rouge, La., 1951. As a result of his original research on land reclamation in Louisiana under the Swamp Land Acts, Robert Harrison concludes that although emphasis has been placed on failures, frauds, and scandals that surrounded the program, this is not the whole story. He points out that the experiences gained under the Swamp Land Acts during the years 1850 to 1880 provided data and knowledge that were very valuable in the formulation of later flood-control programs and to an understanding of the development of the Lower Mississippi Valley.

to other states already admitted and to new states, subject to the requirement that the proceeds be invested as permanent endowment. Beginning with Colorado in 1875, Congress began to specify minimum sales prices or to require sale in accordance with a competent appraisal.

A number of states derived additional funds for the support of common schools from the 3 per cent and 5 per cent grants under the Distribution Acts and from part of the proceeds from swamp and saline grants.

In 1862, following a Presidential veto, Congress passed the first Morrill Act, which granted to each state, including the original thirteen, 30,000 acres for each Senator and Representative to which the state was entitled under the 1860 census, the proceeds to be employed for establishment and support of an institution of higher education to emphasize agriculture and the mechanic arts. States not including sufficient public land might receive land scrip, to be used in other states containing public land, on land open to entry at $1.25 an acre.

Various other special grants were made for the furtherance of institutions of higher education, either through special grants or general allotment grants on the admission of each new state.

*Grants for Internal Improvement.* Although a few special grants were made early in the nineteenth century exclusively for the promotion of internal improvements, such as grants to Ohio and Indiana for particular wagon roads, in general grants for internal improvements were not clearly differentiated from grants for education. For nearly two decades the general policy regarding grants for internal improvements was confused by controversy and clouded by the question of constitutionality. In the 1820's and 1830's, several special grants were made to Ohio, Indiana, Illinois, Wisconsin, and Alabama to encourage canal building and river improvements. In the Distribution Act of 1841, grants of 500,000 acres were made to each of certain states for the promotion of internal improvements, a policy continued on the admission of each new state until 1889. Beginning with 1841, the grants were no longer made exclusively for roads and canals, and the total per state often exceeded the customary 500,000 acres.

Following the Distribution Act, the granting of land for specific internal improvements was virtually in abeyance for a time, except for grants to Wisconsin and Iowa in 1848 for river improvement. In the 1850's and 1860's, grants for canals were made to Wisconsin and Michigan, and in Oregon there was a renewal of grants for wagon roads.

By the middle of the century, however, roads and canals were beginning to surrender supremacy to the railroad, and Congress entered upon a policy of grants for the construction of railways. The first step was the granting of rights of way and terminal sites, together with the privilege of using timber, stone, and dirt along the right of way. Finally, in 1850, strong opposition, partly on constitutional grounds, was overcome, and large grants were made for construction of the Illinois Central to the states through which the road would pass. Each state was supposed to dispose of the land, but was not forbidden to donate the proceeds to the railway corporation. Once the log jam of opposition was broken, there followed in the 1850's a number of other grants, and in 1862, after sectionalism ceased to be a deterrent, grants were made to the Union Pacific and Central Pacific railroad corporations, and during the next 4 years to other Western companies.

As early as 1827, the policy was adopted in canal grants of donating alternate sections for a certain distance on each side of the right of way. This policy was followed in the railway grants, the distance on each side ranging from 6 miles to as much as 40 miles. This policy reflected the lingering influence of the idea that public lands should be a source of Federal revenue, for it was believed the value of the alternate sections retained by the government would increase. This point of view also was reflected in the policy of requiring in most grants a "double minimum" sale price of $2.50 per acre for alternate sections retained by the government.

The desire to protect the interests of settlers on granted lands was reflected in the provision in some of the canal grants, and in railway grants preceding 1864, that after a limited period settlers might have a preemption right to purchase the lands granted, at the usual minimum of $1.25 an acre. The Northern Pacific grant, however, specified a minimum of $2.50.

Growing farmer hostility to railways, dissatisfaction of would-be homesteaders with the diversion of such huge areas to private corporations, and the dilatory tactics of railways in making their lieu selections, which held up the homesteading of the larger areas within which the lieu lands were to be selected, resulted in the virtual abandonment after 1871 of the policy of further grants to railways. In fact, there developed a strong movement to recover the government lands already granted, where nonperformance by the railway appeared to provide legal grounds.

## Quantitative Effects of Disposition of Public Domain

The quantitative influence of the various public-land laws as of 1943 is shown in Table 4. The first part of the table shows, by methods of disposal, the amount of the land grants and the approximate acreage that was sold or disposed of in various ways. Because of the complex methods of disposing of public lands and the overlapping allotments, claims, etc., it is not possible to present figures strictly confined to methods of disposal. However, from the items listed, one can determine approximately the area of land granted for different purposes.

In connection with this part of the table, the chart on page 58 is of interest in that it shows the history of the original entries by years from 1800 to 1943. The table and the chart with accompanying notes should be helpful in a study of our land-disposal policies and programs.

*Table* 4. Disposition of Public Domain

*Million acres*

Approximate area of public lands disposed of under the public-land laws, as of June 30, 1943:*

Granted to states:

| | |
|---|---:|
| For support of common schools. | 77.5 |
| For reclamation of swampland. | 64.9 |
| For construction of railroads. | 37.1 |
| For support of miscellaneous institutions. | 20.6 |
| For purposes not elsewhere classified. | 16.0 |
| For construction of canals. | 4.6 |
| For construction of wagon roads. | 3.3 |
| For improvement of rivers. | 1.4 |
| Total. | 225.4 |
| Disposed of by sales and other methods not elsewhere classified. | 300.0 |
| Granted or sold to homesteaders. | 285.0 |
| Granted to railroad corporations†. | 88.9 |
| Granted to veterans as military bounties. | 61.0 |
| Confirmed as private land claims. | 34.0 |
| Sold under timber and stone laws. | 13.9 |
| Granted or sold under timber-culture laws. | 10.9 |
| Sold under desert-land laws. | 10.0 |
| Total. | 1,029.1 |

Area of public and Indian lands in the public-land states, estimated as of June 30, 1943:*

Area subject to general disposition under public-land laws:

| | |
|---|---:|
| Vacant land outside grazing districts. | 42.8 |
| Vacant land within grazing districts. | 136.7 |

Area not subject to general disposition under public-land laws:

| | |
|---|---:|
| Reclamation withdrawals. | 14.0 |
| Indian reservations. | 53.6 |
| National parks and monuments. | 11.5 |
| Wildlife refuges and game ranges. | 5.1 |
| Oregon and California revested lands. | 2.6 |
| Stock driveways. | 4.7 |
| Power and water reserves. | 6.1 |
| National forests. | 137.5 |
| Other withdrawals and reservations. | 19.2 |
| Area in unperfected entries. | 0.7 |
| Estimated total area of public and Indian lands (excluding overlap). | 413.1 |
| Grand total, United States. | 1,442.2 |

*Table* 4. Disposition of Public Domain.—(*Continued*)

*Million acres*

Area of public, Indian, and other lands in Alaska:‡

| | |
|---|---:|
| Vacant public lands............................................. | 270.0 |
| Oil and gas reservations (including naval)........................ | 48.8 |
| National forests............................................... | 20.9 |
| Fish and wildlife reservations................................... | 7.9 |
| National parks and monuments.................................. | 6.9 |
| Native reservations............................................ | 3.9 |
| Military and naval reservations................................. | 4.1 |
| Other withdrawals, reservations, and uses (including private)......... | 3.0 |
| Total................................................. | 365.5§ |
| Total public domain, United States and Alaska................. | 1,807.7 |

* *Land Management in the Department of the Interior,* U.S. Department of the Interior, July, 1946.

† A deduction of 2.4 million acres has been made to cover recent restoration of certain lands or cancellation of claims of lands by railroads.

‡ Special tabulation of withdrawals and reservations of public land in Alaska, June 30, 1949, by the Bureau of Land Management, U.S. Department of the Interior, subject to revision.

§ Areas estimated in part.

## Appraisal of Land-Disposal Policies

The preceding sketch of the land policies applied in disposing of the bulk of the public domain indicates the specific shortcomings of some policies. An appraisal of the policies as a whole, viewed from the standpoint of the present, should be desirable.

In a sense, criticism of our early land policies may appear merely to bemoan the historically inevitable. In the main, the generations that formulated these policies were neither conscious of nor concerned with the social objectives of the present period. An enumeration of the shortcomings, nevertheless, is worth while, not because a more adequate policy was historically possible, but because these shortcomings are largely responsible for some of the problems of land tenure and land utilization after 1900.

*Absolutism of Private Land Ownership.* Perhaps the most fateful and potentially tragic development was the consistent adoption of alodial tenure in fee simple. This conferred on the individual owner a virtually unrestricted right of use and abuse, limited in practice only by the legal doctrine of nuisance, the tenuous application of the police power, and the power of taxation subject to the constitutional principle of "due process."

Much can be said for the granting of broad fee-simple rights of ownership. These grants fitted in with the virile pioneer spirit and in many ways influenced the rapid settlement and development of frontier areas. They encouraged settlers, and later owners, to develop their lands, to maximize

# ORIGINAL LAND ENTRIES, 1800-1943

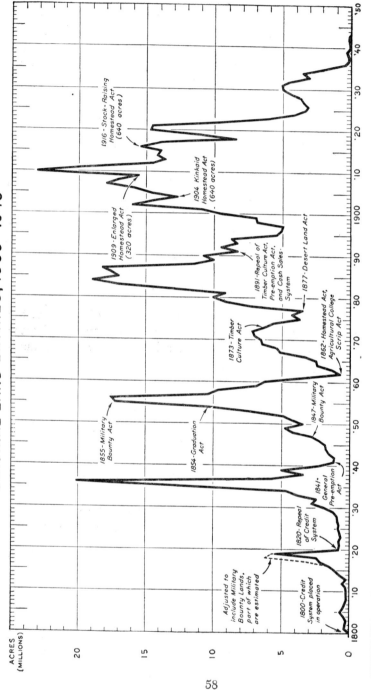

U.S. DEPARTMENT OF AGRICULTURE          NEG. 29225   BUREAU OF AGRICULTURAL ECONOMICS

In the preparation of this chart all the original land entries under the various laws were compiled, in so far as possible. Included are the following types of cash entries, public auction sales, preemption entries, Indian land sales, timber and stone entries under the Act of 1877, mineral-land entries (small), coal-land entries (small), abandoned military reservations, and miscellaneous sales. Also included are entries made with military warrants and various kinds of scrip and original entries under the Homestead, Timber Culture, and Desert Land Acts. It was not possible to secure data concerning all the land entered with scrip and military warrants, the lack of which does not materially affect the picture here presented, since the amount not included in the chart is less than 3 million acres. It should be pointed out that this chart is for original entries. A chart of final entries or one showing the amount of entries going to patent would be substantially different as a large amount of homestead, timber-culture, and desert-land entries never were proved up. The chart does not include lands granted to railroads or states, or certain small grants to individuals. Neither does it include Indian land sales prior to 1879 nor the sale of Indian allotments at any time.

their own interests, and thus, in most cases, to maximize community interests. At the same time, however, the almost unrestricted right of use and abuse of land has resulted in devastation of a major portion of our forests, rapid dissipation of mineral resources, and serious deterioration of a large proportion of our range resources, and the social dislocations that flow from these devastations.

*Failure to Distinguish Various Classes of Land.* The tendency to apply general policies aimed mainly at the disposition of agricultural land to all classes of land, irrespective of whether they were best suited for farming, ranching, forestry, or other purposes, has already been noted. Looking back, it is logical to assert that the land surveyors should have done a more complete job in classifying the public domain and that these classifications should have been used in determining (1) the purposes for which lands were granted or sold, (2) minimum sales prices, and (3) a desirable economic size of holdings. In view of the public interest in rapid disposition and settlement of the public domain, together with the early interest in revenues from land sales, the lack of interest in land classifications and the failure to discriminate against the sale of lands best suited for nonfarm uses for farming were not unnatural.

The need for a rational classification system showed up all too clearly in the arid regions where the homestead unit of 160 acres was far too small for economic operation. It also appears that the indiscriminate disposition of timberlands withdrew from public ownership extensive areas of timberland which should have been retained in the interest of general social welfare. Although there was a tendency to segregate certain classes of mineral land and give them special treatment, not until 1916, well after the close of the laissez-faire period, was the step taken to separate subsurface rights from surface rights.

*Limitations on Acquisition of Land by Settlers.* On the score of ease of acquisition by would-be settlers there was little to object to after the early decades, for Congress gradually took steps to make it convenient for settlers to purchase land, to safeguard occupancy by squatters, and, ultimately, to provide land free on condition of temporary occupancy and improvement.

The principal restrictions on ease of acquisition by settlers were the result of the parallel operation of policies which made it easy for agencies and individuals other than settlers to acquire public domain. The auction policy forced the settler to bid against speculators for the more desirable lands until he was afforded some protection by passage of the Preemption Act. There is much evidence, however, that speculators, through the facilities for acquisition afforded by the auction system, land scrip, bounty warrants, and purchase in large blocks from states and railways, forced settlers to occupy inferior lands or to acquire superior lands at prices materially in advance of the preemption minimum. As a result of the rapid engrossment of the better lands, a considerable amount of tenancy developed in public-land states almost on the heels of the opening of land to settlement.

Easy as it was to acquire certain prescribed areas of land, however, the policy followed by Congress in limiting the size of individual grants caused a considerable problem in areas where larger areas were needed for economic operations. Ranchers and lumbermen frequently found it necessary, as well as profitable, to violate the spirit of the land-disposal laws in order to operate on a commercial scale. The frauds perpetrated by these violations were generally condoned by the spirit of the times. A more reasonable approach, however, would have involved early recognition of the area needs of these operators and the provision of land sales or disposal policies more adequately suited to their needs.

*Failure to Assume Responsibility for the Welfare or Success of Settlers.* Virtually no attempt was made to assure the success of land settlement or to lighten its hardships. There was no assumption of responsibility even for ensuring that the settler obtained land adapted to farming or for preventing occupancy of land better adapted to other uses.[10] The settler was left free to select good land or poor, according to his experience. In fact, under the Graduation Act, provisions were made for peddling out the less desirable portions of the public domain left over in the process of individual selection.

It is true, many settlers developed considerable shrewdness in selection of land, and in this era the practical lore of the countryside served perhaps as well as it could a program of deliberate social selection. The wastefulness of the process and its potential tragedy, also, was less apparent as long as the frontier type of economy prevailed. Nevertheless, the aggregate of hardship from mis-selection was serious, and reached a climax in the occupancy by farmers of the semiarid lands of the Great Plains and Intermountain region, where agriculture was predominantly commercial and capitalistic.

The serious mistakes in selection were aggravated by failure to adjust the maximum size of grants to the capacity of different types of land to support a family. President Hoover's Committee on the Conservation and Administration of the Public Domain reported concerning operation of the Stock Raising Homestead Act that during the period 1918 to 1931 less than one-half of the 133,350 entries had gone to patent. The Committee declared:[11]

[10] In the later decades, of course, certain mineral and forest lands, as well as national parks, were reserved from agricultural occupancy, and in the Grazing Homesteads Act of 1916 prior classification was provided for, but mainly to prevent inclusion of lands adapted to arable farming.

[11] *Report of the Committee on the Conservation and Administration of the Public Domain,* p. 12, Washington, January, 1931.

There are extensive areas in every public land state which have been entered under this act and then abandoned to Russian thistle and other weeds, some poisonous, destructive to ranges formerly valuable to the stock raiser. Ruined fences and abandoned homes dot the landscape for many miles, pitiful evidence of human hopes buried beneath the economic insufficiency of 640 acres in a semiarid section as a stock-raising unit to support a family. It is not fair to our ex-service men and other home seekers to continue in effect an act which has resulted in so many failures and so much misery to settlers.

Long after there ceased to be lands suitable for agricultural settlement under the terms of the Homestead Acts, these Acts continued to serve as a lure to attract ignorant and unwary families to hazard their lives and petty possessions in a struggle against impossible odds, yet the General Land Office was required to continue to advertise the availability of such lands.

A settlement policy characterized by a more definite social spirit would have lessened the economic hazards of settlement by classifying the land in advance, in accordance with its adaptability to different types of farming, and would have adjusted size of holdings accordingly. It also would have sought to mitigate the hardships of settlement by constructing roads, establishing schools and trading facilities, and locating settlers in reasonably compact groups. In the earlier decades, even military protection was left largely to the hardihood and long rifles of the settlers themselves. Gradually, however, there was a tendency for the national government to assume greater responsibility for military protection and to encourage the development of major transport facilities. Nevertheless, the process of settlement was characterized by an incredible amount of hardship and peril. It became a commonplace observation that it required three waves of settlers to settle an area.

The planlessness of land settlement, permitting the widespread dispersion of population, made for excessive costs in provision of roads and schools and, in general, for an illogical and costly pattern of governmental organization.

*Prevalence of Land Speculation.* Nothing was more unpopular in theory than land speculation, and no phenomenon of American economic life was more prevalent. Land speculation was continually decried in Congress, and feeble efforts were made in the later decades to set up restraints. Yet land speculation was probably never more unrestrained than in the last three decades of the nineteenth century. The restraints set up by Congress were largely swept aside by reason of inadequacy of administrative facilities of the General Land Office, its essentially political character, and the generally low level of political morality that characterized the period.

The Homestead Act was generally hailed as a means for bringing to an end the era of land speculation. It was believed that free land for settlers would dry up demand for purchase from speculators. This proved a delusion, for the extensive areas thrown into the hands of speculators by continuance of land sales prior to 1891, huge grants to states and railways, and the tendency of these agencies and the speculators who purchased land from them to select the better and more accessible lands forced settlers to buy from them at advanced prices.

This was deplorable, for it is doubtful that the speculators performed any socially justifiable service. It is possible, however, to exaggerate the seriousness of speculation. Speculators could reap their harvest only by selling the land, their essential aim. It is true, some large estates were retained with a view to yielding continuing revenue from rentals or even from operation by the owners, but in the main these were exceptional; and a loose land policy did not result directly in creating a predominant class of large landlords, as in Europe. In the rapidly developing industrial expansion of the nation, agricultural estates proved less attractive to the moneyed classes than industrial investment. For the most part, agricultural lands first acquired by speculators passed ultimately into the ownership of farmers who established family-sized farms, the predominant type of farm present in the United States.

## CHAPTER 4

*Land Policies in Transition*

Throughout the first 125 years of our national history the primary concern in public land policy centered about the disposal of the public domain. This situation has changed considerably during the past half century. Public land policy today is only slightly concerned with the transfer to private ownership of the remaining public domain. Major consideration goes instead to a variety of policies affecting the use, conservation, and development of the land resources of the nation and to a variety of measures that can be used to implement better land-use practices and to improve the lot of the people who own, occupy, or use the land.

There is nothing unusual about this change in emphasis. Land problems and policies and the attitudes of people toward land may develop slowly, but they always reflect the changing social culture of the time. Land policy is always in a stage of transition because the accomplishment of one set of policy objectives calls for new goals and the recognition of new problems. The shift of emphasis in land policy in this country can be attributed to the disappearance of the frontier and to changing man-land ratios, growing industrialization, wastefulness in the use of natural resources, expansion of the role of government, evolving foreign policies, and changes in political, economic, and social thought.

*Land Policy before 1900*

As the account of the rise and development of land policy in this country reported in Chapters 2 and 3 indicates, American land policy up until the present century was concerned principally with public acquisition of title to lands on the frontier, the sale or granting of these lands to private owners, and the problems of land settlement. Public land policy during this period, however, was by no means static. The actual details of land-disposal policy changed considerably, and during the same period there was a marked change in the attitude of people toward land.

The early settlers in the Thirteen Colonies brought to the New World attitudes toward land that were vastly different from those that prevailed when the nation was established. In the England and Continental Europe of our forefathers, land was the cornerstone of social stability and the focus of an intricate complex of economic and social relationships that determined the position and status of each individual in society, especially in rural areas.

A high proportion of the immigrants and settlers who came to this country, particularly in the years previous to the 1890's, were land-hungry and came in quest of farm land on which they could establish their future homes. Once they had established themselves, however, the magnitude of the available supply of land resources in the country often inspired a gradual but nonetheless definite shift from the idea of land as a place on which to settle and live to the idea of land as a good to be freely purchased and sold. The concept of land as a commodity—as something to be converted into money either through sale or by exploiting its use— came slowly in many cases and still is not entirely accepted by all segments of the farm population. But it was accepted rapidly enough to make the nineteenth century a period of resource exploitation and waste and to pave the way for the present emphasis on conservation programs.

The changing attitude of the American people toward land is reflected in the various shifts of emphasis found in early land policy. The early settlers were hampered in their appropriation and use of land by numerous semifeudal restrictions. The village-type economy of New England was patterned on the villages of the old country, and attempts were made to establish a manorial system in a number of colonies. By the end of the colonial period most of the feudal restrictions concerning the use and disposition of land were abandoned, and a very broad concept of individual property rights in land was accepted. The new national government regarded the public domain as a potential source of revenue, and for over a century lands were offered for sale at public auctions to the highest bidders.

With passing time, numerous changes were made in land-sales policy. Concessions were made to settlers and advocates of family-sized farms through reduction of the minimum size of units purchasable, lowering of the minimum purchase price, use of the ill-starred credit system, and recognition of squatters' rights in the adoption of the preemption principle. The Graduation Act was passed to speed the sale of residual lands. Military bounties were granted to soldiers and veterans and were ultimately modified to facilitate their ready transfer, a situation that encouraged speculation. Swampland, education, and internal-revenue grants were made to the states, to be disposed of by them largely as they saw fit, and lavish grants were made to railroad companies.

The Homestead Act of 1862 and such derivative policies as the Kinkaid Act, the Enlarged Homestead Act, the Stock-raising Homestead Act, and the Timber Culture Act represented a shift in policy in that they made it possible for settlers to earn the title to land by actually living on it and developing it rather than by purchasing it. But it should be remembered that these policies operated side by side with the older sales and grant policies until land sales were stopped in 1891. During the last half of the nineteenth century speculators, timber barons, and others frequently violated both the spirit and purpose of these policies by using them to acquire possession of valuable land, timber, and mineral resources, which they proceeded to exploit for their personal interests.

During the last three decades of the nineteenth century people gradually became aware of the fact that the public interest in land use was not entirely compatible with the policy of freely disposing of the public domain. Public officials and informed individuals such as Major John Wesley Powell pointed out that it was a mistake not to classify public lands according to their best use and develop separate land-disposal programs to meet the needs of each type of land.[1] National leaders began to look askance at the manner in which the nation's forest and mineral lands were being appropriated and used, and sentiment was built up for the public reservation of lands for parks and forest, mineral, wildlife, and other uses. The first of these reservations for other than military purposes came in 1872 with the reservation of the lands in Yellowstone National Park for the future use of the people.

Although the new point of view came into existence gradually, the laissez-faire period of land disposal ended near the close of the nineteenth century. The most significant step in his direction came with the enactment of the Land Reform Act of 1891. This law repealed the Timber Culture Acts, amended the Desert Land Act, repealed the preemption laws, amended the homestead laws to prevent commutation until fourteen months after entry, discontinued the policy of offering lands for sale at public auctions, and authorized the President to set aside timberlands for national parks.[2]

Acting on the authority to reserve land, President Harrison reserved 13,416,710 acres, Cleveland 25,686,230 acres, McKinley 7,050,089 acres, and Theodore Roosevelt 148,346,925 acres.[3] These reservations of forest, mineral, park, and other lands represent a shift in public land policy and

---

[1] Roy M. Robbins, *Our Landed Heritage,* pp. 285–298 and 325, Princeton University Press, Princeton, N.J., 1942.

[2] *Ibid.,* pp. 296–297.

[3] Benjamin H. Hibbard, *A History of the Public Land Policies,* pp. 530–531, The Macmillan Company, New York, 1924.

indicate the rising interest in the problem of conserving and husbanding the nation's resources. After the turn of the century, during the administration of Theodore Roosevelt, this new emphasis in policy flowered in the rise of the conservation movement, in the development of a national forest policy and of the United States Forest Service, and of a national reclamation policy designed to facilitate the construction of irrigation works to reclaim arid public lands.

### Public Land Policy during the First Half of the Twentieth Century

While conservation was probably the keynote in public land policy at the beginning of the present century and while the conservation idea still permeates much of our public policy toward land, this idea has not always dominated the major emphasis placed on land policy since 1910. The past 30 to 40 years have been primarily a period of reorientation in land policy. With the disposal of the better lands, less and less attention has been given to the problems of public land disposal and settlement, while increasing consideration has been given to problems growing out of the development, use, and maintenance of land resources.

Public land policy has spread out to cover a considerable number of subjects. Among these one might list conservation of resources, reacquisition and management of public lands, land classification and resource evaluation, retirement of submarginal lands, reclamation and land- and water-resource development, public planning and control of land-use practices, provision and use of farm credit facilities, land-tenure improvement, and urban and rural housing. A short account of the principal policies and programs applied in these various fields will indicate the breadth of the new developments in land policy during the first half of the present century, and will at the same time provide a framework of reference for the discussions that follow in the remaining chapters of this book.

*Resource Conservation Programs.* Much of the early sentiment for greater public concern over the use and conservation of natural resources crystallized in the conservation movement. This movement had its beginnings around the turn of the century, and was a resultant of a ground swell in national consciousness which arose from (1) an increase in the social outlook that no longer identified general social welfare solely with individualism and *laissez faire;* (2) growing concern over the rapid destruction of natural resources; (3) increasing recognition of public responsibility for the control and management of natural resources, particularly mineral, timber, and water resources; and (4) abandonment of the idea that all public lands should be surrendered into private ownership.

The conservation movement culminated in Roosevelt's 1908 White House conference of governors. For several months after this conference public interest in conservation problems remained at a high pitch; then it began to wane and by the time of the First World War the early conservation era was at an end.

The actual accomplishments of the conservation movement are hard to measure. The national forest program and many of the state forest programs had their beginnings during this period. Several special commissions were appointed to study or act on a variety of conservation problems, and many of these agencies became the forerunners of the present state conservation departments. Because of national concern over a feared shortage of production resources, emphasis was placed also on the need for agricultural research to make two blades of grass grow where one had grown before; a National Forest Products Laboratory was established to find ways of economizing on forest-product use; and the Bureau of Reclamation was set up to construct irrigation works and reclaim public lands. In actual practice the conservation movement became something of a crusade. It floundered and accomplished less than it probably should have because there was no general agreement as to its scope or purpose and "because the fundamentals of economics and of social philosophy, the problems of property, and the legal aspects of conservation were neglected or ignored."[4]

Even though public interest in conservation problems waned during the second decade of the present century, many of the programs started earlier continued and even prospered. More public lands were reserved for forest-, park-, mineral-, and water-power-site purposes, and progress was made in reacquiring lands for state and national forests and game reserves. In 1911, under the Weeks Act, the Federal government began to buy back forest lands to protect the headwaters of navigable streams for the purpose of maintaining the streams in navigable condition. This program also was supported on the ground that it would have a significant effect in retarding floods and in helping to conserve soil resources.

The forest land acquisition program was given further impetus by the Clark-McNary Act in 1924 which authorized the acquisition of lands for timber-production purposes. This change in policy "virtually put the government 'into the business of land management and the growing and marketing of timber on a large scale.' It provided for the extension of national forests over lands already publicly owned, allowed for increased purchases of forest lands within watersheds of navigable streams under the Weeks Act of 1911, and encouraged cooperation between nation and states in forest protection, tree planting, and the acquisition of land needed for reforestation."[5]

With the advent of the New Deal, new emphasis was given to most

[4] Richard T. Ely and George S. Wehrwein, *Land Economics*, p. 469, The Macmillan Company, New York, 1940.
[5] Robbins, *op. cit.*, p. 409.

state and Federal programs dealing with resource conservation. The Bureau of Reclamation continued to operate very much as it had since its beginning; but increasing attention was given by the Department of Interior under Harold Ickes to the problems involved in the conservation of range land, watershed, mineral, and power resources. Various Federal, state, and local forest land acquisition programs were stepped up as large areas of tax-forfeited and purchased submarginal lands became available for public use. More funds were made available for forest-management purposes and considerable forest planting and other work was accomplished by the Civilian Conservation Corps and by the Federal Emergency Relief Administration and other emergency work-relief programs.

The most notable conservation development of the New Deal period came with the new emphasis placed on the problems of soil conservation. A Soil Erosion Service was established in the Department of the Interior in 1933. Two years later the functions of this agency were transferred to the newly created Soil Conservation Service in the Department of Agriculture. This organization deals primarily with the problems involved in conserving and building up the soil resources of the nation. The major emphasis in its program has been on (1) demonstrating the practical effectiveness of soil-conserving programs by actual work in cooperation with landowners, (2) providing technical assistance to soil-conservation districts and individual cooperators, and (3) conducting research on conservation problems. In carrying on its work the Soil Conservation Service has given considerable attention to the problems of flood control and siltation, water facilities, irrigation and drainage, and farm forestry. By the end of 1950, 2,330 soil-conservation districts covering approximately three-fourths of the farm land and two-thirds of the total land had been organized in the various states.

In addition to the work of the Soil Conservation Service considerable credit for the adoption by farmers of soil-building and range-building practices must go to the agricultural conservation programs carried on after 1938 by the Agricultural Adjustment Administration and its successors, the War Food Administration and the Production and Marketing Administration. The agricultural conservation program administered by the Production and Marketing Administration can be properly considered as a part of the Department of Agriculture's production and price program. In 1950, approximately $252 million in assistance payments were paid to 2.6 million farmers for a variety of conservation and land-development practices. Among the more important of these, one might list terracing, spreading limestone, use of green manure and cover crops, crop-residue management, field strip cropping, contour farming, pasture seeding, farm drainage, sodding of waterways, tree planting, and construction of dams for erosion control or for providing livestock water.

*Disposal, Reacquisition, and Management of Public Lands.* The discontinuation of public land sales in 1891 did not mean the end of public land disposition. The nation continued to dispose of its lands at a fairly rapid rate under the various Homestead Acts. As a matter of fact, homesteading did not reach its peak until 1913 when 53,252 entries involving more than 10 million acres were finally approved. Approximately 247 million acres were homesteaded between 1868 and 1946. Three-fourths of this area has been patented, while around two-thirds of the total number of entries have been proved since 1900.[6] Final homestead entries were made at a rate of more than 3 million acres a year in all the years between 1898 and 1926. Except for 1933, they then continued at a rate of more than 1 million acres a year until 1939.

The nation still has some public-domain lands available for private acquisition, but except for the lands in Alaska, most of the remaining lands have been picked over and are of questionable value for farm use. During the early 1930's, the Hoover administration favored granting the remaining public domain to the states. Several objections were raised to this plan, however, and with the advent of the New Deal the tendency was to give more and more attention to the problems of conservation and public land management. New emphasis was given to completion of the project, which had already been begun, of classifying the nation's land resources as crop, range, forest, and mineral lands. A program was started for retiring some 25 million acres of submarginal lands from their current uses. The Taylor Grazing Act of 1934, as amended in 1936, authorized the withdrawal of 142 million acres of vacant, unappropriated, and unreserved public lands for inclusion in grazing districts.

By March, 1935, the remaining public domain was "withdrawn by President Roosevelt in preparation for a nationwide conservation program. These withdrawals, in the words of the President, were made in order to determine 'the most useful purpose for which . . . [the lands] may be put in furtherance of the land programs and conservation and development of national resources.' Most of them would be made into grazing districts; others into national forests, parks, and game reserves; and some converted to water-power development."[7] While this action virtually closed the public domain to further settlement, a small amount of homesteading was still permitted on lands classified and approved for settlement.

The new public land program emphasized public land acquisition rather than land disposal. As has been pointed out, the beginnings of this program are found in the forest land acquisition provisions of the Weeks

[6] *Report of the Commissioner of the General Land Office,* Statistical Appendix, Table 76, 1946.

[7] Robbins, *op. cit.,* p. 422.

Act of 1911 and the Clark-McNary Act of 1924. Under the New Deal, however, new emphasis was placed on several types of public land acquisition. Between 1934 and 1950, 16.2 million acres of forest land were purchased for addition to the national forests. More than 11 million additional acres were acquired by the Federal government under a variety of submarginal land purchase programs between 1935 and 1945. Most of these lands (7.3 million acres) were turned over to the Soil Conservation Service while the remaining lands went to the Fish and Wildlife Service, the Office of Indian Affairs, and other agencies.

Large areas also were acquired for park and recreational uses, for reclamation and valley-authority developments, for consolidation of Indian holdings, and for flood control, rural resettlement, wildlife, and miscellaneous purposes. As a part of the national defense and war program, additional large areas were acquired during the early 1940's for a variety of military uses.[8]

Altogether, the Federal government administered 456 million acres of public domain and acquired lands in 1950. Of this area, some 48 million acres had been reacquired from private owners and from the states. Of the remaining 406 million acres, 57 million acres were Indian lands; 183 million acres withdrawn public lands; 132 million acres vacant, unappropriated, and unreserved lands within grazing districts; and 36 million acres vacant, unappropriated, and unreserved lands not included in grazing districts.

While the Federal government was voluntarily reacquiring lands for public uses, many of the states and local units of government found themselves forced into the position of acquiring a significant share of "the new public domain." Chronic tax delinquency during the late 1920's and 1930's created numerous serious local governmental problems and finally led to the forfeiture and tax reversion of millions of acres of land. Data are not available concerning the total area that reverted for taxes during this period, but the magnitude of the situation is illustrated by the case of the three northern Lake states—Michigan, Minnesota, and Wisconsin—where more than 18 million acres, almost 15 per cent of the land area in these states, tax-reverted during the interwar period.[9]

[8] L. A. Ruess and O. O. McCracken, *Federal Rural Lands*, pp. 19, 22, and 42, U.S. Bureau of Agricultural Economics, June, 1947; also R. D. Davidson, *Federal and State Rural Lands*, 1950, pp. 4, 11–12, U.S. Department of Agriculture Circular 909, 1952. Between 1940 and 1950 the land holdings of the War and Navy Departments increased from 10.5 to 21.5 million acres.

[9] Cf. R. Barlowe, *Administration of Tax-reverted Lands in the Lake States,* Michigan Agricultural Experiment Station Technical Bulletin 225, 1951; R. J. Penn and C. W. Loomer, *County Land Management in Northwestern South Dakota,* South Dakota Agricultural Experiment Station Bulletin 326, September, 1938; and *Tax Delinquency and Rural Land-use Adjustment,* National Resources Planning Board Technical Paper 8, September, 1942.

In most of the states and counties an attempt was made to restore the forfeited lands to the tax rolls. When this effort failed of success, as it did in many areas, many of the reverted lands were incorporated in public forests or were made subject to other types of public land administration programs. In the Lake states, for example, 14 million of the 18 million acres that tax-reverted are now subject to some type of state or county management. Even in those areas where tax reversion did not lead to public land management, considerable sums often have been spent during the past 20 years for the acquisition and blocking up of public forest, recreational, game reserve, and other land holdings.

The growth of the "new public domain" during the past quarter century has necessitated new interest in the problems of public land management. Emphasis has been given to the development of long-term and permanent public land management programs—an attitude that was quite lacking in earlier land programs.

*Table* 5. Public Land Holdings by Federal Agencies, 1950

| Agency | Total acreage held in 1950 | Per cent of total |
|---|---|---|
| Bureau of Land Management | 179,093,483 | 39 |
| Forest Service | 160,582,176 | 35 |
| Bureau of Indian Affairs | 57,279,729 | 13 |
| War Department | 19,332,451 | 5 |
| National Park Service | 13,955,638 | 3 |
| Bureau of Reclamation | 9,927,560 | 2 |
| Soil Conservation Service | 7,415,084 | 2 |
| Fish and Wildlife Service | 4,128,784 | 1 |
| Navy Department | 2,126,004 | * |
| Tennessee Valley Authority | 458,631 | * |
| Agricultural Research Administration | 166,083 | * |
| Farmers Home Administration | 14,198 | * |
| Other agencies (Departments of Justice, Commerce, State, and Treasury, and independent offices) | 1,152,361 | * |
| Total | 455,632,173 | 100 |

* Less than 1 per cent.

Source: R. D. Davidson, *Federal and State Rural Lands*, 1950, U.S. Department of Agriculture Circular 909, 1952.

As Table 5 shows, there are a dozen Federal agencies with considerable land holdings, each of which has a definite land use and management program of its own.[10] Most of these programs involve or contemplate permanent public land management. Among the exceptions one might

[10] For a more detailed discussion of the land programs of each of these agencies cf. Reuss and McCracken, *op. cit.*, pp. 18–49; also Davidson, *op. cit.*, pp. 1–13.

list the Army's disposition of some of its surplus lands after the Second World War, the Bureau of Reclamation's program for turning most of its lands over to farmers once they are subject to irrigation, and the Farmers Home Administration holdings, which have for the most part been liquidated. Many of the lands, such as those administered by the Bureau of Land Management, some of those administered by the Forest Service and the Bureau of Indian Affairs, the Bureau of Reclamation, and the Soil Conservation Service, are included in cooperative grazing districts or may be leased to private parties, groups, or even other Federal or state governmental agencies.

Within the states there is considerable variation in land administration programs. Most of the states have large holdings in highways and roads, and they usually have considerable areas used for institutional and educational or experimental purposes. The largest holdings in most states are in park, forest, and game-reserve lands and are usually administered by a state conservation commission or department, although they may be administered by other state agencies or by the county units of government. In many states various school, educational, and other public grant lands have been retained in public ownership and constitute the largest state holdings. Altogether, exclusive of road right of ways, stream channels, and water areas, some 80.2 million acres of rural lands were held in state ownership in 1950.

*Land Classification and Resource Evaluation.* Considerable attention has been given during the past two decades to the problems of land classification and resource evaluation. There is little that is new in the idea of land classification. Man has used private classification systems of sorts since he first started his use of land resources. The emphasis on public classifications of land resources, however, does represent a relatively recent development in American land policy.

During the nineteenth century several recommendations were made for classifying the public lands and adjusting land-disposal policies to fit various land types. Little action was taken, however, and the use of classification methods was limited to the recorded observations of land surveyors and to the superficial classification that was involved in the swamp and saline land grants and in the Graduation Land Act.

Soil-classification studies have been undertaken over a period of several decades but the first general classification of the nation's resources was completed during the early New Deal period. This classification helped to provide a basis for the new emphasis placed on conservation and public management programs. Since its completion increasing attention has been given to the more detailed classification of the soil, farm crop, grazing, forest, mineral, and recreational land and water resources of the nation. The inventories and classifications of resources that have resulted often have proved useful in directing and implementing public programs dealing with production, conservation, military preparedness, and other programs.

Much of the interest in land classification stems from work carried on by various state institutions. Land-settlement problems caused many states, such as Michigan and Wisconsin, to initate land economic inventories of their unsettled lands during the late 1920's. These inventories were designed to describe the available tracts of unsettled land and to provide prospective settlers with general or specific guides concerning their prospects for successful settlement on these lands.

The problem of farm abandonment in some hill areas of New York in the early 1920's gave rise to a composite land-classification system based on ratings of the size and condition of farm buildings, land cover, and soil types.[11] This land-classification system has been extensively used in a considerable number of New York counties as well as in a large number of counties in other states and in Canada. Originally the classification procedure was designed to indicate possible state forest purchase areas. Land classes I and II represent lands primarily or best suited to forest and recreational uses, while classes III through VIII rate lands for agricultural use according to increasing intensity of use. More recently this classification approach has been used as a guide for various types of programs such as projects for the extension and promotion of hard-surface roads and electric-power lines, adjustments and modifications in farm-mortgage loan policies, and redirection of agricultural-extension programs dealing with rural land-use practices.

Emphasis on land classification and local-resource evaluation culminated in the Land Use Planning Program sponsored by the Federal government in cooperation with the several states between 1938 and 1941. Under this program local groups in practically all the counties in the country were expected to inventory and classify their land resources, study and analyze their problems, and outline or recommend programs that would help to improve local conditions.

During the 1939–1940 fiscal year, 1,195 counties in 47 states were selected for land-use planning. These counties were divided into three groups. Those that were just starting were designated for "preparatory" work. They concentrated on organizing their local committees, starting discussions on local agricultural problems, and getting the committees ready for more intensive work. A second group of counties engaged in

[11] A. B. Lewis, *Methods Used in an Economic Study of Land Utilization in Tompkins County, New York and in Similar Studies in New York*, Cornell Agricultural Experiment Station Memoir 160, 1934; L. A. Salter, Jr., *A Critical Review of Research in Land Economics*, pp. 130–139, University of Minnesota Press, Minneapolis, Minn., 1948; *Land Classification in the United States*, National Resources Planning Board, Washington, March, 1941.

"intensive" planning. Their work consisted primarily of inventorying and classifying their land resources in terms of present and recommended future uses, preparing usable maps, and recommending adjustments in land use and policies that would implement these adjustments.

The third group of counties had committees that had already gone through the first two steps in planning. The committees in these counties were charged with the responsibility for working their recommendations into a "unified program" for local and county planning.[12] These reports were prepared primarily by local people with some technical assistance. They not only concentrated considerable local attention on community and county problems that the people could solve without special state or Federal assistance, but they also focused attention on many issues that had to be dealt with on the state and Federal level.

The local and county land-use-planning movement provided a new and invigorating approach to many local agricultural and other problems. In some areas where genuine attempts were made to get local people to study and analyze their local problems, considerable interest and numerous action programs developed. In other areas, the planning work often was carried on in a superficial manner, and the primary objective sometimes seemed to be the preparation of a land-use map. In these areas local planning often failed to achieve its real end, that of getting local people to recognize their problems and start action to improve their situations.

As one might expect, the land-use-planning movement encountered a certain amount of opposition on the part of other agencies and groups. Because of the political pressure generated by this opposition, Federal participation in the land-use-planning movement ended in 1941. The withdrawal of Federal funds and assistance brought the end of the program in a number of states. In several states, however, interest in local land-use-planning problems has been such that these programs have continued with varying degrees of success.

*Submarginal Land Purchase and Resettlement Programs.* According to classical theory and the principle of maximization, man, in so far as he is a rational creature, will always use his resources in such a way as to maximize the satisfactions he derives from their use—his satisfactions being measured in monetary returns, psychic income, personal pleasure, and other satisfactions. Under this theory man will not long retain land in agricultural use unless it produces at or above the margin of economic use. Ignorance of the facts or errors of judgment can explain the retention of submarginal lands in use over limited periods, but over time these mistakes should be corrected by the operation of individual self-interest.

The general assumption that very few lands used for agriculture are submarginal for this use was challenged during the 1920's by the findings

[12] *Land Use Planning Under Way*, U.S. Department of Agriculture, July, 1940.

of a number of surveys which revealed the existence and persistence of areas where farm incomes and standards of living were far lower than those found in more favorably located or endowed areas. The same studies also indicated that these subnormal income and living conditions often were associated with serious institutional and fiscal maladjustments.

The submarginal-land problem was predominantly an agricultural one, since the populations directly affected were predominantly farm people and the communities concerned were essentially rural. The complex of problems, while largely due to the low economic productive capacity of the lands used for farming and grazing purposes, was also due to or intensified by maladjustments in types of farm organization, size of operating units or holdings, and local fiscal and institutional arrangements. In many cases necessary readjustments were inhibited by overpopulation, land-tenure conditions, excessive indebtedness, and in some instances by physical, mental, and moral disabilities of local people or by their lack of aptitude for commercial agriculture.

One condition that contributed to the awakened interest in the submarginal-land problem during the late 1920's and early 1930's was the overexpansion of the agricultural plant in relation to market demand. This situation prompted suggestions for the elimination of the so-called submarginal farms. Consideration of this idea as a possible means of improving the financial position of agriculture resulted in planks in the platforms of both major political parties and in a number of proposals for the use of public lease or purchase programs to retire submarginal lands from crop production and devote them to forestry and other similar uses.

The submarginal land purchase program undertaken as a part of the New Deal had a threefold purpose: (1) the retirement from cultivation of lands not primarily suitable for cropland use, (2) the movement of people from submarginal land to other areas of economic opportunity, and (3) the reduction of farm surpluses through the retirement of submarginal lands from cultivation. While this last objective appeared plausible, from the standpoint of production-control policy it was subject to two major limitations. To begin with, the average yields on the so-called submarginal lands were low, and any effective program for reducing agricultural surpluses by taking these lands out of cultivation would of necessity involve the acquisition or leasing of millions of acres of these less productive lands. It would also be necessary usually to acquire or lease whole farms, since the remaining land areas, including the farm improvements, would be of little value to the average farmer once his cropland, the most indispensable part of his farm, became subject to the land-retirement program.

A submarginal land purchase program was set up under the terms of the National Industrial Recovery Act of 1933, the Emergency Relief Act of 1935, and Title III of the Bankhead-Jones Farm Tenant Act of 1937. Under the terms of the Bankhead-Jones Act, the Secretary of Agriculture was "authorized and directed to develop a program of land conservation and land utilization, including the retirement of lands which are submarginal and not primarily suitable for cultivation, in order thereby to correct maladjustments in land use."

In the operation of the land-purchase program it was difficult at times to differentiate between areas where handicaps and low incomes arose from a poor natural resource base, from maladjustments in size of holdings or of operating units, or from tenure arrangements and financial disabilities. In many areas the significance of these factors tended to overlap. Two general classes of problem areas were recognized: (1) areas where maladjustments in land use or occupancy were such as to necessitate public action, and (2) areas where individual measures on the part of the handicapped farm families would suffice. With the first class of problem area the retirement of a considerable proportion of the farms from arable farming often seemed desirable. It was mainly with the farms of this area that the submarginal purchase and resettlement programs operated.

Altogether, approximately 11.3 million acres were acquired by the Federal government between 1935 and 1945 under the submarginal land purchase program.[13] In 1950 the Soil Conservation Service had 7.3 million acres of these lands under its administration. An additional 3 million acres were handled by other Federal agencies such as the United States Forest Service, the Grazing Service (now in the Bureau of Land Management), the Fish and Wildlife Service, the Office of Indian Affairs, and the War and Navy Departments. Approximately 1 million acres of these lands were turned over to various state conservation agencies under agreements with the Department of Agriculture.

Approximately 92 per cent of the area administered by the Soil Conservation Service in 1950 was used for grazing purposes, and many of these lands were intermingled with privately owned and with state- and county-owned lands. Around two-thirds of the Soil Conservation Service holdings in 1950 were leased to local and cooperative grazing districts or associations or to local soil-conservation districts. Most of the lands used by other state or Federal agencies were used for forestry, wildlife, or recreational purposes or were added to Indian reservations.

The retirement of submarginal lands from cultivated use and their shift to less intensive uses displaced a number of farm families. Most of these families found new opportunities by themselves. Some of them, however, were assisted under the resettlement program undertaken by the Resettlement Administration and its successor, the Farm Security Administration. These two agencies were authorized to purchase or other-

[13] Ruess and McCracken, *op. cit.*, pp. 42–43.

wise acquire land for use in a program designed to improve the economic position and opportunities available to low-income families.

A number of different projects were sponsored as a part of the re-settlement program. Some called for the settlement of rural people on full-time farms and for fostering dry and irrigated farming developments. Others involved experiments with cooperative farming, low-cost housing projects, and migratory-labor shelters. By 1940 the Farm Security Administration held over 1 million acres. During the years that followed, however, the nonfarm projects—including three green-belt suburban housing projects—were transferred to the Federal Public Housing Administration, and the irrigation projects developed in cooperation with the Bureau of Reclamation under the Wheeler-Case law were transferred to the Soil Conservation Service. Most of the other projects were discontinued, and action was taken to sell the properties that had been acquired.

*Reclamation and Land Development.* Throughout the nineteenth century public policy generally favored the settlement and development of new agricultural lands, but the costs involved in clearing, draining, and irrigating these new areas were borne almost entirely by individual operators or by groups of operators. The enactment of the Reclamation Act in 1902 brought a new era in irrigation development. Under the terms of this law the Bureau of Reclamation has acquired irrigation sites, has constructed dams, reservoirs, canals, and other irrigation facilities, has supplied irrigation water to established farmers in many areas, and has undertaken the development of numerous complex and multipurpose projects.

When the Federal government entered the field of reclamation development, many of the lower-cost and easier-to-develop projects in the West had already been undertaken. The initiative in the development of these projects was taken by (1) individual and partnership enterprises, (2) private cooperative or mutual irrigation companies or associations, (3) local irrigation districts, (4) commercial enterprises which make a business of providing and selling water to farmers who have no direct interest in the irrigation works, and (5) state or city enterprises which supply water to individual farmers.

With the lone exception of the commercial enterprises (which have lost much of their earlier importance), all of these types of organization continued to expand the scope of their operations after the Bureau of Reclamation was formed. Part of the reason for this is found in the Bureau policy of dealing with organizations of water users on Federal projects rather than with individual users. Local irrigation districts or cooperative companies or associations often have been favored by this requirement of group action in contracts involving Federal irrigation facilities. This expansion of non-Federal activity in irrigation developments also has been favored by the concentration of Federal activity in the development of the more complex and expensive projects, while the smaller and more easily developed or financed projects have been left to private initiative.

The 1950 Census of Irrigation classified 26.2 million acres in the 17 Western states plus Arkansas, Louisiana, and Florida as primary irrigation-enterprise lands. An additional 1.7 million acres was classed as supplemental irrigation areas. The Federal government, acting through the Bureau of Reclamation and the Bureau of Indian Affairs, provided water direct for 4.2 per cent of this area. This compares with the 46.2 per cent served by individual and partnership enterprises, 27.9 per cent by cooperative and mutual enterprises, 17.8 per cent by district enterprises, 3.5 per cent by commercial enterprises, and 0.4 per cent by state and municipal enterprises.

These figures credit the Bureau of Reclamation and the Bureau of Indian Affairs only with those projects that they operated in 1950. In addition to the 37 projects which it operated and which provided irrigation water for 682,000 acres in 1950, the Bureau of Reclamation may be credited with the construction of 326 other projects operated by others in 1950. These additional projects supplied water for around 3.7 million acres. The Bureau of Indian Affairs also has constructed some small projects which are now operated as individual enterprises. Between 1939 and 1949 the area actually irrigated increased by between 7 and 8 million acres. Much of this increase, particularly in the West, was made possible by the extension of Federal irrigation facilities.[14]

The Bureau of Reclamation and the Bureau of Indian Affairs, both in the Department of the Interior, are not the only Federal agencies concerned with irrigation developments. The Army Corps of Engineers has been charged in the past with the supervision of Federal investigations and improvements for navigation, flood control, and power developments on rivers and harbors. This responsibility has made the Corps of Engineers a party to the water-resource development programs undertaken in the Tennessee, Missouri, and other valleys. The interests and activities of the Bureau of Reclamation and the Corps of Engineers in irrigation developments in areas such as the Great Plains not only overlap but in recent years have often run counter to each other. The Hoover Commission on Organization of the Executive Branch of the Government recommended that this civilian function of the Corps of Engineers be transferred to the Department of the Interior.[15] Bills were introduced in Congress to effect this change but no action was taken.

[14] Cf. *Irrigation Agriculture in the West*, U.S. Department of Agriculture Miscellaneous Publication 670, November, 1948.

[15] *Report of the Task Force on Natural Resources*, pp. 16–39 and 65–182. For a discussion of some of the issues involved in this possible transfer see Marion Clawson, *Uncle Sam's Acres*, pp. 210–211, Dodd, Mead & Company, Inc., New York, 1951.

In addition to the tremendous increase in public interest and activity in irrigation developments during the past half century, public policy also has favored numerous other types of land- and water-resource development. Federal initiative and support is directly responsible for the resource-development programs undertaken by the Tennessee Valley Authority and now proposed for several other river-basin areas. The large areas included in Federal, state, and local forests attest to the public interest in the development and maintenance of long-term forest-management programs. Similarly, both the Federal and state governments have given considerable attention to the development and management of watershed and range-land resources, particularly in the West.

Public policy also has played an important role in providing flood-control measures and in facilitating the reclamation of wet lands. The Federal government, acting through the Corps of Engineers, has actively participated in flood-control work since 1879 when certain flood-control measures were included in a comprehensive program of navigation improvement on the Mississippi River. The early flood-control projects, for the most part, involved the construction of levees along rivers together with certain channel-improvement measures. More recently the government has constructed numerous flood-control reservoirs to supplement the downstream levees.

The Federal government has greatly expanded its flood-control activities during the past 25 years. Generally speaking, most of the Federal activity in this field has involved little cost to local property owners. Usually some local unit of government or sponsoring agency is called upon to provide the rights of way needed for the project and then is required to take over and maintain the flood-control works once they have been constructed. This responsibility is often assumed by local levee or drainage districts, and their initial costs seldom exceed 10 per cent of the construction costs.[16] These special districts, together with special conservancy districts such as the Muskinghum Valley Conservancy Area in Ohio, are set up under appropriate state legislation as *ad hoc* units of government with the power to levy taxes and borrow money.

The Federal government has played a far less important role in promoting drainage projects than it has in either irrigation or flood control. The leadership in reclaiming wet lands for agricultural use has for the most part been provided by individuals and groups of individuals. Individual action has brought about the drainage of millions of acres of farm land as well as the tiling and drainage of thousands of farms. Group and drainage-district action, however, usually has been called for in the cases of the larger projects and in those cases where conflicts of interests develop out of the private drainage activities of numerous landowners.

Approximately 103 million acres, around two-thirds of the drained agri-

[16] Clawson, *op. cit.*, p. 185.

cultural lands in the country in 1950, were included within organized drainage enterprises.[17] Most of these lands are within local drainage districts which have been set up as *ad hoc* units of government under authority and regulations of the various states. More than one-half of the 103 million acres included in organized drainage enterprises in 1950 was found in the Corn Belt and Lake state regions. Other large drainage enterprises are found along the Mississippi River, in the coastal areas of Louisiana and Texas, and in Florida.

The prospect for additional farm-land development in this country is conditioned by the physical, economic, and institutional framework within which this type of activity takes place. The nation has large areas that can be reclaimed or developed for farm use. But many of these lands are relatively inaccessible so far as their economic location with respect to markets is concerned, while others suffer from unfavorable topographic, soil, or moisture conditions. Some of the arid lands of the West, for example, could be reclaimed were it not for their rough topography or for their lack of an adequate supply of irrigation water. Similarly, many swamplands could be drained, but the advisability of this type of activity is affected by questionable soil fertility or the imminence of reflooding.

Even when the land to be developed is physically suited for reclamation, consideration must be given to the cost of the proposed developments and sometimes to various forms of legislative or group action that may be needed to implement the projects. The Soil Conservation Service's 1945 classification of lands according to use capability indicates that approximately 85 million acres of unimproved land in this country are suitable for cultivation.[18] Much of this area needs irrigation, clearing, or drainage. Altogether around "40 million acres of intrinsically fair to good undeveloped land can be prepared for farming at costs comparable to those of the recent past."[19] Some of this area will doubtless be cleared and developed by private individuals. The relatively high costs associated with the development of many areas and the need for large irrigation and drainage projects, however, suggest that most of this future development will probably involve group action, if not public projects.

One of the critical problems in the reclamation of new lands, particularly high-cost-to-develop lands, involves the question of who will pay the cost of development. Without higher farm prices and higher farm-land values, it is often difficult to justify high-cost developments unless a substantial portion of the cost can be written off as public subsidy or be charged to other multipurpose benefits such as power,

[17] U.S. Bureau of the Census, *Drainage of Agricultural Lands*, 1950, Vol. 4, 1952.

[18] Soil Conservation Service, *Our American Land, The Story of Its Abuse and Conservation*, U.S. Department of Agriculture Miscellaneous Publication 596, p. 5, 1947.

[19] Wooten and Purcell, *Farm Land Development; Present and Future*, p. 4, U.S. Department of Agriculture Circular 825, 1945, and *Farm Opportunities in the United States*, p. 35, U.S. Department of Agriculture, 1945 (processed).

municipal water supplies, or recreational development. As a matter of policy the Federal government has subsidized several developments by underwriting flood-control projects, by charging portions of the cost of constructing reservoirs to other benefits, by providing liberal credit and repayment arrangements to the owners or buyers of lands supplied with irrigation water, and by writing off the cost of some projects.

While most of the states have limited their activities to the administration and disposition of their Swamp Land Grants, the administration of the Carey Act projects, the provision of irrigation and drainage legislation, and the certification of irrigation- or drainage-district bonds, some states have fostered, and in some cases subsidized, irrigation and drainage projects. California, for example, experimented with a state land-settlement program during and following the First World War, while Minnesota during the 1930's assumed the responsibility for paying off the "ditch bonds" issued and later defaulted by certain drainage districts set up under state authority.

*Land-Use Direction and Control Programs.* One of the major land-policy developments of the past half century has come with the increasing emphasis on programs that involve the direction and control of land use.

Man's use of land has always been directed at least to some extent by individual planning and by certain institutional controls such as those provided by laws and customs relating to land ownership. Throughout the nineteenth century there was some group planning of land settlements and reclamation projects, and government land policies did play a fairly important role in directing land-use patterns. On the whole, however, the major emphasis was on a laissez-faire policy that allowed each landowner a wide range of latitude within which he could conserve or exploit his land resources pretty much as he saw fit. Since around 1915, this laissez-faire doctrine has gradually given way to a realization of need for greater social control over individual land-use practices. As a result, more and more emphasis has been given to various types of land-use direction and control—direction and control measures such as those used in land-use planning and in the exercise of the government's tax, eminent domain, police, spending, and public ownership and management powers to encourage, foster, and at times force desired patterns of land use.

Mention has been made of the rise and at least temporary decline of the rural land-use-planning movement.[20] This is only one example of increasing interest in land-use planning. Urban planning problems have commanded considerable interest during the past quarter century, and almost every large city as well as many smaller ones now has its planning board or commission. This need for planning often extends beyond

---

[20] Cf. section on land classification in Chap. 5, and Chap. 6 on Land-Resource Evaluation.

municipal limits and has caused many county and metropolitan areas to set up agencies to plan their over-all development.

The National Resources Committee, later called the National Resources Board and then the National Resources Planning Board,[21] was established during the 1930's, as were a number of state and regional planning agencies. The activities of some of these agencies, including the National Resources Planning Board, were discontinued at the end of the depression. Many of the planning functions performed by these agencies were taken over by other state and Federal agencies such as the state conservation departments and the Federal departments of agriculture and interior. Even so, the void left by the discontinuance of planning agencies has in some cases given rise to new agencies such as state development commissions and the National Security Resources Board.

The rise of land-use and area-development planning has been associated with a variety of land-use direction and control programs. Among the more important are those involved in the zoning of land uses, the prescription of building restrictions, and the setting up of special districts to deal with soil conservation, grazing-land administration, and other comparable land problems.

Types of urban land zoning have been used in this country since colonial times. But the zoning movement did not become really important until 1916 when New York City became the first large city to enact a zoning ordinance. Since then almost every city of any size has established zoning regulations. Rural zoning was first specifically authorized in Wisconsin in 1929; but by 1951 some 38 states had authorized various types of rural zoning. In the Lake states area considerable use has been made of county zoning ordinances in classifying lands for agricultural, forest, and recreational uses and in preventing new settlement and year-round residence on lands considered unsuitable for farm use. A more composite type of zoning, usually involving the application of various urban and suburban land-use restrictions to rural-urban fringe areas and other areas surrounding intensive land-use developments, is now employed in a large number of counties and townships throughout the various states. In addition to the specific objectives secured under these two important types of rural zoning, zoning can be used for a wide variety of other purposes. Important among these are measures designed to secure the orderly development of land and water resources, to regulate the density of popu-

---

[21] See Chap. 14 for a more detailed discussion of the work of this agency. One might question the classification of the National Resources Planning Board as a planning agency. Much of the Board's activity involved making an inventory of problems, of essential public needs, and of board recommendations on public policy. Cf. V. Webster Johnson's chapter, "Planning the Use of Land Resources," in J. F. Timmons and W. B. Murray, *Land Problems and Policies*, pp. 246–247, Iowa State College Press, Ames, Iowa, 1950.

lation within zoned areas, to preserve or promote favorable health and safety conditions—as by prohibiting residence in flood-plain areas—to improve highway conditions, to foster conservation of soil and water resources, and to protect natural scenery, restrict unsightly developments, and in other ways enhance esthetic considerations.[22]

Building codes and restrictions, like zoning regulations, represent an important exercise of the police power in directing and controlling a type of land use. Most cities now have codes that specify minimum standards in building construction as well as fire and sanitation requirements that affect the upkeep and maintenance of properties already constructed. Only a few rural areas are at present subject to restrictions of this type, but the trend is definitely in the direction of further extension of these controls over rural as well as urban uses.

Among other exercises of the police power in controlling land-use practices, one might list the use of timber-cutting regulations, grazing-permit limitations, mining regulations involving health and safety standards, limitations on the volume of oil production, and the powers of weed control and soil-conservation districts to kill noxious weeds and carry on conservation practices at the owner's expense should he fail to carry out these practices himself.

In addition to the public exercise of its police power to secure desired land-use objectives, the government can and does use its taxation, spending, eminent-domain, and land-acquisition powers to secure these ends. Special forest yield taxes have been developed in some states to encourage the private practice of long-term forest-management programs. A somewhat similar objective is secured through the use of mineral severance taxes. Tax policies also are used to foster home ownership in the case of homestead tax exemptions, domestic industries in the case of high protective tariffs, and industrial location in those cases in which tax favors are offered as inducements to get industries to locate at certain spots.

During the past two decades the public spending power has been used as a land-use directive. Various public subsidies, such as the agricultural-conservation payments, have been used to encourage conservation and land-development practices and, during the early years of this program, to foster an over-all reduction in the acreage planted to certain crops. The government also has used its spending power, sometimes in connection with its power of eminent domain, to buy up large areas of submarginal and other lands. These properties have then been diverted to a wide range of particular uses ranging from public forests and military reservations to highways and public housing projects.

---

[22] Erling D. Solberg, *Rural Zoning in the United States,* U.S. Department of Agriculture, Agriculture Information Bulletin 59, pp. 10–11, 1952. For a more detailed discussion of rural zoning see Chap. 14.

*Land Credit, Tenure, and Housing Programs.* Important among the many divergent developments in public land policy in this country during the past 40 to 50 years are those that deal with land credit, land tenure, and housing. Of these, the developments in the field of land credit are probably most significant since they have affected a wide range of operations and have provided a principal means by which the government has influenced tenure and housing conditions.

Throughout the nineteenth century and the early part of this century (and even in recent years in some cases), the scarcity, inaccessibility, and high cost of agricultural credit often have been limiting factors that have prevented the optimum development of farm-land resources. This was particularly true in the South and on the Western frontier where capital was almost always scarce. Public sentiment in favor of more liberal agricultural credit led to the passage of the Farm Loan Act in 1916 and the establishment of the Federal land bank system in 1917. The land banks provided an important source of real-estate credit and brought a loosening up of the farm credit situation in many tight credit areas. The provision of these credit facilities proved of great value to many farmers during the 1930's when land bank loans and the supplementary Land Bank Commissioner loans were used to a considerable extent in mortgage-refinancing operations.

In addition to the long-term credit facilities made available through the Federal land banks, the Federal government has developed a number of other farm credit programs. In 1932 a Reconstruction Finance Corporation was set up, and regional agricultural credit corporations were established in the 12 Federal land bank districts.[23] The following year the control and supervision of these regional corporations was transferred to the newly created Farm Credit Administration. This agency has charge of the land banks which service the local national farm loan associations. Through the Federal intermediate credit banks, it also serves the local production credit associations. In addition to these facilities, it provides emergency crop and feed loans to farmers who cannot secure credit from other sources and it makes loans to farmer cooperative associations.

The Resettlement Administration, established in 1935, started a policy of making rehabilitation loans to dispossessed and destitute farm families who lacked or who had lost their capital and who needed financial help in reestablishing themselves. This agency gave way in 1937 to the Farm Security Administration, which continued the policy of granting rehabilitation loans and which was authorized to start a tenant purchase program. Under this program limited funds were made available for the purchase of farms for selected farm tenants. These loans often involve the full value

[23] E. C. Johnson, "Agricultural Credit," *Farmers in a Changing World, Yearbook of Agriculture,* 1940, p. 745, U.S. Department of Agriculture, 1940.

of the farm and are written at 3 per cent interest with repayment scheduled over a 40-year period. This program has been subject to some
criticism but it has proved of great value to many farm families that
normally would have had few if any sources of real-estate and production
credit available for their use. The functions of this agency were slightly
modified by Congress in 1946 when the agency was renamed the Farmers
Home Administration.

Among the other Federal agencies engaged in agricultural-credit pursuits, one might list the Rural Electrification Administration, which makes
loans for electrification projects, the Commodity Credit Corporation,
which has indirectly influenced land use through its efforts to buoy up
the level of farm prices, and the Veterans' Administration, which guarantees the so-called GI loans. In addition to the activities of the Federal
government, a number of states also have attempted at times to provide
various forms of agricultural credit. Many of these state programs involve
special funds—such as school-land or special endowment funds—and
limited volumes of loan capital. Minnesota, North Dakota, and South
Dakota set up rather extensive rural credit programs in the period following the First World War. Their experience in the agricultural credit business has been far from successful and has involved numerous defaults
and mortgage foreclosures as well as considerable losses to each of
the states.[24]

Governmental activity in the real-estate credit field has by no means
been limited to agricultural credit. The problem of home-mortgage defaults and foreclosures during the 1930's led to the enactment of a number of mortgage-moratorium statutes, which restricted rights of foreclosure, lengthened periods of redemption, and limited the mortgagee's
right to deficiency judgments. The severity of these problems during the
depression years also brought the creation of the Federal Home Loan
Bank system in 1932.[25] This central bank system was set up to serve
mortgage-lending associations in much the same way that the Federal
Reserve System serves commercial banks and the Federal land banks
and intermediate credit banks serve local agricultural lending agencies.

Beginning in 1933 the government encouraged the chartering of
Federal savings and loan associations, and in 1934 a Federal Savings and
Loan Insurance Corporation was established to insure the deposits of
shareholders in savings and loan associations. The worsening of the depression brought the creation of the Home Owners Loan Corporation

[24] *Improving Land Credit Arrangements in the Midwest,* North Central Regional
Publication 19, Purdue University Agricultural Experiment Station Bulletin 551,
pp. 27–29, June, 1950.

[25] For a more complete discussion of the Federal housing credit programs, see
Richard U. Ratcliff, *Urban Land Economics,* pp. 251–279, McGraw-Hill Book Company, Inc., New York, 1949.

in 1933. Between then and 1936, when its loan activities terminated, this agency loaned $3 billion to approximately 1 million homeowners. These loan activities had a far-reaching effect in preventing the complete demoralization of the urban real-estate market. They not only saved thousands of homes from mortgage and tax foreclosure but also saved many loan institutions from imminent collapse and had a marked effect in improving the financial status of many municipalities that had been plagued with tax-delinquency problems.

A major development in the real-estate credit field came with the establishment of the Federal Housing Administration (FHA) in 1934. This agency does not make direct loans. Instead it insures the approved risks taken by private lenders and thereby has provided a more secure mortgage market and has stimulated a freer flow of credit for construction, property improvement, and other mortgage purposes. It has been observed that credit is the lifeblood of the real-estate business. In the field of urban real estate the FHA mortgage has probably done as much as any other factor to promote the relatively free flow of credit that provides the basis for the housing market. A somewhat similar stimulus to the freer use of credit has been provided in the postwar period by the Veterans' Administration's guarantee of GI loans.

Land tenure is by no means a new subject. But it, too, has received increasing public attention during recent decades. Generally speaking, the major public-policy problems in both rural and urban land tenure have been two: (1) fostering the acquisition and maintenance of farm and home ownership, and (2) improving landlord-tenant relations.[26] The attainment of the first of these objectives has involved the extensive use of public land credit programs together with the use of educational programs and programs designed to raise farm incomes and stimulate industrial activity. The second objective has called for better leasing practices, adjustments in state laws governing landlord-tenant arrangements, and in some cases reexamination of the role that governmental agencies play as landlords on certain public lands.

Another major tenure problem that the government has faced during the wartime and postwar period involves control of urban residential rents. Rent controls were instituted during both the First World War and the Second World War to protect tenants against unreasonable rent increases in a period when localized housing problems were often acute and new construction activity was definitely limited. This accent on a concept of distributive justice appears reasonable during emergency periods when most segments of the economy are subject to controls and when they are all geared to some common objective, such as that of winning a war. It is much harder to justify rent controls when other segments of the economy are freed from price controls and other similar

[26] Cf. Chap. 11.

restrictions. Actually, rent controls represent a limitation of what the average American regards as his normal property rights and can affect future investments in residential properties.

For years, one of the major land-tenure problems in many urban areas has been that of finding or providing adequate low-cost housing facilities for the lower-income families. Society often has ignored this problem and assumed that the needs of these families could be met by private enterprise and the workings of the "filtering down" process. During the early New Deal period, the Federal government, partly in an effort to stimulate employment in the construction industry, took the initial steps in the development of a public housing program.

The housing division of the Public Works Administration and the Resettlement Administration both undertook the construction of some low-rent housing. These beginnings were largely experimental and led to the U.S. Housing Act of 1937, which set up the U.S. Housing Administration (since renamed the Federal Public Housing Authority and now the Public Housing Authority). This agency works through local housing agencies set up under state enabling legislation in providing public housing and promoting various types of urban redevelopment. In principle the public housing bill as originally passed and as since revised by later legislation provides Federal subsidies of various types for the construction of low-rent housing facilities. This program has been severely criticized in some quarters. But it will probably continue to attract strong adherents until such time as private industry demonstrates both willingness and ability to provide adequate low-cost housing for low-income families.

## Interrelations between Land and Price Policy

Land policy—principally the problem of public land disposition—was the primary issue in public agricultural policy in this country until around 1915, when the problem of farm credit came to the fore as a leading issue. Since then the field of public agricultural policy has broadened out considerably and has come to include many types of policies and programs scarcely thought of in the past. With these new developments the spotlight of major emphasis—emphasis measured in terms of public discussion and governmental action—has shifted from issue to issue. No issue, however, has commanded more attention since the First World War than the problem of agricultural price policy.

Most issues in farm price policy fall outside the scope of this discussion. Still, it should be observed that price policy has numerous effects, both direct and indirect, upon how land is used and how it is held. Accordingly, it is important that at least passing attention be given to the significance of the interrelations between land and price policy.

The principal farm price policies developed in this country during the past two decades have involved variations of three general approaches: (1) production controls, (2) price supports sustained through the government's commodity loan and storage program and its purchase or agreement-to-purchase activities, and (3) use of government payments to subsidize or induce consumption of agricultural products and to supplement farm incomes and induce program compliance. Each of these approaches has had its impact upon land use.

*Production-Control Programs.* One of the first programs introduced under the Agricultural Adjustment Administration (AAA) in 1933 was that of production controls. At first these controls were in the form of acreage allotments for the basic commodities—corn, cotton, wheat, and tobacco. Later, acreage allotments also were applied to rice, dry beans, peanuts, and potatoes. In the case of tobacco, the allotment system was soon supplemented by the use of marketing quotas. Since the enactment of the Agricultural Adjustment Act of 1938, marketing quotas have been proclaimed for other basic-commodity crops once their supply has reached certain specified levels.[27] Once proclaimed, these quotas are subject to referendum, and with each crop two-thirds of the producers must vote in favor of the quotas before they become effective in controlling the marketing operations of all producers. Once the quotas are voted in for any year, any marketings by producers in excess of quota are subject to specified penalties.

While the use of acreage allotments suggests a logical means for reducing production and thereby fostering higher unit prices, the early use of the acreage-allotment program often failed to secure this end. The actual effects of acreage allotments on land-use and crop-production practices are dependent upon a number of circumstances, including the farmer's capital position, his alternative uses for his land, and his general interests. A farmer with a 40-acre allotment of a crop of which he has normally grown 50 acres may do several things. He may continue to plant 50 acres and forgo price supports; he may till his 40-acre allotment in the way he has always farmed it; or he may intensify his use of this limited area by using more or better inputs of seed, fertilizer, labor, and other factors that might lead to higher acreage yields. He may allow his additional 10 acres—which may or may not be his least productive 10 acres—to lie idle; he may use it to produce substitute crops; or he may carry on a soil-building program on this area which will increase the future production potentialities of his farm.

In actual practice the acreage-allotment program of the 1930's stimulated more intensive land-use practices, with the result that a higher

[27] Tobacco and peanuts were the only crops affected by allotments and quotas in 1951. In 1950 acreage allotments were used for wheat, cotton, corn, dry beans, and potatoes. These allotments were suspended in 1951 because of the emphasis on increased production occasioned by the Korean War and the rearmament program.

total production was secured in many cases from the reduced acreage. For example, the average total production of corn in the six central Corn Belt states in the 1937 to 1939 period was 17 per cent higher than the average for the 1928 to 1932 period, even though only 92 per cent as much land was planted to corn.[28] Similarly, cotton production in the three delta states went up 20 per cent between these two periods, while an average of only 67 per cent as much land was planted to cotton in the 1937 to 1939 period as in the 1928 to 1932 period. This increase in yields can be credited largely to the use of hybrid and improved seed, heavier fertilization, and other intensification practices that probably would have found greater use even if there had been no production-control program. Even so, it must be recognized that acreage allotments do encourage intensification practices, particularly when they are not associated with production or marketing quotas.

The use of an acreage-allotment program for any given crop tends to make land a limiting and strategic factor in the production process unless the farmer has alternative uses of equal value to which he can put his additional land. Because of this situation, most farmers who already have sufficient capital or labor for their normal production programs have found it to their advantage to intensify their land use by building their capital and labor inputs around their rationed land inputs. Except in the case of tobacco, market quotas have been used rather sparingly, and then in conjunction with acreage allotments. Were they used independently, they might encourage less intensive land use, particularly in those cases in which the operator has a plentiful supply of land as compared with his available supply of other productive factors.[29]

In addition to their effect on intensity of land use, production controls have other significant effects on land use. In so far as acreage allotments or marketing quotas lead to a substitution of truck, specialty, or other crops for the controlled crops on the acreage not included within the allotments, they tend to aggravate the surplus production, price, and marketing problems associated with these crops. Unless new production-control and price-support programs are then devised for the substitute crops, some areas normally used for these crops may be forced out of this type of production because changing price conditions make them sub-

[28] Theodore W. Schultz, *Production and Welfare of Agriculture,* tables on pp. 143 and 146, The Macmillan Company, New York, 1949.

[29] This analysis assumes that acreage allotments tend to make land the limiting factor and thus favor intensification of land use to the point where the marginal cost of each input of capital and labor approaches or equals the marginal revenue derived from its use. So long as the farmer cannot substitute highly competitive crops for his controlled crop, marketing quotas are not apt to leave land as the limiting factor. As a result, the farmer may find it to his advantage to use his land resources more lavishly and less intensively at or near the point of highest average return per input unit of capital and labor.

marginal for their old use. In theory at least, this process may start with one controlled crop and have a chain reaction in shifting the margins of crop transference for several crops, as lands that appear submarginal for higher uses are shifted into competition with lands normally adapted for lower uses.

The use of production controls places a natural premium on the ownership or control of properties that have the proper historical base for a sizable allotment or quota. This factor affects land values in the sense that it makes farms with large acreage allotments more valuable than comparable properties with smaller allotments. The effects of this association are most vividly seen in the case of tobacco-growing areas where tobacco often is accepted as the principal, if not the only, commercial crop and where the average acreage allotment covers only a comparatively small acreage. Studies of the land market in these areas show that farm land values are directly associated with the size of the tobacco acreage allotment.[30]

Under the law a farmer may be required to comply with the acreage-allotment, production-goal, and marketing-quota programs if he is to enjoy the benefits of farm price supports. In actual practice, the operations of the average farmer in many areas have not been greatly affected by the production-control programs. The acreage-reduction program of the early AAA undoubtedly had a significant effect upon the operations of some farmers. The programs used throughout the 1930's and the late 1940's also probably had an adverse effect upon some new operators who lacked suitable bases for the profitable commercial production of certain controlled crops.[31] However, the average farmer in established farming areas has often found that the production-control programs have in many cases tended to support the *status quo* so far as production patterns are concerned.

Nevertheless, one should not underestimate the importance of the control programs. During the Second World War and again during the Korean crisis, the acreage-allotment system was suspended for most crops in the interest of promoting increased production. During these periods many farmers planted larger areas, partly in the hope that this larger historical base would give them larger future allotments when and if the allotment system should again go into effect. In the western Great Plains region, for example, large areas of range land were plowed and

[30] John Mason, "Tobacco Allotments and Land Values," *Journal of Land and Public Utility Economics*, May, 1946.

[31] While this was an important problem in some areas during the early years of the program, fairly adequate provisions were made to handle it in later years. Under the Agricultural Act of 1949, 5 per cent of the acreage quotas in each state must be held for new operators.

seeded to wheat during the late war years partly for this reason. Even when production controls are in effect, farmers sometimes choose to remain outside the acreage-allotment and price-support programs while they establish a large historical base that will justify a sizable acreage allotment once they decide to come under the price-support program.

Because of their effect in rationing the land factor, production controls can have an interesting impact on size of farm units. This is particularly true in areas where production centers around one commercial crop and at times when landowners tend to regard the allotment system as a permanent rather than a temporary expediency program. Assuming that the farmer (1) expects no major changes in the allotment system, (2) prefers to participate in the program, and (3) sees only limited opportunity to put the surplus lands not included in his acreage allotment to profitable productive use, he may prefer to sell part of these surplus lands and thus reduce the size of his farm holding. Should he wish to add to the scale of his operations, however, he would find it necessary either to refuse to comply with the program until he could build up a larger historical base or buy properties that do have an allotment base. The purchase of these additional lands usually would involve the associated acquisition of significant acreages of nonallotment lands.

One other effect of production controls on land use is seen in the relatively different manner in which they affect commercial and noncommercial producers. Most of the benefits that production controls have in bolstering farm prices obviously go to the commercial producers who are called upon to reduce their crop acreages and marketings. The small-time or noncommercial operator supposedly benefits very little from price-support and production-control programs because he markets very little produce. Largely because of this assumption, the acreage-allotment and marketing-quota programs often do not affect the small producers. A farmer thus is able to raise up to a specified minimum acreage of most of the controlled crops without an allotment and still benefit from the price-support program.[32] In so far as production controls bring higher farm prices, this situation may encourage an increase in part-time or small-scale farming. While the net effect of the operations of a few hundred operators with minimum acreages is small, a tremendous increase in the number of these operators might, of course, have a significant effect upon over-all market situations and upon the reactions of the commercial producers who bear the brunt of the acreage-reduction program.

*Effects of Farm Price Supports.* Farm price supports, in so far as they

[32] Marketing quotas on corn and wheat, for example, cannot be applied to farms on which the acreage planted to either of these crops amounts to 15 acres or less. Potato-acreage allotments in 1950 applied only to those growers who planted 3 or more acres.

are effective in raising or maintaining farm income levels, add to the
security, stability and profits of farming. Because they do this, they add
to the attractiveness of farm investments both for farm and nonfarm
investors. The prospect of continued price supports in the future has added
greatly to the security of farm ownership. It has encouraged a trend
toward higher land values and it has added to the incentive of some
owners and operators to increase the scale of their farm operations by
buying or leasing more land and thus creating larger farm holdings.

While farm price-support programs generally have the above effects
on land use, the specific effects of price-support programs often depend
upon administrative circumstances and details. The Federal Farm Board
failed in its attempt to hold the farm price line through the use of its loan
operations largely because of the pressure of crop surpluses and world-
wide depression. Under the New Deal programs the concept of parity
prices was introduced into law, and loan and storage programs were used
quite effectively to maintain price floors for selected crops at specified
percentages of parity. Numerous problems have arisen, however, because
of differences between crops and between areas.

The farm price-support program is not applied to all crops in the same
way. During the 1930's varying attempts were made to support the prices
of five basic commodities: corn, cotton, wheat, rice, and tobacco. Since
then peanuts have been added to the basic-commodity list, and a number
of other farm products have been classed as "designated nonbasic commodities" and "other commodities," which also are eligible for price supports. Under the Agricultural Act of 1949 these commodities are or may be
supported at varying levels between 60 and 90 per cent of parity.[33]
Different levels of support prices may, and at times do, favor the use of
land for the culture of certain basic-commodity crops or other high-
support crops when it might ordinarily be used for other crops. Thus
during the low-income years of the 1930's, farmers with allotments for

---

[33] The 1951 support program called for support levels of between 80 and 90 per
cent of parity for the six basic commodities if they had acreage allotments or marketing quotas in effect, 75 to 90 per cent if acreage allotments were not in effect and
marketing quotas had not been disapproved, and 50 per cent (except for tobacco
which would have no support) if marketing quotas were voted on and disapproved.
Mandatory price supports of between 60 and 90 per cent of parity (75 to 90 per
cent in the case of milk and butterfat) applied to the following designated nonbasic
commodities: wool and mohair, tung nuts, and honey. Supports for other nonbasic
commodities were permissive at levels not in excess of 90 per cent of parity. The
exact level of price supports for each commodity is determined by the Secretary of
Agriculture after consideration of the numerous facts involved, including the need
for encouraging increased production of commodities deemed essential for the national welfare. The Secretary has authority to set support levels at more than 90 per
cent of parity if it is determined after public hearings that higher supports are necessary to prevent shortages of commodities needed for the defense program or the
national welfare.

basic-commodity crops tended to grow their full allotment, even though under other circumstances they might have favored other crop or livestock enterprises. More recently, adjustments in support levels have been used to implement increased or decreased production of certain crops.

Changing technology also can create production problems. Under the Steagall Amendment, which was operative during the early post–Second World War period, potatoes, like many other crops, were supported at 90 per cent of parity. Changing technology, however, has favored potato production more than most other crops in the period since the parity base was established. As a result, farmers found it extremely profitable to use their land for potatoes even though their efforts led to a tremendous government surplus of this commodity. This situation was partially rectified when the support price for potatoes was reduced to 60 per cent of parity.[34] Another type of problem occasionally arises in areas where commodity loans cannot be used to support prices because of the lack or inadequacy of local crop-storage facilities.

Price supports are designed to provide a "floor" for farm prices and thus add to the security farm producers have in their expectations. This concept of a price floor is particularly important during periods when relatively low commodity prices are expected. Under inflationary and war-emergency conditions, however, the opposite condition of high-price expectations usually persists. Price ceilings are frequently used under these conditions as a guard against spiraling inflation and runaway prices. Just as high-price supports, or floors, may encourage the production of certain crops during periods of low-price expectations, low price ceilings may discourage the use of lands for some crops during high-price periods. This is particularly true if the farmer feels that he can make more money by shifting from the production of a crop with a low price ceiling to some more promising venture.

*Use of Government Payments.* As a third phase of its farm price-support program, the Federal government has made extensive use of government payments and subventions. Some of these payments have involved consumer subsidies, as in the government purchase of food supplies for foreign relief, its subsidies under the food-stamp plan and school-lunch programs, and its wartime subsidy payments to keep food prices down.[35] Another phase of this program has involved direct payments to farmers. These payments have been generally designed as supplementary farm

[34] Potato prices were supported at 60 per cent of parity during the 1949 and 1950 crop years. In 1951 this support was removed, but a support level of between 60 and 90 per cent of parity could be restored if marketing quotas were permissive and were voted into effect.

[35] Cf. Walter W. Wilcox, *The Farmer in the Second World War*, pp. 253–261, Iowa State College Press, Ames, Iowa, 1947, for a discussion of the wartime food-subsidy program.

income but have been paid specifically as inducements for crop-acreage adjustments and for the adoption of soil-conservation practices.[36]

Most of the consumer subsidy programs have had the effect of raising or stabilizing farm prices and, in this respect, have had about the same effect on land use as the price-support program. The effects of direct payments to farmers on the holding and use of land have been more diverse. During the early 1930's these supplementary income payments were used extensively and with varied success as a means of securing crop-acreage adjustments.[37] After the Supreme Court nullified the processing tax on agricultural products in January, 1936, the emphasis was gradually shifted in the direction of fostering the so-called "conservation practices."

A major issue, so far as land policy is concerned, centers around the questions of who gets the government payments and what effect their receipt has on land values, rents, and tenure arrangements. In 1939, the peak year in government payments, a total of $807 million was paid out to farmers. This sum represents almost 10 per cent of the total cash income (including payments) received by farmers in that year.[38] The bulk of these payments went to the farmers in the higher income brackets who had the larger and more productive farms.[39] In this respect, the government payment program failed to place much supplementary income in the hands of those operators who needed it most. But it did provide some operators with funds that they used in expanding their scale of operations.

No detailed analysis of the impact of the government payments on

[36] Crop-insurance programs, which also have a significant effect on land-use patterns, particularly in disaster areas, might also be regarded as a special type of government payments.

[37] Under the early AAA program, benefit (or rental) payments, derived from a processing tax on agricultural commodities, were paid to those farmers who signed contracts to plant no more than specified percentages of their base acreages of the controlled crops. In 1934 the planting quotas called for respective reductions of 15, 20, and 40 per cent of the acreages planted to wheat, corn, and cotton. It is impossible to indicate the exact effect that the payment program had on crop production. With wheat and corn the drought of the middle 1930's worked hand in hand with the program in reducing surpluses. The cotton and tobacco programs were supplemented after the first year with stringent tax measures that penalized over-quota production and effectively encouraged a high sign-up under the program. Crop surpluses were reduced under the program, but it is questionable how effective the benefit-payments program itself was as a means to this end. (Cf. E. G. Nourse, J. S. Davis, and J. D. Black, *Three Years of the Agricultural Adjustment Administration,* Chap. V, Brookings Institution, Washington, 1937.) Much of the initial reduction in production secured under the AAA programs was lost in later years as intensification practices resulted in higher and higher production from the reduced acreage.

[38] In four states—Alabama, North Dakota, Mississippi, and Texas—these payments accounted for between one-fifth and one-fourth of the total cash income received by farmers in 1939. The payments were reduced during the 1940's, and in 1950 amounted to $252 million, or less than 1 per cent of the total cash income of American farmers.

[39] Schultz, *op. cit.,* pp. 155–156.

land values and rents has been made, but casual observations suggest that the payment program did result in higher land prices. Also, since the payments were supposedly divided between landlords and tenants, they led in some cases to higher cash rents and to greater use of privilege, or bonus, rents on share-rented properties.

The division of payments between landlords and tenants tended in many cases to complicate the problem of landlord-tenant relations. Many landlords insisted on rental agreements that turned much, if not all, of the "government check" over to them. In some cases, landlords even accepted the full government payment in lieu of part or all of the rent the tenant ordinarily would have paid. In both the South and the North many landlords secured their claim to the entire government payment by substituting wage workers or wage managers for tenants or croppers in their farming operations. The decrease in the proportion of farm tenancy in this country between 1935 and 1940 can be partly explained in terms of the tenure adjustments associated with these new arrangements.[40]

*Impact of Land Programs on Price Policy.* The relationship between land and price policy is by no means limited to the effect of price programs on land use. Land programs frequently have a significant counter-impact on the general effectiveness of price programs. The nature of this effect varies with different programs. Some land programs can be used to implement price policy, while others may work at cross purposes with the specific goals of price policy.

During the 1930's the submarginal land purchase program resulted in the retirement of some lands from cultivation and thus tied in with the crop acreage reduction program. After the partial invalidation of the early AAA program by the Supreme Court in 1936, considerable emphasis was placed on conservation-practice payments. This program has helped to advance the cause of soil conservation, but in its early years the government made payments for the adoption of conservation practices and the substitution of soil-building for soil-depleting crops, largely in an effort to reduce the acreages planted to certain basic crops.

Land reclamation and development programs had a quite different impact on the price-support programs of the 1930's. Instead of facilitating the control of production, these programs tended to complicate the problem by bringing new lands into production and by adding to the food-surplus problem. Over a period of time the soil-conservation program, in so far as it leads to the restoration and improvement of soil productivity, may have a somewhat similar effect on production-control programs. Because of their general effect on increased production, land-development programs usually are subject to criticism in periods of crop

[40] John F. Timmons, "Tenure Status of Farm People, 1940," *Land Policy Review*, August, 1941, pp. 29–35.

surpluses. They prove their value, however, during wartime and other emergency periods when increased production is needed.

Land-zoning restrictions thus far have had only a very limited effect on farm price policy. Their more extensive use, however, has been suggested as a possible means of preventing overproduction.[41] While the application of zoning methods on a state or national basis to secure this end would probably not be practicable, the government could substitute the greater use of its police or taxing powers for its recent heavy reliance upon the use of its spending power as a means of inducing compliance with its price programs. While this approach would probably not be popular with producers, it would reduce the cost of administering the price programs.

## Emerging Trends in Land Policy

As the foregoing discussion indicates, the scope of the field of land policy has broadened considerably during the past half century. Further developments—both along present lines and along possible new lines—can be expected in the years to come. The emphasis in future land policy will doubtless reflect the changing economic and social conditions of the times. Increasing population pressure will encourage newland development and more intensive land-use practices. Concern over the future resource base of the nation will sustain public and private interest in conservation programs. Periods of economic distress will stimulate activity in the fields of land credit, land-use planning, and probably land tenure. Surplus crop productions will give rise to various production-control arrangements.

Although it is not possible to spell out the exact direction that land policy will take in the future, it seems probable that most of its present phases will be continued and in some cases expanded. Increasing emphasis no doubt will be given to a variety of emerging land-use problems. Important among these are the rural-urban fringe problems that are mushrooming around our cities, the problem of poverty in agriculture as it relates to land use, the problems of concentration and parcellation in farm ownership, and the land-use problems that may arise from man's effort to control precipitation and weather conditions. Among the other problems and issues that will probably receive serious consideration are the following three aspects of land policy: (1) policy objectives and goals, (2) better integration of land programs, and (3) interest in land policy abroad.

Most of the land policy developed in this country has been developed on a piecemeal basis. Congress and the several state legislatures have

[41] Herbert U. Nelson, "Farm Zoning," *Headlines,* Newsletter of the National Association of Real Estate Boards, Vol. 17, No. 7, Feb. 13, 1950.

enacted legislation from time to time and have authorized various types of land programs. Many of those programs have tended to work at cross purposes. This has given rise to inconsistencies, a certain amount of confusion, and demand for program integration. But while some attention has been given to this need, only limited action has been taken along these lines, and new programs have continued to grow up very much like Topsy.

One of the first problems in program integration is that of determining over-all policy goals and objectives.[42] Once agreement has been secured concerning the content or nature of these goals and the emphasis that should be placed on each goal in directing policy, progress can be made in integrating and coordinating land programs. Considerable thought must still be given to the nature of land-policy goals and to the weighting of these goals in policy decisions, as they affect both present and future policy.

Even after the problem of goals and objectives is considered, however, a serious problem arises in connection with the formal or informal recognition of these policy objectives. Should these statements of goals and objectives be given legal status, or should they be expressed only in the literature and in public thinking? Various organizations already have attempted to state their views of land-policy objectives.[43] Suggestions also have been made that Congress and the various state legislatures should pass joint resolutions declaring the principles and objectives of public land policies.[44] Actions such as these help to focus public interest on land-policy problems and may implement the integration of current programs. Their value over the long run, however, might be questioned.

Congressional action in declaring policy goals might be very important today, particularly if Congress would then take the necessary steps to coordinate all the existing programs into one over-all plan or system. There is no reason to believe, however, that future legislatures will feel themselves bound by present policy statements. The problem of policy direction and program integration is a continuing one. It calls for recurring examinations and appraisals of policy objectives and problems. Just as it takes more than a single housecleaning to set and keep an active household in order, the problem of integrating and coordinating a variety of land programs in a changing world also calls for constant vigilance and action. This does not mean, however, that one can forget or ignore the need for program integration. As land-policy problems become

[42] Rainer Schickele's chapter "Objectives of Land Policy," in Timmons and Murray, *op. cit.*, pp. 5–29.

[43] "National Land Policy," a resolution approved by the Soil Conservation Society of America, *Journal of Soil and Water Conservation*, Vol. 4, No. 1, 1949.

[44] John F. Timmons's chapter "Building a Land Policy," in Timmons and Murray, *op. cit.*, pp. 288–289.

more complex and involved, more and more attention will of necessity be given to their coordination and integration.

Another emerging land problem that in all likelihood will attract an increasing amount of public interest in the future concerns the application of American land policies to the world scene. The Second World War forced the United States into a position of world leadership. In exerting this new leadership, this country has sponsored a number of far-reaching programs such as the Marshall Plan and the Point Four Program. These programs, like many of those conducted under the auspices of the United Nations, frequently involve land-policy issues.

The importance of land policy as a phase of foreign and international policy is often overlooked. As Salter has observed:[45] "In a country as industrialized and as youthful as ours, Americans are prone to forget that in vast areas of the globe and among vast millions of people, rural land problems form the dominant social issue . . . . Even a cursory examination will show that among the real social issues around the globe few are more universal, more frequently strategic, more currently relevant, or more explosive than social relationships in land."

The success or failure of American foreign policy in many parts of the world will be affected to a considerable extent by its general impact on local land problems. The answers to many of our foreign problems lie in measures that will improve living standards and create a climate in which democracy and a freer economy can work. In innumerable cases, the promotion of these ends calls for agrarian reforms and land development and credit programs, working in conjunction with a variety of education, population, industrialization, resource-conservation, and other programs. The development of a positive foreign policy calls for recognition of this network of policies working toward a common end.[46]

[45] Leonard A. Salter, Jr., "Global War and Peace, and Land Economics," *Journal of Land and Public Utility Economics,* November, 1943, p. 393.

[46] See Chap. 15 for a more detailed discussion of this subject.

CHAPTER 5 *Significant Principles
of Land Utilization*

Land utilization is central to all discussions of land problems and policies. As a problem, it involves numerous factors that fall within the economist's sphere of interest. Land utilization, however, cannot be explained entirely in terms of economics. As Ely and Wehrwein observed, it "takes place within three frameworks: the physical, the institutional, and the economic."

Because of the broad nature of land-utilization problems, an attempt will be made here to explore only in a general way the nature and scope of some of the economic factors and relationships that affect the use of land resources. Further consideration will be given to various economic and institutional aspects of land utilization in all the chapters that follow —particularly in the chapters on land-resource evaluation and resource conservation and in the two chapters dealing with institutional arrangements.

From an economic viewpoint, land utilization is concerned primarily with the characteristics and conditions, conflicts, shifts, and adjustments in land use that arise in the utilization of land resources. It includes the study of land resources from the standpoint of their economic contribution to both the individual and society, with a view to determining in what way and for what purpose resources may be used most effectively. It also involves the physical response of land resources to varying applications of capital and labor, the individual and social costs and benefits of land uses, and the operational effect of land policies and programs on the use of land resources.

The field of land utilization is a much broader term than land use, which denotes a type or condition of use. For the land economist, emphasis often is placed on problems that arise within the major classes of land, *i.e.,* cropland, grazing, forest, recreational, mineral, urban, etc.,

99

and within which classes group or public concern is of special significance. This frequently involves a synthesis of physical, institutional, and economic factors that bear on land use, because it is the interrelationship of these factors that is particularly important.

### Principles of Land Use

Any consideration of the economics of land utilization should start with the body of economic theory and principles that governs the utilization of land. This body of theory, for the most part, has been well developed, and no advantage could arise here from a redevelopment of the statements that appear in numerous economics textbooks.[1] It is desirable, however, to review some of the main principles as they relate to land utilization.

The general theory used to explain the appearance of economic rent and land value and man's economic behavior in the utilization of land resources is based almost entirely on the principles that govern the action of entrepreneurs who are seeking to maximize their incomes in a competitive society. Rent theory developed as a part of the explanation of the functional distribution of income, that is, the distribution of total income from production between the factors of production. The value of land in production has been a central theme of discussion, and the value or price ascribed to land is usually regarded as a function of its returns, or economic rent.

The principles of land utilization relate essentially to the combination and proportioning of land with other factors of production so as to maximize net returns to individual operators. In seeking the most profitable combination of the factors of production, this point is reached when the final increment of product from additional units of capital and labor just equals the costs incurred. It is true that land problems and policy are only partly concerned with a determination of what is best use from the standpoint of particular individuals. They are equally concerned with arriving at social judgments as to what is best land use as viewed from the standpoint of what is best for the group. Land should be so used as to contribute to the maximum welfare of people in the present and the future.

*Physical Productivity and Economic Location.* The economic productivity of land depends upon its physical productivity and its location with reference to markets. In the case of agricultural land, physical produc-

---

[1] For examples see John D. Black, *An Introduction to Production Economics*, pp. 129–153, 314–344, Henry Holt and Company, Inc., New York, 1926; Richard T. Ely and George S. Wehrwein, *Land Economics*, pp. 112–155, The Macmillan Company, New York, 1940; Roland R. Renne, *Land Economics*, pp. 153–201, Harper & Brothers, New York, 1947; and Kenneth Boulding, *Economic Analysis*, pp. 459–464, 470–520, Harper & Brothers, New York, 1948.

tivity as reflected through soil fertility and favorable topography and climate is generally a major determinant. With urban areas, location with reference to the most intensively used lands—the so-called "100 per cent spot" location—is of primary importance. Even in the case of agricultural land, however, location is often a strategic factor, for land may be potentially productive but economically unsuited to tillable crop production because of its isolated location. Wherever land of this type exists in substantial amounts, it almost invariably will attract settlers, transportation facilities, and markets, and thus sooner or later be brought under cultivation.

In economic theory there has been a tendency to regard the supply of land as a fixed factor of production, largely of natural origin, with which other factors must be associated in certain proportions. However, as von Thunen first demonstrated, the use value of land is determined to a considerable extent by its location with respect to markets. Location is not a fixed or unchanging factor but instead is a function of transport facilities and rates and of industrial development. The serviceability of land is constantly being modified by technological developments and the distribution of population and industry. As Schultz observes:[2]

People who settled on poor land located in or near the main stream of economic development have benefited from the economic progress growing out of that development as much as have people situated on highly productive land in or near this stream. On the other hand, people who settled on good land that was located away from the centers of active development, and thus at a disadvantage in terms of making the necessary social and economic adjustments, lost ground relative to those people who settled on either poor or good land located in or near the main stream.

*Land-Use Margins.* One of the more important aspects of the economics of land utilization deals with the concept of margins, the so-called extensive and intensive margins of land use. The first of these marks the limit of economic utilization in the extension of particular uses to qualitatively inferior grades of land. The second marks the limit beyond which the addition of more labor and capital to a particular area or unit of land would prove to be economically undesirable. For the most part, the theory of margins has been developed with particular reference to agriculture, although it is applicable to other types of land use as well.

The extensive "margin of cultivation" of classical theory is reached when, by reason of the inferior characteristics of the land, including its location with respect to market, the value of product secured from the optimum combination of productive factors is just sufficient to defray

<hr />

[2] Theodore W. Schultz, "Reflections on Poverty within Agriculture," *Journal of Political Economy*, Vol. 51, No. 1, February, 1950.

their cost. In his original formulation of the concept, Ricardo assumed that the order of utilization of land proceeds from the best land to successively inferior grades until the extensive margin is reached. This assumption, in association with the Malthusian doctrine of population, provided the basis of the well-known pessimistic concepts of distribution developed by Ricardo and his followers and is embodied in the philosophy of *progress and poverty* developed by Henry George. According to Ricardo, as population increases, rents will rise, wages at best will remain stationary but will likely become lower, and profits or return on capital will fall. Inasmuch as his theory assumed that the price of producing food is determined by the capital and labor costs encountered on the margin, any increase in the demand for food leads to price increases, an extension of the margin of cultivation, and an increase in the differential or rent.

This concept of social dynamics was challenged by Henry C. Carey, who pointed out that in the settlement of America the less fertile lands were taken first, and the movement of settlement was subsequently to better lands. However, the less fertile lands that Carey referred to were very often those that seemed best for settlement purposes under the circumstances and at the time. Lands near navigable waters or near streams or springs, for example, were more desirable in the eyes of the early settlers than flat, fertile prairie lands located far away from easy means of communication or a ready water supply.

Friedrich List pointed out how extensively economic diversification and the penetration of industries into areas previously predominantly agricultural modify the relative economic desirability of land. Mill and other followers of Ricardo also recognized that the relative desirability of different units of land was subject to continued change because of modifications in the technology of utilization.

The doctrine of the extensive margin recognizes that at any given time and with reference to any given type of use, various units of land differ in their relative desirability for that use, and some units are subject to a complex of unfavorable conditions as determined by the land itself, its location, and other circumstances that affect its profitable use by private enterprise. Within any one area, differences in physical productivity are usually most responsible for differences in economic productivity; between areas, location and market situation are equally significant factors.

Closely associated with the classical concept of the extensive margin is the concept of the intensive margin. This margin occurs with all grades of land, varying from the most fertile lands to those at the no-rent, or extensive, margin. The intensive margin in land use can be said to occur at that point in the combination of productive factors at which the last input unit of nonland factors barely pays for its cost. In other words, the intensive margin in the productive process occurs at that point at which marginal costs equate marginal returns.

In his application of capital and labor to land, the producer presumably is primarily interested in maximizing his returns. Accordingly, so long as his supply of productive factors holds out, he will tend both to intensify his land use by applying more and more inputs of capital and labor per land unit until he reaches the intensive margin beyond which the total return is no longer sufficient to pay for the cost of additional inputs, and to extensify his operations by pushing out to the lower grades of land or to the less accessible lands until he reaches the extensive, or no-rent, margin.

Under the assumption of perfect competition with complete mobility of capital and labor, the producer will not attempt to intensify his operations by using more and more capital and labor on superior lands if it is more profitable to apply these factors to lands lying near the extensive margin. Similarly, he will not push production on the extensive margin if it is more profitable to use his factors more intensively on the superior lands. Thus it might be concluded that under the assumptions of perfect competition, the returns per unit of labor and/or capital can never be higher at the intensive margin than at the extensive margin, and vice versa.

With the imperfect knowledge, immobility of capital and labor, and fluctuations in returns caused by varying weather conditions found in real life, it is usually difficult, if not impossible, for land operators to identify accurately their intensive or extensive margins. In some areas, lands beyond the extensive margin are used over extended periods before their disappointed owners finally retire them from use. Even on the superior lands, wide differences in individual managerial capacity and the relative immobility of capital and labor contribute to overintensification of use in some cases, while other lands may be used much less efficiently than conditions warrant. Wide ranges exist in the degrees of land-use intensity that apply both within and between areas.

The concepts of extensive and intensive margins are helpful and contribute to an understanding of the conditions of and shifts in land use. However, they cannot be located with any degree of exactness. In real life, economic decisions seldom are made with the precision of economic theory. Often they are conditioned by economic rigidities and non-economic considerations. The actual use people make of land usually reflects their idea of what they think will pay. When better alternative uses beckon, they often will shift to the new use. Many desirable shifts in land use are delayed or prevented, however, because of the operation of economic or institutional factors, such as lack of sufficient capital to finance the shift or the operator's general unwillingness to break away from his habitual way of doing things.

*Intensity and Diminishing Productivity.* From the standpoint of optimum land use, certain lands and types of land use require greater inputs of capital and labor per unit of land than do others. For instance, on an acreage basis, it is rarely necessary to employ as much labor and capital on range lands used for grazing purposes as in raising cotton or tobacco. A relative scarcity of land in relation to the other factors of production tends to place a premium on acres when labor and capital are relatively abundant, particularly with those types of crops or farm enterprises which require large inputs of labor and capital per unit of land. On the other hand, when the supply of land is abundant in relation to the supplies of capital and labor, the operator will tend to center his combination of productive factors around his scarce factors. In those cases in which comparative advantage dictates or favors the raising of a particular crop, the practices adopted in raising it will usually be more intensive in areas characterized by a large supply of capital and labor in relation to the supply of land than would be adopted under the reverse situation.

The optimum combination of the factors of production brings to mind the law of diminishing returns. In most discussions of this law, land is treated as the fixed factor around which the production process is oriented. For this reason many writers relate this law particularly to agriculture. Others, however, hold that there is no need for making a special classification for agriculture, because the process of combining the factors of production so as to yield the largest net returns in agriculture is no different than in any other industry. The aim in either case is to secure the best possible combination of the available factors of production, and usually all the factors may be considered as variables. Land is unique only because of the limitations on its supply and because of the nature of its fixed location. As has been pointed out, the economic supply of land is largely a function of changing population pressure, technological advances, and transportation facilities. As far as most individuals are concerned, managerial ability and control over capital may be just as much the limiting factors as land in the production process.

The principle of diminishing returns can be considered both as a physical law and as an economic law. In its physical setting it often is referred to as the principle of diminishing productivity because it refers to the physical quantity of product produced. In economics its chief application involves the value of the product produced at the margin, and the relationship of this marginal return to marginal cost. This economic concept is based on the application of economic values to physical data. The transition from the physical to the economic concept is important because, from the standpoint of the individual entrepreneur, it is the value of the product and, more important, the excess of value over cost that are significant.

While the principle of diminishing returns usually assumes a given time, place, and supply of productive factors, it was projected over the long run by the classical economists into what is known as the secular law of diminishing returns. As stated by Alfred Marshall, this law assumes that "whatever may be the future developments of the arts of agriculture, a continued increase in the application of capital and labor to land must ultimately result in a diminution of the extra produce which can be obtained by a given amount of capital and labor."[3] Technological advances and a variety of other factors have delayed or postponed the operation of this concept in much of the world. In many of the underdeveloped areas, where technology has yet to make its impact, this concept, together with the Malthusian doctrine of population growth, has tended to exalt the position of the landowner in society. Technology may change the situation in many of these areas. But over the long run, unless the impact of technology by some miracle turns out to have an ever-quickening effect in increasing production, world agriculture can expect to face a problem of diminishing returns.

Much of the universal problem of increasing food production involves ways and means of either bringing new farm lands into use or increasing the intensity with which the currently developed lands are used. This problem of increasing intensity of use sometimes merely involves the application of additional inputs of capital and labor to make lands produce at a level closer to their points of total diminishing returns; more specifically, near the point at which marginal revenue equals or just exceeds marginal cost. On other lands it may involve certain improvements that will lead to more efficient operations. These improvements may lead to higher yields or to lower costs. They frequently involve technological developments such as the use of improved seed, new insecticides, commercial fertilizers, supplemental irrigation, and laborsaving machinery.

A variety of limiting and strategic factors appear at various times in the productive process as "bottleneck" factors that prevent the optimum combination of the factors of production. Management very often appears as one of these limiting factors. As H. C. Taylor has pointed out, the producers with superior organizing ability, in theory at least, should ultimately tend to occupy the better land.[4] Lack of perfect knowledge regarding alternative opportunities, operator immobility, and other factors prevent this theory from working out in practice. There is some

[3] Alfred Marshall, *Principles of Economics*, 8th ed. p. 153, The Macmillan Company, New York, 1938.

[4] Henry C. Taylor, *Outline of Agricultural Economics*, pp. 239–245, The Macmillan Company, New York, 1925.

logic, however, to the assumption that the combination of superior management and superior land should permit, if not justify, the payment of a higher rent than the land would yield under less adequate management. To the extent that this condition tends to prevail in any area, one would expect to find the better lands operated by the best qualified operators, while the operators of less ability would tend to gravitate to the less productive lands.

This hypothesis regarding the affinity of the better operators for the more productive lands must often be qualified in the light of complicating circumstances. A superior operator, for example, may find it more to his advantage to operate a large area of low-value wheat or grazing land than to concentrate on the more intensive culture of a smaller area of highly productive land. Similarly, operators sometimes find that by the advantageous application of good management practices to inferior lands they may overcome many of their natural disadvantages and often secure a higher differential return than they could have expected from a comparable investment in higher-valued properties of greater natural productive capacity. Moreover, the relative difference in the ability of two or more operators may be less marked for the handling of small operating units than for the management of large ones. Thus, in the competition for the better lands, small-scale operators of relatively little or average managerial ability may be able to outbid operators of greater managerial ability who desire large-scale units.

In part, this is a manifestation of the technical distinction between "capacity" and "efficiency." The small-scale operator, handicapped in regard to capacity as a manager, may be less handicapped or even superior in efficiency, particularly in those types of farming that are not readily routinized but which require close attention to every varying detail.

*Efficiency and Capacity.* Because of the significance of variations in land, efficiency and capacity are important concepts. The first may be defined in terms of the effectiveness with which particular land units produce in response to the successive units of capital and labor inputs that are combined with them in the production process. In comparing the efficiency of various tracts of land, it is important that one assume use of the same number of variable-factor input units on each unit of land. Comparison of the respective products of various units of land at their points of least-cost combination provides a fair comparative measure of efficiency only in those cases in which the least-cost combinations involve the same number of variable-factor inputs.

Economic efficiency of land, and particularly its net efficiency, is, of course, not merely a function of its physical characteristics but also of its economic location, the quality of the management applied to it, and the effectiveness of such secondary production as is associated with the primary production process. This last concept refers to aspects of agricultural production such as feeding and managing livestock, handling milk, and preparing products for market, as distinguished from the raising of crops. These aspects of over-all production are not particularly dependent upon the purely physical characteristics of the land itself, but they do have an important bearing on the intensity of agricultural land use.

The capacity of land may be defined in terms of the number of inputs of variable factors that are combined with the land at the point of highest profit combination. Arthur C. Bunce has suggested the usefulness of the concept of elasticity in discussing the question of land capacity.[5] He has defined elasticity as the ability of the farm business or plant to maintain its efficiency as more and more units of variable factors are added. When the marginal and average productivity curves slope downward rapidly, the elasticity might be said to be low; when slowly, the mode of utilization may be said to be elastic. Thus, land having a high elasticity may be able to absorb many units of fertilizer or labor and still show a high relative efficiency. Land with low elasticity is characterized by rapidly diminishing returns as additional inputs of the variable factors are added.

An important factor affecting the elasticity of production for a given farm is the ratio of fixed to variable costs, for a high ratio of fixed to variable costs will incur low elasticity, and vice versa. Moreover, extensive resort to the secondary processes of production may also make for high elasticity. Other things equal, the greater the elasticity, the longer the capacity of the land is likely to remain at the point of highest-profit combination of the factors.

It seems probable that diversity of enterprises and complementary or supplementary relationships with other major types of land use may also be factors that contribute to high elasticity. Thus, through the adoption of secondary processes, development of complementary relationships, and diversification, the potential intensity of cultivation may be amplified. This is a point of significance from the standpoint of social economy as well as private economy.

*Intensity and Land Income.* It is commonplace to expect high land incomes or rents and land values on intensively used lands. However, it has been pointed out that land characterized by a high efficiency may bear a high income or rent for that reason, and yet, because it is low in capacity (as a result of low elasticity), be extensively, rather than intensively, utilized.[6] A stock illlustration of this is the comparatively high rentals and values ascribed to land in the bluegrass region of Kentucky, where,

[5] Arthur C. Bunce, *The Economics of Soil Conservation*, pp. 24–28, Iowa State College Press, Ames, Iowa, 1945.

[6] Conrad H. Hammar, "Intensity and Land Rent: An Overlooked Aspect of Rent Theory," *Journal of Farm Economics,* Vol. 20, No. 4, November, 1938.

from the standpoint of private economy, it has been found possible to utilize land profitably for so extensive a use as pasture.

When high-valued lands are used for pasture, one usually has an impression of an extensive form of land use, because intensity of agricultural land use is usually thought of in terms of cultivation. Actually, large capital expenditures may be involved through investments in purebred stock, in expensive facilities for shelter, in purchasing supplementary feeds, in use of skilled labor management, in advertising and marketing— in short, in the so-called "secondary" phases of operation.

When intensity is reckoned in terms of physical inputs, it is easy to assume that heavy population pressure and a cheap labor force lead to intensive farming. In parts of the Orient, for example, laborious methods of cultivation are commonly employed. Labor is cheap and is used lavishly in agricultural production. From a physical-input standpoint land is used intensively, but the market value of the labor is low, and the total expenditure on variable input factors (capital and labor) is usually small.

The low value of the labor permits a low return from the marginal unit and, therefore, may permit employing a large number of units of labor per unit of land, depending on the elasticity of the type of land use or the particular type of land under consideration. In countries backward in technical advancement and in capital accumulation, the amount of labor employed per unit of land may be quite high, while comparatively little application of capital is made, labor being substituted for capital. The extra labor employed is not an additional cost of production if it has no alternative use.

Technical advances in mechanization have occurred most rapidly in countries like the United States, where land is relatively abundant and the labor supply scarce, in contrast to conditions existing in most other parts of the world where labor is abundant and land scarce.

## Competition of Land Uses

Some of the more important problems in land utilization arise because of competition between land uses. Competition in land use is usually thought of as involving the relative competitive position of various areas or farms at any one time with respect to various specified uses and markets. In this sense competition usually reflects the operation of the principle of comparative advantage and the attendant factors of physical productivity, economic location, the efficiency and capacity with which land responds to the productive process, and the cost of the various factors used in this process. The concept of land-use competition may also involve the element of time. Competition over time, of course, gives rise to problems of conservation and time preference in resource exploitation and use.

*Patterns of Land Use.* According to classical theory, each grade of land normally is put to the type of use for which it is best adapted, and it is employed with a proper degree of intensity and with reasonable, or at least average, efficiency. Occasionally, unstable situations exist because lands are used at other than their "highest and best use." These situations may continue for some time but "over the long run" they are usually cleared up through the operation of competition.

Land-use patterns and intensity of land use depend to a considerable measure upon the income of land or upon its expected income. If the price of the products of land increases relative to production costs or if the producer anticipates an increase in the net return to land, the tendency is to intensify the present use or to shift to a promising higher use. On the other hand, if the price of the products of land decreases relative to costs, the net return to land will decrease and the tendency will be to use the land less intensively or in some cases even to shift to a lower or more extensive use.

The concept of margins of transference is often used to illustrate the comparative competitive positions of different lands and land uses under varying price, cost, and location conditions. This concept has value as a tool of analysis, but it sometimes oversimplifies the over-all picture. The term "margin of transference" implies a definite point of change. Actually, however, it is generally patterns or areas of use that undergo change. The assumption that land income is the primary factor regulating land use also is frequently in error. Other factors, such as size of operative unit, land values, custom, property considerations, and the legal framework within which land is held and conveyed, also have a substantial influence on land-use patterns and practices.

*Impact of Institutional Factors on Land Use.* Man's use of land resources is often affected as much or more by institutional factors as by the economic framework within which his activity takes place. Institutional barriers, together with the failure of the price system always to direct land to its most beneficial use, have created a case for public land policies and public action programs designed to bring desirable adjustments in land uses. Institutional barriers often explain income maladjustments between and within areas as well as the interest or inertia shown by varying peoples in making the changes necessary for progress.

Institutional factors can foster change, *e.g.*, publicly sponsored special incentive programs, but ordinarily they provide obstacles to change. Institutional factors themselves usually are not easily changed. An excellent example of this is found in agriculture, where many farms with fertile land are actually operated on a submarginal basis. The operators of these farms may require relief or subsidies or they may continue their operations by accepting less than commercial wages for their expenditures of labor. They farm on a submarginal basis, not necessarily because their land is incapable of supermarginal production, but rather because of farm units of inadequate size, poor management, inadequate capital, overinvestment in relation to farm value, overvaluation of land, excessive indebtedness, or any of a host of similar factors that cause maladjustments in land use. Similarly, because of the frictional effect of institutional factors, considerable adjustments in farm-product price levels often are necessary before farmers will shift their lands to higher or lower uses as circumstances may direct.

One of the objectives of society and government should be that of helping to bring about desirable adjustments in land use. The aim sought should be to maximize net returns from land for individuals and for society. In seeking this objective, conflicts often arise between individual land uses and the broader social interests of groups or government. If individual interests conflict seriously with the social interest, the former should generally give way to the latter. At times, however, society may be justified in keeping land in or directing it into uses that may not be defended strictly on the grounds of efficiency of use. Among the examples of these situations are the following:

1. The presence of an excessive rural population in areas where a great deal of unemployment or underemployment exists and where there are no alternative employment opportunities. In such a situation it may be sound public policy to contribute substantial aid during a period of adjustment to more favorable conditions, provided the aids do not freeze conditions at *status quo*.

2. The need of retaining certain economic and social values, as, for instance, those that arise in case of the family farm. Family farms can generally compete economically with large-scale commercial farms. But in the interest of agricultural stability and security there may be need at times for special measures to aid in the maintenance of family farms.

3. The need of supplementing or complementing some existing use, such as providing winter feed for the range industry. This is an argument in some situations for subsidies for land-reclamation work. Also, in areas where forestry or mining is predominant, public subsidies and other programs may be used to stimulate food production in the local areas.

*Complementary and Supplementary Relationships.* By reason of complementary or supplementary relationships with other major uses, it is at times desirable to employ a particular kind of land for a use for which it would not be suitable except for these complementary and supplementary relationships.[7] For instance, arable farming may be remunerative on certain land types that would not support commercial production were it not for supplementary income from forest, range use, or urban employment. Similarly, the various complementary and supplementary relationships within a given major use, for example, the various enterprises of

[7] Taylor, *op. cit.*, pp. 37*ff.*

the farm, are such that price changes or changes in cost with respect to any single enterprise will have a far different expansion or contraction significance for the enterprise itself and for the type of farming as a whole than would be the case for a one-crop system lacking in such complementary and supplementary relationships. Price changes also may have widely different effects for systems of farming under which the various complementary and supplementary intrafarm relationships are different.

The presence of complementary or supplementary relationships complicates the problem of determining the economic feasibility of certain types of land development, especially in new and hitherto untried areas. At best, it may be possible to base decisions on the experience of other regions where approximately similar conditions prevail. It is rarely possible, however, to find close similarity in all physical, locational, economic, and institutional conditions. For example, in appraising the economic feasibility of new irrigation development in the Missouri Valley, the effects of complementary and supplementary relationships raise significant and timely problems in land use. From a social point of view it is particularly important that a desirable balance be worked out between the various complementary uses of the land for grazing, fallow, and crop cultivation. The successful integration of these uses would contribute greatly to the stabilization of the economy of the area. We have no experience, however, in a similar area to guide our actions in developing a truly integrated land-use pattern for the area.

### Land Costs

Land costs are of several types. They arise in the development or bringing of new land into use; they are involved in holding and using land in its present use; they are present when land is held for a higher use; and they arise whenever land shifts from one use to another use.

Land costs invariably arise when new lands or underdeveloped lands are brought in cropland use through clearing, drainage, or irrigation. The initial costs of land development become fixed after their investment. But new land costs arise as operating costs occur in the form of interest, additional tax charges, and other direct land-operating expenses. Another type of cost occurs when lands are suspended between a lower and an anticipated higher use, as, for instance, in the holding of a vacant city lot until it is needed for residential or commercial use. Ely and Wehrwein refer to these costs as "ripening costs of land utilization."[8] Another type of cost, a cost of supersession, is incurred when land shifts from a lower to a higher use or from a higher to a lower use. For example, costs arise when land is shifted from grazing to tillable crops or from crop production to forest use. Once a forest has been removed to permit cultivation, it is a difficult, expensive, and time-consuming job to reestablish a forest

---

[8] Ely and Wehrwein, *op. cit.*, pp. 148–149.

economy even when the long-run picture indicates that this is the best economic policy to follow. The structure of land costs in cases of this type may be such as to delay or prevent desirable shifts in land uses. Maximization of the long-term interests of society under such circumstances may require special help or incentives to encourage desirable shifts that do not promise immediate profit to individual operators.

Land costs are either private or social in nature. The private costs are most readily apparent, but examples of social costs are less obvious. Social costs may be direct, as in the case of subsidies for land development or in the case of the reversion of tax-delinquent lands, or indirect, as in the case of irreparable damages to soil because of serious erosion. Except for their fixed and "sunk-cost" nature, land costs are little different from any other type of costs. The fixed nature of land costs, however, is highly significant. They are not particularly important during periods when the price and demand for land and its products are increasing and when the landowner finds himself well able to handle the obligations incurred under a lower price level. Quite a different situation prevails under declining price or depression conditions. The owner then feels the pressure of cost burdens incurred during more optimistic times. Fixed costs then account for a very important part of his budget and definitely limit his expenditures on other items. They materially affect the farmer's ability to absorb the shock of fluctuating income. Debt and tax-payment pressure may force greater intensification in land use. In this sense it has an important and direct bearing on the conservation practices followed by landowners.

So far as the farmer's ability to absorb the shocks of fluctuating income is concerned, it is well known that his net returns from land fluctuate from year to year as a result of climatic conditions and variations in prices and fixed costs. To some individuals fluctuations in incomes constitute a deterring or negative factor to be deducted from the average returns over a number of years. In a high-risk land area, however, where a psychology of risk taking is often prevalent, the high returns of a single good year may cause land to be utilized or retained in use far beyond what would be justified by returns over a period of years. Sheridan County in western Kansas, a county in a high-hazard, one-crop wheat section, for instance, averaged an annual net income of $1,008 per 640-acre farm between 1912 and 1934. The total net income for the period was $21,167, of which $20,472 was for the single year 1920, a year of high yields and exceptionally high prices. The average annual net income not including 1920 was less than $35.[9]

Situations of this type can readily lead to unwieldy private-debt obligations and soil-destructive practices. It has also happened that during the

---

[9] From *The Future of the Great Plains*, Report of the President's Great Plains Committee, pp. 52–53, 1936.

few good years community improvement programs and local government extravagance have led to expenditures that later have resulted in
unreasonably heavy tax burdens. As a net result, the public often is left
holding the bag in relief obligations, reduced tax returns, and increased
tax delinquency.

## Land Classification

The physical, economic, and institutional factors that affect the utilization of land also contribute to significant variations in the productive
capacity and economic value of different areas or bodies of land. In the
field of land utilization, the problem of identifying and describing areas
in terms of land-use capability or suitability has led to the development of
a number of land-classification schemes. In the main, land has been
classified on the basis of five groups of attributes, namely, in terms of (1)
inherent land characteristics, (2) present use, (3) use capability, (4)
recommended use, and (5) program effectuation.[10]

Classification is the process of differentiating phenomena into mutually
exclusive categories, each with distinctive characteristics more or less
homogeneous for the various units included within the category. As
classification is a process of sorting, before objects can be sorted there
must be units of classification. The unit of land-use classification may be
natural bodies of land, as, for instance, a soil type; or a cultural unit, such
as a farm, ownership unit, or unit of the rectangular survey; or some
combination of physical and cultural conditions may serve to define the
unit.

Land may be classified physically in a great many ways. Various areas
may be classified in terms of geological categories significant both for
time and conditions of origin and structural characteristics. It should be
obvious, however, that one does not proceed far with the consideration
of land from the standpoint of its adaptability to particular human requirements without having to take into account, not single physical characteristics, but an entire complex of interrelated physical characteristics.
A soil may be naturally fertile, but unproductive because rainfall is
deficient or is badly distributed seasonally. Another soil, naturally less
fertile but located in an area where precipitation also is deficient, may
offset this disadvantage by reason of its retentiveness of moisture or the
character of its subsoil. Certain types of land may be incapable of continuous use because the combination of topography and soil character
with the current and seasonal distribution of rainfall makes it extremely
erosive.

The validity of judgments of the physical adaptability of types of land
resources to particular human uses depends in large degree on technical

[10] *Land Classification in the United States*, National Resources Planning Board,
Washington, 1941.

progress. Certain semiarid soils, for instance, became useful for wheat raising following the introduction of certain drought-resistant varieties. It is only a short step from the recognition of the significance of technical progress and the importance of the "state of the arts" in determining adaptability of the complex of physical characteristics to human uses to the conclusion that adaptability to use is dependent to a large extent on economic and institutional conditions. As has been pointed out, the factor of location is being continually modified by new transport developments, such as the construction of better highways and the increasing use of motor trucks. These developments have considerable impact on the comparative advantage of different areas and types of land for the production of various crops. Likewise, price changes as they affect both receipts and costs also modify the economic, as distinguished from the physical, adaptability of given resources for human use.

The classification of land according to its adaptability to various human uses, therefore, involves formulation of judgment values based on consideration of the physical characteristics of the land itself and knowledge of its behavior under different modes of utilization. The response of land in the utilization process will vary, of course, according to economic conditions and prevailing institutions.

*Purpose and Objectives.* Land classification may serve two broad purposes, namely, (1) diagnosis of problems and formulation of land-use policy, and (2) the carrying out of particular policies with respect to land use.[11] The following will illustrate the difference: (1) Assuming a need for formulation of new policies with respect to land use in the dry-farming areas of the Great Plains, for example, it is desirable that one know approximately the character and distribution of maladjustments in land use in the region as well as something of the characteristics of the land and its fitness for use. This requires some differentiation or classification of the region according to the magnitude of its land-use "problems" and according to the character of the land as it bears on possibilities and nature of adjustment. (2) Once a definite policy or course of action, such as a decision to replace uneconomic grain farms with a combination of individually operated stock ranches and publicly controlled grazing districts which are to be acquired partly through public acquisition, has been determined upon, it becomes necessary to identify those particular lands which are to be acquired and to differentiate between those to be operated as individual stock ranches, those to be used in common, and so forth.

Within these two broad purposes, the objectives of land classification are analyzed by C. P. Barnes, as follows:[12]

[11] C. P. Barnes, *Land Classification: Objectives and Requirements*, pp. 2–3, Resettlement Administration, Land Use Planning Publication 1, Washington, February, 1936.
[12] *Ibid.*, p. 2.

If land classification is to be advocated in a given situation or area, it should be because it serves a rather specific and definite purpose. A more definite objective than that of "achieving a sound use of land," or adjusting land use to land character, will generally be needed to justify a land classification project and to indicate what its form and requirements will be. Indeed, a clear and definite statement of the purposes for which a proposed land classification project is to be undertaken, will do more to show what sort of procedure should be followed than any treatise on methods that could be prepared. The objective of guiding land settlement and occupancy through zoning, for example, dictated the establishment of land classes or use districts in northern Wisconsin counties and indicated the form which the land classes, or use districts, should take. It is necessary, therefore, to consider the various objectives, rather specifically defined, which land classification may serve, without denying, of course, that it may serve such broad general objectives as attaining the best use of the land, which is in itself only a means toward best serving the general welfare. It will be found, however, that land classification may serve purposes—such as the equalization of tax assessment, and the prevention of losses through credit extension or investment—which, although contributing to the attainment of the best use of land, have more direct usefulness in the conservation of capital.

Most of the questions of procedure in economic land classification, such as the size of the area to be selected for classification, the unit of classification, the degree of intensity of work in classification, the categories of classification, and the methods to be employed, depend on the particular objective or objectives to be achieved through classification.

In general, the finer the distinctions between land types and their use capabilities and the more detailed the mapping of land types, the greater the number of objectives which the land classification will serve. For example, a detailed mapping and evaluation of land types as a basis for tax assessments should also serve, at least indirectly, many of the other objectives of land classification; but use districts for rural zoning may be established, in many cases, with less precise data than would be required for tax assessments. This might seem to imply that land classification should be carried on in such a manner as to serve all probable purposes. As in most other activities, however, the benefits must be weighed against the cost in each instance.

*Classification by Economic Characteristics.* As earlier indicated, an economic land classification involves the formulation of judgments based on the physical characteristics of the land and various economic conditions and institutions that prevail. An economic land classification can be rather simple and reconnaissant in type or very intensive in nature.

In many areas the type of land use is obvious and admits of little doubt. The physical conditions alone may permit only one use, and there may be no alternatives at a given time. At the other extreme, there may be a number of possible uses, the choice among which is affected not only by physical resources but also by economic and institutional factors.

No standard procedure for economic land classification can be set up that will meet all the situations that will occur in different parts of the country. Nevertheless, certain elements of procedure may be standardized, and some uniformity in practice may well be adhered to under most circumstances. The standardization and systemizing of land-classification methods would make greater comparability of findings possible and would add to the facility with which they may be understood. The usefulness of land-classification work in the achievement of consistency in policies, and to some degree its usefulness in the determination of the basic policies themselves, may also be increased thereby.

In choosing the items of information to be collected as a basis for, and in support of, land classification, careful appraisal of the significance of each item, considering the form and objectives of the classification, should determine whether its collection is justified. Among the items that have been useful in economic land classifications are base maps and air photos, soil maps and land-use-capability maps, climatic data, erosion characteristics, land costs and income data, availability of water, land-productivity ratings, carrying capacity and seasonal capability of land for pasture use, forest-site quality, surveys of recreational resources, studies of present land-use practices, ownership-pattern studies and maps, and data relating to community patterns, population distribution, roads, and other public facilities.

As indicated, the finer the distinctions made between the various types of use considered, the more precise and more extensive will be the body of supporting data needed. In long-settled regions, the record of experience in the use of land provides a source of information; in newly settled regions more complete reliance must be placed upon studies of the physical characteristics of land and upon determination of its use capabilities by analyses of expected cost of production and future incomes based upon well-founded assumptions.

In summary, the different types of land classification may vary from simple arrays and arrangements of physical land facts to complex groupings of land uses that are considered desirable as the end product of social planning. Between these extremes, there are a host of different types of land classification. The potential usefulness of any of these approaches depends on the purposes or objectives involved in their use and the extent to which they are to be regarded as useful tools or devices in research, in planning, and in program operations.

No discussion of the economics of land utilization is complete without some consideration of the concept of land value, both as it applies to the income- or benefit-producing capacity of land or specific land improvements and to the market price of landed property. Numerous land-income and -value problems arise in connection with the day-to-day use of land and the various conditions attendant on its operation and use. Land-income and -value considerations also affect and are in turn affected by shifts and trends in land use, land-development programs, and the obligations or burdens placed upon land by various institutional arrangements.

As treated here, the problem of land-resource evaluation covers a broad field. It first involves recognition of the economic concepts of land income or rent and land value. These concepts must then be viewed both from the standpoint of individual operators and of society at large. Finally, they must be applied not only in their usual sense but also in the evaluation of areal resource-development programs.

### Land Values from an Individual Point of View

The classical economists were concerned primarily with an analytical discussion of the forces or principles that determine exchange value and the distribution of wealth. In their analyses they usually divided their factors of production into three classes: land, labor, and capital. It was recognized that, unlike the chemical elements, these factors are somewhat generalized, that they sometimes border upon and overlap each other, and that to a certain extent the factors of labor and capital can often be substituted for other factors such as land in the productive process. Despite these limitations, however, this classification of factors has proved extremely useful in the explanation of the production process and the distribution of wealth. Landowners are able to command economic rent or land income from the use of their factor; while wages are paid to labor; and the use of capital gives rise to interest, dividends, and profits.

*Rent and the Value of Land.* While applicable to certain aspects of the return to any factor of production, the term "rent" is usually used to describe the income to landed property. In this respect it should be pointed out, however, that there are two important types of rent, contract rent and economic rent. Contract rent represents the amount actually paid for the use of land or property. Economic rent, on the other hand, is a more theoretical concept and may be defined as any surplus payment to a productive factor over and above the minimum supply price necessary to bring forth or retain that factor in use. In actual practice these two concepts may and often do approach each other in the case of land or other property. But under some circumstances contract rents may far exceed economic rent, while the reverse situation often applies in other instances.

From the standpoint of classical economic theory, economic rent or the income return to land is generally regarded as a residual payment or as the residue in produce or income receipts that remains after suitable compensation has been made for the use of other productive factors. This concept of rent assumes lands of varying location with respect to market and varying production or use capacity, the operation of the concept of diminishing returns, and the existence of extensive and intensive margins of land use. Under this concept, any appreciable increase in the demand for the products of land compels the use of the more distant or less fertile grades of land or the more intensive use of the better and more advantageously located lands that are now in use. Inasmuch as the market price of land products generally reflects the cost of producing the last units of these products at the extensive or intensive margins, it follows that the market price will be higher than is necessary to pay for the capital and labor used in the production of the crops grown on the more fertile productive land. As Malthus indicated, this "excess of the value of the whole produce . . . above what is necessary to pay the wages of labor and the profits of capital employed in cultivation" is economic rent and as such reverts to the holders of land as an income payment for the use of their factor.

This concept of economic rent as a residual payment to the landlord, or as the differential that remains after the other costs of production have been paid, implies that rent does not enter into the cost of production. From the viewpoint of society at large and of the rent-determination process, this is a perfectly valid concept. Community prices reflect production costs at the margin, and any advantage that thereby accrues to the holders of the more productive lands increases their rental returns without affecting their costs. This same situation applies in the case of landlords who are dependent upon rental incomes to pay their fixed costs of taxes, insurance, and property maintenance. To some extent this situation also applies in the case of many debt-free owner-operators.

From the viewpoint of the individual operator who is bound by contract to specified rent payments or who expects to use his land income to pay for his farm, the economic rent or income of land definitely appears as a factor that enters into cost. It appears in this light because of its effect upon the amount that the operator must pay to obtain the use of his land. Tenants and mortgaged owners must pay their rent and interest charges along with their other production costs. For them the residual factor in the production process tends to be their supply of management and personal or family labor. These operators may or should consider the probable economic rent when they decide how much contract rent they can pay or how much they can afford to pay for land. Once their commitments are made, however, they must meet their contract-rent or interest-charge obligations if they expect to continue operations. If the economic income to land suddenly declines, they ordinarily continue to make their payments on a fixed-cost basis, with the result that the actual decline in income to land results in lower returns to the individual operator for his management and labor.

Economic rent is ordinarily thought of as a surplus arising from the use of land. In modern economic theory, however, the concept of rent as a surplus that arises because a factor can command a return over and above its minimum supply price can apply to other factors than land. The minimum supply price that will command the use of land ordinarily is low and usually is limited to fixed-cost expenditures on items such as taxes and possibly interest on investments in land improvements. Most of the return to the better grades of land thus can be classed as surplus income or as economic rent. The minimum supply prices of capital and labor reflect not only the greater alternative opportunities frequently available to these factors but also the presence of "real" costs that may affect their supply. Thus their supply prices are usually somewhat higher than is the case with land. Technically speaking, society could tax away all the economic rent or surplus of receipts above the minimum supply prices of land and the other factors of production without adversely affecting the physical supply of these factors that would be available for production. Although the inclusion in economic rent of the returns to other factors than land has broadened the theory, it has also provided a distractive element where attention centers on land. Because of the possible confusions suggested by this generalized concept, it is often desirable to speak of the return to land as land income rather than as economic rent.

A definite relationship exists between the market value of land and its annual income-producing capacity. In terms of land income, the value of land is nothing more than the present value of a series of its future incomes. In other words, the value of a tract of land can be described as the total value of its current income plus the value of its incomes for all future years discounted to the present. Since the value of land represents a summation of the present values of its current and future incomes, the primary problem in land valuation is that of estimating future incomes and selecting a proper rate of discount for converting future incomes to present values.

While the theoretic market value of land can be explained largely in terms of the present and future income to land, the actual value of land in the market place is often affected by other factors and considerations. Custom and other institutional factors often have a profound effect upon contract rental rates and land values. For instance, in areas where rack-renting is common, the values assigned to land may appear fabulously high, particularly in terms of the purchasing power of the people who work the land.

Numerous other factors affect land values. Various esthetic and amenity factors, such as type of neighborhood, availability of social services, and the presence or absence of scenic factors such as trees, streams, or pleasant vistas, often have a profound effect upon the desirability and demand for rural as well as urban lands. Speculation motives, anticipated changes in land uses, business-cycle considerations, and the impact of the fixed location of land on its market demand also influence land values.

In summary, one might assert that the market value of farm land is largely determined by three sets of factors: (1) expectations relative to future income from the utilization of land; (2) expectations as to the future course of interest rates, particularly as they affect the discounting of future incomes to the present; and (3) the impact of institutional, amenity, speculative, and other considerations upon the market demand for land.

*Land-Appraisal and Land-Market Information.* Inasmuch as land is an object of value, it is not surprising that considerable attention has been given to land-appraisal methods, to analyses of the land market and its characteristics, and to the collection of data on land values and real-estate market trends. An appreciation of all these factors is essential to an understanding of the workings of the land market.

Land appraisals can be made for a variety of purposes. If a farm is being listed for sale, the central purpose or objective of the appraisal may be that of determining the highest price at which the farm will just clear the market. If the appraisal is made for loan purposes, the objective may be that of determining a safe or conservative long-run value for the property that will guide the lender in the judicious lending of his funds. In appraisals for other purposes, such as forced sales, eminent-domain proceedings, tax-assessment purposes, or determination of the unexpired value of a lease, other objectives may be paramount.

Under each of these types of appraisals varying amounts of stress are placed upon different items. In general, however, the appraisal process involves the single or joint use of the capitalization, sales comparison, or cost-of-reproduction approaches to the valuation of landed property.

The capitalization, or income, approach simply involves the capitalization of the annual income of land into a total-value figure. The simplest formula for this purpose can be expressed as $V = a/r$, in which case $V$ stands for land value, while $a$ represents the annual income to land and $r$ represents an accepted rate of interest. Under the sales-comparison, or market-analysis, approach emphasis is placed upon the comparative market prices for comparable properties. Under the cost-of-reproduction approach, which is used frequently in the valuation of buildings, consideration is given to current reproduction costs with suitable allowances for depreciation. Each of these appraisal approaches has its arguments and advantages. At the same time, each has its disadvantages and weaknesses. Accordingly, many appraisers find it wise to use these methods as a check against each other, and at times as supplements to each other when it appears that the total appraised value should represent a summation of the values of two or more items.

Because of the scattered and localized nature of the real-estate market and the nonstandardized characteristics of the real-estate commodity, it is somewhat more difficult to assemble accurate and reliable data on real-estate prices and trends for large areas than is the case for most market commodities. Yet data of this type are needed to guide people in their appraisals of current real-estate situations and trends. The land value and real-estate trend data collected in the past have proved of value to numerous individuals in their private investments and decisions. They also have been used by public officials as a guide in the extension of credit, in the equalization of property-tax burdens, and in the formulation of other policies bearing on land use and development.

Students of the land market are primarily concerned with the acquisition and assembly of representative data on actual sales, estimates of land values, types of buyers and sellers, the character of the land market, and relationships between net income and land values. In looking ahead to future levels of land values and in evaluations or appraisals of the warranted level of land values, the problem is essentially one of comparing the land market prices prevailing at any one given time with the current and expected levels of land income. The reliability of these projections is, of course, dependent upon the accuracy with which one can assess the current situation and predict future trends. Since no one is infallible in this respect, the best results over time usually call for conclusions based upon familiarity with the best available information regarding prevailing land prices, land incomes, and future estimates of land income, the supply-and-demand aspects of the land market, and the economic and social forces in the economy that influence the general level of land values.

*Situations and Problems.*[1] During the early years of the Second World War, the farm real-estate market was characterized by a much greater degree of caution on the part of both buyers and lenders than had prevailed during the First World War boom. Land values rose slowly at first because of the uncertainty as to the duration of the higher levels of farm income and the recollection of the serious consequences that followed the collapse in income and land values following the First World War. Credit agencies still had a sizable backlog of farms that had been acquired in the 1930's in some parts of the country, and this tended to limit the amount of increase in land values. The intensive campaign conducted by Federal and state agencies to acquaint both buyers and lenders with the dangers of a land boom can also be credited with some effect in preventing a repetition of the earlier First World War experiences. Despite these restraining influences, however, land values rose nearly 60 per cent from 1941 to the fall of 1945, and during the latter part of the period the increase was at the rate of about 1 per cent a month.

Successive years of steadily increasing farm income and the growing pressure of a greatly enlarged fund of liquid assets that had accumulated during the war years when consumer goods were in short supply continued to exert an upward pressure on farm real-estate values for several years following the end of the war. Also, as the expected postwar depression failed to materialize, and increasing international tensions and foreign-aid programs brought about a steadily rising general price level, much of the caution that had prevailed earlier seemed unfounded. Both farmers and nonfarmers continued actively to bid for farm land, even though market prices were approaching a new all-time peak. At the same time, the favorable rental returns from land and the prospects of continued high levels of farm income served to limit the number of owners who were willing to sell. Credit agencies also tended to revise their lending policies in line with the higher level of values, and active competition among lenders maintained favorable interest rates and assured an abundant supply of farm-mortgage credit. Thus, land values rose an additional 34 per cent from November, 1945, to November, 1948. At the end of 1948, the general level of land values in the country as a whole was a little more than twice as high as in 1940 and about the same as the 1920 peak.

[1] We are indebted to William H. Scofield for assistance in the preparation of this section.

The downturn in prices of most farm products, beginning in the fall of 1948 and continuing through most of 1949, served as an effective brake on further increases in land values and brought about the first decline in 10 years. By November, 1949, land values were 4 per cent below a year earlier. This proved to be only a temporary recession, however, for the decline was checked by early 1950 as farm prices and general industrial activity again strengthened, and by July, 1950, about half of this loss had been recovered.

The outbreak of hostilities in Korea in July, 1950, introduced several strong inflationary forces in the land market, which led to a 20 per cent increase in values within the first 16 months. The desire of many people, both farmers and nonfarmers, for the type of inflation hedge that farm real estate provides played an important part in this sudden spurt in values. Higher net farm-income expectations also contributed to the sharp increase in the demand for land. By July, 1952, the national index of values had reached a new all-time high of 213 (1912–1914 = 100), which was 22 per cent above the postwar (November, 1948) peak and 23 per cent above 1920. In terms of the 1935–1939 base period, the national index stood at 263. In a number of states land values were more than three times as high as their prewar average.

With this brief review of the major changes in the land-value structure during the past decade in mind, it may be well to turn to an appraisal of the economic and social consequences which are likely to be associated with that level of values. Specifically, are land values out of line with probable long-term earning capacity? Could several years of sharply lower farm income bring about a repetition of the wholesale foreclosures and debt distress characteristic of the 1920's? Have important classes of potential land buyers been permanently priced out of the market?

An evaluation of the relationship between land values and land income in 1952 indicates that values were not excessive. In fact, if a steadily rising general price level can be anticipated, as some economic forecasters predict, values may actually be low. But even this long-run prospect does not rule out the possibilities of a squeeze developing in which farm costs, including debt-carrying charges and family living expenses, may rise faster than farm income. And the nature of agricultural production practically assures some years of sharply lower income when fixed costs for debt service and taxes can claim a substantial part of the net farm income. A certain degree of instability can be expected, therefore, which is definitely related to the level of land values. Overvaluation of farm lands, particularly when associated with excessive debts and taxes, encourages farming practices that exploit the soil and seriously delays needed changes in land use.

The size and type of mortgage debt load that is created during any period of rapidly rising land values represent a key factor in measuring the general strength or health of the land-market situation. In the aggregate, the mortgage debt load has not shown the alarming increases that were associated with the First World War period, and both lenders and borrowers have exercised generally conservative judgments. Relatively little purely speculative buying took place during the Second World War boom, and the mortgaging of debt-free lands to purchase additional land, a practice that resulted in serious consequences during the post–First World War bust, has not been common. Cash down payments have averaged larger, interest rates have been lower, and a substantially larger proportion of the mortgages have been written for longer periods than during the First World War period. The greater use of fully amortized loans, some with prepayment privileges, will also help to lessen the impact of a temporary reduction in debt-paying capacity. Outstanding farm-mortgage debt was reduced by nearly $2 billion between 1940 and 1946. Although the trend has again been upward since then, it is still only half as large as in 1923 and, in relation to the market value of farm property, was in 1952 the smallest on record.

Although available data indicate that the existing mortgage-debt structure is sound in the aggregate, it is still possible that some individuals have paid record prices for land and have assumed a hazardous debt load. This may be particularly true for short-term production credit. At present (1952) about 60 per cent of the farmers' indebtedness is short-term credit and 40 per cent long-term. In view of the large amounts of money now required for production credit or short-term obligations, as the purchase of a carload of steers, a rather sharp break in prices during the feeding period can readily cause a hazardous debt load. Weather hazards, also, cause some sections of the country to be more vulnerable to a drop in income than others. But the magnitude of future credit problems that can be traced to errors in land valuation and appraisal only during the past decade is certain to be appreciably less than occurred during the 1920's.

Even though present values may not be excessively high in relation to the current level of land income, the present situation also behooves one to look back to what happened following the First World War, when many of the failures, fears, and frustrations of farm families were brought about by the collapse in the land market. This is not to imply that history repeats itself. However, the present level of land values brings to memory what followed after the First World War.

Inflationary trends following the First World War caused values to continue to advance for a time, but after the break in 1920–1921, values declined continuously for more than a decade. Land prices were only 41 per cent as high as they were in 1920, and buyers were reluctant to purchase land during the depression period even at these greatly reduced prices. In the period from 1920 to 1933, the equivalent of more than one-third of the nation's farms changed hands through bankruptcies, fore-closures, forced sales, and related defaults. Farms that changed hands several times would account for some duplication.

Many of the agricultural difficulties that followed the First World War are traceable to the large number of persons who did not properly discount the high wartime level of farm incomes and bought farms largely on credit or who assumed large debts on land for other reasons. During this period farm incomes decreased faster than operating costs. Thus an increased share of farmers' reduced income was required to meet operating expenses and interest payments, insurance, taxes, and other costs of land ownership. Also, trouble was experienced in this period through inability to renew or refinance mortgages when they came due.

In the event of another major war, it is altogether likely that inflationary trends will give rise to demands for land price controls. The most effective means of control calls for measures that would limit farm prices, credit extension, and expendable incomes—in other words, limit the forces that give rise to inflationary trends in the land market. Among the other "measures that might conceivably be used for obtaining a degree of control in the farm real-estate market in an emergency period are: taxes on land transfers; resale gains or war increment taxes; taxes on rents; and taxes on mortgages. The possible variations within each type and the possible combinations of measures are numerous."[2]

The transfer tax is one of the simpler methods of controlling the price of land, and if the rate were graduated upward in inverse relation to time since previous transfer, the tax would discourage land speculation.

If a tax were levied upon transfers, the value of the land would have to be worth more to the buyer than to the seller by an amount at least equal to the tax. In the case of a capital gains tax, the principal purpose is to discourage speculation by taking away a large part of the speculative gains. Thus, it would decrease the demand for land that resulted from speculation and would have an anti-inflationary effect. But the demand that arose from bona fide purchasers seeking a farm for operation or from those purchasing land as a hedge against inflation would not be affected.

In considering the level of land values, not only are there problems relating to the possible loss of farms through foreclosure but also to the effects on a program for increased family-farm ownership. High land values in relation to land income may mean the difference between success or failure of such programs. Not only may high land values make it

[2] Mark M. Regan and Fred A. Clarenbach, "Emergency Control in the Farm Real Estate Market," *Journal of Farm Economics*, Vol. 24, No. 4, p. 875, November, 1942. This article briefly covers the factors to consider and methods of emergency control of land values.

difficult for prospective owner-operators to acquire land at a value and under conditions that can reasonably be expected to pay out, but high land prices may result in a serious threat to the maintenance of the standard of living desired on family farms.

Another problem is the effect of agricultural programs on land values; for instance, the possible impacts of capitalization of allotment and benefit payments into land values.[3] If expected future incomes from acreage allotments or other benefit payments are capitalized into higher land values, they accrue to present landowners and lose much, if not all, of their value as continuing benefits. Subsequent landowners will be obliged to purchase these benefits in the form of higher land prices. Thus benefit payments become no longer a real benefit to the farmer, and may actually become vested interest rights since landowners have purchased them. The cause may be in the system of benefit payments; nevertheless, if the payments are capitalized into land values, it is the resulting level of land values that becomes the real difficulty. The capitalization of benefit payments is a problem that should be studied, as it is most significant in formulating an agricultural program to promote the welfare of rural people.

## Land Values from a Social Viewpoint

It is desirable that we pursue somewhat further than was done in the previous chapter the distinction between individual values and social values, and then consider these distinctions in relation to land.

Valuation analysis has focused attention mainly on explaining values as determined in the market place, and largely in reference to the actions of individuals in regard to the demand for and supply of exchangeable commodities. Value theory has dealt largely with commodities or services which are capable of being, and are, the objects of property rights. There has also been an implicit assumption "that market values correspond roughly with social values, and are an adequate indicator of need for production to follow."[4]

Although market values are the product of social forces, they nevertheless fall far short of registering all the important considerations with which organized society is concerned. It is true that market values measure utilities of goods to people, and thus also represent in the aggregate social utilities; but they do not reflect all social benefits and costs. For instance, attempts at social reforms frequently reflect a concern for social values not adequately reflected in market valuations.

In economics there is a need for a more comprehensive study of social

[3] See John E. Mason, "Acreage Allotments and Land Prices," *Journal of Land and Public Utility Economics,* May, 1946, pp. 176–181.

[4] Henry C. Gray, *Economics for the General Reader,* Chap. 22, The Macmillan Company, New York, 1921.

costs and benefits that arise in the use of wealth and for a more adequate distinction between social values and market values. One of the real gaps is the lack of techniques for measuring social or public values, particularly when social values are intermingled with market values.

*Inadequacy of Market Values as Expressions of Social Values.* There are a number of ways in which market values and social values are not identical.[5] One of the basic distinctions lies in the fact that market values are ratios, and as such cannot measure the true worth of goods and services to all individuals. To be sure, a common denominator or standard of value, such as money, measures values in the market place, but, even so, and with due allowance for fluctuations in the value of the standard itself, the commodities or services that the standard measures are inherently ratios and not necessarily expressions of values either to individuals or to aggregates of individuals. Social values are more synonymous with use values. Use values arise out of choices in judgments and must be "judged in relation to a complex of human purposes."[6]

Differences in the wealth and income of individuals influence greatly the marginal utilities of goods and services; and between individuals and groups there are different degrees of consumer surplus. Thus, a demand that is necessary to clear the market does not measure the aggregate importance or even relative importance to all individuals of a given quantity of a commodity. The value of a given commodity to a group may be materially different from the value for which the commodity may exchange in the market, for its value in use to each member of the group is not the same as its exchange value.

The marginal utilities of different commodities and services to individuals vary greatly because of availability of purchasing power and individual preferences. The concept of aggregate individual subjective values composed of individual utilities multiplied by the number of units of each commodity and service would give a different value figure than the aggregate value as determined in the market.

Because of this fact, the social interest frequently dictates policies that do not permit the distribution of particular commodities to take the course that would result if individuals were left free to compete in the market. For instance, in time of war or in other emergencies that produce extreme scarcities of important necessities of life, governments do interfere with market distribution either by rationing or by the distribution of purchasing power to needy individuals. In the case of rationing, this is

---

[5] For an early review of the status of economic theory on this subject and some discussion on the lack of coincidence between market value and social value, see Benjamin Anderson, *Social Value: A Study in Economic Theory, Critical and Constructive,* Houghton Mifflin Company, Boston, 1911.

[6] J. R. Commons, *The Economics of Collective Action,* Chap. XI, The Macmillan Company, New York, 1950.

done to prevent those in society who possess extensive purchasing power from consuming a larger share of scarce commodities than is justified by the social interest. Another illustration is the provision of free, and even compulsory, education. The interests of organized society do not admit of leaving supply and demand of education to be governed by the free actions of individuals. This, if it were permitted, would inevitably result in numerous parents employing their limited purchasing power in directions other than providing education. Thus the very classes which most need the benefits of education would fail to obtain them.

In contrast, the reflection of values in the market may result in unduly high values for commodities or services which, from a broad social standpoint, are relatively trivial in importance, as, for instance, many of the values which reflect the social psychology of "keeping up with the Joneses." Many individual valuations of commodities or services are made either with a view to emulating divergences from conventional modes of consumption or to conformity with quite artificial conventions.[7] And during emergency conditions, as in times of war, it may be found that the elimination from the national-consumption budget of such items or even of some of the "gadgets of civilization" which were unknown to an earlier generation does not result in a serious recession of actual well-being. Furthermore, market values may even measure social disutilities, as, for instance, the prices placed on narcotics and other injurious items of individual consumption.

Related to the preceding points is the fact that market values may reflect the influence of artifically created scarcities, which interfere with the operation of demand and supply and which permit strategically situated individuals to exercise their acquisitive impulses at the expense of society. The almost intuitive antagonism of public opinion to governmental policies aimed at artifically created scarcities for the benefit of particular classes of citizens, as well as the prevailing hostility to private monopoly, reflects a popular recognition of the important distinction between market values of particular commodities or services and their significance for social welfare. Market prices as determined by administrative action, as in the case of the price of potatoes in 1949, may not reflect the social desirability of the quantity of potatoes produced or the use of land for this purpose.

As use value is the social concept of wealth, then it is the utility of a good to satisfy human needs that measures social values. To the extent that market prices do not accurately measure social values, quantities of goods in relation to the need for them or the service rendered become the more significant measure of social values.

[7] For a good up-to-date discussion on social inefficiency see G. K. Galbraith, "The Unseemly Economics," *Harper's Magazine,* January, 1952, p. 58.

There are other considerations important from a social standpoint that may not find expression in market values. For instance, a venturesome desire to ensure stability may motivate the actions of individuals to take long chances in the hope of relatively large rewards. The rewards sought, however, may not be in the social interest because the chances of loss are great; and if losses do occur, as is frequently the case, society may be called upon to afford relief in one form or another. For instance, men have gambled in the settlement of areas of high climatic hazards and low productivity, leaving society the task of bailing them out when misfortune followed. When society permits hazardous settlement of a substantial amount, not to mention when it is sponsored by some unit of government, it then becomes the duty of government to provide some type of relief.

It is also true that market values do not reflect the presence or absence, adequacy or inadequacy of social institutions or regulations. For instance, protective arrangements against hazardous settlement or for forest-fire protection might have little or no value in the market. The imposition, however, of regulations regarding such protection does result in the emergence of increased market values, as, for instance, a protected forest. Social policy itself does create both market and social values. It can also decrease the sum total of values, provided the regulations are undesirable. The objective of control measures, of course, is to increase total utilities, and unless this follows, they will in the course of time be repealed in a democratic society.

In summary, social values are in part exchange values or give rise to exchange values, but because to a significant degree they are often intangible or nonmonetary in nature, the determination of their power to satisfy wants and desires rests in some type of group decision or public policy and not in the market place. As John R. Commons has stated, social values are often expressed through rationing transactions as contrasted to bargaining transactions. The former is the will of the people in action, the latter is expressed by market price. The aspects of social values that give rise to public policies rest upon what the people want and will support. It is the will of a group in action as expressed by Congress, the executive branch of government, the courts, or any group that exercises moral, economic, or legal power over people that determines social values. And each can and does create economic values of a social nature —values that reflect social benefits over costs.

## Social Costs and Benefits

In dealing with social values, one question that logically arises is: What are social costs? We are interested particularly in the concept as it relates to resource utilization.

It should be clear that social values involve some type of costs. Social values, in fact, become social costs when they are considered from the standpoint of those values that are sacrificed in attaining certain objectives. To a large extent, social costs are opportunity costs in the sense that they are measured by the value of the benefits that society must forgo in order to achieve the objectives decided upon. Costs are benefits forgone. It follows, therefore, that many of the causes of lack of coincidence between market values and social values also result in a similar lack of coincidence between individual costs and social costs.

We are aware of certain distinctions between individual and social costs. For instance, the private economy may not consider the hazards to individual life and limb of the workers until or unless social requirements or regulations compel such consideration; the individual economy may not take into account the social costs of unemployment; and, to a very large extent, as our experience in this country has shown, the private economy may ignore the social costs of natural resources wastefully destroyed or carelessly used. These and other distinctions have given rise to social regulations. The legislation enacted has not aimed primarily at restricting individual initiative, and, generally speaking, this has not been the result. The purpose rather has been to create an environment in which social costs are decreased and private enterprise expanded by the establishment of reasonable rules of conduct. For example, control over waste and sewage disposal in streams and rivers is a highly desired conservational measure in the interest of health and protection of wildlife, but the effects achieved likewise protect and expand individual opportunities and enterprise.

*Governmental Costs.* Perhaps no distinction is more frequently lost sight of than the distinction between social costs and governmental costs. A significant illustration is public opposition to acquisition of land as a means of accomplishing social objectives. From the standpoint of government finance, the purchase of privately owned land involves an expenditure chargeable to government income that may result in an expansion of public indebtedness. From a social standpoint, however, the public purchase of land may entail no social cost if it is assumed that the government will make better use of land than would occur in private ownership, for purchase of land is a mere transfer of ownership. It may involve no destruction or sacrifice of social capital or labor resources. It is true, the employment of taxes or bonds to raise funds to purchase land affects the distribution of wealth or income through the impact of the methods by which the money is raised and paid out. But the effect on distribution of income of the cost of land purchased at any one time could hardly be considered socially injurious. When the conservation of land or its utilization can be achieved better under public ownership than under private enterprise, public purchase in itself represents no sacrifice of essential social resources.

Public funds can be used to correct past mistakes or prevent future ones. Ordinarily an expenditure for the latter purpose should be regarded with more favor than the utilization of public funds in the restoration of, say, forest resources, the restoration of which might have been rendered unnecessary had the government acquired the forests earlier and prevented their wasteful exploitation. However, it is much more difficult to get Congress to appropriate public funds to prevent unsound forest practices than to purchase forest land for restoration purposes after it has little or no commercial forest value to individuals.

In a somewhat similar category, but more widely accepted in the United States, is the fact that unutilized labor involves social wastage. Labor goes irreparably to waste when unemployed, just as water power may be wasted when not utilized. The utilization of either labor or water power may, of course, necessitate the joint employment of other forms of capital, and such capital must be regarded as a cost to be measured against the results achieved, including in the case of labor the benefits of maintaining the morale of the unemployed. Wages paid to unemployed labor for land-resource improvement can be regarded as social cost only to the extent that the labor could be employed for other purposes. The value of such alternative ways of using labor measures the cost of using it. And only on the supposition that society can find no other way to utilize labor—a most unhappy confession of social futility—could the use of unemployed labor by the government for resource development be regarded as costless.

Quite frequently social costs are not taken into account merely because government policy does not assume the responsibility for compensating certain losses to its citizens. For example, permitting private interests to clear-cut a forest area that is basic to the economic life of a community may impose on the citizens of that community heavy personal losses from the necessity of liquidating their private businesses, moving their homes, and reestablishing elsewhere, with the result that existing roads, streets, schools, and other public facilities are rendered more or less useless. To varying degrees this is not untypical of what has happened in many parts of the cut-over areas in the United States. Failure to prevent such situations from arising in the future, either by public acquisition of land or regulation of forest use, may seem to effect certain economies in government expenditure, but these economies may be more than offset by social losses or costs.

A somewhat similar condition exists when public agencies, in the purchase of land for public purposes, require inhabitants to resettle themselves at their own expense. The social cost of resettlement would be-

come a government cost only in case the government assumed the responsibility of the resettlement at public expense; but failure of the
government to assume at least part of the expense does not eliminate the
social costs involved, which may be even greater than if the government
assumed this responsibility in the first instance.

*Benefits and Costs of Land-Resource Development.*[8] Expenditures for
resource-development use or conservation are valuable to individuals or to
society only to the extent that benefits exceed costs. One of the differences,
however, is that for individuals most costs and benefits are tangible and
can be expressed in monetary terms, while for society benefits and costs
are more likely to be intangible and not readily reducible to dollars. And
benefits considered by an individual accrue to him, while the general
benefits to society are often widely diffused.

The costs of land-resource investments are the expenditures for capital
and labor outlays—improvement costs, maintenance costs, and payments
and income losses—that may be associated with adjustments accompanying the investments. For an individual investor such costs are generally
measurable in monetary terms. For society this is also true for funds
actually spent, but, as has been shown, these costs may not represent the
total social costs.

The benefits from a resource-development project are the increased
productivity of goods and services that are the result of or attributable to
the project. For instance, soil saved would be a direct benefit.

Benefits and costs are of different kinds, and it is necessary to distinguish between the various kinds of benefits and costs associated with
development programs. All benefits and costs, regardless of their functional source, their susceptibility to measurement, or the immediateness
of their relation to the project, may be grouped into categories according
to the kinds of effects flowing from a project development. The primary
groups of effects that arise from a project are changes in the provision of
goods and services, changes in time of accrual of goods and services, and
changes in risk associated with the provision of goods and services. Al-

---

[8] The authors have found the report *Proposed Practices for Economic Analysis of
River Basin Projects,* prepared by the Sub-Committee on Benefits and Costs of the
Federal Inter-Agency River Basin Committee, May, 1950, helpful in the preparation
of this section. For an excellent discussion of principles involved in appraising the
economic feasibility of large resource developments and the measurement of benefits and costs both in terms of principles and in relation to specific types of projects,
this report is highly recommended for study. In a number of respects, however, the
analysis here varies from that of this report. Also see M. M. Regan, and E. C. Weitzell, "Economic Evaluation of Soil and Water Conservation Measures and Programs,"
*Journal of Farm Economics,* Vol. 29, November, 1947; and M. M. Regan and E. L.
Greenshields, "Benefit-Cost Analysis of Resource Development Programs," *Journal
of Farm Economics,* Vol. 33, November, 1951.

Obviously, there are many problem situations in resource valuation, and the discussion in this chapter must be largely confined to principles and over-all considerations.

though closely interrelated, each such type of effect may be considered as having a separate or distinct influence on the present worth of the benefits that flow from a project.

Project benefits and costs may be broadly classified into (1) those tangible items that may be reasonably explained in quantitative terms, either monetary or otherwise, and (2) those intangible items that are not ordinarily subject to quantitative treatment. Another significant grouping with respect to immediateness of effects would be (1) the direct and (2) extended or indirect benefits and costs.

From a private point of view, direct benefits are increases in goods and services or reductions in cost to the individuals, while direct costs are the payments they must make in order to secure these benefits. In contrast to direct effects, indirect benefits and costs from a private point of view are those benefits or costs that accrue to individuals usually in an incidental and unintentional manner. An example would be the beneficial effects of increased business for local merchants resulting from an irrigation project.

From a public point of view, the remoteness of the effects of the primary purposes of a project become the basis for grouping both direct and indirect benefits and costs, direct benefits and costs being those that occur in the production of goods and services in the first stages of a project, while indirect benefits and costs are those resulting from successive stages of processing upon the primary goods of the project. Thus the production of citrus fruit from an irrigation project has a direct value to producers, while indirect benefits may accrue to handlers and processors making the product available to consumers.

## Measurement of Social Costs and Benefits

Since many social values are not reflected in market values or prices, their appraisal is likely to involve different principles and procedures than are involved in the simpler task of correctly ascertaining or estimating market values. Economists have perhaps been loath to undertake the task of estimating social values because they involve in part ethical or philosophic considerations not readily translatable into pecuniary terms. An economic consideration of this problem brings up the subject of price levels and discount rates. In regard to prices, it is necessary to project price estimates over the period of the effects of a project. It is not so important, however, accurately to project monetary prices of possible effects —costs and benefits—as to project the relative worth of goods and services in relation to costs during the period of consideration. This should be obvious. The projection of future price levels is most difficult, but analysis can proceed on the basis of reasonable assumptions of relative prices of goods and benefits therefrom.

*Individual and Social Time Preference.* There has been reference to interest and discount rates in determining the value of land resources and in measuring benefits from land-improvement and -conservation practices. It should be clear that the value of land or investment in land, from an economic standpoint, is measured by the present value of future incomes and that in this process a rate of discount must be used in bringing future incomes back to the present for measurement. It should also be clear in comparing the values accruing from investments in land resources that values are comparable only if adjusted to the same time base.

It has been pointed out that social time preference may be different from the time preference of any individual or from the market discount rate. The reason for the differences is essentially that any individual places a value upon the present in terms of his life interests, while society is concerned with the use of resources over a much longer period of time. Some may contend that society is merely the sum total of all individuals, but it is more than this in that society has continuity through succeeding generations.

The report of the Federal Inter-Agency River Basin Committee on *Proposed Practices for Economic Analysis of River Basin Projects* recommends that the interest rate used in measuring the costs and benefits of private and public investments should reflect the long-term borrowing rates applicable. For the Federal government, a rate of 2½ per cent is recommended, as this rate was expected to continue for some time as the long-term rate on government bonds, while for private investments a rate of not less than 4 per cent is recommended for use (1950) in converting deferred private benefits and costs to an annual basis. In determining costs for a private individual or for the government, it is argued that the capital costs should be measured by the price paid for the use of money, which the loan rates reflect. In measuring future benefits the problem for the individual is substantially the same as in measuring costs, in that the cost of a future benefit to an individual reflects current costs. Individual benefits accrue in the relatively near future. However, in the case of measuring benefits that accrue to society, the problem is more difficult.

The cost to the government of borrowing funds is the rate that expresses its position in the market for money in relation to that of private individuals. But the social discount that measures the value of land resources and future benefits from investment, particularly in those arising in the distant future, is not necessarily due to the fact that the government borrows money; nor is the rate of the "proper" social discount for each resource necessarily identical with the rate the government pays on borrowed money.

The differences between present and future social values of specific natural resources are in part independent of a competitive discount rate, and a compound interest rate for anything but a short period of time—

which might be considered by the individual investor—would place an excessive premium on present use and virtually prohibit a provident policy for a remote future. Even a moderate rate of simple interest might make a present expenditure or sacrifice to conserve an exhaustible resource for a remote future appear extravagant.

Individual interest rates and government loan rates reflect the level necessary to call forth the supply of money needed. They are market-exchange valuations. However, organized society must consider the consequences in the future of the destruction of various segments or of even the total supply of various natural resources. Therefore, from the social standpoint, loss in future value is more nearly identical with total utility rather than the product of the various segments controlled multiplied by the value of the marginal segments.[9] The present economic value of benefits grows less significant as the time of benefit accrual moves into the distant future. Both present and future social utilities are likely to reflect quite different considerations from those which serve to explain market valuations.

Moderate changes in interest or discount rates are much more significant than is apparent from a casual appraisal of the difference. As interest rates measure time differences in values, obviously the higher the interest rate, the greater is the premium placed on present values in relation to future values.

*Steps in Measurement.* It is believed that the costs and benefits of land-resource measures and programs can be estimated to a large extent in physical or quantitative terms. The primary responsibility for the type and form of these estimates should be assumed by economists. In such work, however, they should enlist the aid of specialists in such fields as engineering, medicine, psychology and social psychology, ethics and cultural anthropology.

One of the initial steps in the economic evaluation of land-development projects involves the reasonably accurate determination of the effects expected from the project. This early step in the evaluation process thus calls for satisfactory estimates in physical terms of prospective results, such as reductions in water run-off, tons of soil saved, reduction in flood damages, increased yields, changes in intensity of land use, and similar effects brought about by the project. Better and more reliable data of this nature are needed, and in so far as possible they should be assembled in such form that they are subject to economic measurement. Too often the sampling methods used are inadequate, and the effects contemplated are determined in a manner that does not permit their reasonable appraisal.

In so far as possible the physical data collected should be translated

---

[9] As John Maurice Clark has suggested, social values may be "antimarginal." *Preface to Social Economics*, p. 59, Rinehart & Co., Inc., New York, 1936.

into monetary terms. To do this requires well-developed techniques or standards which, broadly speaking, involve the establishment of over-all general principles and the application and modification of these principles to specific situations. The latter is particularly important in the process of evaluation. For the economist to be most effective in the development of valuation standards and techniques he must be alert to new situations and problems and he should work with engineers, applied natural scientists, and others, as a part of a group engaged in appraising benefits and costs.

Thus, the extent to which costs of and benefits from a project can be measured in economic terms depends to no small degree upon the type of data collected and their representativeness of the situation. Unless the economists participate in the process of collecting data, the data assembled may not be in a form most suitable to economic measurement. Through joint participation of all scientists, each group of scientists will contribute to the development of improved valuation standards and techniques.

If well-chosen techniques and methods of investigation are employed, many of the physical effects from a project can be converted, with a reasonable degree of accuracy, into monetary terms. As costs and benefits occur over a period of time, it is first necessary to determine or estimate the time of their occurrence.

Current direct costs and benefits may readily be measured in terms of current price levels, but it is also necessary to appraise future effects in terms of present values. To convert these effects to present values involves the use of reasonable assumptions as to the level of future prices and the use of acceptable rates of capitalization and discount. The future general price level and the prices of particular commodities or services are important in estimating future benefits and costs. And the present value of future goods and services brings up the subject of interest rates to use for valuation purposes. As has been pointed out, for public investments a lower rate of interest is generally used than for private investments, in that government can borrow at a lower rate than can individuals or business concerns; and the appraisal of future effects in terms of present values is a very important step in an economic evaluation of any program, and also in appraising the desirability of alternative types of measures in that it is necessary for comparability of measurement.

To the extent that effects can be reduced to monetary terms and that costs on the one hand and benefits on the other can be so measured, just so much smaller is the area subject to nonmonetary measurement. This is a sound and desirable step in economic evaluation. Furthermore, the effect that cannot be reduced to monetary terms should be quantitatively presented in a form most meaningful for appraisal. If this is done, another significant step in the evaluation process has been taken. It is always well to quantify insofar as possible the economic data. And for those effects—costs and benefits—that are not subject to quantitative measurement, it is well to give as clear a qualitative picture as possible of their character. In some instances, because of the unique significance of the non-quantitative effects, they may be strategic in the determination of policy and thus need to be clearly set forth.[10]

That part of social values that cannot become subject to some type of measurement must obviously become a matter purely of subjective evaluation as determined by the cultural attitudes, the social philosophy, or the political or ethical judgments of a people. And the final evaluation of total social values arising from a public land project or a land-development program is made by the elected representatives of the people and the decisions of those duly chosen for the administration of legislation. Government decisions that are expressed by acts, policies, or programs of the legislative branch of government, at the executive level or by the courts, are the final arbitrators of the social value of any project involving public expenditures. But in the process, economic evaluations are most useful and helpful in choice of projects and in a determination of types of development within a project.

*Valuation Ratios.* To the extent that benefits and costs can be expressed in monetary terms, the relationship between them may be expressed in some form of a ratio. There are in the main three types of ratios: (1) a comparison of total costs with total benefits, (2) the ratio of project benefits to project costs, including operation and maintenance costs, and (3) rate of return on investment or ratio of annual benefits to initial or present value of construction costs.

The primary function of an array of ratios of benefits to costs is to indicate the productiveness of a public investment in a project. If public funds were unlimited, this would not be necessary, but in a world of scarce resources the economic problem is one of choice between different alternative investments.

When the basis for determining project desirability is net benefits, this assumes in effect that funds are available to develop all projects for which benefits equal or exceed costs. For instance, two projects producing the same net benefits, *e.g.*, $1,000, would be equally desirable, although one of the projects cost $10,000 and the other cost $1,000,000. As soon as costs are taken into account the net benefit expression changes its character and becomes a form of benefit-cost ratio.

A project benefit-cost ratio, in which a comparison is made between total project benefits and total project costs, would, in the above example,

---

[10] V. Webster Johnson, "Air Pollution in Relation to Economics," published in *Air Pollution*, p. 37, Proceedings of the United States Technical Conference on Air Pollution, McGraw-Hill Book Company, Inc., New York, 1952.

with each having a net benefit of $1,000, give preference to the project costing $10,000, the benefit-cost ratios being in the proportion of 10,000 to 11,000 and $1,000,000 to $1,001,000, respectively. "If the sum of all beneficial effects were compared with the sum of all adverse effects for a project, the ratio of the benefits to the costs would reflect the effectiveness with which all the resources involved were being used."[11]

A ratio of benefits to costs constitutes a good measure of the efficient use of funds in resource development. The emphasis is on high returns from a project, but not necessarily on the efficient use of resources other than those required directly by the project. Where extensive employment of resources for project development is desired, selection should include a sufficient number of the projects with the most favorable ratios to make up the desired amount of public-works expenditure.

When the emphasis is on the rate of return on the investment, the desirability of a project is determined by the relation of the net return from a project, excluding interest costs, to the initial investment. The soundness of the investment may be measured by comparing the prevailing rate of interest on government loans with the calculated return on a project. The use of the rate of return on investment for selection of projects favors projects with a low initial investment and high annual cost for operation and maintenance. "The method has a limited usefulness, as for example, for determining relative desirability of projects when construction funds are limited and when the relative cost of operation and maintenance is considered of secondary importance."[12]

## Purposes of Evaluation

Among the functions performed by an economic evaluation of a land project or land-development program, to the extent that economic evaluations are determinant, are (1) economic justification for project costs, (2) appraisal of the desirable type and size of project development, (3) estimate of the relative desirability of several projects, (4) determination of the equitability of cost allocation between geographic areas, between public and private interests, and among types of beneficiaries, and (5) determination of the basis of repayment amounts and schedules.

Since many of the resources essential for project development have other profitable uses, an economic analysis of any particular project must include a measure of the relative productivity of the use of the capital and labor that go into that project in comparison with alternative uses for them. The use of capital and labor for irrigation, for instance, might

---

[11] *Proposed Practices for Economic Analysis of River Basin Projects,* Report to Federal Inter-agency River Basin Committee, p. 14, Washington, May, 1950.
[12] *Ibid.,* p. 14.

well be compared with the results achieved from the use of a similar amount of capital and labor for drainage, or vice versa. In any particular project the expected returns from land resources with and without a project furnish a measure of the economic justification for the expenditures and a basis for comparisons between projects of the relative desirability of projects.

There is no single method for land development and conservation, and assuming that some type of project is socially justifiable, the analysis of costs and benefits is particularly significant in project formulation and design. The aim is to develop a program that will make for the most effective use of the resources, and do so in a manner that will maximize the excess of benefits over costs. Thus, one very significant purpose of an economic evaluation is to determine the combination of resources and the degree of development which will result in maximum net benefits. In doing this it is necessary to consider alternative uses for funds and to choose between types of projects and their sizes for different purposes.

In order to justify a project from a social point of view it is necessary that total benefits attributable to the project exceed the total costs and that these costs be not in excess of alternative costs for obtaining the same result. And the justifiable degree of intensity of phases of a project should be established by the relationship between costs and benefits of incremental segments. In other words, separate analysis of benefits and costs of independent segments should be made. If a segment of a project cannot bear the additional cost of providing for it, it is not strictly economically justifiable. It is recognized, however, that the feasibility of project development is not determined solely on economic grounds. For example, it is practically politically impossible to refuse to irrigate good land lying near a dam behind which millions of acre-feet of water are impounded, even if the farm products to be produced exist in surplus quantities. Nevertheless, a sound economic appraisal should go far in weeding out costly and inefficient projects or segments thereof.

Often public policy requires that groups or individuals directly benefiting from a project assume a share of the project costs. In the allocation of these costs it is necessary that an evaluation of costs be made for beneficiaries. If the beneficiaries bear a part or all of the costs, it is necessary to know costs for cost-allocation purposes; and even when costs are nonreimbursable, it is necessary to an appraisal of economic feasibility that cost be known for each group of beneficiaries. For instance, if the benefits from a project accrue to a relatively small group of individuals, the question of the economic feasibility of such a project in comparison with one with a similar cost structure, but which has a wide diffusion of benefits, is material in determining economic feasibility.

## River-Basin Development

The developments that are taking place in river basins focus attention on land-resource evaluations, the need of doing a better job in project evaluations, and the fact that land-development work in river-basin areas constitutes one of our major land-resource evaluation tasks. The Federal government is engaged in a broad program of resource conservation and development on public and private lands. The program consists of numerous projects and lines of activity for flood control, navigation, hydroelectric power, reclamation, soil conservation, forest improvement, range management, recreation, wildlife, and other purposes. Some 40 billion dollars of Federal expenditure was under consideration in 1949 for multiple-purpose water-resource projects and related developments.[13]

Most of the elements within the Federal resource-conservation and -development program may be expected to influence agricultural land use and agricultural production in one way or another. As one illustration of a major influence, 5.6 million acres of land in the Western states is scheduled to come under full or supplemental irrigation by 1955 under a program of the Bureau of Reclamation.[14] This will expand the irrigated area of the West by about one-fourth. Millions of additional acres throughout the country will become suited for higher or more productive uses through the reclamation, soil conservation, flood control, and other agricultural-resource activities of the Federal government. On the other hand, some areas, such as reservoir overflow lands, will be retired from agricultural production.

The vast number and complexity of land-development programs gives rise to many problems of evaluation. A significant problem, and one which is of growing importance as government enters more and more into the economic life of the people, is the task of appraising proposed accomplishments in relation to their costs. Arising from development programs are the benefits that accrue to particular individuals or groups and those that are diffused throughout society. Thus one of the valuation tasks is to determine the part of the costs of a program that can be borne, for instance, by landowners or land operators and the part for which public assistance is necessary in the interest of national welfare. A large part of the costs is not directly repayable to the government, and thus, as in the case of irrigation and flood control, economic feasibility must be measured in terms of social or public benefits—benefits diffused throughout an area, region, or nation, and which to a substantial degree are not

[13] A. B. Roberts, *Certain Aspects of Power, Irrigation, and Flood Control Projects: A Report with Recommendations,"* Task Force Report on Water Resources Projects, Appendix K, p. 6, prepared for the Commission on Organization of the Executive Branch of the Government, Washington, January, 1949.

[14] *The Reclamation Program: 1948–54,* p. 2, Washington, 1948.

measurable in market transactions. Nonreimbursable public expenditures are justifiable social contributions if the social benefits exceed the public or social costs.

It might be well also to add that for those values that are public in nature, the task of seeing that they are widely diffused and that costs are equitably borne is particularly related to social organization. We need to know where the alleged benefits fall, how best to distribute their costs through tax or special charges, and how to organize most effectively and democratically to do the job. And "individuals and governments dealing with fundamental questions of adjustments in land use want to know . . . how best to go about toward getting land use changes . . . [some of which are quite drastic] without disturbing in a fundamental way the system of rights, freedoms, and forms which characterize their particular society and form of government."[15]

*River-Basin Problems.* Essential to an economic appraisal of benefits and costs is a clear understanding of the problems and conditions existing within an area. In river basins many problems are encountered in supplying water to dry land, removing excess water from wet land, and protecting land from overflow and flooding. The problems are associated with engineering operations or are in the nature of related problems that arise in erosion control, restoration of forests, and bringing about necessary shifts in the use of land. It is possible here to merely mention some of them.

At the present time, most of the large-scale land-development projects are phases of multiple-purpose development; consequently, the land factor is only one of several factors to be considered. In some of the projects power development may be the strategic and propelling force. When such a situation exists, and the project is highly desirable, and there is land that is suitable for agricultural development, it becomes an exceedingly difficult task, as has been indicated, to stave off agricultural development even though this phase of the project may not be economically justifiable under existing conditions. Agricultural development in such instances is determined largely by political considerations rather than by economic feasibility. Of course, the project justifications may be based upon conclusions drawn from unsound and unwarranted uses of techniques and methods.

In the evaluation of benefits in relation to the costs that arise from land development, it is first necessary to get a good picture of existing land-use conditions, that is, of the type and range of products grown, nature of the cover, degree of erosion, and productivity of the land under existing

---

[15] Robert W. Harrison, "The Role of the Agricultural Economists in the Formulation of Land Use Policies in River Basins," *Journal of Farm Economics*, Vol. 31, p. 405, February, 1949.

land-use practices. Such information needs to be by land classes or group-ings of a size that permits rather careful observation and study. It is from this base that one must proceed to develop plans and programs. In this task, among the things it will be necessary to explore are (1) programs for conservation and improvement measures on crop- and grassland, (2) programs for forest development, (3) programs for flood control and water retardation, and (4) institutional adjustments needed to achieve desired objectives.

Land and water programs for conservation and development of re-sources take various forms, as improved land-use practices, terraces, strip cropping, farm ponds, and very large dams and engineering structures. It is also necessary to consider institutional changes that will be involved in the execution of the program, and those additional changes or shifts in emphasis that are needed in present programs for the acceleration of operations. Furthermore, attention must be given to educational and re-search activities. What needs to be done cannot be separated from the operating mechanics of doing the job and from getting the job incor-porated as a part of the thinking of the people who are directly involved.

To be somewhat more specific, let us look at a few of the development problems that are present in the Missouri Basin. For example, the irriga-tion of land raises questions of economic feasibility which necessitate an analysis of data on type and character of soils, type of farming, size of farm, crop yields, price levels, land values, irrigation-district organization, and other related factors. As irrigation in the region involves the storage of water, this in turn means the inundation of large areas of land. In these situations it is necessary to consider problems that arise in connec-tion with damages resulting in inundation of reservoir areas, government programs to reduce the impacts of adjustments, and reestablishment and relocation of people residing in inundated areas. Generally, inadequate attention has been given to inundation problems and the social costs involved.

In areas such as the Missouri Valley, one of the significant problems is the integration of irrigated agriculture with the surrounding nonirrigated land. In other words, to what extent is it economically feasible and prac-ticable to stabilize the productivity of the area and reduce distress through integrated land use and thus increase the efficiency of the com-bined utilization of irrigated and nonirrigated lands?

The uncertain growing conditions in the Upper Missouri states because of the semi-arid climate make it imperative that this large agricultural area of the nation be developed in such a way as to stabilize its production and con-tributions to the national welfare as quickly and as completely as possible. Large public expenditures for relief and feed and seed loans in the Upper Basin states were necessary in past years when adverse weather and business conditions and severe insect pest ravages occurred. Development programs that will help stabilize farming and ranching operations in these states will relieve the government of future relief and emergency expenditures. More important, sound agricultural development programs will permit the Missouri Valley with its great grain and meat production capacities to make its maximum contribution to the national welfare.[16]

Problems that arise in river-basin development work in their broad aspects must not only deal with measures that are advanced for the conservation and development of resources in the particular area under consideration, but also the relative need for a program in comparison with conditions existing in other areas. As development generally means an increase in agricultural production, it is necessary to take into consideration the present and long-time demand for agricultural products. And it is of the utmost importance to be sure that the development of resources means their conservation and not their exploitation, both of which may occur through development. If the latter occurs and if at any given time we are not in need of additional production, it may be by far the best policy to hold the land in reserve for a future use. Of course, it is realized that the need for additional agricultural products is not the only reason for bringing land into use; but in the absence of evidence to the contrary, there is no social justification for society to spend money to bring into crop production land the products of which exist in ample supply.

It is also necessary to consider the administrative or organizational devices that implement land programs and, in this connection, the issues that arise in Federal-state relationships and interagency conflicts. A phase of this problem is the question of centralized or valley-authority control versus coordination through committees. In this area there are many difficulties and conflicts that arise in (1) the coordination of the separate activities of Federal agencies, (2) the determination of policies that are necessarily national and policies that ought to be determined on a regional or state basis, (3) the unification of administrative responsibility while retaining the values associated with the functional type of departmental organization, (4) the impact of a multiplicity of valley authorities on present Federal structures, (5) the synthesization of national programs with local administration, and (6) the representation, powers, functions, and responsibilities of a board created at a high-level status for dealing with land- and water-resource problems.

River-basin programs also require adjustments in the organization, functions, fiscal matters, etc., of state and local governments, especially at the local levels. For instance, because of the inundation of some lands

[16] Roland R. Renne, "An Economist's Appraisal of the Missouri River Development Program," *Journal of Farm Economics*, Part 2, Vol. 31, No. 4, p. 1018, November, 1949.

and more intensive development of others, studies need to be directed to public service and to revenue and expenditure problems of local government. Furthermore, it is necessary to keep abreast with changing demands on group-enterprise organizations for both irrigation and drainage. New situations are constantly arising that make necessary changes in regulations and rules of operation in water districts.

*Framework of Investigations.* It is beyond the scope of this discussion to suggest a framework of economic investigations related to Federal conservation and development work. The solution to this problem depends largely upon the solution to the larger problem of providing a more effective organization for Federal conservation and development planning and the establishment of a national water-resource policy.[17]

The Hoover Commission found no effective agency within the present organization of the Federal government either for the screening or the reviewing of proposed water-development projects or for determining their economic and social worth.[18] Neither did the Commission find that any adequate check was being made upon the validity or timing of development projects in relation to the economy of the country.[19] The Commission's proposal for the solution of this and related organizational problems was (1) to transfer the rivers and harbors and flood control activities of the Corps of Engineers to the Department of the Interior, (2) to establish a drainage-area advisory commission for each major drainage area (composed of representatives of the proposed Water Development and Use Service of the Department of the Interior, of the proposed Agricultural Resources Conservation Service of the Department of Agriculture, and of each state), (3) to establish a Board of Impartial Analysis in the Office of the President, and (4) to require a report on each irrigation or reclamation project from the Department of Agriculture.[20]

The current Federal resources project investigations ostensibly reflect economic justification from a broad public viewpoint, but, in fact, reflect limited and heterogeneous private and public perspectives which vary, depending upon (1) the varying geographic scope of the investigations, (2) the varying functional authorizations of the respective agencies, (3) the varying economic interests of the segments of the population most directly concerned, and (4) the varying extent to which estimation of public gains or losses is attempted in the investigations.

[17] In this connection, see Vol. I of *A Water Policy for the American People.* Report of the President's Water Resources Policy Commission, Washington, December, 1950. The summary statement on pp. 1 to 19 is particularly pertinent.

[18] The Commission on Organization of the Executive Branch of the Government, U.S. Department of the Interior, *A Report to the Congress,* p. 26, March, 1949.

[19] *Ibid.,* p. 2.

[20] *Ibid.,* pp. 2–6, 26–39.

Perhaps the most serious effect of deficiencies in the present framework of economic investigations regarding Federal resource projects is that attention is distracted from the extent to which the less expensive means available to the Federal government with which to influence agricultural resource conservation and development—research, education, extension, laws, regulations, etc., not ordinarily investigated on a project basis—might be substituted for the more expensive project-type measures involving Federal capital expenditures, subsidies, or grants. Another serious effect is that attention is distracted from the extent to which alternative substitute action may be taken in guiding the resource program most effectively and efficiently toward desired goals of public policy.

These deficiencies in the program of economic investigations in connection with Federal resource projects cannot be overcome merely by developing uniform interagency standards of benefit-cost analysis at the individual project level. Coordination and improvement of individual project investigations would indeed be helpful, particularly in appraising individual projects and alternative choices of operation in a particular situation. But needed also is an expanded investigative framework under which individual project investigations will be complemented by coordinated investigations of the public-welfare aspects of these projects from regional and national perspectives. It is difficult to see how alternative choices of projects between areas and even of methods of development within a given area can be adequately appraised except in a framework that will give due weight to the national and regional public-welfare aspects of the development programs.

# CHAPTER 7 *Economics of Land Conservation*

In this chapter we are concerned with land conservation, particularly as it is related to soil conservation. There is an advantage in centering our thinking around one aspect of conservation in the exploration of relationships and factors that bear on conservation. As there are many meanings of "conservation," it is difficult to generalize. The concept has different meanings as related to different types of resources because some are renewable while others are nonrenewable, and these characteristics affect the future importance of a resource in relation to the present. In the case of some minerals, the conservationist may wish to save by drastically curtailing utilization, while in the case of water power one may save by putting the resources to use as promptly as possible, or again in the case of trees it may be well to use only the annual increment in growth by the practice of sustained forest management. In a broad sense, conservation means "best land use," and this is a focal point of attention throughout the book.

The demands of the Second World War on our natural resources, and throughout the world the drain on land resources to meet the needs of a rapidly growing population and to increase the level of living of the peoples of the world—all of this under conditions of a possible third world war and of a struggle in many parts of the world for the use, ownership, and control of land resources—focus attention on conservation problems and the development of land resources to a degree not equaled in any other period of the history of mankind. A social consciousness has arisen among people and nations of the importance of doing much more than is being done to deal with soil conservation and related problems. Even in such an agriculturally rich and productive nation as the United States, the conservation of the land is an important problem, because soil erosion in many areas is serious and because of our increasing responsibility not only to our own people but to the people of the world in providing food. Food is not only a nutritional product and an implement of war; it is also a real weapon for peace.

146

The problem of conservation is encountered in the utilization of natural resources when it is desirable or necessary to consider the future availability of those resources. This element of futurity is the basis for consideration of physical, social, and economic forces and instrumentalities that would not be encountered when the point of view is confined to current utilization. However, even in current utilization, not involving questions of conservation, it is frequently necessary to incur expenditures with a view to future benefits, as in the construction of relatively permanent improvements.

## Nature of the Problem

In dealing with economic problems in soil conservation, it is necessary to recognize the limitations that are imposed by physical, social, and institutional forces in the maintenance of soil resources and the level of productivity. For instance, it has often been pointed out that geologic erosion is one of the great natural processes in soil formation. Erosion is not always destructive nor can it be completely prevented. Some of our most fertile soils are alluvial and loessal areas created by water or wind erosion. But the creation of such fertile soils is likely to be the product of the removal of soils from areas many times greater.

Like many other forms of deterioration, soil depletion is a cumulative process. The removal of the humus layer greatly reduces the water-storage capacity of the soil and increases the volume of run-off and its abrasive power. It also lessens the capacity of the soil to maintain reserves of water to meet plant requirements in periods of moisture deficiency. The removal of humus lessens the beneficial activity of the biotic processes that contribute to soil fertility; and the layers of soil and subsoil beneath the humus cover are commonly more erosive in character. The combination of these various types of deterioration in turn reduces the density of vegetative cover and thereby lessens the benefits of the most important factor contributing to soil conservation. As the vegetative cover is lost, gullies are formed, and more and more the water is concentrated in channels, which in turn leads to an extension and increase in size of the gullies through accelerated washing and caving.

Soil deterioration is cumulative also in its economic and social aspects. As physical deterioration proceeds, profitable operation becomes less and less practicable, and expenditures for retarding further deterioration become more and more costly and therefore less possible. Social deterioration of the family and community may likewise be cumulative, as land or farm abandonment reduces the population available for participating in community life, and as a decrease in tax revenue reduces income available for the support of community services.

Such factors as low farm incomes, small and inadequate operating units, and fluctuating and unstable incomes are bound to lead to undesirable soil-management practices. If units are inadequate in size or inefficiently operated, the result is low net returns and likely little, if any, financial reserve to invest in conservation. Under such conditions, not only is there a tendency but often it is absolutely essential to continue to drain the soil resources in order to eke out an existence. Furthermore, from the standpoint of broad social interests, changes in size of farms and operational efficiency occur slowly and are often retarded for long periods in many areas because of population pressures and the institutional pattern of land use.

Unsatisfactory tenure patterns, inequitable landlord-tenant relationships, and excessive taxation of land also have a direct bearing upon the degree and type of soil conservation which is economically feasible. Serious erosion and depletion of the productivity of the soil are often only symptoms of underlying maladjustments in the social and economic system. When such situations become evident, it may mean the presence of an excessive population on the land, accompanied by poverty, poor health, ignorance, and a lack of understanding of the full value and need for soil conservation. Such environmental factors place the people in a physical and mental state that is not conducive to the practice of soil conservation. This necessitates public expenditures not only for soil conservation but first for rehabilitating groups whose cultural development has depreciated and has become as impoverished as their soil resources.

Problems of soil conservation have many facets, and they are much broader than the returns from saving soil from the viewpoint of an enterprise. This should be obvious. Thus, in an economic analysis of conservation problems it is essential that the problems studied be approached broadly. In analyzing problems, the limitations of economic analysis should be duly recognized. Relationships can best be ferreted out and the solution to problems determined by a broad-gauged social-science approach and by social scientists working in cooperation with other scientists, or vice versa.

It is necessary to recognize that conservation is a part of the life of a people—their social philosophy, cultural attitudes, and practices followed in regard to use and control of land resources. In the end, the desire to conserve must become a part of the institutions, customs, and thinking of a people. Aldo Leopold, in discussing the economics of conservation, has this to say:[1]

A system of conservation based solely on economic self-interest is hopelessly lopsided. It tends to ignore, and thus eventually to eliminate, many elements in the land community that lack commercial value, but that are (as far as we

[1] Aldo Leopold, *A Sand County Almanac*, p. 214, Oxford University Press, New York, 1949.

know) essential to its healthy functioning. It assumes, falsely, I think, that the economic parts of the biotic clock will function wihout the uneconomic parts. It tends to relegate to government many functions eventually too large, too complex, or too widely dispersed to be performed by government.

And further on he states:[2]

It is inconceivable to me that an ethical relation to land can exist without love, respect, and admiration for land, and a high regard for its value. By value, I of course mean something far broader than mere economic value; I mean value in the philosophical sense.

## Meaning of Conservation

Various definitions of the term "conservation" as applied to soil resources have been used. The emphasis in some has been in terms of physical concepts; in others, the emphasis has been on economic and social aspects; while physical, economic, and social considerations are combined in still others. Definitions that have been used include the prevention of waste, the maintenance of productive capacity of the soil for sustained production, and the utilization of resources so as to maximize the present value of future returns.

Broadly used, the concept "conservation" is here considered to mean a process of preventing a reduction in the quantity or a deterioration in the quality of a stock  of natural resources existent at a given time. However, not all avoidance or prevention of wasteful use of natural resources should be designated as conservation, for to do so would be to give the term conservation so broad a connotation that it would become almost synonymous with economics.

For instance, to sow poor seed, to use soils for crops for which they are not adapted, or to employ a particular acre of arable land for a type of product not justified by conditions of comparative advantage are all forms of economic waste in land use—waste of natural resources and probably of human and capital resources as well. But the mere avoidance of inadequacy of use or of uneconomic use can hardly be called conservation, unless the inefficiency avoided would have resulted in a reduction in quantity or deterioration in quality of the resources employed. To be sure, sometimes it is possible to avoid or lessen the depletion of the stock of natural resources that would otherwise be necessary by a more efficient use of the resources employed. For an example we might take a nation whose wheat requirement is a million bushels and that one-half of that is being produced by inefficient technical methods or unsuitable economic process without depletion of natural resources, while the other half is produced by methods of production that result in soil depletion. Now, if

---

[2] *Ibid.*, p. 223.

better technical methods or an improved combination of the factors of production could double the volume of production on the lands employed without depletion, it would be possible to meet the nation's requirement for wheat without using the soils that are being depleted. Thus there may be an interrelation between economic waste in general and the specific form of waste that results in the depletion of natural resources.

From an economic standpoint, however, we may say that not all economic waste takes the form of depleting natural resources. On the other hand, the avoidance of depletion—that is, conservation—is frequently wasteful from the standpoint of private economy because the avoidance costs more than the value of the resources conserved. This may be true also from the social standpoint, although there is frequently no coincidence from the two standpoints in the respective valuations of the costs of avoiding destruction.

Some such question may confront an individual or a social group in the case of virgin-soil fertility. Should the original level of fertility be maintained by restoring it as rapidly as it is depleted, or should we enjoy the benefit of the stored-up fertility in the form of bumper crops and low costs and then undertake to stabilize the stock of fertility at a lower level? Assuming that continued utilization without replacement of fertility results in a gradual decrease in productivity, it has been suggested that an entrepreneur would be justified in pursuing this course so long as the value of each unit of depletion is greater than the cost of replacing it. In other words, why purchase replacements as long as there is available a stock of fertility—the value of which exceeds the cost of restoring it? Up to the point where the unit of fertility removed could be replaced at a cost that does not exceed its value, assuming it can be restored, the maintenance of the original stock of fertility unimpaired would be from the standpoint of private economy uneconomic. And to reduce the level of fertility to the point where replacement cost balances its value is physical depletion but not economic depletion. To lower the level of fertility still further, however, represents not only physical but economic depletion, for we are proceeding to the stage where it will cost more to replace what is removed than we derive from its removal.

*Depletion versus Soil Deterioration.* As soil resources may under certain conditions of use be utilized continuously without necessarily becoming exhausted, some writers have distinguished between fertility depletion and soil deterioration. Both fertility depletion and soil deterioration result from exploitation and are accelerated by careless and unsound land-use practices. The former refers to losses which temporarily lower production but result in no irreparable impairment of capacity to produce. However, soil may deteriorate through erosion to such an extent that not only is there an impairment of the elements of fertility but also damage to the soil structure that may be more or less irreparable. The distinction is relative and not absolute; nevertheless it has practical significance.

Declines in fertility that can be restored would not necessarily reduce basic productivity capacity. Only in the case of a permanent loss in soil productivity, such as deterioration in soil structure, would such capacity be adversely affected.[3] Through the loss of fertility, however, it may be impossible to maintain the protective land cover necessary to control erosion and soil destruction.

It has been suggested by Bunce that the distinction between fertility depletion and soil destruction is related to a still broader one, namely, between a fund of resources and a flow of resources, a distinction that may be broadly applied to the conservation of natural resources in general. The distinction is both physical and economic, although Bunce tends to emphasize the economic distinction.[4]

In the case of certain fund resources the physical supply may be predetermined by nature, and no substantial addition in total supply or local supply can be expected. In this case, depletion or deterioration through use or other causes is absolute. For many resources, however, the extent or quality of the stock at a given time, physically considered, may be a function of the balance of the building-up forces and the destructive or deteriorative causes. Thus nature may gradually restore or build up fertility from the action of solutions, the disintegration of rocks, etc., while man may be restoring or enhancing fertility, at least in a given locus, by growth of legumes, animal and green manures, drainage, and other methods, at the same time drawing on the fertility for crop production. For instance, nature or man, or both in combination, may bring about the reforestation of an area depleted of forest growth. During the process of growth, the extent of depletion or of conservation at any given time will be a resultant of the growth process on the one hand offset on the other hand by destructive natural forces or by human appropriation.

*Rate of Utilization.* Conservation of the soil involves consideration of the rate of utilization. Exploitation, maintenance, and improvement represent the three types of conditions that characterize the rate of use of soil resources. The objective should be to so use the soil as to maintain it. However, in practice this is not always possible under conditions of tillable crop use, fluctuating prices, and institutional barriers. To an individual, the optimum economic rate of utilization is the one that will maximize the present value of future net returns. The present value of future net incomes can be estimated by discounting to present value future net incomes as determined on the basis of assumed yields, assumed prices,

[3] *Economics of Agricultural Land Use Adjustments*, Iowa Agricultural Experiment Station Bulletin 209, March, 1937.

[4] Arthur C. Bunce, *The Economics of Soil Conservation*, p. 7, Iowa State College Press, Ames, Iowa.

and estimated costs of production. It is necessary, however, to bear in mind that individuals place a premium on present use or value in determining their actions in the utilization of land resources. This is a natural response of man to land because of the uncertainty of life.

If the returns from land provide an income adequate to maintain the productive capacity of the soil, conservation is then economically feasible. If not, the maximization of returns results in exploitation and to an operator a conservational rate of use would be uneconomic. From a social point of view, exploitation would be economic or uneconomic—depending on future need for the soil resources—and a controlled rate of exploitation may be economically sound, as, for instance, in the case of the extraction of minerals.

Conservation may involve no significant sacrifice or cost from the standpoint of private economy because it may be consistent with the most profitable type of present use. Examples of this occur under those types of farming which incidentally tend to conserve the soil and still prove most profitable under existing conditions of comparative advantage. The individual practice of conservation, however, does not always pay, and thus conservation is very much a social problem. Bearing on this point, a question that may be raised is: Would farmers have achieved the conservation results attained during the past 15 years without the financial aid of soil-conservation programs? A good deal of land conservation has been obtained through state and Federal conservation programs. Certainly farmers have borne a large share, and likely could have borne more; but much that has been achieved would not have been forthcoming without direct help from the conservation programs.

### Classification of Natural Resources

Natural resources may be classified by the relation of use to exhaustion as follows: (1) resources not exhaustible through use, as, for instance, water power; (2) resources necessarily exhausted by use, such as minerals; (3) resources exhaustible by use but replaceable by growth, such as forests and wildlife.

In the case of water power and certain other resources, waste may take the form of inadequacy of use in the sense that as long as a waterfall is allowed to continue without being harnessed to useful machinery it may be said to be physically wasted, although in a particular time and place its utilization might be subject to costs which exceed the benefits to be derived.

The appropriation of minerals by mining results in depletion of the local supply, and it would be absurd to expect that other minerals would be brought from a distance to replace at point of origin those appropriated. Something like such a process, however, does occur when industries dependent on local supplies of minerals bring minerals from other localities to keep their factories in operation once the local supplies are exhausted. To a certain extent, also, minerals already utilized in the process of manufacturing are more or less recoverable, as, for instance, by the scrap-iron industry. The exhaustion of minerals may also be retarded by various technical methods of preventing waste and by the substitution of more abundant types of minerals for those which exist in limited supply. With due regard to these special considerations, however, minerals within a given area are a fixed stock which cannot be increased by human action, while their extraction and use result in a diminution of the supply.

Such resources as forests, range-pasture grasses, and fish and game may exist at a given time as a stock, or stored supply, accumulated in the past, which is depleted more or less by appropriation and utilization, but may be restored or even increased, so far as a given location is concerned, by measures to promote growth of trees or grass or by multiplication of animals. Whether this is found practicable, however, will depend largely upon economic and social considerations.

Soil is a type of resource that may be utilized, to all practical purposes, continuously without exhaustion, although its conservation may not be consistent with the most profitable present use. Moreover, it is possible to increase the supply of soil adapted to use by various types of land reclamation and to improve the quality of soil in use by changes in use or soil-improvement practices.

*Resource Exploitation*

An exploitation of land resources has characterized American agriculture since the beginning of settlement. For instance, the early policy of making available free of charge publicly owned natural resources to whoever succeeded in first appropriating them contributed much to our social philosophy of exploitation. On this subject, much has been written, and it is hardly necessary to review the story. However, as the soil is a basic resource and as our focus of interest is land, a simplified statement of the physical conditions or situations responsible for soil-resource deterioration should be helpful to an understanding of the economic phases of problems of land conservation.

The virgin soils which the white man found available for his use on this continent have been thousands of years in the making. Unfortunately, only a few generations, and in some areas less than a generation, have been required to effect their widespread depletion. In many respects soil depletion is an insidious process and therefore at times is not readily recognized even by technical specialists. It is likely to become apparent to the man on the street only when the process of destruction has reached an extremely advanced stage. When a forest is cut down the amount of depletion is obvious and can be accurately calculated. The potential supplies of mineral resources are less readily estimated, but their rate of depletion can be determined fairly definitely. In the case of soil, however, aggregate resources, except in terms of area, are difficult to estimate, and the rate of depletion is still more difficult to determine.

*Causes of Soil Deterioration.* Soil resources may deteriorate in productiveness in a number of respects, which in turn are more or less interrelated by way of intensifying one another. Among these causes are the following:

1. Removal of one or more of the essential elements of plant food through their appropriation by crops or pasture grasses. The elements commonly required in largest quantities for plant growth are nitrogen, phosphorus, potash, and calcium; but numerous other elements are more or less influential, some of them in relatively small quantities. The basic elements appear in various forms and chemical combinations, some of them more readily available than others for appropriation by plants. Some of the requisite elements may exist locally in such abundance that the process of removal is not significant for continued use. The various chemical constituents necessary for plant growth are so interrelated, however, that the removal of one essential element or its reduction to an insufficient amount, even though the other remaining elements are still ample, may result in seriously reduced productivity.

2. Necessary elements may be gradually lost through evaporation of moisture in which elements of fertility are in solution, or the exposure of soil through cultivation without adequate cover may result in consumption of humus through acidification and oxidation. Thus the store of organic materials accumulated through thousands of years is literally burned up. In the process the nitrogen supply in the organic material is consumed.

3. Bacteriological conditions unfavorable to plant growth may result from continued or improper use, especially through lack of diversification. Many types of bacteria are salutary in creating conditions favorable to plant growth, especially the nitrogen-forming bacteria, but certain other types of bacterial action may be harmful.

4. Stores of plant food may be destroyed by fire. Fire may be especially destructive of the humus so important to fertility and water-storage capacity.

5. Toxic substances such as alkali or selenium may be deposited in the soil, usually as a result of the contrived application of water-containing mineral salts, or they may have accumulated prior to human use of the soil.

6. The physical structure of soil may be modified through excess mois-

ture, resulting in puddling and the consequent impairment of suitability for plant growth.

7. Elements of plant food may be carried to depths inaccessible by plant roots through leaching or carried away entirely through underground drainage.

8. Productive soils may be buried beneath infertile soils or other materials deposited by the action of water or wind. A single heavy rain has been known to bury soils beneath a deposit of sand and gravel as much as 2 feet in depth.

9. The physical structure of the soil, including elements of plant food, may be washed away through water erosion or carried away by wind erosion. This type of deterioration, as contrasted with the mere depletion of chemical elements without impairment of the physical structure, may be irreparable; consequently it constitutes the more serious challenge to national policy. Sometimes the washing away of a surface soil may uncover a subsoil potentially as fertile, except for organic matter, as the portion of the soil removed, but in general there results a deterioration of productiveness.

10. Related to both the chemical impairment through removal of requisite chemical elements by plants and to the physical impairment through erosion is the destruction of the humus—the more or less disintegrated organic material deposited from decaying crop residues, roots, weeds, leaves, etc. More or less fibrous and spongy in character, humus has a most important function in regulating moisture content of the soil. When precipitation is excessive, the humus may store much of it, releasing it later for the use of vegetation when the moisture supply would be otherwise deficient. By storing appreciable amounts of excess moisture, the humus content may lessen to that extent destructive run-off that would increase erosion and siltation and, when concentrated in the streams, result in floods. Humus appears to be important also in keeping open the tiny pores of the soil within which is stored the supply of oxygen requisite for the roots of plants. Without the all-important humus these pores or tiny channels tend to become sealed up by the deposit of sticky clay or other substances, thus impairing the circulation both of air and water. Humus aids the small rootlets to penetrate the soil, especially heavy and more or less impervious soils. Finally, through decay, it may gradually release its store of nitrogen for plant use.

*Extent of Soil and Forest Depletion.* Conservation is a real problem to the extent that land resources are being impaired to the detriment of our future well-being. It is contended by some that the conservation movement in its various aspects has awakened us none too soon to the serious extent to which our pioneer prodigality has proceeded in impairing our heritage of natural resources, while for others conservation problems are far from being as serious as the "alarmist" would lead us to believe. However, it is not necessary to try to weigh carefully the degree to which conservation is a problem, provided we recognize that our land resources have been exploited and that the public should be concerned about this exploitation. This is not to minimize the importance of making an inventory of our land resources and keeping it up to date, but we are not so much interested in the protection of "every acre of land" as we are in moving forward on a substantial front in the interest of land-resource conservation.

The existing condition of our land resources is revealed by the inventory surveys of the Soil Conservation Service and the Forest Service of the U.S. Department of Agriculture. On the basis of present trends, the Soil Conservation Service estimated in 1950 that in the United States about 115 million acres of cropland was being damaged by serious erosion; and that over 50 million acres of land in cultivation should be shifted to grass or trees by 1970 or 1975. Of the land in crops, more than half was subject to erosion in greater or lesser degree. It is estimated that the gullies caused by man's misuse of the land are equivalent to an area about as large as the state of Virginia, or in the neighborhood of 25 million acres.

In regard to our forest resources, the Forest Service estimates that between 1938 and 1950 the quantity of standing saw timber declined 9 per cent. The annual cut of saw timber, together with natural losses during that period, exceeded the growth of saw timber by 50 per cent. In the eastern half of the United States, where there are millions of acres of forest land, the growing stock is inadequate to sustain the rate of cutting. During the Second World War it was found that many kinds of lumber, especially of good quality and large size, were no longer readily available.

Three-fourths of our land suitable and available for growing commercial timber—345 million acres—was privately owned in 1950. This included the best growing sites and the most accessible locations. These privately owned forests have furnished some 90 per cent of our timber needs, but the growth on these lands is now less than one-half of their productive capacity. In the development of these lands we are faced with an enormous task. It is a difficult problem, intensified by the fact that 75 per cent of the private forest land is in the hands of more than 4 million small owners; and the cutting practices and the conservation land-use practices on these lands are far from what is desired. In addition to the need for better management of our timber resources, we also are not effectively using forest lands for their watershed and soil protection, forest range, and fish, game, and recreation values.

Although the resource exploitation situation in the United States is not alarming, these inventory estimates do indicate that conservation is a real social problem and that programs of public action are truly needed.

*Methods for Soil Conservation*

The methods for soil conservation are in part the reverse of those factors causing soil deterioration. Nature's method of building and maintaining soil takes the form of the disintegration of rock; the growth of a vegetable cover which supplies physical protection against the destructive action of water and wind and contributes all important organic material; bacterial action in transforming the organic materials derived from vegetation into appropriable chemical elements; the action of water in creating a favorable physical structure in the soil and subsoil by bringing to the topsoil elements of fertility from the subsoil or the parent rock and depositing chemical constituents of rain or snow; and to a degree the action of other forms of animal life, such as the penetration of earthworms or the deposit of manure by the higher forms of animal life.

Some of these processes may be unfavorable to the creation or maintenance of soil fertility, according to whether they are excessive or deficient. Excessive water may be a source of destruction, and a deficiency of water may handicap nature in soil building and maintenance. The balance is often a delicate one, and nature itself may be so handicapped that it fails to create the basic conditions of fertility. The altitude may be so high that vegetation does not flourish, and we have rocky and barren mountaintops practically lacking in soil. Rainfall may be so deficient that vegetation cannot flourish, and nature may succeed in developing only a sandy desert when the creation of a soil is further handicapped by the action of wind in continually shifting the surface sand. The slope may be so steep or the rainfall so severe that nature finds it impossible to stay the action of erosion and succeeds at best in creating only a shallow, infertile soil.

The structure of the soil and subsoil may be very important in determining the erosion rate. Some soils are less resistant to erosion than others. In general, a high capacity of the soil for water storage or for underground drainage, as determined by its depth, the supply of humus, the texture of the soil and subsoil, the absence of hardpan, and the number of tiny channels, limits materially the amount of water that will have to run off the surface and therefore the erosive effect of a given amount of precipitation.

Vegetation is nature's most important method of soil conservation, a method which likewise contributes to soil building. For example, the forests hold back water by their large surfaces of trunks and branches; by the deep penetration of the roots and their binding qualities, especially near the surface; by the obstruction to the flow of water offered by logs and limbs; but above all else by the spongy and moisture-retentive forest litter, which absorbs vast quantities of water, thereby supplementing the storage afforded by the soil and subsoil. In particular, the protective covering of litter prevents silt or clay-burdened water soaking into the tiny soil channels and sealing them or clogging them so that the percolation into the soil is impeded.

Grass is likewise potentially effective in conserving and improving soils by providing surface and subsurface storage, retarding run-off, intercepting water-borne soil materials, and reducing the abrasive effect of the water and its content. The effectiveness of grass depends on the type of grass employed, density of stand, and the manner in which it is utilized. It is when man works against nature, such as in following a one-crop system, especially when it consists of row crops or other crops that provide a minimum vegetative coverage, that destructive soil deterioration results.

From a conservational standpoint, land-use practices, supplemented by engineering structures, terraces, check basins, etc., as needed, are essential; but without a conservational pattern of land use, nature is such a persistent force that any man-made structures sooner or later must lose their conservational effectiveness. And considering how delicate is the balance even in nature between the constructive and the destructive forces, human action in the attempted utilization of soil can readily be a potent factor in intensifying the destructive processes. The types and processes of land utilization in the United States have often so disturbed the natural balance that the destructive forces have been much accentuated.

### Measuring Economic Values

If it were possible to measure and attach economic values to all the various public and private benefits and costs associated with different types of land utilization, economic analysis could serve as the principal basis for determining desired conservation practices; that is, it would then be possible to measure the effects of different land practices and programs. However, the process of valuation in economics is very much confined to monetary values. Furthermore, a basic limitation of economic analysis is the inadequacy of data concerning the effects of given measures on physical production and other related results, and the absence of sufficiently comprehensive social-accounting techniques to allow proper weighing of the social or public values involved. Thus, economic analysis can at best be only one of the means of studying problems associated with the relative desirability of various alternative management practices and uses of land resources.

In the case of soils, adequate data for estimating the expected physical effects of various soil-conservation measures, applied to varying degrees of intensity and in varying combinations, are a primary requirement for economic analysis, from either a private or a public point of view. The absence of such data is due in part to the length of time required for observation and experimentation, but perhaps in even larger part to the lack of well-oriented purposes toward which such data would contribute. Collection of data with definite purposes in mind, rather than the collection of all available information with the hope that answers to specific questions will be forthcoming, should be the method adopted. The provision of adequate economic data is the joint responsibility of economists, soil scientists, engineers, etc., with emphasis on obtaining types of basic data adapted to economic evaluations or measurement for purposes sought.

Even though adequate physical data were available, the satisfactory conversion of such data into economic terms would still constitute a major obstacle. The basic difficulty stems largely from the absence of adequate criteria and standards for fully reflecting the social values involved. Such standards are needed to provide a basis for determining the extent of social responsibility for programs and measures in the interests of conservation and for establishing arrangements that will be effective in achieving the desired levels of conservation.[5]

Although research is making progress in certain aspects of these limitations, the rate is slow, and it is also true that completely acceptable bases for adequately weighing total social effects can never be achieved. Even though complete coverage of all effects is not feasible, an increase in the proportion of effects subject to quantitative treatment would constitute a definite contribution toward guiding soil-conservation policy.

## Individual and Social Interests

As has been indicated, the feasibility and desirability of conservation, at any given time, is to a large degree a function of numerous factors, which may be considered either from the standpoint of private or entrepreneurial economics or from the standpoint of broad social interests. From either standpoint a most significant consideration is the value of the resources concerned in relation to the costs or other sacrifices requisite to conserve them. As has been pointed out, market values and social values may be determined by very different considerations, while the elements entering into the costs of conservation may also differ, as between the private economy and social economy.

If a particular type of natural resource or certain units thereof are to be reserved or preserved for use at some future time, it is clear that willingness to take such steps, other things equal, will depend to a substantial degree on the value unit of the resource for present use as com-

---

[5] In the previous chapter some principles and considerations were discussed for measuring social values which are equally applicable to land conservation.

pared with the value of a corresponding unit at a future time or times with reference to which conservation of the resources is being considered. Omitting for the moment the consideration of the discount on the future, which is partly a function of duration of time, it is clear that willingness to refrain from present use will depend on the extent to which anticipated future value exceeds that derived from its use in the present. Moreover, willingness to incur costs to preserve a resource from impairment due to current use or other causes, assuming costs are constant, will depend on the future unit value of the resource to be conserved.

Consequently, in a country or region where a particular class of resource is very abundant, the resource is likely to be used very prodigally or wastefully because it is so cheap that consumption is stimulated. Moreover, when such resources exist in great abundance, the foresight of individual entrepreneurs is not likely to be sufficient to recognize prospective future scarcity, and the present cheapness of the resources makes it appear uneconomical to incur the necessary costs of preventing depletion or waste. This situation is likely to prevail in new countries when population is sparse and current profligacy and wastefulness in utilization are likely to be further stimulated by uncertainty concerning the extent of the available resources and the prospective requirements of subsequent periods.

In American agriculture soil exploitation has been due partly to the lack of strong economic incentives for increasing costs to prevent waste in methods of utilization. Soil was a resource to be mined. Land operators, and even economists, were long in the habit of overlooking the depletion of the soil as a cost of production, the emphasis being on the maximization of current net farm income through adequate-sized operating units and efficient management. This may be a desirable objective from the standpoint of the individual farm—provided costs of soil depletion are shifted; but when costs fail to take into account soil deterioration and this results in a social loss, as a people we need to reconsider our concept of efficient production. In industry, the maintenance of the plant is considered a cost of production; likewise, similar land costs should so be considered.

*Individual versus Social Exploitation.* If soil exploitation is confined to the flow resource, and depletion stops short of any permanently harmful effects on the fund resource, it may be economic both for the individual and for the public as well, and the two interests would be compatible. The short-term benefits to the individual and society from using up the stored fertility of the soil make possible the filling of special needs such as those occurring during the recent war period, yet permit restoration of this depleted fertility at a later date.

However, if depletion extends to the point of deterioration or loss of the fund resources, the problem is much more serious from the social viewpoint. Fund resources may be destroyed either by erosion or by a breakdown in soil structure. In such instances, a gain for the individual may mean a permanent loss to society. Such a loss from soil destruction may cause an increase in the cost of producing needed food and fiber or it may result in a decrease in the food and fiber production below the requirements necessary for the well-being of mankind. This difference in evaluation, as has been indicated, results because the individual's estimates of benefits give greater weight to returns receivable in the near future, while social values give greater weight to more widespread current effects as well as to those expected to occur in the more distant future.

From the standpoint of society, the extent and permanency of soil deterioration are exceedingly important. Exploitation of the soil may not be a burden upon farmers because of their ability to shift the costs to other individuals or to society. As has been pointed out:

Many a land user sees exploitation as economic to himself because the capital loss resulting from the declining productivity can be shifted to society or another individual. A tenant on a year-to-year arrangement—a holder of a life estate in farm land—an operator heavily indebted and about to lose the place to his creditor—will find it economically advantageous to turn the productivity of the property into cash just as far as possible before relinquishing it because the landlord, the succeeding heirs, or the creditors bear the capital loss.[6]

Thus, the economic and institutional framework in which the productive process functions may cause depletion beyond the point at which fertility maintenance is economic.

Continuous returns from the land arise either by maintaining the land in a *status quo* condition or by adding to or subtracting from the fund or flow resources of the soil through exploitation or improvement. The fund and flow resources of the soil are variables that may be added to or subtracted from in relation to one another. When land is exploited, it is often overvalued for a significant period of time in relation to the returns to the land if operated under a system of sustained production. Thus high fixed land costs to meet mortgage payments or pay for improvements may force land operators to continue exploitation even though they recognize the need for conservation.

[6] Maurice M. Kelso, *Research Needs in the Economics of Soil Conservation*, address presented at the annual meeting of The Soil Conservation Society of America, Omaha, Nebr., December, 1947.

## Investments for Conservation

*Private.* In so far as conservation is dependent on the actions of private individuals, it is more likely to be associated with periods when social demand for the resources in question has increased to the point where unit values have become sufficient to make conservation appear worth while. High values of natural resources in the present, particularly if not encumbered with high fixed costs, tend to promote conservation because they imply probability of high values at subsequent periods and represent a greater justification for the incurring of costs to prevent waste.

At any given time, the amount that an individual can afford to invest in soil conservation depends on the cost of capital and labor investments as compared with the additional income expected from following such conservation practices. Investments in soil conservation are capital and labor outlays on land. They differ little from any other type of real-estate improvement except in the degree to which they may depreciate under adverse economic circumstances. For instance, if depreciation extends into the fund resources, the result socially is significantly different from that in the case of the deterioration of farm buildings, because of a much greater problem of replacement, if it is indeed possible at all.

Investments in conservation measures may be made either to increase the present level of income from the land or to avoid a decrease in the future returns below the present rate. As has been stated:[7]

Financial outlays for soil conservation represent additions to the capital investments in land. Justification for such capital additions must be based on one of two possible conditions. First, the expected future incomes will be sufficiently expanded by the proposed conservation practices to justify the additional capital. Or secondly, the additional investment is necessary to prevent the depreciation of the [present] income stream, even though no additional income may be forthcoming.

In the first case, a positive return over existing levels is expected by the individual who invests in conservation facilities. In the second, investment in conservation is made, not to increase present income levels, but to prevent the size of subsequent returns from diminishing or disappearing. In both instances, the income to be realized with conservation is greater than would have been expected without. Whether conservation investments are made to prevent future decreases in productivity or to repair damages arising out of neglect or failure to maintain soil resources makes little difference in the soundness of the investment. It is recognized that the time element of the increase in income would need to be taken into account.

[7] Everett C. Weitzell, "Credit for Financing Soil Conservation," *The Appraisal Journal,* January, 1948.

In determining the benefits or incomes attributable to the conservation measures for comparison with their costs, the results of soil-conservation measures should be calculated over the expected life of the improvement. And in measuring the extent to which conservation investments pay, any investment in soil conservation that is of a permanent nature need return only upkeep and a reasonable interest on the capital outlay. In other words, it is not necessary to pay back the principal investment for a permanent improvement. As the improvement is permanent, it becomes capitalized in whole or in part in the market value of the land, and thus is a capital asset to the landowner. However, although it is not necessary from an economic standpoint to pay back the investment in order for it to be a sound investment, it is desirable to do so, as a debt load is an obstacle to satisfactory weathering of fluctuations in farm income without impairment of basic resources.

Whenever investments in conservation are of relatively short duration, the returns should be sufficient not only to cover maintenance and upkeep during the life of the improvement and to pay interest on the remaining investment, but also to return the cost of the initial improvement. Annual charges for maintenance and replacement may become sizable with such conservation practices as terraces and waterways, but may be smaller for concrete structures and other more durable improvements.

A number of conditions determine whether an individual will make investments for soil conservation and the extent to which he will do so. These include the time of benefit accrual in relation to that of costs; the availability of credit on terms suitable to requirements of conservation investments; the risks attached to the realization of potential returns; and the attitudes toward conservation. There is also the need for demonstrating that such investments are profitable. There is thus a significant place for demonstrational and educational work in developing greater interest in conservation-investment possibilities. Such educational work, by necessity, becomes primarily the responsibility of the government, even when conservation measures are applied entirely by the individual at his own expense.

*Public.* In the United States private rights and interests in land have, for the most part, been placed above public interests. It has been pointed out that our philosophy of fee-simple ownership of landed property was based on the belief that privately held land yields most to the general welfare, and that landowners, either spontaneously or with a limited amount of social persuasion, will use their land in the general public interest. There are exceptions to this general statement, but it has been our guiding principle, set aside or modified only for very good reasons. One of these reasons is conservation.

Whenever conservation activities have value to society over and above their value to the individual, the public should assume part of the financial responsibility for their maintenance. And in such instances, government may need to exercise controls over the conditions of use and the occupancy of land resources. Thus, conservation is often very much a social problem. Good land-management practice by individuals alone will not do the job.

Public concern over present depletion or deterioration stems from the public interest in assuring adequate agricultural production for the present, for tomorrow, and in perpetuity.[8] Whenever individuals are not able to bear all the costs of desirable conservation measures, it becomes a public problem. Moreover, even when financially profitable as well as in the public interest, individuals are not always in a position to rehabilitate badly eroded land or even land of moderate erosion. The individual may lack interest, technical ability, and the capital required to carry out economically desirable conservation practices, thus making necessary public aid if the job is to be done.

Public interest also arises when damages are inflicted by soil washing downstream from one person's land on to the property of another. One individual alone may be unable to avoid such damage, and when it is not a possible or reasonable obligation of any one individual to remedy this problem, it becomes a joint private and social responsibility, or even a social obligation, to see that conservation measures are adopted.

The amount and type of public action to bring about conservation will depend upon the extent of the needs and public awareness of the necessity for protecting soil resources. Because of the extensive nature of soil-conservation problems and national and world-wide interest in maintaining agricultural production, public assistance in the planning and development of soil-conservation programs is usually necessary to obtain the scope of development justified and needed to protect the public welfare. Wise husbandry demands that conservation measures be installed long before hunger and starvation become immediate possibilities or realities.

Public considerations of soil-conservation problems include the amount and the way in which public funds should be used to encourage needed programs. As public funds are limited, there is always the need to choose between alternative types, amounts, and areas for public investment in soil conservation. Greatest benefit from public expenditures usually results when public funds are used to supplement private efforts to install needed conservation measures rather than when the government tries to do the entire job alone. When costs of soil conservation are shared with

---

[8] For a discussion of the relation of interest and discount to the conservation problem see L. C. Gray, "The Economic Possibilities of Conservation," *Quarterly Journal of Economics*, May, 1913.

private individuals, cooperative arrangements between the government and the other beneficiaries should ensure stability and continued operation of the land resource in a way that will realize the maximum potential public and private benefits from the land.

Furthermore, the amount of the investment in soil conservation should, in so far as feasible, be geared both to the needs for the conservation expenditure and to the economic conditions that affect resource-employment levels. Timing is indeed important, and it is particularly so whenever and wherever conservation investments can be part of a public-works program. Thus, desirable expenditures for soil conservation can have a double-edged effect by saving our land resources and helping to stabilize the economy—two very worth-while social objectives. Such stabilizing effects from proper timing of expenditures for needed conservation measures will be in addition to the benefits that will accrue from maintaining for posterity an adequate and productive agricultural economy, capable of meeting recurring as well as emergency needs of people.

CHAPTER 8 *Population and Land*

Few relationships in life are more significant or more fundamental than those that exist between man and land. Man is the chief recipient of the benefits and fruits of land. Land provides him with living space, with the organic elements so necessary for the production of most foods and fibers, and with the raw materials he uses in his home and industries.

Not only does man benefit from the use of land in the production process, he himself enters into this process. Man supplies the ingenuity, integration, and know-how that makes land valuable in the production process. In effect, he provides or makes available the labor, management, and even the capital that must be combined with land if economic goods are to be produced. Here again the relationship between man and his land-resource base is important. The heights to which any people may rise, the extent of the benefits they reap from their environment, and the relative intensity with which they use their land reflect (1) the nature of the human resources found in the population, (2) the quantity and quality of the land resources available for use, and (3) the interaction of such other factors as the culture of the people, the state of the arts, and the use of technology.

*Population and the Demand for Land*[1]

The adequacy of any land-resource base and the intensity with which it will be used are a direct function of the effective demand for land and its products. Population pressure is the most important single factor involved in any computation of this demand for land.

The exact nature of the general demand for land differs, of course, with varying types of land use. So far as the production of food crops is concerned, the general demand situation is largely a function of population pressure and nutritional standards. The demand for food thus is de-

[1] The term "demand" is used here in its generalized sense, not in the more specialized sense in which economists often speak of demand, as the schedule of amounts that buyers would be willing to purchase at all possible prices at any given instant of time.

166

termined by the size of the total population and the amount and type of food consumed by the average individual. This over-all demand situation is influenced by a number of economic and institutional factors. Among them emphasis may well be placed on such factors as family budgets and incomes, dietary tastes and customs, food-rationing programs, movements to maintain or improve diets, international trade balances and "dollar shortages," and national self-sufficiency programs.

While nutritional standards have an important influence on the demand for food-producing lands, they have only a very limited effect upon the demand for land for urban and residential uses or for the production of fiber crops, forests, and minerals. The demand for land in these cases involves the interaction of population pressure with a variety of factors, such as stage of industrial and technological development, consumer incomes and tastes, and the impact of climate and custom upon clothing and housing needs.

Constant relationships between the supply and the demand for particular types of land may be retained over varying periods. Over the long run, however—and indeed, in many cases, even over the short run—neither the demand for land resources nor the impact of this demand upon the available supply can be regarded as constant or static. The concept of demand as it applies to land is an ever-changing and dynamic one. Population numbers may increase or even decrease; individual consumption patterns change with adjustments in family budgets; technological developments may point the way to more intensive land use and greater food production or they may give rise to new uses and result in greater demand for mineral, forest, and other resources.

*Examples of Relationship between Population and Demand for Land.* Excellent examples of the potentialities that exist in the relationships between population pressure and the demand for land are found in the cases of western Europe, the United States, and some of the "vegetable-civilization" areas of southeastern Asia.

Throughout the dark Middle Ages the total population of western Europe was held pretty much in balance by the positive checks of war, pestilence, and famine. The average real income per family was small, and new technology had but small impact. The over-all demand for land during this period fluctuated from time to time but tended to be somewhat constant. People wanted more food and higher and better living standards. But they lacked the leadership, know-how, and energy to acquire them.

The agricultural and industrial revolutions brought a marked change in this situation. Agricultural production increased with the introduction of new crops and improved cultural practices. This increase in food production permitted higher dietary standards, even with a considerable increase in total population. More important, together with growing industrialization, it permitted higher worker productivity, higher standards of life, and a steady expansion in the effective demand of individuals for economic goods and services. With these changes the over-all demand for land resources soared to tremendous new heights, and the land and labor resources of western Europe were used more intensively and more effectively than ever before. At the same time, through the development of new trade channels the industries and peoples of Europe were able to draw raw materials and land products from the far corners of the earth.

The rise of industry and trade in the United States has followed a pattern somewhat similar to that of western Europe. Several significant differences exist, however. The beginnings of the agricultural revolution found Europe with a more or less stabilized population that in many respects already was pushing against a somewhat limited land-resource base. New techniques and developments permitted more effective use of the available land and labor resources; and over time both the high mortality and high birth rates of this earlier period were reduced to their current levels. The increasing demand for land and its products throughout all of this developmental period, however, was always modified or checked by the somewhat limited supply of available land resources.

In the case of the United States, there was little or no problem of population balance once the coastal colonies were firmly established. Birth rates and mortality rates were high, as they were in Europe, but there was no land-resource barrier to discourage a rapid rate of population increase. The virile foreign populations that colonized these shores looked upon population growth as eminently desirable. There was little reason for worrying about the impact of population pressure against the food supply. The land resources of the New World were such that man could easily satiate his needs and demands for land. As a result, the early American tended to use land somewhat lavishly in the production process.

This tendency to regard other factors than land as the scarce or limiting factors in production has persisted to the present day. The American economist still thinks of agricultural efficiency in terms of return per man-hour or return per unit of capital invested. His European contemporary is more apt to measure agricultural efficiency in returns per land unit. Another example of the key importance of the man-labor factor in America as compared with the land factor in Europe is seen in the contributions American inventors have made in producing laborsaving devices and in the parallel emphasis that European inventors have placed on developing material-saving techniques.[2]

[2] Erich W. Zimmermann, *World Resources and Industries*, pp. 28–29, Harper & Brothers, New York, 1933.

Much of the wealth and industrial might of the United States can be traced directly to the fact that its resource base has been able to provide for most of the demand of its people for a wide variety of land resources and products. In this respect, it has enjoyed positive advantages over most of the other nations of the world.

By way of contrast, one might look to the so-called "vegetable civilizations" of southeastern Asia, which Zimmermann has aptly described as "Monsoonia."[3] This area has an "abundant food supply with commercial fringes and some industrial veneer." As Irene Taeuber observes:[4]

Southeastern Asia is the paradox of demographic and economic development. Here are crowded areas and empty spaces. Islands whose multiplying peoples would have made Malthus even more sorrowful than he was lie adjacent to historic islands of depopulation. Economic expansion and population redistribution can solve the immediate problems of the relation of people to resources. To those who have studied the demography of the area, however, optimism concerning the possibilities for economic development in the short run is tempered by the knowledge that economic development in the past has served primarily to increase the number of the people and so to render continually more difficult economic development whose goals are the increase in individual welfare rather than the increase in total product.

Population pressure has increased considerably in many of the countries in this area during the past century. In most cases, however, this increase has been associated with only limited additions to the total economic supply of land and with little appreciable increase in worker productivity. The increase in total population, which has come largely as a result of man's success in reducing mortality rates, in many areas has brought smaller and smaller per capita shares in the tillable land áreas and in the products derived therefrom. The net result has been a continuing low standard of life that has caused some observers to despair of the advisability of applying new techniques or developments that would lead only to greater population pressure and the aggravation of human misery.[5]

The people of this area have the same desire for full stomachs and more adequate living standards as the people of most other parts of the world. Their effective demand for food and other products of the land and their ability to raise themselves "by their own bootstraps," however, are very definitely limited by their available supply of land resources.

[3] *Ibid.*, pp. 144–145.
[4] Irene Taeuber, *The Population of Southeast Asia*, paper presented at the Conference on World Land Tenure Problems, University of Wisconsin, Madison, Wis., Oct. 18, 1951.
[5] For example, see William Vogt, *Road to Survival*, Chap. I, William Sloane Associates, New York, 1948.

Whether or not the rising tide of nationalism in this part of the world and the determined effort of many of the people to throw off the shackles of feudalism and colonialism will give them the leadership, drive, and access to know-how and materials that they need to better their individual living standards yet remains to be seen. Their success or failure in this endeavor will be determined largely by their ability to maintain their populations at their present levels while they take measures to stimulate trade and industry and to increase crop and other production. Only by producing a larger surplus over and above what they need to maintain a Malthusian survival state of existence will these people be able to accumulate the capital and the training they need to finance their progress to a better life.

As the comparison of these three examples suggests, high-population pressure in and of itself does not necessarily lead to high effective demand for land. Heavy population pressure is usually accompanied by intense desire for more food and other goods, but when the population presses against a limited land- or natural-resource base, the effective demand for land may often be described in terms of the minimum areas or amounts necessary to maintain life.[6] The greatest relative demand for land and its products occurs in industrialized societies. Demand in these areas is measured not in subsistence diets and the bare necessities of life but rather in the vast array of raw materials needed for rich diets, extensive wardrobes, comfortable homes, automobiles, electrical equipment, and the thousands of other articles used by the average individual in modern society.

## Ratio of Population to Land

*Population Density.* Land-use policy and practice, and through it the contribution of land to the over-all well-being of the economy, is determined to a considerable extent by the ratio of population to land resources. A very common expression of this relationship is found in the often-quoted data on population densities—number of persons per square mile, square kilometer, or some other areal measurement. Inasmuch as this index involves only population numbers and total land area, it is a

---

[6] Zimmerman, *op. cit.*, pp. 87–93, comments on the fact that only about one-third of the physically cultivable land is actually cultivated in China. Much of the reason for this situation is found in the time and labor requirements associated with the hand-labor economy. It takes the average man about 15 days to spade an acre of land, and comparable labor requirements are often involved in the planting and harvesting of crops. As a result, "the average agricultural laborer in southern China cultivates a plot of less than 250 feet square. To support the laborer and his dependents, such a small piece of land, even when intensively cultivated, must possess a high degree of natural productivity and must respond most readily to the cultivating effort." Thus only the more fertile lands are used, and many potentially productive lands remain out of cultivation because they cannot be used to advantage under a hand-labor economy.

simple matter to rate countries from high to low as in Table 6, which reports the population densities for 35 selected countries.

For purposes of analysis, the simple concept of population density is often both unrealistic and misleading. Examples of misleading conclusions that may be based on casual use of this index are not hard to find. One might assume from the figures in Table 6, for example, that the problem of population pressure is more than twice as serious in Belgium and the Netherlands as in Haiti or India, or between six and seven times as serious as in Indonesia, or more than a dozen times as serious as in Egypt. Actually, the problem of population pressure, except in times of war and blockade, is much less acute in Belgium and the Netherlands than in any of these other areas. The principal reason for this is found in the industries of these two countries and in their use of international trade to supply themselves with the raw materials and land products produced in many other parts of the world.

*Table* 6. Population Densities in 35 Selected Countries

| Country | Persons per square mile* | Country | Persons per square mile* |
|---|---|---|---|
| Belgium | 734 | Greece | 158 |
| Netherlands | 648 | Spain | 146 |
| Japan | 566 | China | 123 |
| United Kingdom | 534 | Indonesia | 105 |
| England | (809) | Thailand | 91 |
| Italy | 399 | Turkey | 70 |
| Switzerland | 294 | Egypt | 52 |
| Haiti | 290 | United States | 51 |
| India | 290 | Sweden | 40 |
| Denmark | 258 | Mexico | 34 |
| Pakistan | 214 | Soviet Union | 24 |
| Poland | 206 | Argentina | 16 |
| France | 195 | Brazil | 16 |
| Israel | 179 | Paraguay | 9 |
| Romania | 173 | Saudi Arabia | 6 |
| Yugoslavia | 170 | Iceland | 4 |
| Philippines | 169 | Canada | 4 |
| Bulgaria | 167 | Australia | 3 |

\* Population densities computed from total area and population figures reported in 1952 World Almanac.

Population-density figures also ignore the importance of the type, quality, and distribution of land resources. Egypt with a population density of 52 persons per square mile would not seem to have a population-pressure problem. When it is remembered, however, that only 3 per cent of the land in Egypt is cultivated and that the remaining 97 per cent is largely unpopulated desert, the relationship between Egypt's 20 million people and its limited area of irrigable land along the Nile takes on a very different complexion. The presence of large desert areas explains the low population densities found in Saudi Arabia, Lybia, Australia, and in parts of China, the Soviet Union, and the United States. Other types of population deserts are created by the probably irreclaimable jungles of eastern Brazil and by the subarctic and arctic wastelands of Alaska, Canada, Greenland, and the Soviet Union.

*Man-Land Ratios.* A much more realistic measure of the ratio between population and land resources is provided by the so-called man-land ratio. On the land side this ratio differentiates between various types of land use and the relative value or productivity of available lands for these uses. On the man or population side, this ratio is concerned not only with numbers of people but also with their state of economic and industrial development, their ability to make intensive use of the land, and in some cases, with their relative dependence upon the direct use of land. On this last point, for example, it is desirable in some discussions of man-land ratios to consider only the agricultural portion of the total population or only those people who are directly involved in the cultivation and use of the land. In this sense, man-land ratios often refer to the relationship between specified segments of the population and certain types of land— as in the ratio between farm population and total area in cultivation.

Because of the large number of variable factors involved, it is not easy to compute man-land ratios or to express them in numerical terms. The scope of the problem is exemplified by the difficulties that arise in devising a satisfactory index or measure of land resources. Efforts have been made to assign weights to the areas found in cultivated crops, fallow lands, pasture and grazing areas, forests, and other uses, so that rational comparisons might be made between areas with differing proportions of lands in these various uses.[7] While these indices simplify the problem of area comparisons, they are limited primarily to agroforestal production and do not measure the resource advantages associated with presence and use of minerals and water power, transportation advantages associated with favorable locations, or the relative ability of a people to profit

[7] None of the indices developed to measure land productivity have as yet received much attention in this country. One of these approaches, first given currency around 1936 by W. Staniewicz of Poland, assigns a value of 1 to an acre of average cropland. Fertile garden lands may be assigned a value of 3 if they are considered three times as productive as the average cropland. Other land uses such as hay or meadowland, permanent pasture, and forest land may be assigned values of 0.4, 0.2, and 0.15 per acre, respectively, depending upon their relative productivity. With these weights, assuming that they are uniformly applicable to all areas considered, it is possible to compute the number of "statistical acres" there are per person in any area or country. Cf. Charles L. Stewart, "Population and Land Resource Relationships," *Land Policy Review*, Vol. 7, pp. 15–20, Winter, 1944. Another measure which involves "arable equivalents" based on crop and pasture-land areas is also used by some writers. Cf. Wilbert E. Moore, *Economic Demography in Southern and Eastern Europe*, League of Nations, 1945.

from international trade and the importation of food and other resources from other areas.

Man-land ratios can follow a number of significantly different patterns. Five basic extreme positions may be recognized:

1. *Sparse populations with a poor or limited resource base.* The best examples of this ratio between population and land resources are found in the cases of the Eskimo communities of Alaska, northern Canada, and Greenland; the desert nomads of the Sahara and Arabian deserts; and the native populations of some of the smaller mid-Pacific islands and of the jungles of Central America and western Brazil. Any notable increase of population pressure in these areas will probably be associated with the establishment of extractive industries or the building of military installations.

2. *Sparse populations with rich or potentially rich land resources.* Excellent examples of this relationship are found in the cases of the American Indians in what is now the United States and southern Canada, and the early settlers in this country, Patagonia, and Australia. This relationship is typical of the early stages of development of a new country. If this relationship continues over any period of time, it is usually because the inhabitants and prospective immigrants fail to recognize the value of the resource base. Otherwise, their policies will probably favor the rapid settlement and development of the land resources and the expansion of the resident population.

3. *Dense populations primarily dependent upon agriculture with limited land-resource bases.* Two of the best examples of this situation are found in the lower Nile valley of Egypt and in Java and Madura, both of which areas have a population density of more than 1,000 persons per square mile. Other good examples are provided by a number of the Caribbean islands, such as Barbados with its 1,193 persons per square mile, Martinique with a population density of 689, and Puerto Rico and Jamaica with densities of 644 and 315, respectively. The cropland resources of these areas often are productive but they are physically limited in amount. Population pressure against the available resource base already constitutes a serious problem, but improved cultural practices, sanitation- and medical-improvement programs, industrialization, and increased use of international trade have permitted and will permit further population increases.

4. *Dense populations with a limited resource base but with strong industrial and trade ties to larger resource areas.* Perhaps the best examples of this situation are found in the British crown colonies of Hong Kong and Singapore. Both of these colonies are small in area but with the all-important help of foods and raw materials imported from other places they support large populations which are engaged primarily in industrial

and commercial pursuits. The strategic military bases at Gibraltar, Malta, the Panama Canal Zone, and Guam provide comparable examples of large populations that are primarily dependent upon the goods and materials brought in from other areas.

In many respects the problem of dense populations with limited local resource bases is the problem of every large city that must look to a hinterland for its raw materials and means of sustenance. The problem appears more difficult, however, in those areas where population centers are separated from their resource areas by national political boundaries than in countries such as Canada, China, the Soviet Union, or the United States, where the hinterland area often is found in the country itself. Great Britain, the Benelux countries, Germany, France, Switzerland, Italy, and Japan are important examples of industrialized nations with relatively high population pressures whose economies are largely dependent upon active trade with other areas.

5. *Large populations with good resource bases.* None of the nations in the world today provide really good examples of this situation. China has a large population and what is thought to be a potentially rich resource base. Much of the population, however, exists on a near hand-to-mouth basis while many of the country's resources remain underdeveloped. The United States and the Soviet Union have large national populations and good resource bases, but the potentialities for population growth in both of these countries are still high. Perhaps the best example of this situation is provided by the British Commonwealth of Nations which links the livelihood and day-to-day economy of approximately one-fourth of the world's population to the distribution and use of the resources found on slightly less than one-fourth of the world's surface land area.

Most of the countries of the world have man-land ratio problems that are not typical of any of these five extremes but which tend to lie between them. Very often, particularly in the larger countries, the problem of man-land ratios varies considerably by areas within countries. In Canada, for example, the great majority of the population live in a relatively narrow belt that stretches across the nation and extends only 200 to 250 miles north of the nation's southern border. A progressive and industrialized economy has been developed within this zone. The vast subarctic and arctic land mass that lies north of this narrow band is sparsely populated and, although it does hold promise of mineral wealth, it is poorly suited for crop-production purposes.

A similar wide range of situations applies in the United States. Some of the desert and mountainous areas of the West are sparsely populated and have a precarious resource base (situation 1). Historically, this country, and the Western frontier in particular, has been popularly regarded as a land of opportunity where the supply of resources has exceeded the needs of a still sparse population (situation 2). Some communities in the southern Appalachians suffer from excess poverty and underemployment in agriculture—in other words, from high-population pressure with respect to available agricultural resources (situation 3). On the other hand, many of the industrial centers of the country are located in counties and states that are far from agriculturally self-sufficient and that draw upon the entire nation and many other parts of the world for food and the raw materials they use in their industries (situation 4). Finally, when the country is viewed as a whole, it can be regarded as one of the world's richest resource areas and as an area with a large and steadily increasing population (situation 5).

*Rationalization of the Man-Land Relationship.* Most populations find their plans for development and use of their land resources limited by the available supply of these resources. The relationship between population and land, however, is by no means fixed or unchanging. There is much that the average people can do in rationalizing its resource base—in putting the available supply of resources to more effective and more efficient use.

Several approaches may be followed by a nation or a people in rationalizing its economic supply of land to provide either a larger total product or larger per capita shares in this product. Among these the following might be listed:

1. *Intensification of land uses.* This process involves more intensive culture and use of available cropland, forest, mining, residential, and other sites through the use of improved cultural practices; the use of more fertilizer, insecticides, better seed or livestock; the development of timber-stand improvement and selective-cutting programs; the construction of multistoried structures on urban lots; and other similar measures. As a general rule, intensification involves the application of additional input units of capital and labor. As was pointed out in Chapter 5, when land is the scarce and limiting or fixed factor of production, it is profitable to apply the variable inputs of capital and labor up to the point at which the marginal product secured from their application barely pays for the cost of the last input. When increasing population pressure leads to greater effective demand for the products of land, product prices often rise and the rise in price justifies more intensification in land-use practices.

2. *Development and creation of "new lands."* Just as more intensive land-use practices add to the productivity of available supplies of land, the development of new lands and the bringing of new lands into use on the extensive margin also add to total production. New lands can be developed or "produced" by the clearing, drainage, irrigation, or terracing of potential croplands; by planting of forests on wastelands; by under-

taking mining operations; by filling in waterfront and rough areas for urban and transportation use; and by other similar approaches that add to the economic supply of land by bringing areas into new or higher uses.

3. *Removal of obstacles to better land use.* Closely associated with efforts designed to intensify and extensify land use are the possibilities for recognizing the limiting and strategic factors that often constitute barriers to better land use. Recognition of the need for railroads, better highways, or cheaper means for transporting products to market; for improving credit or marketing facilities; for supplying surface or sprinkler irrigation; for clearing, draining, or leveling lands; for supplying commercial fertilizers; or for better landlord-tenant relations can lead to higher total production and the maximization of the interests of society. This approach to increasing food production is often used in combination with programs designed to intensify the use of land now in cultivation and to bring new lands into use.

4. *Industrialization and development of international trade.* Countries not well blessed with natural resources, or endowed with good supplies of only certain types of resources, often can maximize their interests and make the best use of their domestic labor supplies by importing various raw materials from other areas, processing them at home, and then selling manufactured products in the world market. In a real sense, the development of industry and world trade along this line really enlarges the economic resource base upon which a country and its people may draw. The successful use of this approach often depends upon a number of factors. Usually the country must have a comparative advantage for the production of the goods which it wishes to produce. This means that it must have a skilled labor supply, an available supply of venture capital and management, favorable production or market location, access to sources of energy (waterpower, oil, coal, etc.), and/or access to the raw materials used in the manufacturing process. It is not necessary for a country to possess all of these advantages. As a matter of fact, the industrial economies of countries such as Great Britain, Italy, and Japan are very much dependent upon the importation of basic raw materials from other areas. In the final analysis, however, those countries that make successful use of this approach must have some production advantages that permit them to compete on a profitable basis with other producers in the world market.

5. *Military conquest of additional resource areas.* In times past military conquest often has been used as a means for extending dominion and economic and national control over natural-resource areas. While this approach is frowned upon in many quarters, one should not forget that the rise of many nations to world power has been associated with conquests and the subsequent administration or colonization of subjugated

areas. The Second World War was precipitated largely by the expansionist policies of the Axis powers. The conflict between the "have" and the "have-not" powers is not as much a world problem now as it was during the 1930's, but world politics are still very much concerned with problems such as the control of the oil resources of the Middle East or the surplus rice-producing areas of the Far East. In many respects, the problem of economic domination of foreign market and resource areas might be likened to the problem of military conquest, which involves political as well as economic control. Much the same results can be attained under either type of program. Military conquests, however, are frowned upon, while programs of economic domination, although occasionally criticized, are still regarded as respectable.

6. *Population-control and migration programs.* Populations with limited supplies of land resources available for their use may rationalize their situations by voluntarily checking their rates of population increase or by encouraging the migration of their surplus numbers to other areas. In modern times, birth control has never been popular as a political issue. Nevertheless, it is well to recognize that numerous societies in the history of mankind have looked with some favor on the use of measures such as infanticide, abortion, sex taboos, genocide, exposure to plagues, and wars as means of limiting population growth.

A notable example of an area that has alleviated some of the worst features of its man-land ratio problem in modern times is provided in the case of Ireland. In 1846, just before its famous "potato famine," Ireland had a population of approximately 8.3 million people as compared with a total of 4.3 million in 1951. Between 1846 and 1851 the total population declined by 1.7 million people, largely because of the ravages of famine and diseases associated with malnutrition and because of widespread migration to other areas. In the years that followed, thousands of Irishmen migrated to other areas, and the man-land ratio advantages thereby secured were maintained by a voluntary population-control policy.[8]

Voluntary population-control policies are at work in a number of other countries where fertility rates have declined almost to the population-replacement level. At the same time, population-migration policies are recognized and favored in areas such as Italy as a means for reducing increasing population pressure. Neither of these two policies affect the economic supply of land, but by reducing the population pressure against land, they may contribute to more efficient land use and to larger per capita shares in the available supply of land and its products.

[8] This policy of family limitation operates within a cultural framework which generally opposes the use of birth-control techniques. The fertility rate among married couples is relatively high in Ireland, but the total rate of population increase has remained low because of delayed marriages and the failure of a large proportion of the population to marry.

*7. Shifts to lower nutritional standards.* When populations with relatively limited land resources fail to increase food and other production as fast as they increase their population numbers, they obviously must reconcile themselves to the acceptance of smaller and smaller per capita shares in the products of land. So far as the food supply is concerned, this need not mean starvation diets. It may involve shifts from diets rich in livestock and other products secured from a somewhat extensive type of land use to diets composed largely of cereals, vegetables, and other foods produced under more intensive-type farming methods. Over time, many of the densely populated areas of Asia have probably made dietary adjustments of this general type. The new diets, while perhaps less appealing than the old, suffice to maintain larger populations on what may actually be a smaller land-resource base.

*The Drive for Lebensraum.* A cursory review of the man-land ratios found in various parts of the world indicates that the populations of some areas are far better endowed with land resources than are the peoples of other areas. Much of this present relationship between population pressures and the relative allocation of resources can be explained in terms of historical accident and development.

Prior to the industrial revolution, areas with the best potentialities for agricultural production under existing cultural practices were favored for settlement. Since then many of the advantages of favorable location have accrued to countries with mineral and energy resources and with ocean-going fleets of commercial ships.

Those countries that were first affected by the industrial revolution definitely enjoyed a head start over other countries both in reorienting their own economies and man-land relationships and in seeking and securing economic and political colonies and spheres of interest in other parts of the world. This early start fortified the economic position of countries such as England, France, and Holland and permitted them to develop hinterland resource and market areas that have provided bulwarks for their national economies in times past.

Perhaps it is inevitable that the favorable position of the countries that have acquired sizable shares of the world's land resources should be challenged from time to time by the "have-not" powers. The history of the last three centuries is replete with wars, struggles, and diplomatic arrangements that have involved quarrels over and transfers of important colonies and other resource areas. This contest for resource and market areas extends to the present day. Prior to the Second World War the world was extremely conscious of Germany's drive for *Lebensraum*, or "living space," and of the demands of Japan and Italy for "a place in the sun." The insistent demand of the Axis powers for colonies and economic and political expansion helped to set the stage for the Second World War.

Just as the clamorous demand of the latecomers among the world's industrial powers for colonies and larger shares in the world's land resources has served to disturb the *status quo,* so also does the current rise of nationalism in many of the underdeveloped areas of the world suggest further dissension over the allocation and control of resources. This probable dissatisfaction will not necessarily be limited to the development and economic control of the resources within these areas. Covetous glances will probably be cast in other directions. Recognition of the fact that European peoples have settled and claimed a major share of the world without settling it as fully as most Asiatic peoples would may lend support to an Asiatic *Lebensraum* doctrine. One of the first things that the exponents of such a doctrine may argue for will be the removal of the immigration quotas and restrictions that largely exclude Asiatic migrants from settlement in Australia and parts of Africa and the Americas.

The significant factor that should be recognized here is the fact that several of the world's industrial economies have been built up largely with the help of raw materials drawn from vast hinterland areas. Most of the advantages associated with the production of these materials often have gone to the people of the industrial countries. Very often their monopoly rights to these advantages have been protected by rigid immigration, tariff, and export restrictions.

Other nations in their climb to industrial power have at times demanded similar advantages and have achieved varying degrees of success. With the current rise of nationalism in the Far East and in the Moslem world and with the emphasis now being placed on the development of underdeveloped and backward areas, one may expect demands on the part of native populations for larger shares in the advantages associated with the production and development of land products (oil, minerals, plantation crops) in their countries and possibly even other areas. The achievement of these demands may partially undermine the economies of some industrial nations. In the final analysis, however, it will lead to wider distribution of the advantages associated with the use of the world's land resources.

### Population Trends

Much of the future problem of man's relationship to land depends upon world and national population trends and man's ability to control or direct population growth. As the data on world population growth reported in Table 7 indicate, the population of the world and of all its major land areas has increased considerably since 1650 and particularly since 1900. In 1950 the world had an estimated population of 2.4 billion people, more than twice its population in 1850 and more than four times its estimated total for 1650.

Between 1920 and 1950 the total population increased an estimated 566 million persons, or at a rate of slightly less than 1 per cent per year. This means that the world's population is increasing at a rate of between 20 and 25 million people each year. Continuation of this trend could easily bring a doubling of world population within a century.

*Table* 7. World Population Growth, 1650 to 1950
(In millions)

| Area | 1650 | 1750 | 1800 | 1850 | 1900 | 1920 | 1930 | 1939 | 1950 |
|---|---|---|---|---|---|---|---|---|---|
| Africa.......... | 100 | 95 | 90 | 95 | 120 | 136 | 155 | 175 | 198 |
| America........ | 13 | 12 | 25 | 59 | 144 | 207 | 244 | 274 | 328 |
| Asia*.......... | 330 | 479 | 602 | 749 | 937 | 997 | 1,069 | 1,162 | 1,272 |
| Europe*........ | 100 | 140 | 187 | 266 | 401 | 485 | 530 | 573 | 589 |
| Oceania........ | 2 | 2 | 2 | 2 | 6 | 9 | 10 | 11 | 13 |
| World total.... | 545 | 728 | 906 | 1,171 | 1,608 | 1,834 | 2,008 | 2,195 | 2,400 |

* In the population estimates for the 1920 to 1950 period, the entire population of the U.S.S.R. is reported in the European totals. The population of the Soviet Union, which has not been reported on a continental basis, was officially estimated at 193 million at the end of 1946. This figure is used in the 1950 world estimate. In 1951 the population of the Soviet Union was estimated as 207 million persons.

SOURCE: 1650 to 1900 data from A. M. Carr-Saunders, *World Population: Past Growth and Present Trends*, p. 42, Oxford University Press, New York, 1936; 1920 to 1950 data from *Demographic Yearbooks*, 1949–1950 and 1951, Statistical Office, United Nations.

*Theories of Population Growth.* Numerous theories have been introduced at various times to explain the potentialities of population growth. Some of these have been mechanistic in their approach, while others have involved naturalistic and economic explanations. Perhaps the most notable of these theories is the now famous Malthusian doctrine which was introduced by the Reverend Thomas Robert Malthus in his *Essay on the Principle of Population* in 1798.

Up until the time of Malthus—and indeed since then, in most areas with expanding economies—increasing population pressure generally was regarded as desirable. Malthus challenged this idea with his thesis that "population invariably increases where the means of subsistence increase . . . . unless prevented by some very powerful and objective checks." The implications of this doctrine are clear. Man, because of his prolific nature, will always tend to increase his numbers until they press against the food supply. Accordingly, even though he may temporarily succeed in increasing his means of subsistence, he is doomed over the long run to a bare subsistence standard of living.

Malthus listed "all unwholesome occupations, severe labor and exposure to the seasons, extreme poverty, bad nursing of children, great towns, excesses of all kinds, the whole train of common diseases and epidemics, wars, and famine" as the powerful and objective checks that are primarily responsible for limiting population growth. He also recognized the possible use of preventive checks—voluntary abstinence, moral restraint, postponement of marriages, and other tamperings with the sex instinct—but he rejected them as conducive to vice and misery. Without the operation of his objective checks, he argues, population would tend to increase in a geometric ratio, while the means of subsistence would increase at a slower arithmetic rate.

A review of the world scene at the time of Malthus provides considerable evidence to support his generalization regarding population growth. Throughout the Middle Ages and up until the beginnings of the agricultural revolution during the seventeenth century, the population of Europe was relatively constant. Fertility rates were high, but so were mortality rates. Almost every upward surge in population was checked by the ever-prevalent threats of famine, malnutrition, and gnawing hunger; disease, pestilence, and periodic plagues such as the Black Death of the fourteenth century; and intermittent warfare and strife. When increasing agricultural production and the beginnings of industry and trade lessened the dangers of famine after 1650, the population of Europe responded by almost doubling itself by 1800.

Throughout the years that have elapsed since Malthus first published his population theory, its general applicability has been demonstrated time after time in many parts of the world. Total population pressure in many areas has pressed against the means of subsistence and has been held in check primarily by the contributions of famine, disease, and war to high mortality rates. The introduction of agricultural improvements, increasing trade, and improved sanitation and medical practices to some of these areas seemingly has resulted only in higher population pressures with little or no improvement in the status of the average individual.

Despite the logic of its theory and its general application to the conditions prevalent in many parts of the world, the Malthusian doctrine has not always stood up in practice. Throughout most of the industrialized countries of the Western world it has been discredited in two important ways: (1) birth rates and the rate of population increase have been reduced largely by voluntary choice and by man's use of preventive measures, and (2) technological advances in agriculture, industry, and medicine have greatly reduced the importance of famine, plague, and war as objective mortality checks against population growth.

Several important factors have contributed to the failure of the populations of these countries to breed to the Malthusian limit. Technological developments have permitted better diets and higher living standards and, at the same time, have contributed to increasing worker productivity and higher real incomes. These developments, together with the changing economic asset value of children and the progress made in reducing mortality rates, particularly among children, have brought an important reorientation in the thinking of the average family regarding its optimum or most desirable size. The desire to maintain a high standard of living, the ascendancy of woman in modern society, the spread of education and culture, and the dissemination of knowledge regarding birth control—all of these have contributed to a generally declining birth rate and with it to man's success in avoiding, or at least postponing, the operation of the Malthusian principle.

Because of its failure to provide a completely satisfactory explanation of the problems of population growth, the Malthusian doctrine is often regarded in this country as an interesting and provocative but still somewhat discredited theory. It still has numerous adherents, however, who take a dim view of man's long-run ability to maintain or improve his living standards in the face of increasing population pressure. Because of its association with the critical problem of world food shortages, this pessimistic neo-Malthusian point of view received considerable popular attention in the years immediately following both the First and Second World Wars.

In addition to the Malthusian doctrine, a number of other theories have been advanced to explain human population growth. Generally speaking, these theories fall into two groups: those that involve a naturalistic or biological approach and those that involve social or cultural approaches. Among the more important biological theories, brief passing attention might be given to the views advanced by Sadler, Doubleday, Spencer, Gini, and Pearl.

Sadler argued the existence of a direct relationship between the fecundity of a people and the fertility of its land area.[9] Doubleday related fertility to nutritional standards and argued that human fecundity decreases with increasing food consumption.[10] Spencer related declining human fecundity to the increasing complexity and development of society.[11] He observed "an inverse proportion between the power to sustain individual life and the power to produce new individuals." Gini described the growth of national populations in terms of rising and falling fertility cycles.[12] Pearl experimented with the growth of yeast cells and population increases among fruit flies. After comparing his results with other data on

[9] Michael Thomas Sadler, *The Law of Population*, London, 1830.

[10] Thomas Doubleday, *The True Law of Population Shown to Be connected with the Food of the People*, London, 1841.

[11] Herbert Spencer, "A Theory of Population Deduced from the General Law of Animal Fertility," *Westminster Review*, April, 1852; also his book *Principles of Biology*, Vol. 2, D. Appleton & Co., 1867.

[12] Corrado Gini, *Population, Lectures on the Harris Foundation*, University of Chicago Press, Chicago, 1930.

vegetable, animal, and human population growth, he asserted that population growth logically takes the form of a flattened and sloping S curve.[13]

The exponents of the social and cultural approach discount the strictly biological approach and deny the necessity for men acting like fruit flies. Their explanations of population growth rest on man's reaction to a variety of economic, social, and political factors. Many of the writers in this group, including William Godwin, Karl Marx, and Henry George, deny the existence of any natural law that would prevent man from permanently bettering his conditions. Dumont advanced a theory of social capillarity which made population growth largely dependent on economic conditions. He suggests that the individual who is striving upward through the "wick" of society will lose interest in procreation and the rearing of families.[14] Carr-Saunders has indicated that man can control his numbers but that his decision to do so is conditioned by attitudes of mind and a desire to achieve an optimum population level.[15]

There is no need here for further examination of these theories or for attempting to set up an all-inclusive theory of population growth. All the theories described contain elements of truth. The important thing to recognize, however, is that the problem of population growth is extremely complex and that it is not readily explainable in terms of a few simple factors. The average demographer of today who attempts to predict population trends concerns himself with the age, sex, marital, occupational, and other composition characteristics of the total population, with changing trends in birth and mortality rates, and with the effects of migration on population patterns.

Rates of population change depend primarily upon the number of births as compared with the number of deaths. In the main, births are dependent upon the number of married women of child-bearing age and the desire of families to have children or their inability to control births. With accurate estimates of the number of married women of child-bearing age both now and in the foreseeable future, and with reasonably correct calculations regarding the trends in fertility, mortality, and migration, it is possible for demographers to predict the probable population for various periods in the not-too-distant future. The principal difficulty involved in

[13] Raymond Pearl, *The Biology of Population Growth*, Alfred A. Knopf, Inc., New York, 1925.

[14] Arsène Dumont, *La Morale Basée sur la Démographie*, Schleicher Frères, Paris, 1901.

[15] Alexander M. Carr-Saunders, *The Population Problem: A Study in Human Evolution*, Oxford University Press, New York, 1922. For a more detailed discussion of the above and other population policies, cf. Warren S. Thompson, *Population Problems*, pp. 18–42, McGraw-Hill Book Company, Inc., New York, 1942; Edward B. Reuter, *Population Problems*, pp. 132–186, J. B. Lippincott Company, Philadelphia, 1937; and Edmund Whittaker, *A History of Economic Ideas*, pp. 320–358; Longmans, Green & Co., Inc., New York, 1947.

these predictions centers around the demographer's inability to predict accurately future fertility and mortality trends. As the experience of many population forecasters during recent years clearly indicates, one cannot safely base predictions for the future on projections of past trends.[16]

*World-Population Outlook.* Much of the concern evidenced in recent years regarding the world's ability to support a larger population is premised on the assumption that world population will continue to increase at a fairly rapid rate. As has been pointed out, world population is now increasing at a rate of approximately 1 per cent per year, a rate that could easily lead to a doubling of population numbers in less than a century. The extent to which this trend will continue depends largely upon fertility and mortality trends throughout the world.

In their studies of world population trends, many demographers now classify the various countries into three groups: the incipient-decline group, the transitional-growth group, and the high-growth-potential group.[17] The first of these groups is made up of those areas where mortality rates have been reduced to a low level and where fertility rates also have declined considerably from levels that have prevailed in the past. This classification includes most of the countries of northwestern and central Europe plus Australia, Canada, New Zealand, South Africa, and the United States.[18] Altogether, this group accounts for approximately one-fifth of the world's population.

Because of the approaching balance between births and deaths in these countries, they would seem to offer a lower potential for rapid population increase than other areas. During the 1930's and 1940's many population experts predicted that most of these countries would soon reach a point at which their total-population levels would be generally stabilized. These predictions were based largely on the experience of the 1930's, a period of relatively low fertility rates, during which some of these countries reported small net losses in their total population numbers. The decade of the 1940's witnessed an increasing margin of births over deaths in these countries and thus somewhat postponed their prospects for population stability.

The transitional-growth group, which also accounts for roughly one-fifth of the world's people, is made up of those countries that have suc-

---

[16] Joseph S. Davis, "Our Amazing Population Upsurge," *Journal of Farm Economics,* Vol. 31, pp. 765–778, November, 1949.

[17] Cf. Frank W. Notestein, "Population: The Long View," in *Food for the World,* University of Chicago Press, Chicago, 1945; also Conrad and Irene B. Taeuber, "World Population Trends," *Journal of Farm Economics,* February, 1949, pp. 237–250.

[18] While the United States and other outlying English-speaking areas were originally included in this classification, the high rate of population increase in these areas during the 1940's suggests that they might properly be classed as in the transitional-growth group.

ceeded in reducing their mortality rates but which still must experience considerable reductions in birth rates if they are to achieve population balance. This group is composed of countries such as Japan, the Soviet Union, eastern and southern Europe, and parts of Latin America. By and large, the industrialization and urbanization movements had a later start in these countries than in the incipient-decline countries.

Acceptance and use of modern medical and sanitation practices has put these two groups roughly on a par with each other so far as mortality rates are concerned, but too little time has yet elapsed since the initial industrialization of the transitional-growth areas to permit the gradual reduction of fertility rates that has been observed in the incipient-decline areas. If the transitional-growth countries follow the expected trend, they too will join the incipient-decline countries in another two or three generations as areas where the population increase will probably not much more than exceed the numbers needed to maintain a stable population. Before this situation becomes a reality, however, the transitional-growth areas will probably experience considerable increases in their total-population numbers.

The final group—the high-growth-potential group—accounts for the remaining 60 per cent of the world's people. Included in it are the populations of China, southern and southeastern Asia, the Near East, most of Africa, and most of Latin America. For the most part, these countries are just beginning to feel the impact of industrialization and they still have both high birth rates and high mortality rates. They represent the real danger spots in world population growth because they represent (1) the areas with the highest birth rates, (2) the areas where population pressure is already greatest against the food supply, and (3) the areas where the prospects for definitely improving the living standards of the average individual seem most remote. In the not-too-distant future, considerable progress will probably be reported in the reduction of mortality rates in these areas. This action should logically be associated with simultaneous efforts to effect commensurate reductions in birth rates. Famine and widespread malnutrition are common sights in many of these countries, and while considerable progress may yet be made in increasing the food supply, the eventual improvement of individual living conditions calls for population balance. As Notestein has observed:[19]

It is not the problem of doubling, or perhaps even tripling, the product of backward regions that staggers the imagination; it is the need for an indefinite continuation of such an expansion in order to keep up with an unending growth. The demographic problem is not that of putting an immediate end to

[19] Frank W. Notestein, "Problems of Policy in Relation to Areas of Heavy Population Pressure," *Demographic Studies of Selected Areas of Rapid Growth*, p. 152, Milbank Memorial Fund, New York, 1944.

growth, but of checking growth before the populations become unmanageably large—for example, before the present numbers are doubled.

Assuming a world-wide goal of peace, prosperity, and higher standards of life for all people, the prospect of tremendous population increase in the high-growth-potential areas provides a problem that indeed challenges the ingenuity of man. Historically, declining birth rates have usually followed declining mortality rates; seldom, if ever, have the two dropped at the same time. Yet the orderly advance of society in the high-growth-potential areas—and to some extent, even in the transitional-growth areas —suggests the need for almost simultaneous action.

This calls for the development and application of definite population policies. The goal of these policies admittedly is that of reducing birth rates to levels that will permit population balance in the not-too-distant future. A variety of methods or approaches involving birth control, rapid industrialization, and popular education might be used. Kingsley Davis, in his discussion of this problem in India and Pakistan, writes:[20]

Theoretically, there are two conceivable ways of reducing fertility quickly. One—the direct method—is to bring birth control immediately to the people. The other—the indirect method—is to industrialize at once and thus create overnight the conditions that will cause people voluntarily to limit their fertility. . . .

Those who zealously wish to start an all-out birth control campaign in India and Pakistan are impelled not only by humanitarian motives but also by a greater appreciation of technology than of sociology. Forgetting the cultural obstacles, they are tempted to believe that if a quick, easy, inexpensive, and semi-permanent contraceptive could be found which, like an injection or a pill, would produce harmless sterility for six months or more, it could be brought to the Indian and Pakistan population much as smallpox vaccination has been brought to them. From a purely physical point of view birth control is easier than death control. It involves the management of only one type of germ and only one kind of contagion, as against hundreds of types in health work. . . . It involves relatively simple and easy principles that the layman can grasp, as against complicated ones that he cannot grasp in general medicine. The money it requires cannot compare to that required for other kinds of medical attention. Indeed, so simple is the process of contraception, so clear the principle, that it is absurd to think that science, which has accomplished so much in so many more complex matters, cannot find suitable techniques for accomplishing this goal. In fact, we know that when there is a will to limit family size, even crude techniques will greatly reduce fertility.

But the simplicity of the problem from the *physical* point of view merely underlines the fact that the obstacles are not primarily technological but sociological. An immediate birth control campaign in countries like India and Pakistan would leave social conditions the same. The people's old values and

---

[20] Kingsley Davis, *The Population of India and Pakistan*, pp. 226–227, Princeton University Press, Princeton, 1951.

sentiments would remain intact, as would their old illiteracy and conservatism. They would, therefore, lack the incentive to adopt contraception even if it were handed to them. They would not have the habits and personal circumstances that go with family limitation. In other words, the very forces responsible for the current high fertility would make the adoption of such a policy difficult and unlikely, in spite of its demographic advantages.

Rapid industrialization offers a possible solution to the high-birth-rate problem, particularly if it is associated with rising worker productivity, increasing standards of living, and an educational movement designed to reorient popular attitudes regarding optimum family size. The general effectiveness of this approach will be conditioned by a number of important factors. Among them one might list (1) the decision as to whether or not this approach should be associated with a direct birth-control program, (2) the relative speed with which the industrialization movement can affect the habits and thinking of the mass of the population, and (3) the general problem of initiating rapid-industrialization programs in backward and underdeveloped areas.

One additional approach to the problem of reducing high-fertility rates in the high-growth-potential areas is suggested by workers in the field of nutrition. Following the hypothesis developed by Doubleday more than a century ago, workers in this field have found that diets of low-protein content (the typical diets of the high-growth-potential areas) tend to stimulate sexual desire and activity and thus contribute to high fertility.[21] This observation regarding the "fertility of hunger" suggests a vicious cycle in which hunger breeds overpopulation, which in turn aggravates the prospects for additional hunger.

The exponents of this thesis assert that sudden improvements in nutritional standards among the world's hungry populations will be followed by declining birth rates. This view lends support to the assumption that the long-run solution to the problem of securing world population balance lies in the rapid acceptance and development of programs that will bring higher living standards and new attitudes of mind to the millions of families living in the less developed areas of the world.

*Population Trends in the United States.* The United States provides an excellent example of a population that has experienced tremendous growth in the past and that may level off in the next half century but which still has great potentialities for further increase. As the trend data reported in Table 8 indicate, the population of this country increased almost thirtyfold between 1800 and 1950 and approximately doubled between 1900 and 1950. Most of this increase has resulted from a marked

---

[21] Cf. Josue de Castro, "The Fertility of Hunger," *Collier's*, Vol. 129, No. 3, pp. 14–15, 56–57, Jan. 19, 1952; also his book *The Geography of Hunger*, Little, Brown & Company, Boston, 1952.

surplus of births over deaths. Immigration, however, has been an important factor both in adding to the amount of population increase and in contributing to high birth rates.

While there have been considerable variations in the rate of population increase from decade to decade, the past century has been generally characterized by a declining rate of population increase. This observation together with the low fertility rates of the 1930's, the drying up of immigration, and the assumption that the mortality rate had approached its absolute minimum led many observers to predict an early leveling off of total population numbers. One widely accepted forecast of the late 1930's, for example, suggested that the population of the United States would rise to a peak of slightly over 139 million around 1960 and thereafter decline. This estimate was raised in later forecasts, but "as late as mid-1950, the standing official estimate of our peak population was 165 million, and a decline before this century's end was indicated."[22]

The downward trend of the 1930's was followed by an upward surge during the 1940's. This trend resulted in the addition of 19 million people to the total population. While this was the largest increase reported in any decade of the nation's history, the rate of increase was not large by past standards. Actually, the 14.5 per cent rate of increase exceeded the rates reported in only one other decade, that of the 1930's. Nevertheless, the population increase of the 1940's seemed somewhat amazing at the time —amazing because it so far exceeded expectations.

In retrospect, it is easy to credit the upward surge in population growth during the 1940's to factors such as the maturing of the "surplus baby crop" of the 1920's, the impetus that the war gave to marriages that might otherwise have been delayed, the impact of the war and postwar business boom on marriage and birth rates, and continued progress in the reduction of mortality. But what, one might ask, does this portend for the future? Will the total population continue to increase at a fairly rapid rate or is the current upward trend a temporary one that will be followed by a cycle of declining fertility? The answers to these questions lie in the future and they will be determined to a considerable extent by the age distribution of the population, future fertility and mortality rate trends, immigration policy, general economic conditions, and the rational desire of families to increase or limit their family size.

In the three years following the 1950 census, total population increased by an estimated 7.9 million people. Continued increase at this rate could almost bring a doubling of the national population before the year 2000.

[22] Joseph S. Davis, *Our Changed Population Outlook and Its Significance*, address to the Stanford Research Club, Nov. 14, 1951, published in *The American Economic Review*, Vol. 42, No. 3, pp. 306 and 308, June, 1952. Cf. population forecast of W. S. Thompson and P. K. Whelpton in *The Problem of a Changing Population*, pp. 22–27, National Resources Committee, Washington, 1938.

*Table* 8. Population Trends in the United States, 1790 to 1953

| Year | Total population (continental U.S.) | Increase | Per cent of increase | Immigration by decades |
|---|---|---|---|---|
| 1790 | 3,929,214 | | | |
| 1800 | 5,308,483 | 1,379,269 | 35.1 | |
| 1810 | 7,239,881 | 1,931,398 | 36.4 | |
| 1820 | 9,638,453 | 2,398,572 | 33.1 | |
| 1830 | 12,866,020 | 3,227,567 | 33.5 | 151,824[a] |
| 1840 | 17,069,453 | 4,203,433 | 32.7 | 599,125[b] |
| 1850 | 23,191,876 | 6,122,423 | 35.9 | 1,713,251[c] |
| 1860 | 31,443,321 | 8,251,445 | 35.6 | 2,598,214[d] |
| 1870 | 39,818,449 | 8,375,128 | 26.6 | 2,314,824[e] |
| 1880 | 50,155,783 | 10,337,334 | 26.0 | 2,812,191 |
| 1890 | 62,947,714 | 12,791,931 | 25.5 | 5,246,613 |
| 1900 | 75,994,575 | 13,046,861 | 20.7 | 3,687,564 |
| 1910 | 91,972,266 | 15,977,691 | 21.0 | 8,795,386 |
| 1920 | 105,710,620 | 13,738,354 | 14.9 | 5,735,811 |
| 1930 | 122,775,046 | 17,064,426 | 16.1 | 4,107,209 |
| 1940 | 131,669,275 | 8,894,229 | 7.2 | 528,431 |
| 1950 | 150,697,361 | 19,028,086 | 14.5 | 1,035,039 |
| 1953[e] | 159,473,000 | | | |

[a] Oct. 1, 1819 to Sept. 30, 1830.

[b] Oct. 1, 1830 to Dec. 31, 1840.

[c] Calendar years.

[d] Jan. 1, 1861 to June 30, 1870. All other immigration data are for periods beginning July 1 and ending June 30.

[e] Census Bureau's estimate, July 20, 1953, including armed forced overseas.

It seems probable that this rapid rate of population increase will decline somewhat during the next decade as the women who are now in the child-bearing age group are replaced by the smaller number of women born during the 1928 to 1941 period when the birth rate stood at less than 20 births per 1,000 population.[23] This may be only a temporary respite,

[23] The crude birth rate in the United States stood at 25 births per 1,000 people in the population in 1915. It remained above 20 until 1928. During the depression it reached a low of 16.4 in 1933. Since 1942 it has been above 20 in every year except 1945. In 1947 and 1949 it exceeded 25. The effect of this birth cycle on the present and prospective number of women of child-bearing age is indicated by the 1950 census, which reports the following percentage distribution of females by age groups: under 5 years, 10.5 per cent; 5 to 9 years, 8.4 per cent; 10 to 14 years, 7.5 per cent; 15 to 19 years, 7.1 per cent; 20 to 24 years, 7.7 per cent; 25 to 29 years, 8.1 per cent; 30 to 34 years, 7.7 per cent; 35 to 39 years, 7.5 per cent; 40 to 44 years, 6.6 per cent; 45 years and over, 28.8 per cent. The relatively small proportion found in the 10-to-24-years groups as compared with those found in the 25-to-39 and 0-to-9 years groups indicates a prospective decline in the number of potential new mothers during the next 10 to 15 years.

however, because the large baby crop of the 1940's and early 1950's suggests another baby boom in the late 1960's. The extent to which these trends develop depends largely upon the future course of fertility rates (number of births per 1,000 women of child-bearing age), mortality rates, and immigration. Increasing fertility rates, of course, may keep births moving at an even keel during the next decade, while declining fertility rates may negate the current prospects for a baby boom in the late 1960's.

In 1950 the Census Bureau published three "illustrative projections of population of the United States, 1950 to 1960," using the assumptions of low, medium, and high rates of increase.[24] As the graphic presentation of these data in the accompanying illustration, which unofficially projects them to 1975, indicates, the assumption of a low rate of increase suggests an early leveling off of the population with totals of 161.7 million in 1960 and 165.6 million in 1975. The medium projection rate suggests population totals of 169.4 million in 1960 and 190.1 million in 1975. The high projection rate, which most accurately describes the population-growth trend to date (mid-1953), points to a population of 180.3 million in 1960 and 225.3 million in 1975.

The high projection rate shown in the illustration involves a somewhat more rapid rate of increase than has generally persisted since 1900. This suggests that the increase rate of the early 1950's may not continue and that some slackening off can be expected. Nevertheless, it is well to recognize that the projection of this high rate of increase does not overly exaggerate the population-growth potential of the United States.[25]

The extent to which the families of the nation choose between the high projection rate or some lower rate in the decades to come will be determined to a considerable degree by family attitudes, general business conditions, and the prospects for economic security and rising standards of living. Depressed business conditions, economic pessimism, and fear of

---

[24] Jacob S. Siegel and Helen L. White, *Illustrative Projections of the Population of the United States, 1950 to 1960*, Bureau of the Census Series P-25, No. 43, Aug. 10, 1950. These projections include armed forces overseas. Cf. also Margaret J. Hagood and Jacob S. Siegel, "Projections of Regional Distribution of Population," *Agricultural Economics Research*, Vol. 3, p. 47, Table 3, April, 1951. These projections were revised in *Provisional Revision of the Projections of the Total Population of the United States, July 1, 1953 to 1960*, Bureau of the Census Series P-25, No. 58, Apr. 17, 1952. In its revision, the Bureau suggests population totals of 165.2, 171.2, and 179.8 million persons in 1960 under the low, medium, and high projection rates.

[25] Many demographers regard the present high birth rate as a temporary phenomenon and assume that the United States may soon take its place among the incipient-decline countries. Joseph S. Davis (*Our Changed Population Outlook and Its Significance*, pp. 314–315), however, asserts that by the year 2000, our total population "is likely to be between 200 and 300 million, and an excess over 300 million seems . . . as conceivable as a falling short of 200 million." Unless catastrophies more severe than the Second World War intervene, "indeed, our population in 1980 seems . . . more likely to be over 200 million than under it."

insecurity played a leading role in reducing fertility rates during the 1930's. In the 1940's booming business and economic optimism, coupled with the government's military family-assistance programs and special veterans' programs, gave considerable impetus to a rising flood of births.

A recurrence of the conditions of the 1930's could again depress fertility rates. So long as business conditions are favorable and the population does not seem to press against the available food supply, however, it

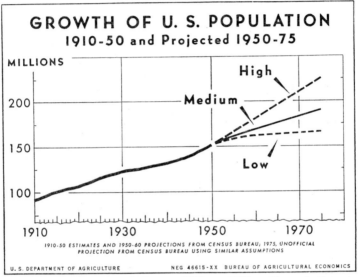

**GROWTH OF U. S. POPULATION**
**1910-50 and Projected 1950-75**

Population trend in the United States, 1910 to 1950, with projections to 1975, assuming high, medium, and low rates of increase.

seems probable that family attitudes will favor steady increase toward a higher optimum population level. As Davis observes:[26]

> Marriage and children constitute an integral part of the real standard of living of most Americans. Under economic pressure, either or both will be deferred and the number of children restricted. But if economic and social conditions permit gradual increase in consumption levels and improvements in working conditions, the gains from higher productivity will be taken, on the average, partly in more goods and services, better housing, shorter hours of labor, earlier marriage, somewhat more living children per family, and greater ease in old age. No one can safely forecast the changing proportions to which such gains will be devoted, or how seriously our international obligations will restrict the net total. But the evidence of recent years strongly suggests that if goods become obtainable with less and less effort, the competition between wants for goods and wants for babies, which depressed marriages and births in 1925–40, will be less powerful than it was then.

[26] *Ibid.*, p. 318.

If and when it becomes obvious that future population increase will lead only to decreasing standards of life for the existing population, the American people will have a real incentive for family limitation and population stability.

### Future Man-Land Adjustments

The increasing population pressure felt in most countries of the world during recent years carries with it a certain ominous significance. Numerous reactions to the over-all problem are possible. But whether one tends to "view with alarm" or to face the future with hope and optimism depends largely on his individual point of view.

Those who concern themselves largely with the biological aspects of population growth can build up a good case for grave forebodings regarding man's future ability to feed himself. The fact that the population of the world increased by approximately 25 million persons in 1951 and that around one-tenth of this increase occurred in the United States cannot be taken lightly. With this rapid rate of increase, the ugly head of Malthusianism again raises itself with its prediction that all countries, even those with a bounteous resource base such as that possessed by the United States, must trudge their way along a "road to survival" and face the specter of eventual want and hunger.

On the other hand, those who look to the world of new scientific and technological developments can easily be carried away by the tremendous prospect for increased production of natural and synthetic foods, fibers, and other products. As these observers see it, man can easily produce sufficient food to care for a growing population and still provide a higher standard of living.

A realistic approach to the problem of future man-land relationships calls for balanced consideration of the potentialities for both increasing population and increasing food production. While the prospect for increasing population pressure, both on the world and the domestic front, has serious implications, the situation is by no means hopeless. Man, in so far as he is a rational being entrusted with some power for shaping his future destiny, does have the ability to limit his numbers at some point short of a Malthusian level of survival. He also can take such steps as are needed to provide for the growing land requirements for living space and for food, fiber, forest, fuel, mineral, and other products of land.

In so far as these land requirements are reflected in the effective economic demand for land and its products, action can and probably will be taken to increase the production of the needed land products. This production process may call for bringing new lands into use or for the up-grading of some land uses. It might also involve the application of more intensive land-use practices, an increasing use of new technological developments, and the substitution of capital or labor factors for land inputs in the production process.

Science and technology promise to play an increasingly important role in implementing production. One must recognize, however, that although the future of technological developments in this field is bright, it is altogether possible that an eventual point of diminishing returns may be reached. But this is not a problem of immediate concern. The world today can produce sufficient food and fiber to feed and clothe its present population and even a reasonable addition to its present numbers. The big problem is not can it feed itself but rather are the nations and peoples of the world willing to accept the economic, political, and social adjustments that may be necessary if the resources of the earth are to be used to give all of its people a fuller and better life.

In many respects the problem of securing long-range balance between population pressure and the food supply is essentially one of balancing the economic supply of land against the demand for land and its products. As a first step in this equation process it is necessary to determine the extent and nature of the effective demand for land and to gauge this demand in terms of land-area requirements. Once these area requirements have been determined, the problem is one of finding sufficient land to meet them. This process may call for allocation of the existing economic supply of land, additions to this supply, or recalculation of the area requirements in terms of the price levels or institutional controls that may be needed to bring new lands into use or to make the available supply suffice.

The primary emphasis in this chapter will center around the extent of the physical and economic supplies of land that are available for use in the United States and the extent to which this supply can fill the nation's demand for food and other land products. In the discussion of land requirements, major emphasis will be placed upon the requirements for food production. Consideration also must be given, however, to the land requirements for the production of fibers, other nonfood crops, and forest products, plus the provision of needed watershed and water reserves, recreation and wildlife areas, and the reservation or provision of lands for other essential uses. Some of these requirements involve multiple land uses. Others involve interchangeable uses or uses that may be in conflict with each other, depending upon the extent of the demand for each use and the relative emphasis that is placed upon conservation practices.

## The Supply of Land

When it is viewed in the aggregate, the economic supply of land must be measured in terms of use or production capacity rather than in terms of physical area. The extent of this supply is dependent upon the operation of numerous variables. It reflects the physical supply of land that is both available and suitable for cropland or other uses, its native productivity, the intensity with which it is used, man's use of technology in its culture, the effect of variable weather conditions, insects, pests, and plant diseases upon crop yields, and man's decision to carry on exploitive or conservational measures. It also reflects the operation of several important economic and institutional factors. Among the more important of these are land-product price levels and the effect of prices in allocating resources, production limitations or controls and production-subsidy programs, land-development costs and programs, the structure of transportation costs, trade restrictions, international-exchange problems, and the demands of growing nationalism or industrialization.

*Supply and Use of Agricultural Lands in the United States.* The total land area of the continental United States is approximately 1,934 million acres. Of this area approximately 30 million acres are classified as inland water area, while 1,904 million acres, or 98 per cent, is dry land and land temporarily or partially covered with water. This total area comprises the physical supply of land in this country. The economic supply is somewhat more limited in that it involves only those areas that are put to economic use.

As the land-use data reported in Table 9 indicate, slightly over nine-tenths of the total land area of the United States is used for the three principal agricultural uses—cropland, pasture and grazing, and forest.

Cropland acreages have remained fairly stable for several years. The enormous crop yields of recent years have been produced on only a little more than one-fourth of the total land area. In the 1949 cropping season, cropland accounted for about 478 million acres, of which total 386 million acres were actually cultivated, including land being fallowed.

Permanent pasture and grazing is by far the largest single item of land use. This use involves about 950 million acres, or over 50 per cent of the land. Included are 631 million acres of nonforested pasture and grazing land and 320 million acres of grazed forest land. Approximately one-third of the pasture and range land, most of it located in the arid and mountainous portions of the West, is in public ownership.

For the most part the areas now classified as pasture and range land have a lower productivity potential than the areas in cropland use. Large areas are grazed because this is the highest and best use—sometimes the only feasible use—for these lands. When converted to cropland equivalents based upon the acreage of tame hay needed to provide the same quantity of feed supplied by pasture, all of the pasture and range land can be considered as the equivalent of about 150 million average acres of cropland. This qualitative comparison lessens the quantitative importance of the large area in pasture and range. At the same time, however, it must be remembered that these lands represent a significant portion of the

*Table* 9. Major Uses of Land in Continental United States, 1950

| Land use | Acreage, millions | Percentage of total |
|---|---|---|
| Agricultural use: | | |
| Cropland: | | |
| Land used for crops[a] | 386 | 20.2 |
| Cropland used as pasture | 69 | 3.7 |
| Idle cropland | 23 | 1.2 |
| Total improved land available for crops | 478 | 25.1 |
| Pasture and grazing land: | | |
| Nonforested pasture and grazing land | 631 | 33.2 |
| Agricultural service uses[b] | 12 | 0.6 |
| Forest[c] | 606 | 31.8 |
| Nonagricultural use: | | |
| Special-use areas[d] | 93 | 4.9 |
| Miscellaneous other land[e] | 84 | 4.4 |
| Grand total | 1,904 | 100.0 |

[a] Land used for crops in 1949, including cropland harvested, crop failure, and fallow.

[b] Farmsteads, feed lots, gardens, farm roads, etc.

[c] Excludes 14 million acres withdrawn from forests for parks and other special uses. The total forested area, including the withdrawn land, is 620 million acres.

[d] Urban areas, rural villages and industrial sites, highway and railroad rights of way, parks, wildlife refuges, airports, military reservations, reservoirs, and other similar special-use areas.

[e] Includes wasteland, rock, desert, and miscellaneous other areas.

Source: Estimates based on data assembled in a Bureau of Agricultural Economics land-use inventory project, January, 1953.

agricultural land supply of the nation. More than half of the farms and ranches depend largely on grassland for feed. Pasture and range lands supply more than one-third of the feed for livestock in this country.

Forest and woodland, including 320 million acres of grazed forest land, comprise 606 million acres, or approximately one-third of the total land area. Of this, over one-third is publicly owned. Much of the land classified as forest and woodland is in hilly and mountainous regions, wet and swamp areas, and on sandy lands.

The area devoted to agricultural service areas on farms is estimated at about 12 million acres. This area includes land devoted to farmsteads, feedlots, small gardens, roads, lanes, and other farm-service uses. An estimated 10 million acres is used for farmsteads and feedlots.

The remaining 177 million acres is used neither for agriculture nor forestry. These lands represent two extremes in use capacity. On the one hand, 93 million acres are used for a variety of intensive and high-value uses, such as urban, residential, commercial and industrial purposes, parks, highways, railroads, and airports. On the other extreme, some 84 million acres are mostly barren, waste, rock, and desert areas, which have low surface use for agriculture but may have value for wildlife, recreation, or watershed use.

## Land Use, 1880 to 1950

The period 1880 to 1920 was characterized by expansion of agriculture. Cropland acreage more than doubled (Table 10). Grassland available for grazing declined somewhat as sod lands were plowed up and nonagricultural uses increased for urban areas, parks, and roads. Shifts in land use of considerable regional and local importance occurred—new cropland was developed in some areas, and in others submarginal land was converted to pasture or allowed to revert to forest—during the 30-year period 1920 to 1950, but the period was one of relative stability in the over-all acreages devoted to the major land uses.

Available records show that land in farms increased steadily from 1880 to 1950. Farms and ranches included 28 per cent of the total land in 1880, 50 per cent in 1920, and over 60 per cent in 1950. More of the Indian lands and public and private grazing lands not enumerated previously as land in farms are now included. The changes in acreage of land in farms therefore represent mainly agricultural development of the country, but partly changes in the method of classifying and reporting land.

While notable shifts in the use of land have occurred since 1900, and especially beginning about 1910, they have been counterbalanced by regional changes. For example, cropland and improved pasture acreages have increased generally in the West and in the Lower Mississippi Valley, whereas there have been decreases in cropland in many parts of the Northeast and Southeast.

Large transfers between uses have also taken place. While cropland increased over 60 million acres, total pasture and range land decreased by over 100 million for the country as a whole in the 40-year period 1910 to 1950. Forest and woodland acreages remained about the same. Although there has been much land cut-over and cleared, a large acreage of crop and pasture land in the East has reverted to forest.

The combined acreage used for crops, pasture, and range was slightly lower in 1950 than in 1910, but the composition of this area changed significantly over the period. In 1910 less than 24 per cent was cropland; in 1950 cropland made up 28 per cent. Land used for agriculture (all land in farms plus nonfarm grassland and forest-land grazed) has declined slightly since 1910 as the nonagricultural uses have increased. Similarly, total land used for agriculture and forestry has become smaller.

At present, annual new farm-land development only about equals the shifts to other uses, including forests, areas absorbed by urban and industrial growth, by airports and reservoirs, etc. The areas occupied by

*Land Problems and Policies*

*Table* 10. Trend in Land Utilization, United States, 1880 to 1950
(In millions of acres)

| Land use | 1880 | 1890 | 1900 | 1910 | 1920 | 1930 | 1940 | 1950 |
|---|---|---|---|---|---|---|---|---|
| Cropland[a]..................... | 188 | 248 | 319 | 347 | 402 | 413 | 399 | 409 |
| Available pasture and range (non-forested)[b].................. | 935 | 892 | 831 | 814 | 750 | 708 | 723 | 700 |
| Forest and woodland[c].......... | 628 | 604 | 579 | 562 | 567 | 607 | 602 | 606 |
| Other[d]....................... | 154 | 161 | 176 | 182 | 186 | 177 | 181 | 189 |
| Total..................... | 1,905 | 1,905 | 1,905 | 1,905 | 1,905 | 1,905 | 1,905 | 1,904 |
| Land in farms.................. | 536 | 623 | 839 | 879 | 956 | 987 | 1,061 | 1,159 |
| Land not in farms.............. | 1,369 | 1,282 | 1,066 | 1.026 | 949 | 918 | 844 | 745 |
| Total..................... | 1,905 | 1,905 | 1,905 | 1,905 | 1,905 | 1,905 | 1,905 | 1,904 |
| Pasture and range land available for grazing[b] (grassland and grazed forest)............. | e | e | 1,131 | 1,121 | 1,066 | 1,042 | 1,065 | 1,045 |
| Land used for crops and pasture... | e | e | 1,450 | 1,468 | 1,468 | 1,455 | 1,464 | 1,454 |
| Land used for agriculture[f]....... | e | e | 1,607 | 1,618 | 1,617 | 1,565 | 1,565 | 1,559 |
| Land used for agriculture and forestry[g]..................... | e | e | 1,782 | 1,780 | 1,777 | 1,773 | 1,768 | 1,759 |

[a] Cropland harvested, crop failure, and cropland idle or fallow, but does not include cropland used only for pasture.

[b] Grassland pasture, including cropland used only for pasture, and other nonforested grazing land. Includes idle grassland which probably existed in significant acreages only prior to 1900.

[c] Exclusive of forest land in parks, game refuges, military reservations, etc. Includes commercial and noncommercial forest land and including woodland grazed.

[d] Includes "special land-use areas," such as urban areas, highways and roads, farmsteads, parks, game refuges, military reservations, etc., and also land having slight surface-use value except for wildlife and watershed protection and recreation (desert, rock, sand dunes, etc.).

[e] Data not available.

[f] All land in farms plus all nonfarm land grazed by livestock.

[g] All land in farms plus nonfarm grazing land and forest land.

urban centers, towns, parks, and other special uses have increased greatly since 1910, rising from 53 million acres to 93 million acres in 1950.

From 1930 to 1950, there was a net decrease in the total acreage of cropland of 4 million acres, due mainly to conversion to other uses.[1] New cropland development in the 20-year period 1930 to 1950 is estimated to have been about 20 million acres. However, shifts of cropland to

[1] Before the AAA program began in 1933 farmers usually thought in terms of "gross areas," which did not make allowances for land occupied by ditches, fence rows, turn rows, and building sites. In later years they have thought more in terms of "net acres." This change in method of reporting undoubtedly had some effects on recent estimates of acreages of individual crops and of total cropland.

permanent pasture, woodland, and nonfarm uses more than offset the new land. In other words, there possibly has been a gross shift of 24 million acres of cropland to grazing, forestry, and nonfarm uses and new land development of 20 million acres, resulting in a net decrease of 4 million acres or more in cropland.

A large amount of the new land development occurred in the Lower Mississippi Valley by drainage, flood control, and clearing. A relatively large acreage of new land also was developed in the 11 Western states by irrigation and land clearing. In the Great Plains and Mountain regions several million acres of grazing land were plowed for wheat after 1945. While this new land was being developed in the Mississippi Delta and in the West, large acreages of hill lands in some of the Eastern and Southern states were being shifted from cultivated crops to pasture and to forest. Abandonment of cropland was especially rapid in some of the poor, cotton-land hill areas, where population was moving out to the developing industrial centers and to the Western states.

*Sources of Additional Cropland.* The Soil Conservation Service, which classified the lands of the country according to their use capability in 1945, estimated that approximately 80 to 85 million acres of unimproved land are suitable for regular cultivation under good practices. This estimate includes lands which need drainage, irrigation, and clearing, as well as some additional acreages of grazing lands suitable for cultivation under good farming practices. A considerable area could be put in cultivation as a result of land-clearing operations. Many of the lands needing clearing, particularly in the South, also need drainage or flood protection.

The bulk of the unimproved land most suitable for development is included in drainage, flood control, and irrigation-development projects which are already authorized or under construction. Even so, many years of work will be needed to bring the suitable land under cultivation. The completion of these projects calls for large expenditures of labor and materials as well as considerable planning and organization. The justification for the development of some of these lands should depend upon the marketing prospects for the products from the new land.

A considerable part of the irrigation, drainage, and flood-control development under way and planned will be primarily of benefit to existing farms and ranches, although considerable land in undeveloped areas also will be benefited. Much of the development involving drainage and clearing is primarily a matter for local district action or for community group or individual initiative, there being no special government program for this purpose at present. Most of the undeveloped land suitable for development is privately owned.

The development of new lands will not necessarily result in a net addition to the total cropland area. In many instances, lands ill-suited to farming because of soil and slope are being farmed with only meager returns. Some land cultivated during the war cannot be permanently maintained in cultivation because of erosion, poor soil, climatic conditions, and lack of sufficient water. This will add to the problem of shifting land uses within the next decade. Also, while some lands are being reclaimed, the fertility of other land is being exhausted through nonconservative farming. Much of this land should be taken out of regular cultivated crop production and restored by revegetation measures.

In some ways, the recurrent use of land for field crops, then pasture, and then forest, which has occurred especially in some areas of the East and South and to a lesser extent in other parts of the country, amounts to a long-time cycle of depletion by cropping and/or grazing followed by restoration by forest and other vegetative growth. The economic and social costs of such extreme land-use changes might be reduced either by the use of conservation practices on lands already in cultivation or, when demand lags, by retirement of this land from crop use.

A recent survey by the Soil Conservation Service shows that over 45 million acres of poor land now used for crops are ill-suited for regular cultivation because of severe erosion, steep slopes, and poor soil conditions. Thus, the need for retiring poor cropland to other uses may be one of the major justifications for bringing into cultivation an equivalent productive acreage of new land.

Estimates by the Soil Conservation Service indicate that if present conversion trends continue over the next decade, about 20 million acres of suitable grassland and woodland will go into cultivation, and approximately 26 million acres of adapted woodland will be converted into grassland pasture. At the same time a large acreage of poorly adapted cropland will be shifted to grass and to woodland.

It has been estimated that over 700 million acres of land in the United States are physically capable of being used for cropland purposes.[2] This provides a fairly substantial reserve beyond the 478 million acres now classified as in cropland use. With the present demand and price conditions, much of this land, of course, is not available for cropland use. However, should increasing population pressure, increasing demand, higher prices, or other conditions warrant such action, part or all of this reserve area probably could be brought under cultivation.

This potential reserve of land for cultivation includes approximately 100 million acres of pasture and grazing land and over 100 million acres of forest or cutover land physically capable of producing crops without drainage but requiring clearing. About 17 million more acres in the Western regions of low precipitation could be irrigated; and more

[2] *Report of the Land Planning Committee*, Part II, pp. 127–132, *National Resources Board*, Washington, 1934.

than 20 million acres of wet land (other than tidal marsh), some of it of potentially high fertility, might be drained at various levels of cost. Much of this land is used at present for grazing, timber production, and as wildlife habitats, and its use as cropland would involve a proportionate reduction in land used for these purposes.

*Trend toward Increasing Productivity per Acre.* The past several decades have been characterized by an almost fabulous increase in agricultural production in this country. Brewster has indicated that total agricultural production increased 370 per cent between 1870 and 1950, while the size of the farm labor force increased by only 4 per cent.[3] Much of this increase has resulted from the impact of mechanization on individual productivity; much of it also from the effect of new technology on crop yields and average production per acre.

The increased farm output from 1870 to 1950 was associated with an increase in cropland used for cultivated crops from 165 million acres to 386 million, an increase of 134 per cent. Much of the increase in cropland occurred prior to 1920. The employment of other resources increased sharply after 1900, except labor, which was roughly the same in 1920 as in 1900. Since 1920, however, neither depressions nor prosperous periods —low farm prices or high prices—have resulted in as highly significant changes in cropland used for crops as in other factors of production (Table 11). Acres used for crops decreased from 1919 to 1923, but increased slightly in the 1929 to 1933 depression, and increased again in the war period 1939 to 1943. Labor employed in agriculture dropped in 1929 to 1933 and again in 1939 to 1943. The quantity of power and machinery increased greatly between 1940 and 1949. Most current input expenses increased, such as for fertilizer and seed. Crop production per acre increased by over 28 per cent from 1935–1939 to 1945–1949.

These data seem to indicate that the supply of land used in agriculture has a relatively low price elasticity. In the short run this is in large part owing to the quickly available alternative substitute materials, and to a less extent because of the small changes that can be made readily in a short time in the quantity of land through investment and disinvestment, such as by development of new land or by exhaustion of productivity.[4]

Some of the greatest increases in crop yields came during the decade of the 1940's. Many of the advances up until then sufficed only to

[3] John M. Brewster, "Farm Technological Advances and Total Population Growth," *Journal of Farm Economics*, Vol. 33, p. 129, February, 1951. Brewster indicates that "from 1870 to 1920, total population growth was faster than farm technological advance, as reflected in output per farm worker, with the result that agriculture was an expanding industry in terms of both total output and farm employment opportunities." Since 1920, farm technological advance has outraced total population growth.

[4] For a discussion of this subject refer to D. Gale Johnson, "The Supply Function for Agricultural Products," *The American Economic Review*, September, 1950, pp. 539–564.

Table 11. Total Acreage of Cropland Planted, Farm Employment, Volume of
Farm Power and Machinery, Fertilizer Used, and Farm Output,
United States, Specified Years 1910 to 1951
(1935–1939 = 100)

| Year | Total acreage of cropland planted or used[a] | Man-hours of farm work[b] | Power and machinery[c] | Fertilizer and lime consumed[d] | Insecticides and fungicides[e] | Total input[f] | Farm output[g] |
|---|---|---|---|---|---|---|---|
| 1910 | 88 | 107 | 105 | 61 | ... | 91 | 79 |
| 1912 | 90 | 111 | 110 | 64 | ... | 94 | 87 |
| 1919 | 100 | 112 | 124 | 67 | ... | 102 | 85 |
| 1923 | 98 | 110 | 118 | 75 | ... | 104 | 90 |
| 1929 | 101 | 110 | 118 | 101 | ... | 108 | 97 |
| 1932 | 103 | 108 | 113 | 55 | ... | 104 | 101 |
| 1939 | 97 | 99 | 105 | 109 | 106 | 106 | 106 |
| 1943 | 101 | 100 | 120 | 168 | 118 | 110 | 128 |
| 1945 | 100 | 95 | 126 | 195 | 126 | 115 | 129 |
| 1949 | 103 | 90 | 156 | 270 | 131 | 128 | 140 |
| 1950 | 100 | 84 | 163 | 301 | 178 | 130 | 138 |
| 1951 | 101 | 89 | 170 | 330 | ... | ... | 146 |

[a] Total acreage of cropland planted and fallowed, or all cropland used (includes acreage multiple-cropped, only one time).

[b] Man-hours of farm work.

[c] Volume of farm power and machinery valued in 1935 to 1939 dollars.

[d] Fertilizer used in tons.

[e] Insecticides and fungicides volume in dollars.

[f] Total inputs of labor, power and machinery, fertilizer consumed, insecticides and fungicides, etc.

[g] Farm output measures the volume of production available for eventual human use through sales from the farm or consumption in farm households.

SOURCES: *Agricultural Outlook Charts*, U.S. Bureau of Agricultural Economics, 1952; pp. 10, 18, 22, 24, October, 1951; *Farm Production Practices, Costs and Returns*, Statistical Bulletin 83, pp. 6, 26, 32, 49, 74, October, 1949; and *Farm Labor*, January, 1952.

counterbalance and offset losses resulting from soil deterioration and the ravages of insect pests and diseases. During the 1940's, however, agricultural technology really came into its own. The introduction of improved crop varieties, the use of conservation measures and better tillage practices, the development of improved methods of combatting plant diseases and insects, the increased use of drainage and irrigation practices, and increasing dependence upon the use of lime and commercial fertilizers brought notable increases in the average acreage yields of many crops.

Five-year moving averages of wheat and oats yields, from 1885 to 1933, indicate that the average yield of these crops changed but little during that period, although there were downward fluctuations in abnormal years. The yield of corn likewise decreased, especially during the 15 years 1920 to 1935, and during the drought years 1933 to 1937, when the average yield was lower than in any preceding 5-year period since the Civil War. Cotton yields also declined, notably as a result of the ravages of the boll weevil from 1910 to 1925. Composite yields of 12 crops for the period 1900 to 1935 showed a considerable downward trend, largely because of the influence of drought, pests, and land deterioration.

During the 1940's, however, wheat yields averaged more than 25 per cent above the preceding 20 years. Better growing weather, hybrid seed, fertilization, and other factors have boosted corn yields since 1940 by over 25 per cent, about the same as the increase in wheat yields. Cotton yields increased to a level that was almost double that which prevailed between 1895 and 1915. Since 1940, the general trend in average crop yields per acre has been upward, and with increasing acceptance of technological improvements the prospects appear good for even more increases in average acre yields.

The possibility of high average yields when necessity compels their achievement is shown by recent results obtained in the United States and in some of the west European countries that are subject to heavy population pressure. Average yields of small grain and potatoes in such west European countries as Germany, Great Britain, and Belgium before the Second World War were considerably more than double the averages for the United States, although in part this superiority was offset by a higher yield of corn in this country as compared with small grains. Crop yields in the Corn Belt and other good farming regions of the United States, however, compare favorably with those of western Europe. The high yields mentioned in Europe, however, involve much larger inputs of labor than would be regarded as either desirable or practicable in this country under present economic conditions.

In the United States rapid strides have been made in economizing the use of land for feed crops by measures such as the addition of high protein concentrates to the corn rations used in feeding livestock and by the wider use of legumes in hay crops, pastures, and meadows. It has been estimated, for instance, that under the former method of fattening hogs mainly on corn, it required from 11 to 12 bushels of corn to produce 100 pounds of live weight, while with the addition of supplementary proteins and minerals to the corn ration it is possible to produce 100 pounds of pork with 7 to 8 bushels of corn.

Great progress in the economy of crop and pasture land also is being achieved by development of more efficient strains of livestock and by the selection of individuals capable of more efficient use of feed. As a result of the combined practices of selecting better animals and employing more efficient methods of feeding, it is estimated that milk production per cow has more than doubled since 1910.

Since 1944 the level of agricultural production has been more than 35 per cent above prewar and nearly two-thirds more than that in 1913 to 1915. The startling changes that have taken place in farming in the last two decades are illustrated by three index series—production per acre, production per animal unit of livestock, and production per worker. All three of these indicate a considerable increase in output from about the same area of land. In addition to better farm practices several other factors have contributed to the higher farm output. Not only have crops been shifted to the best lands both on an individual farm and area-wide basis, but considerable areas have been improved by drainage, irrigation, and soil-building measures.

A great deal of research work has been done on soil problems, and many significant facts are being uncovered in tests of fertilizer materials and in the composition of crops grown under different conditions. It has been learned, for example, that the need for minor elements by plants is increased as acre yields are stepped up by use of heavier applications of liming materials and fertilizers and by growing higher-yielding hybrids. These higher yields increase the requirements for the minor elements that are needed by plants and decrease the plants' content of those minor elements needed only by animals. Similarly, the stepping up of milk production per cow requires that larger amounts of the minor elements that are essential to animals and man be contained in the feed.[5] Results of recent studies indicate that as higher and higher yields per acre are produced by hybrids and other means, the composition of the plants are changed, with less protein and carbohydrates and substitution of more elements having lower food and feed value per unit. Evidently high-yielding hybrids require carefully balanced application of certain minor elements to soils or the addition to feeds of essential elements for animals.

The influence of weather still is an uncertain factor in production. There is a question also as to whether improved technology can give rise to the same continuous progressive advances in production during the next decade as in the 1940 to 1949 period. Already there are some indications of a diminishing rate of increase. For example, crops are now pretty well concentrated on the best lands, and only moderate gains can be expected from additional shifts to new lands.

Continued mechanization is expected, but additional mechanization cannot release the same large acreages from feed to food crops as it has

[5] Firman E. Bear, "A Survey of the Minor Element Situation," *Journal of Soil and Water Conservation*, January, 1950, pp. 11–12.

during the last two decades. As the limit of substitution of mechanical power for horsepower is approached, more new cropland will likely be required. Hybrid corn seed is now used for most of the corn crop; accordingly great additional increases in yields cannot be expected from this source. Inadequate or poorly balanced supplies of the moisture needed for plant growth now limit corn and other crop yields in many areas. Much remains yet to be done in checking certain disease and insect pests as some of the new control measures appear not to be as effective after a few years' use as when first tried.

This statement merely is intended to call attention to some of the problems that will arise in expansion of the already high level of production on present croplands. The improvements must be continued and expanded if production is to be maintained and increased without substantial additions to our crop acreage.

*The World's Agricultural Areas.* Competent estimates show that the total land area of the earth that is suitable for economic cultivation is definitely limited. These estimates vary greatly, partly because of the varying assumptions made regarding economic conditions. Carl Alsberg, for example, estimated that 6.4 billion acres could be used for crops if necessary.[6] O. E. Baker has estimated that about 4.4 billion acres is suitable for wheat, rice, or other cereals.[7] Recently Pearson and Harper concluded that only 2.6 billion acres,[8] or about the same as was cultivated at the beginning of the Second World War, could be used to grow crops. On the other hand, Kellogg and Salter have indicated that between 2.6 and 3.6 billion acres are now cultivated and that an additional 1.3 billion acres could be added to this present cropland area (Table 12).[9]

Besides land in crops, permanent pasture and range grazing lands are an important source of our food supply. Alsberg estimated that the land area suitable for pasture alone was about the same as the 6.4 billion acres of potential cropland.

Nearly one-half the land area of the world is made up of snow and ice fields, tundra, desert or semidesert, and high mountains. Yet these lands are not unimportant agriculturally. Many semidesert and mountain areas

[6] Carl Alsberg, "The Food Supply in the Migration Process," in *Limits of Land Settlement*, p. 43, Council on Foreign Relations, New York, 1937.

[7] O. E. Baker, "The Population Prospect in Relation to the World's Agricultural Resources," *Maryland,* the alumni publication of the University of Maryland, College Park, Md., 1947.

[8] Frank A. Pearson and Floyd A. Harper, *The World's Hunger,* p. 48, Cornell University Press, Ithaca, N. Y., 1945.

[9] Charles E. Kellogg, "Food Production Potentialities and Problems," *Journal of Farm Economics,* Part 2, Vol. 31, No. 1, pp. 251–262, February, 1949; and Robert M. Salter, "World Soil and Fertilizer Resources in Relation to Food Needs," *Science,* Vol. 105, No. 2734, pp. 533–538, May 23, 1947.

furnish grazing to domestic animals and feed for wildlife. Also, some tracts of arid and semiarid land are irrigated by waters collected from the high mountains and other areas not intensively used for agriculture.

*Table* 12. Cultivated and Arable Land of the World

*Acreage of cultivated land,*
*billions*

Estimates of cultivated cropland, 1937 to 1939, compiled by State
    Department, assisted by Office of Foreign Agricultural Relations\*. . 2.6

Estimates of cultivated land, 1947, by R. M. Salter and others of
    Bureau of Plant Industry, Soils and Agricultural Engineering†. . . . 3.2
Estimates of additional land which could be cultivated if needed
    (somewhat similar to or better than that in cultivation in the Phil-
    ippines and in Finland)‡. . . . . . . . . . . . . . . . . . . . . . . . . . . . . . . . . . . 1.3
    Total cultivated land and additional areas suited to cultivation. . . . 4.5

\* Cropland planted and fallow. Data are believed to be somewhat comparable to the total of cropland harvested, failure, and fallow for the United States. Cropland harvested 1935 to 1937, about 2.4 billion acres. Estimates of cropland used, 1935 to 1937, compiled by O. E. Baker, for a World Atlas of Agriculture, also totaled about 2.6 billion.

† From address by R. M. Salter at the annual meeting of the AAA, Boston, Mass., December, 1946. Subsequently published in proceedings. The estimate was given as a range of 7 to 10 per cent of the world land area, cultivated, or from 2.6 to 3.6 billion acres. Arable land as used here evidently includes some pasture and grazing land judged to be tillable but not actually cultivated. Estimates from various atlases and articles in geographic journals place the arable-land figure at 4 to 6 billion acres, or about 15 per cent of the world's land area. (Land area of world is 35.7 billion acres.)

‡ Estimate of additional arable land is based to some extent on both physical and economic possibilities as judged after review of what is being done in land use in various countries of the world. This estimate is not the limit of physical possibilities, however, if additional land is needed. More land could be brought into cultivation by drainage, irrigation, and addition of fertilizers, etc.

These calculations deal with immense areas and probably are correct only within a very wide margin. The extent to which land areas are used or are available for use in agriculture reflects not only the physical characteristics of the land but also the state of the arts and general economic conditions. All use of land for crops requires at least some improvement and preparation involving work and materials—very little new land is simply waiting for the plow. Most of it requires clearing, much needs drainage, and some must have irrigation to make it productive. Most of the undeveloped land is far removed from present transportation and other facilities, and roads, electric power, medical facilities, telephones, and local industry must go along with land development and settlement. Many areas will need terraces and contour farming to prevent erosion. Large acreages will require cover crops, lime, and fertilizer.

Much new land is being added gradually to the areas under cultivation in the United States, Canada, Mexico, Brazil, Australia, Indonesia, Finland, the Philippines, the Soviet Union, India, Pakistan, some of the African states, and several other countries.

For many countries such as the United States, the over-all prospect for increasing agricultural production will probably depend more upon efforts to raise crop and livestock-product yields on lands now in use than upon possible extensions of the area of cropland. It has been estimated that it would be practicable to increase production of most agricultural items in the United States by about 20 per cent under economic conditions of full employment.[10] Considering the relative state of the agricultural arts throughout the world, equivalent or greater increases could be secured in most countries from the better application of known techniques. According to Kellogg, the estimated food needs for the world in 1960 can easily be handled by production from the new areas that can be brought into use and the more intensive or improved use of the lands now under cultivation. From a physical standpoint, there is little reason for assuming that the world cannot supply sufficient food production to support a population of around 3 billion persons by the year 2000.

Recent publications have questioned, however, whether technological advances in agricultural production and land improvement for the world as a whole are keeping pace with needs as they have in the United States.[11] And after reviewing estimates of the productive land resources of the world and potential trends in population, Black and Kiefer conclude that "except in the newer countries and in those with possibly expanding frontiers, the foods needed for a continuously expanding population cannot be produced. In some of them the foods needed for adequate diets for their present populations cannot be produced within their own boundaries."

It must be recognized that although the world still has a great potential for increasing its total food supply, this potential is not evenly distributed on either an area or a per capita basis. As a matter of fact, the prospects for increased production often appear greater in sparsely populated areas than in areas with dense population. The extent to which this potential is uti-

[10] *Production Adjustments in Agriculture,* Land Grant College, U.S. Department of Agriculture Report, 1947; and *Peacetime Adjustments in Farming: Possibilities under Prosperity Conditions,* U.S. Department of Agriculture, Miscellaneous Publication 595, 1945.

[11] Cf. John D. Black and Maxine E. Kiefer, *Future Food and Agriculture Policy,* pp. 119–138, 146–147, McGraw-Hill Book Company, Inc., New York, 1948; *The State of Food and Agriculture, 1948: A Survey of World Conditions and Prospects,* Report of the Food and Agriculture Organization, pp. 24–32, September, 1948; Fairfield Osborn, "Crowded Off the Earth," *Atlantic Monthly,* March, 1948, and "The Country That Can Feed the World," *Atlantic Monthly,* April, 1948; William Vogt, *Road to Survival,* William Sloane Associates, New York, 1948; Pearson and Harper, *op. cit.*

lized will depend upon a combination of factors—economic, political, and social. The relative intensity with which the peoples of various countries will use their lands will depend upon the interaction of the factors of supply and demand and upon their ability to employ capital, labor, and technological know-how in their development and use of the earth's resources.

### Crop and Pasture-Land Requirements

Consideration already has been given to the problem of population pressure and the joint effect of population numbers and nutritional standards on the demand for food and other land products. This over-all demand factor is particularly important in the computation of agricultural land requirements because it provides a measure of the total food and other production that is desired. With this production goal established and with the available data on land productivity, it is possible to indicate the approximate acreages needed in production.

In this discussion of land requirements, attention will be given to (1) the changing demand for crop and pasture lands, (2) the numerous factors that affect the future requirements for these types of land, and (3) the general outlook on cropland requirements.

*Changing Demand for Crop and Pasture Lands.* The population upswing of the 1940's was accompanied by significant gains in the dietary and other living standards enjoyed by the average American. These gains add up to an increasing demand for agricultural products.[12] Far from suggesting long continuation at any one time of the problem of farm surpluses that plagued American agriculture throughout most of the interwar period, this trend suggests that the demand for food products and, more particularly, "our demand for milk, meat and other animal products will become such as to put pressure upon our ability to expand output of these products."[12]

During temporary periods, as in 1949 and again in 1953, stocks of specific agricultural products may be larger than required for the current year; but generally, as indicated by recent trends in production and requirements, fairly good stocks are in the public interest, to avoid shortages in periods of drought and to provide the needed reserves for national defense.

In addition to the trend toward increasing demand for land products, the decade of the 1940's witnessed a number of other significant trends and developments that also affect the demand for crop and pasture lands. Among the most noticeable changes in farming were the increased use of farm power and machinery, the decrease in number of farm workers, the

[12] Joseph S. Davis, "Our Amazing Population Upsurge," *Journal of Farm Economics*, Vol. 31, pp. 765–778, November, 1949.

decline in number of farm work stock, and the increase in use of fertilizer and lime. Also important were the increase in acreages planted with improved seed, the substitution of legume hay for grass hay, and improved pastures and better feeding practices for livestock.

An insight into the changing land requirements for food production in this country is provided by the following comparison of some basic data for the two 5-year periods 1918 to 1922 and 1940 to 1944, both of which were periods of high farm and industrial activity. During the 1940 to 1944 period the total population of the United States was approximately 26 per cent larger than during the 1918 to 1922 period. Yet on the average, each person in the later period consumed nearly 10 per cent more farm products than in the earlier period, and at the same time harvested acreages for all uses decreased about 3 per cent.

More than 50 per cent of the increased production available for the larger population has come from improved crop and livestock yields. About 30 per cent resulted from the crop acreage formerly required for feeding the large number of horses and mules needed before substitution of tractors, and about 20 per cent from acreages required in the past for producing products for export.

Another significant change appears in the fact that the number of persons living on farms in 1950 approximated 25 million, some 7 million fewer than in 1910 when the total population was about 92 million. In other words, less than 1 person in 6 is now a farm resident, while 40 years ago 1 out of 3 lived on a farm. Farm employment in 1950 was between 11 and 12 million persons, including family laborers and part-time workers. A large number of those now living on farms are engaged in other than agricultural work and in the strictest sense of the term are not full-time farmers.

*Acreages used as cropland.* The general trend in cropland use for specified purposes between 1910 to 1949 is shown in Table 13. During the 1945 to 1949 period an average of 375 million acres were used for crops. Of this total 297 million acres were used for food, fiber, and tobacco for domestic consumption, 48 million for producing export products, and 30 million for producing feed for horses and mules. Of 365 million acres used for crops in 1920 to 1924, 55 million were used for producing export products, 85 million for feed for horses and mules, and 225 million for producing food, fiber, and tobacco for domestic consumption.

Among the outstanding facts shown by Table 13 are the general stability in the cropland requirement for domestic consumption, around 2.1 to 2.3 acres per capita from 1910 to 1949; the great decrease in cropland acreage required to feed farm work stock; and the wide fluctuation in cropland used to produce export products. The cropland requirements for domestic consumption, exclusive of feed for work stock, averaged 2.06 acres per

*Table* 13. Average Acreage and Utilization of Cropland for Specified Purposes (Harvested Cropland, Failure, and Fallow), United States, 1910–1914 to 1945–1949°

| Year | Total cropland† | | Acreages used for producing export products, millions | Acreages used for producing— | | | Total population July 1, millions |
|---|---|---|---|---|---|---|---|
| | | | | Feed for horses and mules, millions | Food, fiber, and tobacco for domestic consumption | | |
| | Million acres | Per capita | | | Millions | Per capita | |
| 1910–1914 | 337 | 3.55 | 44 | 90 | 203 | 2.14 | 95 |
| 1915–1919 | 359 | 3.49 | 52 | 92 | 215 | 2.09 | 103 |
| 1920–1924 | 365 | 3.32 | 55 | 85 | 225 | 2.05 | 110 |
| 1925–1929 | 374 | 3.14 | 48 | 74 | 252 | 2.12 | 119 |
| 1930–1934 | 381 | 3.05 | 34 | 64 | 283 | 2.26 | 125 |
| 1935–1939 | 373 | 2.89 | 24 | 55 | 294 | 2.28 | 129 |
| 1940–1944 | 371 | 2.75 | 20 | 42 | 309 | 2.29 | 135 |
| 1945–1949‡ | 375 | 2.60 | 48 | 30 | 297 | 2.06 | 144 |

* Cropland acreages planted or seeded, and cultivated or fallow land, excluding cropland used as rotation pasture and cropland temporarily idle.

† Five-year averages of total cropland acreages for chart, p. 21, *Changes in American Farming* by S. E. Johnson, U.S. Department of Agriculture Miscellaneous Publication 707, December, 1949, and revised table on utilization of harvested cropland, June 27, 1950.

‡ The acreage figures shown for export products, feed for horses and mules, and for domestic products, 1945 to 1949, are preliminary and subject to revision.

capita during 1945 to 1949. Total cropland acreage for all purposes averaged 2.6 acres per capita.

*Acreages used as pasture.* In the development of the United States the relative importance of pasture lands has gradually declined as more and more of these lands have been pressed into cultivation. To some extent this tendency has been offset by the general expansion of the farm pasture area at the expense of lands not in farms. The area used exclusively for pasture in the United States decreased from over 1 billion acres in 1880 to about 800 million acres in 1949, or from about 20 acres per capita to a little over 5 acres per capita. In addition to the 800 million acres of grassland and arid woodland, there was some grazing on about 220 million acres of forest and cutover woodland and on about 80 to 100 million acres of cropland temporarily used as pasture, such as winter grain, stubble fields, harvested cornfields, and hay aftermath (Table 14).[13]

Conversion of the acreage figures on our semiarid and arid grazing lands

[13] This area of 800 million acres excludes commercial forest and farm woodlands pastured but includes considerable brush and semiarid shrub land.

Table 14. Pasture and Grazing Land, Continental United States, 1950*

| Land use | Acreage, millions | Percentage of total |
|---|---|---|
| Cropland used as rotation pasture†...................... | 69 | 6.8 |
| Permanent farm pasture............................... | 416 | 40.8 |
| Grazing land outside farms‡........................... | 215 | 21.0 |
| Total nonforested pasture and grazing land............. | 631 | 61.8 |
| Arid woodland, shrubs, and brushland................... | 100 | 9.8 |
| Total land used chiefly for pasture.................... | 800 | 78.4 |
| Woodland and forest grazed........................... | 220 | 21.6 |
| Grand total.......................................... | 1,020 | 100.0 |

* Estimate January, 1952.

† Cropland used for pasture is included also under cropland in Table 9, p. 196.

‡ Federal, state, and private land. Other public and private lands grazed are included in arid woodland and forest grazed.

to the equivalent carrying capacity of the humid and subhumid pastures indicates that our total pasture area would represent an equivalent of about 2.0 acres of humid and subhumid pasture per capita (not counting land in hay aftermath, stubble fields, and winter grain pastures, nor pastured forest lands). In Germany, a roughly corresponding figure for 1935 was only about $\frac{1}{10}$ acre per capita, while in England, where pasture economy is much more prevalent than in Germany, the per capita area of pasture, including "rough grazing," was approximately $\frac{1}{3}$ acre, and in France, including alpine pastures, a little over $\frac{1}{3}$ acre per capita. The low per capita pasture figures in the European countries is made possible in part by employment of feed crops and imported feeds to supplement pasture. They also have a lower consumption of dairy and beef products per capita.

## Future Requirements for Crop and Pasture Land

As was pointed out earlier, the amount of land devoted to the production of food and agricultural raw materials depends principally upon our habits of consumption, the size of population, the productivity of our land, and the extent of our foreign trade in farm products. In determining our future requirements for crop and pasture-land use, it is first necessary to explore somewhat further the effect that these factors are likely to have on future needs.

*Population and Diets.* During the years that are ahead the population of the United States can reasonably be expected to exceed substantially the 1953 population of 160 million. If a high level of employment and income is maintained throughout the next two decades, there will also be further advances in dietary levels, including the spread of better diets to all income groups.

Much work has been done in recent years by the Bureau of Human Nutrition and Home Economics and other groups in planning and testing different-cost adequate diets. Three standard diets have been generally accepted in studies of food and land requirements, namely, a liberal-cost adequate diet, a moderate-cost adequate diet, and a low-cost adequate diet. Of these three different-cost diets, the most expensive would satisfy food preferences most fully.[14]

A study by the Bureau of Agricultural Economics of the food resources available to meet these different diet standards concludes that with average recent yields, about 160 million people could be furnished the average 1943 to 1945 civilian diet from the cropland equivalent then available.[15] Furthermore, assuming the extension of the 1941–1945 average yields in those cases where more production may be necessary, from the available cropland resources about 140 million people could be supported with the liberal-cost adequate diet, about 170 million with the moderate-cost, and 200 million with the low-cost adequate diet suggested by the Bureau of Human Nutrition and Home Economics.

An adequate diet at moderate cost, for the 1952 population of 157 million people, would require the equivalent of over 90 per cent of the present cropland acreage with average recent crop yields, but some shifts would be desirable between crops to allow for greater amounts of livestock products, fruits, and vegetables. The liberal diet for the 1952 population would necessitate considerable increase in consumption of livestock products, particularly milk and milk products and high-grade meats, and probably would require an increase of 25 million acres in cropland to allow more land for hay, rotation pasture, fruits, vegetables, and other necessary uses.

From 70 to 80 per cent of the harvested cropland of the United States is employed in the production of food for human use or feed for livestock. Of the total used for food or feed, about three-fourths is employed for

[14] *Planning Diets in New Yardstick of Food Nutrition: Low Cost, Moderate Cost, and Liberal,* p. 14, U.S. Bureau of Human Nutrition and Home Economics, 1941 (processed).

[15] Raymond P. Christensen, *Efficient Use of Food Resources in the United States,* U.S. Department of Agriculture Technical Bulletin 963, pp. 35–44, 1948. In this study, pasture was converted to a harvested-cropland-equivalent basis by computing the acreage of tame hay that would be required to provide the same quantity of feed as that supplied by pasture. Average 1941 to 1945 crop yields were used. About two-thirds of the 2.7 acres harvested-cropland equivalent per capita in 1943 to 1945, or 1.8 acres, were cultivated crops; one-third, or 0.9 acre, was the cropland equivalent of pasture.

producing livestock or livestock products for food. Hence changes in diet affecting the consumption of livestock and livestock products exert a preponderant influence on land requirements. Between 1910 and 1940 a number of significant changes occurred in the character of American consumption of farm products (see accompanying illustration). A marked decrease occurred in consumption of cereals and potatoes for human food. Meanwhile, the per capita consumption of fruits and vegetables increased. This increase in fruits and vegetables, however, has involved only a small acreage of cropland. There has been a considerable increase in consumption of dairy products, fats and oils (including butter and margarine), meat, poultry, eggs, and fish, especially since 1940.

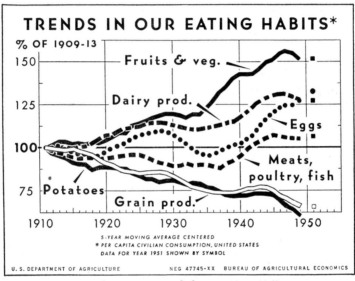

Trends in our eating habits, 1910 to 1950.

Although our food habits have changed significantly, the per capita acreage required for our food needs, as earlier indicated, has changed very little during the past 40 years. The use of more livestock products that require larger acreages of land for their production has been offset to some extent by increased crop and livestock production per unit.

As it is always possible that population pressure might necessitate economies in consumption of products that require large areas of land in proportion to the amount of food produced, it is of interest to explore the possibilities in this direction. The greatest possibility for economy in land requirements by changes in consumption takes the form of less consumption of those products which require large areas of land per capita to produce a given quantity of food value. Present statistics indicate a wide range in per capita crop- and pasture-land requirements for various important classes of food products in supplying the number of calories required for the average individual's consumption (about 1,200,000 to 1,300,000 calories per year).[16]

For example, sufficient calories could be obtained to support a person with present production rates from about 0.3 acre of sugar cane or sugar beets; 0.5 acre of potatoes or corn; 1.0 acre of wheat; 2.1 acres of cropland for feed to produce pork and lard; and 7.5 acres for feed to produce dressed beef plus 2.3 acres of pasture.

From the standpoint of land requirements beef is evidently the most costly type of food, and a country characterized by heavy population pressure is likely to reduce greatly the per capita use of beef in favor of the consumption of more pork products and poultry. Lamb, except as a by-product of wool production, is also likely to be greatly economized except in so far as it can be produced on wastelands unsuitable to cultivation. Milk and its products are more economical per crop acre than swine as a source of protein but require a considerably larger area of improved pasture. Nevertheless, dairy products constitute so important an element in the diet, particularly of young people, that a considerable quantity of milk is likely to be retained in the diet even in countries subject to serious population pressure. To a considerable extent maritime nations will replace meat and milk by a large consumption of fish. Tree fruits require much more land than bush fruits or vines, which is one of the reasons for the extensive consumption of the products of the grape in the southern European countries.

Wheat is the most expensive of the cereals, in terms of land requirements. In countries subject to severe population pressures it is likely to be displaced in considerable measure by potatoes or rice, or by such other cereals as rye and oats which yield a larger cereal product per acre, especially on inferior lands. As a source of human food, corn is much more economical than the small grains and apparently about on a par with potatoes. By adopting the average European diet with its larger dependence on cereals and vegetables and relatively smaller dependence on meat and other livestock products, it would be possible to reduce very sub-

[16] *Nutritive Value of the Per Capita Food Supply, 1909–1945*, U.S. Department of Agriculture Miscellaneous Publication 616, pp. 6–11; and *Supplement for 1949 to Consumption of Food in the United States, 1909–1948*, U.S. Department of Agriculture Miscellaneous Publication 691, pp. 18–19.

From 1909 to 1949 the number of calories available from the per capita food supply ranged from 3,200 per day to 3,510. The daily average was more than 3,400 during most of the years from 1909 to 1931, with the exception of a short period during and after the First World War. From 1933 to 1938 the average each year fell below 3,300, with the low at 3,200 in 1935, a year of both economic depression and drought. From 1940 through 1945 the average number of calories each year fluctuated between 3,340 and 3,430 per capita per day. The average calories per capita for the 1945 to 1949 period was 3,310.

stantially our per capita arable acreage requirements. Let us trust, however, that this will not come to pass.

*Crop and Livestock Production per Unit.* More crop production was secured per acre in the United States in 1948 than in any other year through 1951. The sharp increase in production per acre and per animal unit of livestock from 1940 to 1948 has been a major factor in the high levels of farm production during the past decade. While numbers of livestock have increased, total acreage of cropland has changed very little since 1920 (Table 15 and the accompanying figure). Changes in acreage of cropland and in production per acre, however, have not been

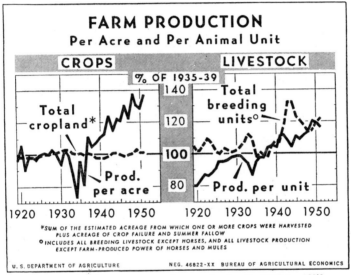

Farm production per acre and per animal unit, 1920 to 1950.

uniform among the geographic divisions of the United States. Over the last quarter of a century, the acreage of cropland has increased on the fertile soils in the Mississippi Delta and in the Western states and decreased in the poor-soil areas in the eastern part of the country. The net result has been relative stability in acreage for the country as a whole with an upward trend in production of crops per acre.

The production per acre and per unit of livestock averaged 28 per cent and 13 per cent greater, respectively, for the 5 years 1945 to 1949 than for prewar years 1935 to 1939. These increases in productivity constitute an unprecedented break from previous trends (Table 15). Because of the nature of the factors leading to increased production per acre during the past 10 years, agriculture has definitely moved to a higher production plane from which it will probably not recede.

*Table* 15. Production per Acre and per Animal Unit, 1910 to 1951
(1935–1939 = 100)

| Years | Total cropland | Crop production per acre | Animal units | Production per animal unit |
|-------|----------------|--------------------------|--------------|----------------------------|
| 1910–1914 | 90 | 100 | * | * |
| 1915–1919 | 96 | 98 | * | * |
| 1920–1924 | 98 | 98 | 105 | 85 |
| 1925–1929 | 100 | 101 | 101 | 95 |
| 1930–1934 | 102 | 92 | 107 | 95 |
| 1935–1939 | 100 | 100 | 100 | 100 |
| 1940–1944 | 99 | 117 | 119 | 108 |
| 1945–1949 | 101 | 128 | 118 | 113 |
| 1950 | 101 | 128 | 119 | 119 |
| 1951 | 101 | 128 | 122 | 116 |

* Not available.

SOURCE: *Agricultural Outlook*, p. 10, U.S. Bureau of Agricultural Economics, 1952.

The possibilities for further expansion of production within the next few years have received considerable attention in recent years.[17] It has been estimated, for example, that the wartime volume of farm output could be increased by 20 per cent under average weather conditions if improved production methods now available were adopted to the extent profitable, if farm prices averaged parity, and if necessary soil-conserving practices were put into effect. A 10 per cent increase in food output from the 1943 to 1945 average may be considered reasonable by 1960. This moderate increase would be only about 5 per cent greater than the average production for the 1945 to 1949 period. On the other hand, there is a possibility that over-all food production might be cut by as much as 10 per cent for a few years because of severe droughts, disease, or insect damage. Between these two extremes is the possibility that food production under normal weather conditions during the 1950's may average about the same as in the 1945 to 1949 period.

*Requirements for Pasture Lands.* Theoretically, crops, pastures, and forests compete for specific areas of land surface on the basis of comparative advantage. Locally such competition may at times be significant, particularly as between cultivation and use as high-grade pasture. Even in a country as crowded as England it is found that pasture is more profit-

[17] Cf. *Peacetime Adjustments in Farming: Possibilities under Prosperity Conditions, op. cit.*, U.S. Department of Agriculture Miscellaneous Publication 595, 1945; also *Long-Range Agricultural Policy: A Study of Selected Trends and Factors Relating to the Long-Range Prospect for American Agriculture*, pp. 43–47, U.S. Bureau of Agricultural Economics, for the Committee on Agriculture of the House of Representatives, 80th Cong., 2d Sess., Committee Print, Mar. 10, 1948.

able than cultivation on considerable areas of high-grade land. Nevertheless, from a broad national standpoint, crops usually have first choice, while pasture or grazing uses and forests are the residual claimants.

To a considerable extent crops and pasture are complementary uses, in the sense that they jointly contribute to production of livestock and livestock products and are capable of being used more or less interchangeably in the process. It was estimated in 1947 that 34 per cent of the total feed units employed for livestock were supplied by pasture. When all pasture and range land is converted to a cropland-equivalent basis, this area equals 152 million acres. The area of land employed for pasture in the production of livestock products may be greatly economized by employment of supplementary feed produced on arable land, or vice versa. Therefore, pasture requirements are somewhat less absolute than those for arable uses.

Any substantial increase of pasture area would come at the expense of either cropland or forests. The replacement of large areas of crops by pasture is unlikely, other than temporarily in periods of surplus crop production, except for arable areas which have deteriorated seriously from erosion or overcropping and some of the high-hazard cropland in the western edge of the Great Plains. However, there are good possibilities for increasing pasture acreage and production in parts of the United States, as in the Southeast, by improving, fertilizing, and reseeding present pasture, as well as by clearing and seeding abandoned cropland, brushland, and suitable bottomland areas.

The carrying capacity of our humid and subhumid pastures is considerably less than that of England and Wales, Germany, France, Denmark, and other countries of western Europe. This suggests the possibility of meeting some of our pasture requirements by improved methods of utilization. Pasture- and grazing-land resources, their requirements, present and future, and the means to develop and maintain them deserve continuous study in connection with current agricultural programs.

*Situation with Regard to Conservation Measures.* Land-use capability and soil surveys show that about 90 per cent of the estimated permanently arable area of the United States will require much more protection than it now receives if it is to remain continuously in cultivation. According to conservation-needs estimates prepared by the Soil Conservation Service, the following protective measures involving use of the cropland are essential: (1) cover crops are needed annually on 34 million acres, (2) green-manure crops on 55 million acres, and (3) crop rotations on 213 million acres. In order to carry out these measures, a reduction of grain and other soil-depleting crops on present cropland will be necessary to permit the planting of cover and green-manure crops and installation of rotations containing hay and pasture crops.

If these soil protection and maintenance measures are carried out, it will be necessary to lengthen the rotation of grain crops and many other crops, such as cotton and soybeans, and develop additional cropland to permit longer rotations and increased production. It is estimated that an equivalent of 20 to 40 million acres of cropland would be fully occupied every year by cover crops, green-manure crops, and other needed conservation measures. In other words, an allowance of a minimum of 20 million acres in cropland is necessary to permit proper use to maintain and increase production.

*Exports and imports.* An additional factor that must be considered in any projection of future land requirements involves the special circumstances that affect the exchange of products with other regions of the world. An active export program can have a significant effect upon both agricultural prosperity and agricultural land requirements. On the other hand, any marked recession in the export demand for farm products may contribute to agricultural surpluses and to lower returns to the agricultural enterprise.

The intensification of nationalism in the period between the First and Second World Wars, which took the form of many obstructions to the flow of commerce, together with the increased potency of competition from countries producing for export and the increased self-sufficiency of buying countries, led to a notable decline in value of agricultural exports from the United States. The acreages of cropland used to produce export products decreased from an average of 55 million acres in 1920 to 1924 to 24 million acres in 1934 to 1939, then fluctuated between 20 and 48 million acres during the war and postwar years 1940 to 1949. Most of the decline between the two world-war periods occurred after 1929, when the requisite area was about 50 million acres.[18] In addition to the cropland areas used for the production of exports, some pasture lands also are employed for this purpose.

In the past, two products, wheat and cotton, have accounted for much, if not most, of the acreage employed for export production. Tobacco, vegetables, and fruits are of considerable importance so far as value of product and the employment they afford to farm population are concerned, but they represent a relatively small amount of arable land. Other than fats and certain special items, we have ceased to employ any considerable amount of land for exported livestock products except in periods of unusual circumstances, such as war or other calamities. Only about 10 per cent of the total acreage of arable land in use (including rotation pasture, fallow, crop failure, and idle land) was used for producing ex-

[18] *Farm Production Practices, Costs and Returns*, U.S. Bureau of Agricultural Economics Statistical Bulletin 83, pp. 22–23, October, 1949. (Crop acreages harvested adjusted to exclude duplication due to double cropping and to include land being fallowed preparatory to planting.)

ports from 1945 to 1950. It appears improbable that we shall soon witness any marked increase in the proportion of our arable land needed for this purpose, particularly judging from past trends in exports, the recovery of agriculture in Europe, and the decrease in the expenditures for foreign aid programs.

In addition to our production for domestic use and export, the United States also obtains certain agricultural products from abroad. Coffee is one of the most important of our agricultural imports, and it cannot be produced effectively in the continental United States. It is physically possible to produce silk and tea, but at such excessive costs that we are unlikely to do so, and besides, the manufacture of silk substitutes is quite successful. We produce a part of our sugar supply but only under a quota system with tariff protection, and it does not seem likely we shall greatly expand the cultivated acreage devoted to this purpose in the interest of materially lessening our dependence on foreign sources of supply. While this country produces a plentiful supply of cotton both for domestic use and for export, it imports small quantities of a few special classes of cotton. The United States is self-sufficient in production of certain types of wool but finds it economically desirable to import considerable quantities of other types.

*Outlook for Crop- and Pasture-Land Requirements.* In view of our knowledge and assumption regarding (1) population numbers in the United States and the medium projection rate for population growth by 1960 and 1975, (2) current domestic consumption levels, and (3) average yields and their effect on the general cropland requirements for various purposes, it is now possible to give objective consideration to the outlook for the future crop- and pasture-land requirements of this country. The estimated cropland requirements for domestic consumption and other purposes in 1960 and 1975, assuming continuation of the 1945 to 1949 consumption and acreage-yield levels, are summarized in Table 16.[19] The estimated cropland requirements for the same periods with the assumption of certain specified upward adjustments in consumption levels and acreage productivity also are indicated.

Assuming the same cropland rate per capita as employed in the 5 years

[19] Cf. Byron T. Shaw, *The Job Ahead for Agriculture,* Testimony before the House Subcommittee on Agricultural Appropriations, Feb. 5, 1952, and *The Role of Research in Meeting Future Agricultural Requirements,* paper presented at the forty-fourth annual meeting of the American Society of Agronomy, Cincinnati, Ohio, Nov. 18, 1952 (processed); *A Water Policy for the American People,* Vol. 1, pp. 154–166, The President's Water Resources Policy Commission, 1950; *Agricultural Production in the Defense Period,* Land Grant College, U.S. Department of Agriculture Report, 1952; and *Reserve Levels for Storable Farm Products: A Study of Factors Relating to the Determination of Reserve Levels for Storable Farm Products,* Supplement I, "Historical Variations in Crop Yields and Production," pp. 17–30, 82d Cong., 2d Sess., S. Doc. 130, 1952.

*Table* 16. Projected Cropland Acreage Requirements for 1960 and 1975
assuming 1945 to 1949 Consumption Levels and Acre Yields
(In millions)

| Item | 1935–1939[a] | 1945–1949[a] | 1960[b] | 1975[b] |
|---|---|---|---|---|
| Population[c] | 129 | 144 | 171 | 193 |
| Cropland, acres: | | | | |
| Cropland for domestic consumption— | | | | |
| food, feed, fiber, and tobacco[d] | 294 | 297 | 352 | 398 |
| Other cropland requirements: | | | | |
| Export | 24 | 48 | 40 | 40 |
| Feed for horses and mules[e] | 55 | 30 | 15 | 7 |
| Cover and soil-improvement crops[f] | 35 | 31 | 25 | 25 |
| Total cropland requirements | 408 | 406 | 432 | 470 |
| Cropland equivalent of pasture and grazing land[g] | 156 | 150 | 164 | 183 |
| Total cropland equivalent | 564 | 556 | 596 | 653 |

[a] Actual cropland acreage requirements, including cropland harvested, crop failure, summer fallow, cover and soil-improvement crops, etc.

[b] Projected cropland acreage requirements, including items specified in footnote a.

[c] Population estimates and projections are from census data presented in the President's Materials Policy Commission Report, Vol. 5, p. 63, and the President's Water Resources Policy Commission Report, Vol. 1, p. 154.

[d] Includes acreage for growing feed for livestock used in producing livestock products and relatively small acreages used for producing certain industrial products.

[e] Requirements for feed for horses and mules: 10 million head, 1945 to 1949; 6 million, 1960; 4 million, 1975.

[f] Reserve for cover and soil-improvement crops. Includes idle cropland in 1935 to 1939 and 1945 to 1949.

[g] Cropland equivalent of pasture is in terms of feed produced. Requirements for 1960 and 1975 are in proportion to 1945 to 1949 requirements.

SOURCE: Unpublished data and calculations from the U.S. Department of Agriculture. Compare President's Water Resources Policy Commission, *A Water Policy for the American People*, p. 159, 1950.

1945 to 1949—2.06 acres for domestic consumption—352 million acres of cropland will be required for the expected population of 171 million in 1960.[20] In addition, the acreage required for feeding necessary workstock is estimated at 15 million acres for 1960. Maintenance of our cropland makes it necessary to allow 25 million acres for cover and soil-improvement crops. Production of crops for export possibly would add 40 million additional acres, to bring the total cropland acreage required to 432 million by 1960. This is 26 million acres greater than the average acreage employed during the 1945 to 1949 period.

Moving on to 1975, if we follow the present trend in production and

[20] Total planted cropland and fallow acreages, without cover- and soil-improvement-crop acreage and the equivalent of pasture acreage.

consumption levels and population growth that has been taking place, approximately 470 million acres of cropland will be needed to supply necessary products for the expected population of 193 million people and to meet other requirements. To supply an adequate diet as defined by the Bureau of Human Nutrition and Home Economics to the whole population expected in 1975 possibly would raise the present consumption level by about 15 per cent. This would add another 70 million acres of cropland and make the total required 540 million acres (exclusive of the cropland equivalent of pasture).

If crop yields and livestock production efficiency should be increased by 15 per cent from 1950 to 1975, then the cropland acreage required might be only about 50 million acres above the amount used 1949 to 1951. Thus even with allowance of a substantial increase of 15 per cent in productivity per acre, an adequate diet for the whole population would require 460 million acres of cropland in 1975, instead of the 406 million acres in the 1945 to 1949 period. A gain of 25 per cent in productivity per acre, or an average increase of 1 per cent per year, would be necessary to supply our food and fiber needs in 1975 from the cropland area available in 1950.

Because of our dependence upon livestock and livestock products for a substantial portion of our food supply, it is necessary to consider the requirements for pasture and grazing land as well as cropland. The cropland equivalent of pasture and grazing land based on feed value was estimated at 150 million acres for the period of 1945 to 1949. When the cropland equivalent of pasture required at the 1945 to 1949 production level is added to the cropland acreage projections based on 1945 to 1949 consumption levels and acre yields (Table 16), it gives a total cropland equivalent of 556 million acres in 1945 to 1949, 596 million acres in 1960, and 653 million acres in 1975. In other words, to maintain present consumption levels we shall need an increase of approximately 20 per cent in pasture production by 1975, either from a gain in productivity per acre or from a greater improved pasture acreage, possibly both.

Shifting from assumptions based on the current situation to assumption of a 15 per cent increase in both consumption and productivity, a total cropland equivalent of 638 million acres would be needed in 1975. The gain in productivity, however, is contingent on comparable improvement in farm technology. Much depends upon research to improve crops and livestock and to control pests, as well as upon rapid dissemination and acceptance by producers of modern methods. Likewise, improvement of dietary standards depends upon maintenance of a high level of average income among all workers and the widespread adoption of more adequate diets by large groups. While these figures are only projections of current trends and are based on stated assumptions as to production, consumption, and population changes, they do indicate the magnitude, the complexity, and the urgency of the problems involved in future agricultural land requirements.

Maintenance and improvement of the present cropland and pasture base to provide for the needed expansion in production in the next decade will be highly desirable from a national standpoint. Over the longer-run period 1950 to 1975, it will be desirable to improve systematically for cultivation and rotation pasture from 50 to 60 million additional acres of the best undeveloped land to ensure its availability for crops when needed and to increase its carrying capacity as pasture. This goal could be accomplished by development of 2 to 2.5 million acres per year. Moreover, more efficient methods of producing, processing, storing, and distributing food products should be sought because they would make profitable a larger volume of production and enable consumers to have more food for the same, or possibly less, expenditure.

### Forest Land Requirements

Forests are a basic resource, and the country needs a continuing supply of forest products for industrial and other uses. The forest products industries are themselves an important segment of America's industrial strength. Each year they produce several billion dollars' worth of lumber and other commodities. The forestry industry as a whole, including harvesting, manufacture, transportation, and use of wood products, is a source of livelihood for several million people. In 1946 it afforded work equivalent to 3.3 million full-time jobs and wages totaling 6.3 billion dollars.

Productive forests also are needed for much besides their timber. Today, more than ever, the country needs to protect its soils and watersheds, to guard against rapid run-off, erosion, and damage to water supplies. Growing forests help to provide this protection and at the same time provide the nation with definite recreational and scenic values. Because of their multipurpose use and value, it is to the national interest to encourage and foster forest production just as it is to the national interest to encourage food production.

The Forest Service, through its forest survey, has been working on a national inventory of the forests for two decades, but the job is far from done. Only two-thirds of the 620 million acres of forest land in the United States has been initially inventoried. Resurveys of one-half the area previously inventoried are needed to bring the results of the initial survey up to date. This is especially necessary because heavy cutting during the war period, combined with normal depletion and growth before and since, have brought marked changes in the forest-cover and timber volume.

With minor local exceptions, it is neither desirable nor necessary to use lands needed for cultivation or pasture for forest purposes. Some of the land now in cultivation, however, may so deteriorate that forest cover may be found desirable, temporarily at least, as a means of protection or restoration. The use of many of the less productive crop and pasture lands for forests is not practicable. Most of the 588 million acres of arid and semiarid pasture, for example, are not capable of growing commercial timber trees, although over 100 million acres do support growth of forest shrubs, such as pinyon-juniper and chaparral, and other noncommercial forest plants. The distribution of forest land is shown in Table 17.

*Table* 17. Distribution of Forest Land of Continental United States by Regions, 1950
(In million acres)

| Region | Commercial forest | Noncommercial forest | Total |
|---|---|---|---|
| North.......... | 146.5 | 9.1 | 155.6 |
| South.......... | 206.7 | 35.7 | 242.4 |
| West.......... | 104.0 | 118.0 | 222.0 |
| Total........ | 457.2 | 162.8 | 620.0* |

* Includes about 14 million acres of forested land in parks and other areas withdrawn from commercial timber production.

Source: *Forests and National Prosperity*, U.S. Department of Agriculture Miscellaneous Publication 668, p. 15, 1948, and subsequent related reports.

*Land Available for Forest Use.* In spite of the widespread clearing of forest lands for crop and pasture use in years past, the nation is still abundantly provided with lands that are primarily suitable for forest use. It has been estimated that around 262 million acres find their "absolute," or optimum, use in forestry. A somewhat comparable acreage is physically capable of employment for other purposes but under present conditions is retained in forest. During the next 25 years about 25 to 30 million acres of the more fertile of these lands may have to be diverted from forest to crops and improved pasture.

With the continuing programs of forest improvement and management, a reduction of up to 10 per cent in the commercial forest area need not seriously affect our future timber supply. Tree planting and natural restocking on abandoned farm land in the hill and mountain areas of the Eastern states will in part offset the land clearing in the Coastal Plains, the Mississippi River Delta, and the Pacific Northwest.

According to official estimates the nation had a total commercial forest area of 457 million acres in 1950 (Table 17). In addition it had about 163 million acres of noncommercial woodland, including arid woodland such as pinyon-juniper, chaparral, and mesquite. Thus, the estimated area physically suitable and available for growing commercial timber represents about three-fourths of the total forest area. The better and more accessible forest sites are of course in this class. Of the 457 million acres of commercial forest land, 205 million acres are covered with old-growth or second-growth saw timber. About 71 million acres are classed as poorly stocked, seedling and sapling and denuded area; about 86 million as fair to satisfactory restocking seedling and sapling area; and 95 million acres as pole timber and cord wood, some of which, however, could grow into saw timber if permitted. The entire stand of timber on commercial areas, including trees 5 inches in diameter breast high and over, is estimated at 470 billion cubic feet, of which 154 billion cubic feet is pole timber. In terms of saw timber there are approximately 1,600 million board feet.

The forest area, physically suitable and available for growing commercial timber, is therefore not quite 3.1 acres per capita. This is far more ample than the corresponding available area in western European countries where there is less than half an acre of forest land per capita. At the same time, it is less ample than in Canada and some of the predominantly forested regions of northern Europe.

*Forest Drain and Growth.* The per capita rate of consumption of forest products is very largely a function of the relative opulence of the supply, for it is possible to get along with relatively small amounts by employment of substitutes. In this country the per capita drain on forests has been much higher than in most nations of advanced economic development. This situation can be attributed largely to (1) our relatively high per capita area of forest land, (2) high-volume production based on the liquidation of already mature forests rather than operations conducted strictly on a "sustained yield basis," and (3) the relative cheapness of forest products and the effect of this price factor in inducing wasteful methods of appropriation.

Since 1906 the rate of forest drain has tended to decline, although with considerable fluctuations attributable to changes in business conditions. This decline has come as a result of increasing population pressure, the cutting out of the more available supplies of timber near the centers of consumption, and a general upward trend in finished timber prices. Per capita consumption of timber is likely to decrease even more in the future when the present period of liquidation of accumulated forest resources is replaced by more complete dependence on annual growth. The costs associated with reforestation and the holding of growing timber will doubtless lead to higher prices, which in turn will tend to reduce consumption, unless public subsidies are made available in the interest of lessening the cost of timber or stimulating consumption.

In 1944, the total annual drain was estimated by the Forest Service at 13.7 billion cubic feet and the annual growth 13.4 billion feet. Return of private building activity since the war probably has resulted in an increase of the drain to about 15 billion cubic feet in 1950. About nine-tenths of the drain is due to cutting. The remainder is the work of fire, insects, diseases, and natural causes.

Whereas our long-range need is to build up productive growing stock, the past trend of timber volume has been in the other direction. The 1945 figures show 43 per cent less saw timber than was given in reports by the Department of Commerce for 1909, and 9 per cent less than was estimated by the Forest Service for 1938. The decline since 1909 probably has been greater than indicated since early estimates necessarily were incomplete as to small properties and tree species and sizes then considered of non-commercial value.

About 80 per cent of the present drain is in saw timber, particularly the better softwoods, whereas much of the growth is in small low-grade trees and inferior hardwoods. Nearly half the drain is occurring in the South, which has only 28 per cent of the nation's timber, while about one-fourth each occurs in the North and West, which have 21 and 51 per cent of the timber, respectively. Growing stock east of the Great Plains is badly depleted, and the land generally is understocked.

Comparison of growth and drain is an instructive but often overworked criterion of the nation's forest situation because of the great difference between regions as to forest conditions, forest species, stage of depletion, and demand for timber. The near balance between timber drain (13.7 billion cubic feet) and timber growth (13.4 billion cubic feet) is deceiving. These figures mask the fact that for softwoods the demand is great, resulting in a drain of 21 per cent more than growth, while for hardwoods, with a smaller demand, the drain is 17 per cent less than growth. Furthermore, four-fifths of the drain is in saw timber. Saw-timber drain is more than 50 per cent greater than saw-timber growth. The nation cannot be satisfied with a balance based on poles and saplings when its building and forest industries depend so largely on saw timber.

Assuming an average annual drain of 15 billion cubic feet, or about 100 cubic feet per capita, an annual drain of about 17.5 billion cubic feet would be required for a population of 175 million. Provision for this volume of timber on the present forest area calls for a material increase in production by improvement in average rate of growth, prevention of losses by fire, insects, and disease, and reduction of waste in cutting and use. Such an increase appears practicable in view of what is being done on many well-managed forests and the good possibilities for increasing timber production on farm woodlands through better practices.

On areas where good growth is occurring, particularly on those where the species and quality of timber are desirable, it is known that rate of growth could be accelerated by affording greater protection against fire, disease, and insect enemies, and by other types of improved forest management, such as thinning, removal of weed trees, and planting desirable species.

Thus it appears probable that when necessary readjustments are effected to increase the rate of growth in relation to the acreage employed, an area even smaller than that physically adapted to forest growth will be sufficient to satisfy our reasonable requirements for forest products. In fact, it is doubtful that the diversion to cultivation of present forest and cutover lands which are characterized by soil and climate suitable for farm crops will necessarily reduce the forest area below that capable of satisfying the probable demand for forest products. The accomplishment of these results, however, will require significant readjustments in our forest policies and programs and in the attitude of the public toward the care and management of forest land.[21]

### Requirements for Other Surface Uses of Land

In addition to the land requirements for cropland, pasture, and forest use, considerable areas are needed for certain other purposes, such as residential, industrial and commercial, transportation, mining, recreational, and a variety of service uses. It has been estimated that by 1975 approximately 80 million acres will be required for urban, suburban, transportation, mining, and service-area purposes. In addition, it is estimated that approximately 42 million acres will be required for national parks and for state and county parks, an increase to approximately double the area devoted to these purposes in 1950. Wildlife refuges are estimated to justify the employment of approximately 38 million acres of land, which is a very large expansion beyond the approximately 5 million acres used for this purpose in 1950.

Much of the increase in lands for recreation and wildlife may consist of multiple use of some present forest and grazing areas and of wastelands that would not be suitable for timber production or crop and pasture use. They are an addition, also, to extensive provisions in publicly owned forests for recreation and wildlife conservation. Over and above the lands suitable for the various uses which we have discussed, there will remain a total area of about 50 million acres the surface of which is capable of little or no agricultural use. This area is made up of desert lands not grazed, swamps and tidal marshes not used, beaches and sand dunes, rock and other barren land.[22]

[21] Much of the information contained in this section on forest-land requirements was obtained from the following publications: *Forests and National Prosperity, A Reappraisal of the Forest Situation in the United States,* U.S. Department of Agriculture Miscellaneous Publication 668, 1948; and *Basic Forest Statistics for the United States,* 1950.

[22] The above estimates for needed parks and wildlife areas are from the National Resources Board, *Report on National Parks and Public Works in Relation to Natural Resources,* pp. 108–109, December, 1934. While the above estimates are made as of 1960, it is doubtful that material change in the figures would occur as of 1975.

## General Outlook

Because of the nature of world food needs, there is a general feeling that several long-range measures must be adopted to maintain land resources in productive condition. Many farmers, as well as technicians, feel that the recent drain on soil must be eased and a better balance attained between row crops, close-growing crops, legumes, and grasses. Some ground was lost in soil and water conservation during the Second World War. Increased hay and pasture will mean less cultivated cropland and require more roughage-consuming livestock. Similarly, some of the semi-arid lands and the hill lands plowed for crops during the war should be returned to grass. At the same time, development of new cropland will continue through irrigation in the West and by clearing and drainage, particularly in the Mississippi Delta and the Atlantic and Gulf Coastal Plains. On many farms wet lands can be drained and profitably used for crops, and adjoining erosive hill lands can be returned to grass or forests.

Recent research shows that with the technological advances being made, the prospect for agricultural land utilization is generally favorable. Only moderate increases in the amount of improved land devoted to agriculture will be needed in the United States during the immediate future.[23] In their analysis of the agricultural production and food situation, Black and Kiefer assert that the cropland of the United States can range, without difficulties, except those of readjustment, from 300 to 400 million acres, and that no great obstacles stand in the way of expanding it to 500 million acres and even more.

The food situation in the United States appears favorable when the average consumption level is compared with diets in some areas. Nevertheless, there are serious deficiencies among the low-income groups, in both urban and rural areas. New-land development and improvement, adoption of more diversified systems of farming, an increase in productive efficiency, increase in the number of family farms, and a more adequate average diet are among the major fields in which an advance should be made.

The world has many hunger areas where increased production from new land and technical improvements are urgently needed. Without sufficient food for the population of the world, peace is uncertain, and sustained progress toward a better standard of living for the average citizen of the world unlikely. No country or people can expect permanent

---

[23] Cf. Charles E. Kellogg, *The Soils Men Live By,* lecture for the Graduate School, U.S. Department of Agriculture, Nov. 15, 1948; Robert M. Salter, *New Horizons for Agriculture,* address at the American Farm Bureau Federation Annual Convention, Atlantic City, N.J., Dec. 13, 1948; Christensen, *op. cit.,* pp. 15–17, 54–58; "Food Production and Civilian Food Consumption Per Capita, United States, 1925–48," *The National Food Situation,* October–December, 1948–1949, U.S. Bureau of Agricultural Economics Outlook Issue for 1953; and Black and Kiefer, *op. cit.*

security while others live in continual dread of hunger or of displacement by less fortunate population hordes who are seeking to better their lot. If the world is to be adequately fed and clothed, there must be a continuation of the search for increased efficiency in agriculture and greater production at lower costs per unit of output.

The land supply and production potential is great enough to provide for all the people of the earth in the next century if the land is properly developed, maintained, and used. But it does not follow that this is an easy job or that it will be achieved. Many social, economic, and political obstacles to world-wide improvement in use of land resources as well as physical problems must be faced and must be dealt with before the world can be fed adequately. In the case of improvement in production techniques, the United Nations, including the United States and many other countries, stand committed to the principle of helping farm people everywhere to help themselves, so they and their countrymen can live in health and enjoy increased happiness.

## CHAPTER 10

*Development and Settlement*

*of Agricultural Land*

Attention has been given in the two preceding chapters to the problems of increasing population pressure, agricultural land requirements, and the supply of land available for human use. Most analysts agree that considerable areas, both in the United States and in the world at large, can be developed for commercial agricultural use. The process of converting undeveloped and underdeveloped lands into productive fields, pastures, and forests or woodlots, however, often is an expensive one. Land seldom becomes a productive economic factor without considerable expenditures of time, effort, and money on its development.

*Land-Development Costs*

The development and settlement of new land areas almost invariably involves large cost outlays. These costs can be classified as (1) capital investments, (2) time costs, and (3) social costs.

The importance of investment and working capital in the land-development process is especially apparent in the world today. It makes little difference whether an individual farmer is using a bulldozer to clear a few acres of land, or a drainage district is using power equipment to dig or dredge its ditches, or the Federal government is erecting a mammoth dam to provide and store water for irrigation or other purposes. In almost every case, considerable capital outlays are needed for the equipment and personnel used on land-development projects.

Most of the frontier lands in this country were settled and developed by people who had very little cash to invest. With this fact in mind, it may seem somewhat paradoxical that major emphasis should now be placed on the capital-outlay aspects of land-development costs. It should be recognized, however, that the pioneer settlers usually paid dearly in time, hard work, and privation for the farms they carved from the wilderness. The old saying that "it takes three generations to make a farm" implicitly recognizes the importance of land-development costs.

Much of the frontier was settled by people who were content to live and work on a near-subsistence basis while they developed their farms and waited for thriving communities to arise and for markets to develop for their produce. These settlers were usually motivated by other than strictly commercial and profit incentives. Today the situation is somewhat different. Desirable "free" and low-cost lands are no longer available. The easiest-to-develop lands are, for the most part, already in production. Development of the areas that remain almost invariably calls for large capital expenditures—very often expenditures that cannot be justified on a private-investor basis if the investor thinks in terms of early returns or profits from his investment. This high-capital-cost aspect of new land development is accentuated by the current emphasis on commercial developments and expectations of early returns. Very few land developers are willing to wait years, if not generations, for their projects to pay out.

Those costs that arise from the accumulation of tax and interest charges and the forbearance of profits on funds invested in new developments are called "time costs."[1] These costs usually accumulate between the initial investment of funds in a project and the time when the project begins to pay its way.

If time costs involve merely the time period required for clearing land, growing a crop, erecting a building, or laying out and constructing an irrigation project, they are called "waiting costs." Sometimes these costs accumulate over relatively short periods of time. But in the case of growing forests and huge reclamation projects, many years may pass before the forest crop can be harvested or the project can be put into operation.

When additional time costs arise because no effective demand has as yet developed for a new project or because of upward adjustments in tax assessments based on anticipated higher values, etc., the costs can be described as "ripening costs." High ripening costs are experienced in all premature developments. Numerous premature subdivisions were laid out in the post–First World War period with the hope that the newly developed lots would soon be sold. In those cases where the hoped-for ready markets failed to materialize, subdividers frequently found their initial investments as well as their anticipated profits swallowed up by mounting ripening costs.

Farm-land developments also have been plagued at times by the specter of ripening costs. Excellent examples of this situation appeared all along the frontier during every business-depression period of the nineteenth century. Land speculators and settlers on partially developed farms

---

[1] Cf. Richard T. Ely and G. S. Wehrwein, *Land Economics*, pp. 145–150, The Macmillan Company, New York, 1940.

frequently lost their properties through tax reversion or abandonment because they could not pay the ripening costs that accumulated during the years they had to wait for changing price and demand conditions to ripen their lands for economic development. A more recent example may be found in the various cutover regions where hundreds of once optimistic settlers have abandoned their cabins and clearings and where numerous investors have lost money speculating on cutover lands. The original error in these cases may be traced to the overoptimism of the early settlers and investors regarding the prospects of these lands for economic development. Over the long run, the problem of the cutover regions may be simply one of premature development and excessive ripening costs.

Another type of cost concept which sometimes is associated with time costs is that of "supersession costs." These costs have some of the characteristics of time costs, but they really represent a special type of development cost that arises from shifts in what appears to be the optimum use of land. Because of their cost nature, supersession costs frequently loom as an important factor in operator decisions relative to land-use changes. A dry farmer, for example, may hesitate to shift to irrigation, even though it may be economic over a period of time for him to do so, because of the initial cost of providing his land with canals, lateral ditches, and the equipment and know-how needed for successful crop cultivation. Similarly, a grain farmer may hesitate to shift to dairying even though his land may be ripe for this use because of the cost of supplying dairy buildings, starting a herd, and shifting from his established pattern of farming.

In some cases, as in the tearing down of a house to make way for a commercial establishment, supersession costs also may involve the writing off of old investments. Supersession costs actually represent a forbearance of income if the individual fails to change to the higher use and capital-outlay costs plus the possible writing off of past investments if he should decide to do so. Supersession costs can have more than a temporary effect in discouraging or preventing changes in land use that may seem economic and desirable. In some cases, they can prevent desirable changes for long periods until new owners with greater foresight or investment capacity take over.

The problem of social costs frequently is ignored in discussions of land development and settlement. These costs often seem subtle and incidental but they are nonetheless real. The settlement of any new area calls not only for settlers who will uproot themselves from their past surroundings and face the necessary readjustments, uncertainties, and possible perils of the new area; it also calls for the establishment of new communities and community services.

It would be difficult indeed to place a monetary value on the various social costs that accompanied the settlement of the United States. Not only did the pioneers have to start from scratch in developing farms and villages and in providing houses, schools, roads, communities, and community services, they also faced the prospect of Indian wars, plagues, and at times near-famine. The importance of these costs often was overlooked in the new settler's enthusiasm for acquiring land and helping to build a new world. Nevertheless, it should not be forgotten that most of the progress made in capital accumulation along the frontier found its roots in self-effort and privation.

While there may be some tendency to minimize the social costs associated with past land settlements, the problem of social costs assumes paramount significance in considerations of prospects for large-scale new land settlements in areas such as the tropics or Alaska. Not only is there the problem of recruiting and transporting settlers to these areas and then providing markets for their produce; there are also numerous critical problems involving the development and maintenance of transport and communication facilities, and the provision of adequate community, health, and housing facilities. These social cost factors—in combination with other development-cost and economic and political factors—provide an important barrier to the immediate development of the more promising undeveloped sections of the world.

## Prospects for New Land Development

In the light of this brief discussion of the nature and importance of land-development costs, consideration should be given to the general prospects for new land developments in the United States.

*Amount of Land Available.* In 1950 the United States had an estimated 40 million acres of fair to good undeveloped land that probably could be developed at costs not unreasonable in relation to costs of the recent past. As Wooten and Purcell have observed:[2]

Of this total, some 20 million acres which need clearing and drainage, scattered over the country, could be made into arable farm land by measures that seem feasible; five million acres of fertile Mississippi River Delta land can be made available by clearing, drainage, and additional protection from floods; and it is estimated that possibly as much as 15 to 20 million acres of dry land can ultimately be reclaimed through irrigation and related improvement.

These figures represent the estimated limits of physical development for perhaps 25 years or more. Under conditions likely to occur in the foreseeable future, not more than half of this further potential for irrigation and drainage will probably be developed. Even if economic conditions warrant, development probably could not be pushed to such a point for some years because of

[2] H. H. Wooten and Margaret R. Purcell, *Farm Land Development: Present and Future*, U.S. Department of Agriculture Circular 825, p. 4, October, 1949.

the time, materials, machinery, and manpower required for providing necessary public services and for improving the land.

Surveys have indicated that there is, from a physical standpoint, a significantly larger acreage that could be cleared, drained, or irrigated for crop production. In many instances, however, the quality of these lands would be lower than that of present cropland, and costs of development high or very high. Part of the land that could be developed at moderate costs is already in farms and is used for pasture or allowed to grow up into brush and trees. In all probability, there are more than 85 million acres of undeveloped lands in need of clearing, drainage, or irrigation that would be more productive for crops than much cropland now in cultivation.

The development of new cropland areas gives rise to problems of interarea competition. The justification of new developments depends both on their prospective competitive position and on the subsidies required for their development. Even if the crop-production prospects of a new area suggest that it can compete with or undersell the crops grown in already developed areas, questions may be raised regarding the desirability of using large public subsidies to bring new lands into use when their development will result in immediate losses to already developed areas because of the competition from increased production. Obviously, some new lands can and probably will be developed without any form of public subsidy, but this is not true for major developments.

While it may be possible to grow certain crops, such as potatoes and sugar beets, more economically in new areas than in areas where they are now grown, this fact in itself does not necessarily justify subsidies to bring new areas into production. This is particularly true where the crops produced are already in surplus supply. Too much of a commodity is certainly enough without more of it. The imminent need for greater food supplies, because of threats of war, crop failure, trade disruptions, or increasing population pressure, however, may justify the development of areas that will probably be needed for food-production purposes in the not-too-distant future.

Some will contend that the answer to the interarea-competition problem is not to grow more potatoes or sugar beets but rather encourage diversified and soil-conserving crops. Unfortunately, however, grains, pasture, and the extensive types of crops usually provide lower returns per acre than the more intensive culture crops. When and where high development costs arise, land settlers usually find it necessary to rely to a considerable extent on intensive crop culture. The per-acre cost of development is a determining factor. It is not practicable to spend as much as $300 or $400 an acre to irrigate pasture land.

*Irrigable Areas.* Approximately 26 million acres of harvested cropland and pasture were irrigated in the United States in 1950 as compared with about 21 million acres in 1940. During the past 10 years the average annual increase in acreage under irrigation has been around 500,000 acres.

The two principal potentials for further irrigation in the United States are (1) development of new areas in the arid parts of the country, and (2) supplemental irrigation in areas of inadequate or poorly distributed rainfall. Irrigation in these areas reduces the hazards of drought and assures larger yields than natural rainfall will produce.

An early inventory of lands in the West estimated that ultimately about 51,535,000 could be irrigated. This exceeds by over 25,000,000 the area now irrigated.[3] Most authorities now feel that this early estimate is too high and assume that a potential of 15 to 20 million additional acres of Western lands can be irrigated. To assure a dependable source of water for this acreage, it will be necessary to protect the watersheds by sound management practices. Many more thousands of acres of land in the Western states are suitable for irrigation than there is accessible water to irrigate them.

As of 1948, the Bureau of Reclamation had in projects under construction, authorized, being investigated, or proposed for irrigation development some 13.2 million acres of new land, plus about 7.8 million acres to which additional water would be supplied. The breakdown by states is shown in Table 18. It may be noted that big new-land irrigation developments are planned for Montana, Nebraska, North Dakota, South Dakota, and Wyoming in the Missouri Valley, and Oregon and Washington in the Columbia Basin. In the other major basins, a higher proportion of the proposed developments are designed to provide additional water to establish irrigation areas. The present expansion of irrigation in the 17 Western states should bring 5 to 10 million additional acres into production during the next 25 years.

Some of the new developments in the Missouri Basin are in the sub-humid region. Undoubtedly, much will be learned from these projects regarding the problems that will arise from the operation of irrigation projects on a standby and security-against-drought basis. Some of the problems that may arise are: Will the farmers keep up their ditches when not needed? Will the hope for rain delay the application of water beyond the critical time most needed? What about costs when water is not regularly used?

The area in the humid region subject to supplemental irrigation has expanded tremendously since the Second World War. Between 1939 and 1949 the area east of the Mississippi actually irrigated by this means increased from 166,000 to 518,000 acres. Farm equipment was available for the supplemental irrigation of a somewhat larger acreage in both of these years but was not used because of favorable rainfall conditions. For many

[3] *Ibid.*, p. 7.

Table 18. Summary of Estimates of Potential Irrigation Development, United States, by Regions and States
(In acres)

| Region and state | Area irrigated, 1949* | Further development under way and proposed by Bureau of Reclamation, 1948† | |
|---|---|---|---|
| | | New lands | Supplemental water |
| Pacific: | | | |
| Washington.................. | 618,129 | 1,546,800 | 108,170 |
| Oregon....................... | 1,337,517 | 1,065,580 | 211,700 |
| California.................... | 6,598,839 | 1,763,500 | 2,110,000 |
| Total...................... | 8,554,485 | 4,375,880 | 2,429,870 |
| Mountain: | | | |
| Idaho....................... | 2,167,879 | 792,390 | 978,430 |
| Nevada...................... | 722,896 | 97,800 | 99,780 |
| Arizona...................... | 979,114 | 254,535 | 607,660 |
| Utah........................ | 1,166,972 | 158,647 | 271,725 |
| Montana..................... | 1,808,576 | 1,037,160 | 342,900 |
| Wyoming.................... | 1,474,835 | 838,100 | 332,710 |
| Colorado..................... | 2,943,895 | 722,045 | 1,882,315 |
| New Mexico................. | 691,476 | 210,287 | 146,250 |
| Total...................... | 11,955,643 | 4,110,964 | 4,661,770 |
| Plains: | | | |
| North Dakota................ | 35,759 | 1,222,810 | 0 |
| South Dakota................ | 84,356 | 1,013,110 | 23,300 |
| Nebraska.................... | 887,239 | 1,137,840 | 20,960 |
| Kansas...................... | 140,992 | 237,020 | 830 |
| Oklahoma................... | 44,209 | 231,592 | 600 |
| Texas....................... | 3,150,527 | 881,200 | 624,300 |
| Total...................... | 4,343,082 | 4,723,572 | 669,990 |
| Total 17 Western states..... | 24,853,210 | 13,210,416 | 7,761,630 |

* Bureau of the Census, *Irrigation of Agricultural Lands*, 1950, Vol. 3.
† Data from Bureau of Reclamation as released through the National Reclamation Association, January, 1948.

crop areas in the humid region, this type of irrigation has little to offer. For the areas and growers of specialty crops plagued by occasional, if not frequent, critical shortages of plant moisture, however, supplemental irrigation not only guarantees crop production but often permits higher yields than could be expected under normal rainfall conditions.

Interest in supplemental irrigation stems from (1) development of new types of portable, lightweight irrigation equipment, (2) advances in farm techniques, (3) increased application of high-grade fertilizers that require more moisture for optimum use than is supplied by natural precipitation, and (4) the postwar levels of farm income that have both permitted and favored substantial investment in new equipment.

*Clearing and Drainage Areas.* Recent major developments in the clearing and drainage of land are of interest because of what has taken place in different parts of the country. Most of the new land development in the Northeastern states has involved the addition of small acreages to truck, fruit, potato, dairy, and poultry farms through the removal of brush, stumps, trees, or stones. In the level coastal-plain area of Delaware and Maryland, however, farms have benefited from drainage. The major emphasis in land-development work in this area has been on the enlargement and improvement of existing farm units.

In the Lake states area there has been a general increase in the average size of farms. Much of this increase has resulted from a reduction in the total number of farm operating units and the addition of the holdings of earlier operators to adjoining farms. Farm enlargements also have resulted in many cases—particularly in the cutover counties—from land-clearing and -development activities on existing farms. There has been some development of new full-time farm units.

Land-clearing activities also have been important in the Pacific Northwest where considerable new farm acreages were developed during the 1940's. Rather large areas have been reported cleared under the agricultural conservation program of the Federal government. Numerous families that were attracted to the coast before and after the Second World War have cleared new farm lands either because of a real desire to establish permanent homes or as a possible hedge against unemployment.

The Mississippi Delta promises more in the way of new land development through clearing and drainage activities than does any other area in the United States. As has been pointed out, this area has thousands of acres of potentially good crop and pasture land that must be cleared, drained, and protected against flood and backwater-overflow conditions before it can be made productive. During the past 20 years several million acres of agricultural land have been developed for farming in this area.

An example of the general problem involved in developing the delta lands is provided by a recent report on methods and costs of clearing land in northeast Arkansas.[4] This study indicates that "thousands of acres

---

[4] George F. Jenks and Robert W. Harrison, *Methods and Cost of Clearing Land in Northeast Arkansas*, Arkansas Agricultural Experiment Station Bulletin 495, June, 1950. For other descriptions of land-settlement and -development problems along the lower Mississippi, see Robert W. Harrison and Walter M. Kollmorgen, "Past and Prospective Drainage Reclamations in the Coastal Marshlands of the Mississippi

of bottomland" have been reclaimed since the Second World War and that this has resulted in the development of many new farms and the enlargement of hundreds of established farms. Landowners and farmers have made substantial investments in land-clearing equipment, such as tree saws, stump saws, bulldozers, and winches. Almost all clearing is being done by local interests. Only in a few instances are the clearing activities sponsored by corporations or holders of tracts of unusual size. Little attempt has been made to develop lands for sale.

The ownership of undeveloped land in eastern Arkansas is widely distributed. Many homesteaders of depression days continue to hold woodlands purchased from the state. Frequently, holders of this type have developed the higher land along the streams and now hope to clear the remaining low-lying woodlands. As the undeveloped holdings of these farmers are naturally small, the question of economic size in relation to clearing machinery and methods is of great importance.

Many owners of commercial farms hope to shift production to new land where yields are high and to retire their older fields to pastures or other uses. Much undeveloped land has been purchased in anticipation of this adjustment.

A large proportion of the new land settlers in the delta area during the depression period found by their third or fourth year of operation (the first or second payment year) that they were unable to clear land, construct buildings, and pay for their farms at the agreed purchase rate. Many of them had to give up their farms when the first payment fell due even though they already had built a shack to live in and had cleared several acres of land. When mortgage holders foreclosed and got the land back, the work performed by the settler, of course, added to the value of the land. This additional value represented part of the loss suffered by the unsuccessful settler and was, in fact, a "subsidy" to those who foreclosed.

Sometimes the second or third settler on a particular farm merely took over the original contract, perhaps paying the former settler a small amount of cash for the improvements. Often, however, these settlers bought from the people who had foreclosed on the previous settlers, paying higher prices than for uncleared land, because of the value added by the other settlers' uncompensated work.

*Impact of Economic and Institutional Factors.* The prospect for new agricultural land development in the United States is affected as much by economic and institutional factors as by the physical availability of

River Delta," *Journal of Land and Public Utility Economics,* Vol. 23, pp. 297–320, August, 1947; also their study *Drainage Reclamation in the Bartholemew-Boeuf-Tensas Basin of Arkansas and Louisiana,* Arkansas Agricultural Experiment Station Bulletin 476, April, 1948.

new land areas that are susceptible of development. On the economic side, the question of whether new lands will or should be developed depends to a considerable extent upon the market demand or anticipated market demand for the products from the additional land. So far as institutional factors are concerned, new land developments can be fostered, directed, or controlled by rural zoning ordinances, public land-ownership or management programs, specific reservations of undeveloped areas for special uses, and credit, subsidy, and other programs designed to foster land settlement or development.

Market prices and the demand for the products of new lands may have only a limited effect upon subsistence operators. In our present commercial market economy, however, the usual operator is interested in profits either now or in the future. Accordingly, new lands will not be developed, or once developed will not be maintained, if the anticipated returns from these lands fail to justify their development or maintenance. True, submarginal lands have been brought into use. Usually, however, these lands have been developed by overoptimistic or misguided settlers, groups, or agencies.

Practically all of the low-cost and easy-to-develop agricultural lands in this country have already been brought into agricultural use. Most of these lands have remained in developed farms or pastures. Some of the less productive lands, however, have been abandoned and have slipped back to less intensive uses. In some areas submarginal land purchase programs, zoning ordinances, public land-management programs, and other institutional measures have been employed to take or keep the less productive and less advantageously located lands out of farm use.

In any over-all analysis of the prospects for new land development, it is wise to remember that the economic justification for the development of any particular tract of land can change rapidly with changes in market demand, development costs, and technology. Increasing population pressure and an increase in the market demand for agricultural products may make it economically profitable to develop many areas now regarded as submarginal. Similar adjustments may result from a reduction of development costs or from the introduction of new practices that lead to higher yields or lower costs. On the other hand, just as higher farm prices, bigger yields, or lower costs may push down the economic margin of production, lower prices or yields or higher operating or development costs may encourage the retirement of additional marginal lands from use.

*Land Improvements on Existing Farms.* As the foregoing discussion suggests, a substantial portion of the land area that can be brought under cultivation at reasonable cost is already in existing farms. From the beginning of colonization in this country, it has been a common practice for settlers to buy or purchase more land than they have expected to use for intensive crop culture. Over time, most of the lands in these farms have been put to agricultural use, but many potentially productive croplands are still used as woodlots, unplowed pasture or meadowland, and as open range.

Most of the lands within established farms that are considered suitable for cultivation under present conditions can be brought into use rather easily through land clearing and plowing. The problem with these lands often is one of individual initiative and owner or operator estimates regarding the potential productive value of the land. Not only must the owner feel that the land to be cleared is potentially productive, he also must feel that it would be desirable so far as his farm program is concerned to put his land to a higher use. This means that he must weigh his need for more cropland against his need for pasture or a woodlot. With the present emphasis on livestock programs and on conservation practices, he may prefer to leave his land in its present state. In some cases he may choose to bring new lands into use but at the same time retire some of his fields that are now in cultivation to less intensive uses. Because of the spatial distribution of the various grades of land, it is inevitable that the operators of the best lands will tend to hold some of their lands out of cultivation for other less intensive uses, while operators in poor land areas will have comparatively inferior lands in cultivation.

A surprising amount of land-clearing activity has taken place in recent years. Land-clearing operations have been going on for years in many areas, but the increasing use of tractors, bulldozers, and other power equipment during recent years for removing stumps and rock piles and for land leveling has somewhat simplified the problems of land clearing and development. During the 1935–1950 period the Department of Agriculture made agricutural conservation payments for land-clearing operations on 2,454,161 acres (391,810 acres in 1950).

Many of the most significant land-development and -improvement activities on established farms center in the use of practices designed to step up or upgrade the productive capacity of already partially developed lands. Among the more notable examples of these measures are the recent advances in the use of commercial fertilizers, liming, green-manure crops, crop rotations, terracing and strip cropping, field tiling and drainage, flood-control measures, and irrigation practices. In many cases these land-improvement programs have been sponsored by individual initiative and financed entirely on a private basis. Many of the improvements have resulted, however, from the payment and acceptance of agricultural-conservation payments for specific practices. In 1950, for example, payments were made for the application of lime to 11,390,829 acres, phosphate to 21,895,229 acres, potash to 8,437,616 acres, and for the leveling of 377,439 acres for irrigation purposes. Many of these activities also are promoted and carried on by group organizations such as those represented by soil conservation, flood control or levy, drainage, and irrigation districts.

### Land-Settlement Program Following the First World War

In the settlement of the Eastern colonies and the Western frontier most of the initial new land development came at the hands of the settlers themselves. Group action and the assistance and direction provided by governments, railroad colonizers, and settlement-promotion companies were important. But the decision of the settlers to move to new areas and the progress they made in clearing, reclaiming, and developing "their" lands stemmed largely from individual initiative.

Colonization offices often were set up by state and local governments. Favorable land-disposal policies were put into operation. Special military bounties were granted to veterans, and large land grants were made for educational purposes and for the building of railroads and other internal improvements. But up until the present century the activity of the government and of many of the colonization agencies engaged in the settlement movement ended with the encouragement and provision of lands for settlement. The problems of developing the land almost always were left to the settler.

Since the enactment of the Reclamation Act, and more particularly since the First World War, public interest in land settlement has tended to shift from the mere provision of raw land in prospective settlers to the provision of partially, if not completely, developed farms. The nature of some of the problems that have arisen is described in the sections that follow.

*Federal Programs.* During and immediately following the First World War, a number of proposals were made for Federally sponsored land-settlement programs designed to aid veterans. Settlement plans were recommended as early as 1915, and in 1918 a postwar land-settlement plan was developed by representatives of the Departments of Agriculture and Labor, and the Reclamation Service of the Interior Department.[5] Under the plan developed and submitted to Congress, the state governments were to furnish the land, and the Federal government was to provide $100 million to be used in reclaiming land, improving it, and providing farm buildings.[6] The plan visualized the development of about 25,000 new farms, with full payment for the land to be spread over 40 years at 4 per cent interest.

[5] E. Jay Howenstine, *The Economics of Demobilization*, pp. 80–81, Public Affairs Press, Washington, 1944.

[6] *Annual Report of the Secretary of the Interior*, 1918, pp. 32, 36.

In spite of the widespread publicity and early support received by the plan, it did not receive favorable consideration in Congress. Opposition to the proposal grew among farmers and farm organizations. Many people felt that the government already had gone too far in encouraging land settlement—often on lands upon which it was impossible to make a decent living. Shortly after 1920, mounting farm surpluses provided an additional argument against furtherance of the settlement movement. Established farmers were not in favor of an expansion of the agricultural area to their own detriment.

Another deterrent factor centered in the fear that the settlement plan had inadequate safeguards to prevent speculation and to provide for sound farm-community development. Many people felt that there was greater need at the time for improving existing rural communities than for establishing new ones. There was also considerable doubt that substantial numbers of war veterans were seriously interested in clearing, draining, and improving new land in order to get established on a farm. Many veterans seemed to be more interested in speculation or the wishful hope that something worth while might accrue to them through an opportunity on a land-settlement project.

Although a Federal land-settlement program for veterans did not develop after the First World War, provision was made for the training of disabled veterans for work in agricultural occupations, including professional work, and under certain conditions aid was given in buying equipment and livestock. Preference also was given veterans in the homesteading of public lands and in obtaining farms on reclamation projects.

*State Settlement Programs.* After the First World War a number of states undertook active programs to provide new-land farms for veterans. Through state land-settlement departments and often with the assistance of state colleges of agriculture a number of projects were launched for the development of farms on cutover, drained, and irrigated lands. It was argued that great opportunities were to be found on the land and that its "best use" was for agriculture. Legislatures appropriated money for the distribution of literature on agricultural opportunities through state land-settlement departments or state Departments of Agriculture, and this thesis was further expanded by advertisements in the press, in farm journals, and in Chamber of Commerce literature. Several states also had farm credit programs to enable veterans and, in some cases, others to buy farms. In brief, many states sponsored an aggressive promotion of land settlement, often on lands unsuited to tillable agricultural use. Also, they placed altogether too many persons on the land who had neither the experience nor aptitude for successful farming.

At times the settlement promoters were unscrupulous money grabbers who engineered high-pressure sales campaigns. Most of the land boomers probably expected great developments. But regardless of whether they did or did not, many of them still operated on the philosophy of getting all possible while the getting was good and let the buyers beware.

State encouragement was given to many private colonization schemes, and private promoters usually backed the state settlement projects and, more particularly, the state programs for assistance in colonization and settlement. In California, for example, private colonization efforts prompted the establishment of a state Land Settlement Board in 1917. This Board made liberal funds available on relatively low-interest terms for the provision of land and homes for settlers.

The well-known Durham and Delhi projects were established in California through the use of these funds. These two projects started out under fairly favorable circumstances. Troubles started, however, as soon as farm income levels dropped during the agricultural depression of the 1920's. Once their incomes started to decline, the settlers found it difficult, if not impossible, to maintain reasonable standards of living. Discouragement followed, and many settlers soon became delinquent in their payments. Under these circumstances few new buyers were attracted to the projects. By 1928, only 54 per cent of the land in the Delhi project had been sold.

Interestingly enough, less than 10 per cent of the settlers on the Durham project were war veterans, while only about half of them were experienced farmers. On the Delhi project the proportions were about a third and two-fifths, respectively. These data seem to support the concern felt by some members of Congress that veterans were not particularly interested in developing farms in new land areas.

In 1931, the California legislature decided that the state should write off its $2.5 million investment in the Durham and Delhi projects and withdraw from the land-settlement business. This loss was unfortunate, but losses on land-settlement projects are by no means unusual. Indeed, they occur in a high proportion of the total cases, particularly on those projects started or developed during periods of unfavorable price conditions.

Several reasons can be given for the short-run losses experienced on many new-land-settlement projects. Often they grow out of mistakes in selecting lands of limited rather than high productive capacity for development. They also result from the difficulties associated with the recruiting of suitable settlers. One other serious problem stems directly from the emphasis placed upon commercial developments. The development of new farms as going concerns, if accomplished over a short period of time, generally costs more, even in the best agricultural areas, than the new farm is worth in the market once it is developed. The process of reclaiming land, laying out farms, erecting houses, service buildings, and fences, and installing necessary improvements is at best an expensive one. Investments in new farms often are justified over extended periods. In the short run, however, it is not at all surprising that they often seem high in relation to the market values placed on comparable farms developed in earlier periods.

A 1944 survey of the Durham project showed that the size and type of farm did not differ much from that originally planned.[7] However, there had been some consolidation of units on the poorer soils and some subdivisions on the better soils. Approximately a fourth of the units were still owned by the original settlers. In general, the level of well-being appeared to be about as good as in other areas in the state of similar type of farming. In the Delhi project area the settlers did not do as well as in the Durham settlement because of poorer soils and small acreage allotments. But the general appearance of the area was found to be similar to that of other settlements in the same locality.

Numerous land-settlement projects were undertaken with public approval or backing during the years following the First World War.[8] Some of these projects were mildly successful; others failed. The two projects described above and many others like them cannot be regarded as complete failures because they ultimately did become more or less going concerns. Often, however, these projects did involve major losses, both direct and indirect, for the settlers. They also involved substantial losses in public funds. From examples such as these one might ask: Is it to the social interest to grant subsidies to the end that people may suffer losses, endure hardships, and experience failures? Admittedly, many of the mistakes after the First World War grew out of overenthusiasm for bringing more land into agricultural use. Perhaps one of the principal values of this experience is found in the lessons it provided for the revival of settlement plans after the Second World War.

## Land Programs for Veterans of the Second World War

Aside from the settler colonization that has taken place on some of the large irrigation projects in the West, the last 10 to 15 years have not witnessed any spectacular new-land-settlement movement. Few land-settlement promotional efforts comparable to those that followed the First World War have arisen since the Second World War. Land-settlement proposals designed to reward veterans by providing them a place on the

[7] *Farm Opportunities in the United States,* pp. 90–93, U.S. Department of Agriculture, Interbureau Committee on Postwar Agricultural Programs, July, 1945.

[8] For further material see W. A. Hartman, *State Land-Settlement Problems and Policies in the United States,* U.S. Department of Agriculture Technical Bulletin 357, May, 1933; and W. A. Hartman and J. D. Black, *Economic Aspects of Land Settlement in the Cutover Region of the Great Lake States,* U.S. Department of Agriculture Circular 160, August, 1931.

land have not been seriously sponsored by either the Federal or the state governments. Attention has been given, however, to the development of a number of land and credit programs that have affected the acquisition and development of new farms and farm lands.

*Federal Programs.* The most direct Federal land programs that relate to veteran settlement concern the allotment of homesteads. Veterans have first priority in the allotment of the somewhat limited number of homesteads that remain. The Bureau of Reclamation reports that 296 public-land farm units comprising 30,728 acres on five Federal irrigation projects were opened for homestead entry during fiscal year 1949. As the Columbia Basin and other current projects are completed during the next 10 years, it is expected that some 5,000 to 6,000 additional irrigated farm units will be available for allotment to veterans and others from publicly owned lands. Veterans and other residents in the region where the projects are located often have the best opportunities for filing applications and receiving favorable consideration.

A few hundred additional homesteads are granted from the remaining public domain each year as suitable spots are located, classified, and made accessible by roads and other facilities. In 1949 there were 884 original homestead entries and selections. Of these, 376 were in Alaska. Applicants for these lands must qualify for final entry, or title, by maintaining the required period of residence on their tracts and by meeting minimum improvement and use standards. Most of the homesteads go to qualified veterans of good character and farm experience who wish to farm permanently and have the necessary minimum capital for their farm operations.

Another important type of Federal assistance to veterans centers in the credit facilities provided by the Veterans' Administration and by the Farmers Home Administration. The so-called GI or VA loan program, authorized under the Serviceman's Readjustment Act of 1944, permits the Federal government, operating through the Administrator of Veterans' Affairs, to guarantee 50 per cent of veterans' loans on amounts of up to $4,000.[9] These loans can be made for numerous purposes, including the acquisition of homes, farm land, or equipment, the construction of farm improvements, and the development of farm lands.

GI loans bear interest at not to exceed 4 per cent per annum and are payable in full over a 25-year period. The government pays the interest for the first year on that portion of the loan which it guarantees. On those loans made for farming purposes, certain requirements relating to the farming ability and experience of the applicants, the necessity for the loan, the bona fide character of the farming operations, the value of the farm, and the purchase price paid, or to be paid, for the farm, must be met before a loan may be approved.

[9] Public Law 346, 78th Cong., 2d Sess., 1944.

Through its production loan program the FHA of the Department of Agriculture offers financial assistance supplemented by on-the-farm guidance to farmers, including veterans, who cannot secure adequate credit on reasonable terms elsewhere. Operating loans are based on farm and home plans developed by borrowers with the assistance of field employees. These operating loans are made for the purchase of workstock, other livestock, equipment, feed, seed, and other farm and family needs. They bear interest at the rate of 5 per cent per annum and are repayable within a maximum period of 7 years, the repayment period being shortened wherever it is consistent with the borrower's ability to repay. These loans are limited to not more than $7,000 to one person in any fiscal year.

Although not related directly to land settlement or development, it is worth noting in this connection that under Title I of the Bankhead-Jones Farm Tenant Act, which is also administered by the FHA, loans not to exceed the average value of efficient family-type farms for the county in which the farm is located are made to individuals to finance the purchase of family-type farms. Such loans may be for the full purchase price plus necessary improvements. They are repayable over a period of 40 years and bear 4 per cent interest. Annual interest and principal payments may vary with changes in net income, *i.e.*, more may be paid in good years and less in bad years so long as the debt is fully retired in 40 years. Each loan must be approved by a committee of three farmers who live in the county. They consider the character, ability, and experience of the applicant, the adequacy of the farm he wants to buy, and the reasonableness of the price to be paid. The farm is then operated under a plan mutually developed by the borrower and the FHA.

Under the Servicemen's Readjustment Act of 1944, veterans are made eligible for tenant purchase loans, the same as if they were farm tenants. The 1950 appropriation act provided $15 million for direct loans by the FHA for the purchase, enlargement, or development of efficient family-type farms. Almost all of this amount was earmarked for veterans' loans. Only negligible amounts were used for subsequent loans to current borrowers. Because of the policy of veterans' preference, the great majority of the direct loans have gone to veterans. Between 1945 and July 1, 1950, a total of 9,651 loans involving $74,161,395 were made to veterans under this program.

Approximately 24 per cent of the money loaned has been for the purpose of repairing or constructing buildings or for the development of land. Since the war an increasing number of loans have been made for the enlargement of presently owned inadequate farms and for the development of owned farms of adequate size that lack the facilities or improvements needed for their efficient operation.

In addition to the funds appropriated directly by Congress for loans for the purchase, enlargement, or development of efficient family-type farms, the FHA since 1946 has had authority to insure similar loans involving funds advanced by private leaders. By mid-1950 approximately 700 veterans' loans made from funds advanced by banks, insurance companies, or individual lenders had been insured by the government.

The veterans' farm training program also has some bearing on farmland improvement and development. Under this educational program, veterans are provided an opportunity to study farm practices and efficient farming methods. The administration and supervision for the program is provided by state agencies, usually the state board of vocational education. For a veteran to qualify for aids under the training program, he usually must operate, either as owner or tenant, a farm that is an economic unit or an area of land that can be made into an economic unit. In a few cases, however, aids have been granted to farm laborers working under the supervision of approved farmers. The aids vary according to the number of dependents the veteran has but usually approximate $90 per month. Veterans generally attend classes two nights a week.

All participants in the program are required to develop farm plans that conform physically with the general standards recommended by the Soil Conservation Service or some local advisory committee. The operational arrangements outlined in these plans often are in line with the policies the FHA advocates in its tenant purchase program. As the program is under different state and local supervisors, the standards met vary somewhat by states. Broadly considered, however, it is the opinion of those who have observed the program at close range that much has been achieved from its educational training phases and that substantial improvements and developments in land use also have resulted. By 1950 more than 600,000 veterans had enrolled in the program. Around 360,000 of these were still participating under it.

*State Programs.* After the Second World War, a number of the states took steps to assist veterans to acquire farms. A Veterans' Farm and Home Purchase Act adopted by the California legislature in 1943 provides for acquisition and resale of farms and homes to veterans under provisions similar to those of the original act following the First World War. In 1946 Texas provided for the extension of credit to veterans of the Second World War for the purpose of buying farm land.[10] In both instances, the legislation was designed to help finance farm and home purchases rather than to promote land development and settlement.

Nearly all the states arranged through the State Extension Services for county agricultural agents and advisory committees to assist veterans by furnishing information on such matters as suitable types of farming,

[10] John H. Southern and Joe R. Motheral, "Land for Texas Veterans," *Southwestern Social Science Quarterly*, Vol. 28, pp. 225–243, December, 1947.

amount of capital required, sources of credit, size and productivity of adequate units, equitable leasing and purchasing arrangements, and good farm practices and management. Many state agricultural colleges, experiment stations, and extension services issued publications dealing with farming opportunities and factors to consider in the purchase of farms. These publications are definitely not of the promotional type that followed the First World War. Their primary purpose has been that of providing helpful suggestions on available farming opportunities, cautioning veterans against possible pitfalls, and providing them with a sound basis for deciding whether or not they should farm. Generally, these publications have discouraged veterans from undertaking unnecessary risks in seeking new opportunities on the land.

## Success Factors in Land Settlement

The outlook for increasing population pressure both in this country and in the world at large points very definitely to a growing need for intensification of food and agricultural production activities both on the lands now in use and on many lands yet to be developed. Some of the new lands that will be developed are potentially very productive; others are probably of marginal value at the present time. Many of these new lands will be developed within already established farms. Considerable new land areas, however, will call for land settlement and colonization activities.

Those who are charged with the engineering, planning, or leadership of the new settlement movements can, if they will, find much in our past experiences with land settlement that will guide them in the successful direction of their projects. Many factors in these past experiences also can be identified as factors responsible for project failures. From these past experiences, the following success factors are recommended for consideration in future land-settlement programs.

1. *Productive farms of economic size.* The availability of productive land in farm units of economic size is one of the most essential and most basic requirements for the successful colonization of settlers in new land areas. The land should be of a quality that will respond to good farm-management practices and be adapted to the type of farming planned. It also should be located in an area that has ready access to adequate farm marketing facilities.

It is often wise for the average settler to go through some of the growing pains of developing land rather than be provided with a complete farm unit that is overdeveloped in relation to surrounding communities and improved beyond his own personal experience. When the farm is provided with improvements and equipment, these provisions should be adequate but not excessive.

New areas proposed for settlement should be classified as to their use capabilities and the productive capacity of the land. Only those lands that give promise of being productive over extended periods should be developed for settlement. Lands not adapted for agricultural use might well be zoned against future settlement. Many of these areas are in public ownership and should be retained and developed for other useful purposes.

2. *Overinvestment in relation to returns.* A common reason for failure or slow progress in land-settlement projects can be traced to the fact that real-estate values and loans have been high in relation to the earning capacity of the developed farms. This is sometimes caused by overimprovement of farm units, although it often results from the high costs now associated with most new-land-development programs. It might also result from land speculation and unjustifiable inflation of land values.

Little can be done about the high cost of land development. In most cases the easiest-to-develop lands already have been brought into use and only the higher-cost or less promising lands remain. The long-run inflationary trend in general price levels over the past century in this country also has had the effect of making land development more expensive in terms of net cash outlay than it has been in the past. However, the problem can be met to some extent by limiting expenditures to essential items and by exploring fully the probable relationships that will exist between costs and benefits before development work is undertaken.

The problem of inflationary land values can provide a serious obstacle to the successful settlement of farmers in new land areas. Usually these inflationary tendencies involve the premature or excessive capitalization of the anticipated value of new land developments and capital improvements. This problem may be particularly important if speculators are permitted to push land prices up in advance of government development.

For the successful settlement of any project, it is essential that the prices assigned to the lands offered to settlers be kept in line with their long-run productive capacity. The achievement of this goal may call for land-inflation control measures. In cases where the cost of land development has been high, it may call for partial subsidization of the total development cost.

3. *Inflexible fixed costs.* Many settlers in new land areas have experienced difficulties because of the necessity for meeting high principal and interest payments during the early years while they are still developing their farms into going-concern units. The settler's prospects for success can be enhanced if his fixed costs are held down during this period or

made flexible in relation to his earnings. A policy of permitting payment postponements during the early years and during other periods of low income would help to assure the success of many settlers.

4. *Selection of settlers.* The success or failure of many land-settlement projects rests squarely on the choice of settlers. The experience of settlement agencies, both public and private, in the United States and in other countries shows that settlers who have (*a*) a knowledge of and skill in agriculture, (*b*) physical capacity and fitness, (*c*) adaptability and desire for farm life, and (*d*) some capital of their own are more likely to succeed than persons deficient in one or more of these characteristics.

Many projects have enjoyed indifferent success primarily because they were settled by misfits who were in no way particularly qualified for their new calling. Individual settlers who have appeared to be well qualified also have failed in many cases because their wives or other members of their families have not been temperamentally suited for life as a settler. The problem of screening prospective settlers often is a difficult one both because of the complexity of individual applicants and the deficiencies of those in a position to pass judgment on their qualifications as prospective settlers. Even so, it is desirable that settlers be carefully selected in the first instance. In some cases it has been suggested that the screening process should extend to a trial or probationary period that the settler must pass before receiving title to the land.

5. *Information on settlement opportunities.* It is usually desirable to provide prospective settlers with as much information as possible regarding farm opportunities on new lands and on existing farms. This information should be largely factual and objective rather than promotional in character. Prospective settlers should be provided with accurate data regarding such factors as soils, number and type of available farms, land values, credit facilities, probable system of farming, land incomes, and community facilities. Every attempt should be made to have each settler go into the venture with his eyes open to the facts and without any false illusions or ideas concerning the problems he will face.

6. *Cost of group versus scattered settlement.* Experience has shown that group settlements of new areas are usually more costly than scattered or infiltrated settlements in old areas. This is true because of the incurrence of additional costs for the provision of the public and community services not usually found in the new areas and because of the greater risks often associated with group settlement. Farmers who settle in scattered areas not only benefit from the community facilities already provided in their areas; they also find that they are on their own and that they, rather than the group, must take the responsibility for success or

failure. This placing of responsibility on the individual sometimes inspires more effort and initiative on his part than he would show under a group-settlement arrangement. Of course, it is recognized that group settlement does have a place in the development of substantial areas of new farm land.

Generally speaking, success in land settlement depends upon getting qualified settlers on productive farms of economic size. Success can be further assured by protecting settlers during their early years against excessive fixed-cost payments and by providing them with a farm-price structure that will assure them the opportunity to realize reasonable farm incomes.

CHAPTER 11   *Land Tenure*

Land tenure has been defined as "all the relations established among men determining their varying rights in the use of land."[1] The scope of these relations covers a multitude of type situations. In the broadest sense, land tenure involves the holding or use of all or any portion of the "bundle of rights" represented by landed property. It deals with the allocation of rights in land and involves control over land resources. It arises out of man-to-man and man-to-society relationships with respect to the ownership, control, occupancy, transfer, and use of land, and it refers to the manner in which rights in land are held and also to the period of time over which these rights are held.

Land-tenure discussions frequently center about the problem of farm tenancy. Significant as it is, the term "tenancy" is more limited than "tenure" and applies only to the leasing or sharing by a tenant of a portion of the rights in land held by the owner or landlord. Tenancy represents only one type of tenure relationship, and its importance is more than balanced by the problems involved in the acquisition, holding, and transfer of ownership rights. In addition to the problems of land ownership and operatorship, land tenure also involves a number of public-private, debtor-creditor, and at times employer-employee relationships.

American land policy has been directly influenced by the tenure system developed in this country. This system is the outgrowth of a long period of development. Like land policy in general, it reflects the fact that the nation is rich in land resources and has been settled during a comparatively recent period. Beyond this, it has been profoundly affected by a number of important policy developments of the past. Significant among these are (1) the settlement of the frontier by a people who made little or no attempt to assimilate or absorb the native Indian population and its culture, (2) the adoption of the Anglo-Saxon legal concept of

[1] George S. Wehrwein, *Research in Agricultural Land Tenure:* Scope and Method, Social Science Research Council Bulletin 20, p. 2, April, 1933.

251

property rights, (3) the acceptance of the principle of alodial tenure
—land ownership in fee simple—in public and in most private land sales,[2]
(4) the rapid disposition of the public domain, and (5) the use of public
land and credit programs to advance the cause of the family farm.

## Land-Tenure Situation and Trends

*Present Land-Ownership Situation.* All of the land in this country is
held under some form of tenure and is subject to some type of ownership, either private or public. Of the 1,904 million acres in the United

*Table* 19. Major Land Uses by Types of Ownership, United States, 1950

| Land uses | Total area | | Private land | | Public land | |
|---|---|---|---|---|---|---|
| | Million acres | Per cent | Million acres | Per cent | Million acres | Per cent |
| Cropland................ | 408 | 21.4 | 401 | 29.9 | 7 | 1.2 |
| Pasture and grazing...... | 700 | 36.8 | 450 | 33.5 | 250 | 44.5 |
| Forest and woodland*.... | 605 | 31.8 | 405 | 30.2 | 200 | 35.6 |
| Special-use areas†........ | 105 | 5.5 | 27 | 2.0 | 78 | 13.9 |
| Barren, brush-, swamp-, and wastelands....... | 86 | 4.5 | 59 | 4.4 | 27 | 4.8 |
| Total................ | 1,904 | 100.0 | 1,342 | 100.0 | 562 | 100.0 |

* Excludes 15 million acres of forested land reserved for parks, wildlife areas, and
other special purposes.

† Includes urban areas, industrial sites, highway and railroad rights of way, parks,
wildlife areas, military posts, airports, farmsteads, etc.

Source: H. H. Wooten, *Inventory of Major Land Uses in the United States*, 1950,
Table 14, unpublished manuscript for revision of U.S. Department of Agriculture
Miscellaneous Publication 663.

States, approximately 1,342 million acres, or 70.5 per cent, are held in private ownership. A breakdown of the 29.5 per cent in public ownership
shows that 20.9 per cent is Federally owned and 3.0 per cent is in Indian reservations, while an estimated 5.6 per cent is held by the state
and local units of government. As the data reported in Table 19 indicate,
only slightly over 1 per cent of the area in public ownership is used for
cropland. Approximately 80 per cent of the public lands are classified as
forestry and grazing land, while around 14 per cent are used for service-
area purposes, and 5 per cent are classified as barren, brush-, swamp-, or
wastelands.

An estimated 107 million acres were held and administered by the
states and local units of government in 1950. These lands are subject to

[2] Marshall D. Harris, *The Genesis of the Land Tenure System of the United States,*
University of Illinois thesis abstract, Urbana, Ill., 1945.

various types of administration. In general, however, except for the areas used for highways and roads, most of these holdings are administered as (1) forestry, conservation, park or recreation areas, (2) lands leased out or otherwise held in trust for public schools, (3) lands used by schools, hospitals, prisons, and other institutions, and (4) lands held for disposal.

Of the 1,342 million acres in private ownership, 30 per cent is cropland, 34 per cent pasture and grazing land, and 30 per cent forest and woodland. The remaining area is used for urban and other special uses, or it represents wasteland. Approximately four-fifths of the privately owned area is in farms. This accounts for more than nine-tenths of the 1,159 million acres reported in farms in 1950. Most of the additional lands in farms are publicly owned but are operated by individuals on a leasehold basis.

According to the Agricultural Census of 1950 approximately 717,485,000 acres, 61.9 per cent of the total area in farms, were owned by a total of 3,915,000 owner-operators, while approximately 410,039,000 acres, 35.4 per cent of the total farm area, were reported under lease.[3] Much of this leased area undoubtedly was rented from individuals who owned but one farm. Many of the tenants, however, rent land from more than one owner, and many landlords have more than one farm. This situation complicates the task of computing the number of landlords owning leased farm land. Altogether, however, it is estimated that the nation's farm land is held in slightly over 5 million separate ownership units. Many of these units are owned jointly by husband and wife, by family groups or other partnership combinations, or are held in undivided or unsettled estates. Approximately 95 per cent of the privately owned farm lands are held by individual owners, while around 5 per cent are owned by corporate and institutional owners.

The agricultural census of the United States deals almost entirely with farm operating units and, at best, gives only a partial picture of the farm-ownership situation. A more complete picture of the over-all situation is provided by the nation-wide survey of agricultural land-ownership conditions conducted by the U.S. Bureau of Agricultural Economics in 1946. This survey shows that 89 per cent of the individual owners were men and that they owned 92 per cent of the acreage and 91 per cent of the value of the individually owned farms.[4] From a legal standpoint, 82.0 per cent of the owners held their lands in full ownership, 2.5 per cent had life estates, 4.4 per cent had undivided interests in their farms, 5.4 per

[3] The 1950 Census of Agriculture provides only approximate totals on the areas of farm lands owned and leased by operators. Data are not available regarding the ownership of managed lands and the ownership of lands leased to others by part owners. In 1945, 60.7 per cent of the farm land was owned by owner-operators and owners of managed farms, while 39.3 per cent was held under lease.

[4] Cf. Buis T. Inman and William H. Fippin, *Farm Land Ownership in the United States,* U.S. Department of Agriculture Miscellaneous Publication 699, 1949.

cent had purchase-contract rights, and 5.7 per cent had combinations of the above ownership interests.

Classification of the individual owners by tenure status indicates that 55.7 per cent of them were owner-operators, 10.9 per cent part owner-operators, 15.3 per cent operator-landlords, and 18.1 per cent nonoperating landlords. Of the 11 per cent of the owners who were women, 48 per cent were nonoperating landlords. Only 44 per cent of the nonoperating landlords reported living on farms. So far as major occupations are concerned, 65 per cent reported that they were farmers, 8 per cent retired farmers, 3 per cent housewives, 10 per cent business or professional men, and 14 per cent laborers. Only 26.6 per cent of the owners were under 45 years of age, while 24.5 per cent were in the 45-to-54-years age bracket, 24.3 per cent between 55 and 64, 17.6 per cent between 65 and 74, and 7.0 per cent over 75.

A survey conducted by the Forest Service in 1945–1946 shows that 206 million of the 285 million acres of privately owned land not in farms could be classified as commercial forest land.[5] Of this area, 122.3 million acres were held by approximately 1 million owners in holdings of less than 5,000 acres, 32.9 million acres by 3,200 owners in holdings of 5,000 to 50,000 acres, and 50.7 million acres by 398 owners in holdings of over 50,000 acres. A large proportion of these forest holdings, particularly the larger ones, are owned by lumber companies, pulp companies, and other corporate owners. Little data are available concerning the ownership of the remaining 79 million acres of privately owned land, but most of this area is used for grazing or recreational purposes.

*Major Tenure Groups.* The classification of farm tenure groups is complicated by wide ranges of variations in case types and by differences in classification objectives. The classification system most generally used in this country is that developed by the Census Bureau which has collected and reported data on the tenure status of farm operators in every decennial census since 1880 and in the special agricultural censuses conducted every 5 years since 1920. In classifying tenure groups the census divides farm operators into owners, managers, and tenants. The owner group is then subclassified as full owners and part owners, and the tenants are subclassified by method of rental payment as cash, share-cash, and share tenants, sharecroppers, and other tenants. Some data also are reported on hired laborers and unpaid family workers in connection with the tabulations on the farm labor force.

Valuable as this tenure-classification system is, it often masks the wide ranges in individual net worth and economic well-being found within

[5] *The Management Status of Forest Lands in the United States*, p. 6, U.S. Department of Agriculture, Forest Service, 1946. This survey reports 139.1 million acres of commercial forests included in farms.

each tenure group.[6] Also, it has not always been as meaningful as it could be because prior to 1950 no particular effort was made to differentiate between ownership and tenancy on the large-scale commercial farms, on the family-sized farms, and on the subsistence, residential, and part-time farm units.

Since the tenure classifications used by the census apply only to farm operators, there is no occasion for dividing the owners into full landlords, owner-operating landlords, and owner-operators. The *full owners* are those operators who own all the land they use regardless of whether or not they rent out land. Most of them hold their farms in fee-simple ownership and thus have exclusive, although not absolute, individual ownership interests in their lands.[7] During their lifetime these owners can sell, give or bequeath, mortgage, lease, or subdivide their farms pretty much as they please. Their power to use or abuse their land is limited only by the state's exercise of its power of police, taxation, and eminent domain. As reported by the census, full owners range in importance from owners operating large commercial farms and cattle ranches down to subsistence farmers and the owners of rural residences,

Quite similar to the full-owner group are· the *part owners*. These operators own some land and rent in additional lands. Sometimes their owned holdings are small in comparison with their leased holdings, sometimes large. Many of the part owners have growing families and rent in additional lands so as to adapt the size of their farming operations to their expanding farm family-labor supply. Others rent lands in addition to those they own because they find it more economical to rent land and invest their capital in equipment and livestock than to buy land. In

[6] Failure to recognize this fact has led some people to assume that the various tenure rungs on the "agricultural ladder"—family laborer or wage hand, tenant, mortgaged owner, full owner—can be rated in hierarchical importance, with each successive status level being higher and superior to all lower ratings. While this hypothesis might be justified in some individual cases, it does not apply in all individual cases, and it does not provide valid criteria for comparisons between operators. The nature of the classification system also suggests a rural class system to some people, while it suggests a nation-wide agricultural ladder to others. Actually, neither assumption is completely correct. The tenure process is a dynamic one, and changes in tenure status often come with changes in economic conditions and institutional settings and with the operator's accumulation over time of capital and experience. In some areas, as in parts of the Middle West, a substantial portion of the operators do progress up an agricultural ladder. In other areas and communities, some operators are seemingly born to ownership, while many of the laborers and tenants find it almost impossible to climb successfully to a higher status level.

[7] In addition to the owners in fee simple, many owners—often widows—hold only life estates. While these owners are free to use their farms, they cannot sell, devise, or assign more than their limited life interests in the land. The ownership of entailed estates is possible in some areas but is not at all common. Cf. John F. Timmons, "Farm Ownership in the United States: An Appraisal of the Present Situation and Emerging Problems," *Journal of Farm Economics*, Vol. 30, p. 81, February, 1948. In general, the census treats all owners of freehold estates as full owners.

1950 slightly more than one in every five owner-operators was a part owner. As a group, however, the part owners operated more farm-land area, harvested almost as much cropland, and controlled land and building investments valued at almost two-thirds as much as those operated by full owners.

The *farm manager* group is of small importance from a numerical standpoint. But the fact that the managers usually are found on the larger and better-equipped farms, ranches, and plantations, and in many cases have had special training or are otherwise specially fitted for their jobs makes them important as a tenure group. This is particularly true when consideration is given to the contributions of the manager-operated farms to the nation's total agricultural production. In 1949, for example, the manager group accounted for 4.8 per cent of total commercial farm production but for only 0.4 per cent of the farm operating units.

The *tenant* group makes up the residual group of farm operators. All the members of this group rent in the farm land they use. But as individual operators they vary from the not-so-prosperous tenants and croppers operating small units on an almost primitive basis to large scale operators who find it to their advantage to invest their capital in equipment and rent rather than buy the land they need.

*Cash tenants* are sometimes regarded as the highest and most efficient group of tenants because they own their livestock and equipment, take all the risks of farming, and make a money payment for the land they rent. The *share tenants* operate more on a partnership basis with their landlords, with the landlords supplying varying amounts of power, equipment, livestock, feed, seed and fertilizer, production costs, and management. Under the share system the landlord receives his rent in kind and thus assumes part of the risks of operation.

Numerous sharing arrangements have been worked out with the distribution of shares in the crop depending upon the crops involved and the separate contributions made by the landlord and the tenant. One of the most important share-tenancy arrangements is the "third and fourth" system, which is customarily used in large areas of the South. Under this arrangement the tenant usually provides the power, equipment, and labor, together with a share of the production expenses, and pays the landlord a third of the corn crop and a fourth of the cotton and other specialty crops. Some "third and fourth" tenants are free to exercise considerable independence of management, while others work under the close supervision of their landlords.

A popular share-tenancy arrangement in the Middle West calls for equal division of the farm produce between the landlord and tenant. When only crops are involved, the tenant usually supplies the power and equipment, while the landlord pays a share of the production expenses. When livestock are involved in the lease, the tenant often supplies at least part of the livestock in addition to the power and equipment. *Cash-share leases* represent a combination of the cash and share systems, as in the case where the cropland is rented on a share basis with cash rent being paid for the use of pasture land.

The *sharecroppers* are found mostly in the South and the census data reported for this tenure group applies only to the Southern states. As a rule, the cropper has but little opportunity to show independence or to assume the responsibilities of management. He usually works a tract of farm land under landlord supervision and is dependent upon his landlord for work stock or power, equipment, capital required for crop production, and money grants for family-living use during the crop season. Ordinarily, the cropper contributes little except his own and his family labor toward crop production. For this he receives half of the crop from the landlord. In most respects, the average cropper is more a laborer being paid in kind than a tenant paying rent. In many states, his legal status is that of a laborer rather than a tenant. Still, he does bear some of the risks of farming, and he is treated as a type-of-farm operator by the census.

During recent years many croppers have enjoyed moderate farm incomes. With the farm prices that prevailed during the 1930's, however, the farm incomes received by most croppers were too low to permit a moderate standard of living, to say nothing of the capital savings needed for advancement to a higher tenure status. Slightly over half the share-croppers reported by the census are Negroes, and about three-fourths of them grow cotton as their principal crop. In some areas cropper status carries with it a stigma of legal, social, and economic inferiority. In other areas, particularly in those places where farm boys often start out as croppers and later become owners, sharecroppers are usually treated on the same basis as other tenants.

The classification "other tenants" includes those paying "standing rent"—a fixed quantity of produce such as 3 bales of cotton or 500 bushels of corn—those who perform certain services for the landlord in lieu of rent, those who have their farms rent-free, and—up until 1950 when they were reported separately—tenants of undetermined status.

In 1950 share tenants accounted for almost two-fifths of the total number of tenants and were found concentrated in the Corn Belt, the Great Plains area, and the Mountain states. Slightly over one out of every seven tenants rented for cash, while almost one out of every seven rented on a share-cash basis. The cash tenants were concentrated mostly in the Lake states dairy region, the Northeastern states, and the Far Western states, while share-cash tenants were the prevalent group in many of the North Central states. Croppers accounted for about a fourth of the tenants and were found on the cotton and tobacco farms of the South.

*Tenure Status of Farm Operators.* Various measures can be used in describing the farm-tenure situation and tenure trends. Five of these measures—the proportionate distribution of tenure groups by number of farm operating units, acres operated, cropland harvested, value of real estate operated, and composition of total gainfully employed farm population—are reported in Table 20. From this table it appears that slightly

*Table* 20. Percentage Distribution of Tenure Groups in the United States by Various Significant Measures, 1950

| Tenure group | Farm operating units | Acres of farm land | Cropland harvested, 1949 | Value of farm land and buildings | Gainfully employed farm population |
|---|---|---|---|---|---|
| All owners............. | 72.7 | 72.6 | 68.3 | 71.5 | 37.8 |
| Managers............. | 0.4 | 9.1 | 2.1 | 4.0 | 0.2 |
| All tenants............. | 26.9 | 18.3 | 29.7 | 24.5 | 14.0 |
| All laborers............ | .... | .... | .... | .... | 48.0 |
| | | | | | |
| Full owners............ | 57.4 | 36.2 | 35.3 | 44.0 | 29.8 |
| Part owners............ | 15.3 | 36.5 | 33.0 | 27.5 | 8.0 |
| Managers.............. | 0.4 | 9.1 | 2.1 | 4.0 | 0.2 |
| Cash tenants.......... | 4.0 | 3.6 | 2.8 | 3.3 | 2.1 |
| Share-cash............ | 3.6 | 4.2 | 8.8 | 7.1 | 1.9 |
| Share................. | 10.0 | 7.5 | 13.7 | 10.7 | 5.2 |
| Croppers.............. | 6.4 | 1.2 | 2.4 | 1.5 | 3.4 |
| Others and unspecified.. | 2.9 | 1.7 | 1.9 | 1.9 | 1.5 |
| Unpaid family workers.. | .... | .... | .... | .... | 25.7 |
| Hired laborers......... | .... | .... | .... | .... | 22.3 |

SOURCE: Data on gainfully employed farm population and hired labor force from *Agricultural Statistics*, 1951, Table 625, p. 543. All other percentage data computed from preliminary reports on 1950 Census of Agriculture.

less than three-fourths of the farms were owner-operated in 1950, while slightly more than one-fourth were tenant-operated. Owner-operators accounted for approximately the same proportion of farm land and harvested cropland area and real-estate value as they did number of farms. The farm-manager group, though relatively small in size, accounted for over 9 per cent of the farm-land area and 4 per cent of the real-estate value. Tenants operated almost 30 per cent of the harvested cropland but had only 18 per cent of the land in farms. The final column in the table indicates that the gainfully employed farm population in 1950 was made up 38 per cent of owners, 14 per cent tenants, 26 per cent unpaid family workers, and 22 per cent hired laborers.

Farm-land tenancy reached its peak in the United States in the early 1930's. At that time there was a larger number of tenants, and they accounted for a higher proportion of the total number of operators and the total area in farms than at any other time. Since then, the trend has been reversed, and the proportion of farm tenancy has dropped to a point lower than it has been at any time during the past 60 years (cf. Table 21).

*Table* 21. Farms Operated by Tenants, United States and Major Regions, 1880 to 1950
(In per cent)

| Census year | United States | North-east | North Central | South | West |
|---|---|---|---|---|---|
| 1880 | 25.6 | 16.0 | 20.7 | 36.2 | 14.0 |
| 1890 | 28.4 | 18.4 | 23.4 | 38.5 | 12.1 |
| 1900 | 35.3 | 20.8 | 27.9 | 47.0 | 16.6 |
| 1910 | 37.0 | 18.2 | 28.9 | 49.6 | 14.0 |
| 1920 | 38.1 | 17.2 | 31.1 | 49.6 | 17.7 |
| 1925 | 38.6 | 13.0 | 32.0 | 51.1 | 18.7 |
| 1930 | 42.4 | 12.5 | 34.1 | 55.5 | 20.9 |
| 1935 | 42.1 | 13.8 | 36.3 | 53.5 | 23.8 |
| 1940 | 38.7 | 12.6 | 35.4 | 48.2 | 21.3 |
| 1945 | 31.7 | 8.6 | 29.1 | 40.4 | 14.5 |
| 1950 | 26.8 | 6.8 | 24.2 | 34.1 | 12.9 |

Between 1935 and 1950 the proportion of farm tenancy in the country dropped from 42.1 to 26.8 per cent, and the number of tenants decreased by 1.4 million operators, or by approximately one-half. During this same period there was a considerable decrease (6.8 to 5.4 million) in the number of census farms, but only a slight change in the total number of farm owners. Between 1935 and 1940 the number of owners dropped by over 200,000, while the number of tenants dropped a half million. In the next 10-year period, however, the number of owners increased again to almost the 1935 level, while the number of tenants dropped by almost a million operators.

Much of the decline in the number and proportion of tenants since 1940 has resulted from the effect that higher farm-income levels have had in making it both possible and profitable for many tenants to become farm owners. The wartime and postwar demands of industry and the military services for manpower have at the same time drawn large numbers of tenants, hired workers, and farm-family workers away from farms. The reason for the decrease in the number of operators between 1935 and 1940 is less obvious.[8] The reported increase in the number of hired farm laborers from 2.4 million in 1935 to 2.6 million in 1940 suggests that some owners and tenants may have become hired workers. But the majority of the displaced operators probably went into nonfarm employment.

*Table* 22. Farm Land Operated by Tenants and Held under Lease, United States and Major Regions, 1900 to 1950
(In per cent)

| Census year | United States | North-east | North Central | South | West |
|---|---|---|---|---|---|
| Proportion operated by tenants | | | | | |
| 1900 | 23.3 | 22.6 | 24.9 | 24.2 | 14.5 |
| 1910 | 25.8 | 20.2 | 28.0 | 28.0 | 14.8 |
| 1920 | 27.7 | 19.0 | 32.2 | 30.6 | 15.2 |
| 1925 | 28.7 | 15.1 | 34.5 | 31.7 | 16.0 |
| 1930 | 31.1 | 14.1 | 36.2 | 36.6 | 17.3 |
| 1935 | 31.9 | 14.7 | 37.5 | 37.5 | 17.8 |
| 1940 | 29.4 | 13.6 | 37.5 | 33.2 | 14.4 |
| 1945 | 22.0 | 9.2 | 30.1 | 26.3 | 8.9 |
| 1950 | 18.3 | 7.3 | 25.4 | 20.7 | 8.2 |
| Proportion held under lease | | | | | |
| 1925 | 39.1 | 17.2 | 44.8 | 36.8 | 38.2 |
| 1930 | 43.7 | 17.2 | 48.9 | 42.7 | 42.4 |
| 1935 | 44.7 | 18.0 | 50.0 | 43.9 | 43.1 |
| 1940 | 44.1 | 17.3 | 51.6 | 41.8 | 40.9 |
| 1945* | 39.3 | 14.7 | 46.4 | 36.1 | 38.2 |
| 1948*† | 38.1 | 13.8 | 42.3 | 38.9 | 34.9 |

* Includes land in manager-operated farms that is rented, as well as the areas leased to tenants and part owners.

† 1948 data from the Enumerative Survey of Agriculture conducted by the Bureau of Agricultural Economics in April, 1948. Buis T. Inman, "Current Farm Tenancy Trends," *Agricultural Economics Research*, Vol. 1, p. 95, July, 1949. Detailed data on farm-land areas under lease are not available from the 1950 census.

The trend toward fewer and fewer tenant-operated farms also has affected the proportion of farm-land area under lease. As Table 22 indicates, the proportion of the farm area operated by tenants was less in 1945 and 1950 than it had been at any time since data were first collected

[8] Some of this decrease may be attributed to the fact that the 1935 Census of Agriculture was taken in January instead of April. The data were gathered on a slightly different basis from the other censuses, and the findings on total number of farms and operators probably involve overenumeration of farms.

on this point in 1900; and the proportion of the farm area reported held under lease in 1948 was less than it had been at any time since tabulations were started in 1925. The decrease in tenancy between 1945 and 1950 would have brought a considerably larger decline in the proportion of the farm area held under lease had it not been accompanied by an increase during this period of from 11.3 to 15.3 per cent in the proportion of farm operators who were part owners.

This over-all statement concerning the farm-tenure situation is not really descriptive of any of the four principal regions of the United States. In the Northeast region, for example, tenancy has never constituted the problem it has in the South. Around 1900 almost 21 per cent of the farms in the Northeast were tenant-operated. Since then, the proportion has dropped to 7 per cent, while the proportion of the acreage under lease has dropped to less than 14 per cent.

Tenancy is much more common in the North Central region. This is particularly true of the Corn and Wheat Belt sections of the region where farming is often highly commercialized, although not so true in the Lake states dairy area. Between 1880 and 1935 the proportion of farms operated by tenants in the North Central region increased from 21 to 36 per cent. During the decade and a half that followed, the proportion of tenancy dropped to 24 per cent, while the proportion of the area under lease declined from 52 to around 42 per cent. Enlargement and consolidation of farms in this region between 1935 and 1950 brought a reduction of almost 370,000 in the number of tenants and 19,000 in the number of owners.

The West, with its large areas of ranch land and irrigated and dry farms, has been settled for the most part since 1880. This settlement movement brought a sevenfold increase in the total number of farm operators between 1880 and 1935. Between 1935 and 1950, the proportion of tenancy in the West declined from 24 to 13 per cent, and the proportion of the land area operated by tenants dropped from 18 to 8 per cent. Approximately 35 per cent of the farm-land area in the West is under lease, most of it being leased to part owners. Part owners are important in many parts of the country, but they are most important in the ranching and dry-land areas of the West where a high proportion of the owners make a regular practice of supplementing their holdings by leasing large tracts of grazing land (or securing grazing permits) from agencies of the state and Federal governments.

In the South the total number of tenants more than tripled, and the total number of farm operators more than doubled between 1880 and 1935. Between 1935 and 1950 the number of tenants dropped by 926,000, or by almost half, while the number of owners and managers increased by 157,000. This has brought a reduction in the proportion of tenancy in this region from 56 per cent in 1930 and 54 per cent in 1935 to 40 per cent in 1945 and 34 per cent in 1950.

The highest proportion of farm tenancy in the country is found in the South, particularly in the eight Cotton Belt states—South Carolina, Georgia, Alabama, Mississippi, Arkansas, Louisiana, Oklahoma, and Texas—where considerable use has been made of sharecropping and the "third and fourth" share-tenant arrangements. All of these states reported more than 60 per cent of their farms tenant-operated during the 1930's.[9] It was the depressed living conditions of the tenants and croppers in this area, depressing conditions resulting largely from low farm incomes, lack of stability, and an often unfavorable environmental situation, that gave rise to much of the surge of national interest in the farm-tenancy problem during the late 1930's. Higher farm prices and other factors such as the demand for industrial labor, the government's farm price-support program, its payments to farmers, and its tenant-rehabilitation program have brought a marked reduction in the number of share tenants and croppers in these states in the years since 1935.

*Size of Farms.* The size of the average farm in the United States has increased considerably during the last half century. As Table 23 shows, the average farm in 1950 contained 215 acres, an increase of 70 acres over the 1925 average. Here again, however, the national average does not describe the situation in the separate regions or in the individual states. Average size of farms by states in 1950 ranged from 67 acres in North Carolina to 3,834 acres in Arizona. By regions the averages varied from 111 acres in the Northeast, 212 acres in the North Central and 148 acres in the South to 703 acres in the West.

In all of these regions, the size of the average farm has tended to increase, particularly in the period since 1935. Most of this increase, however, has come in the size of the units operated by part owners and tenants. The average farm operated by a full owner in 1950 was almost 14 acres larger than it had been in 1935. It still remained smaller, however, than the averages reported for 1910 and 1920.

The increase in average size of farms has been favored by two factors: increasing farm mechanization and the consolidation of grazing-land holdings in the West. Farm mechanization has made it possible for many owner and tenant families to expand their farming operations and has made it desirable from an economic standpoint to buy or rent additional land. The fact that many owners have chosen to rent rather than buy additional land explains the large holdings and growing importance of the part-owner class. The consolidation of ranch-land holdings and the organized administration and leasing of public grazing lands—lands that

---

[9] Mississippi reported 72.2 per cent of her operating units (census farms) tenant-operated in 1930. This is the highest proportion of tenancy thus far reported by any state.

*Table* 23. Average Size of Farms by Tenure of Operator, United States and Regions, 1900 to 1950

(In acres)

| Census year | All farms | Full owner | Part owner | All tenants |
|---|---|---|---|---|
| United States | | | | |
| 1900........................ | 146.2 | 134.7 | 276.4 | 96.3 |
| 1910........................ | 138.1 | 138.6 | 225.0 | 96.2 |
| 1920........................ | 148.2 | 137.0 | 314.2 | 107.9 |
| 1925........................ | 145.1 | 126.6 | 354.9 | 107.6 |
| 1930........................ | 156.9 | 127.9 | 374.5 | 115.0 |
| 1935........................ | 154.8 | 121.8 | 386.2 | 117.6 |
| 1940........................ | 174.0 | 123.9 | 488.3 | 132.1 |
| 1945........................ | 194.8 | 124.9 | 562.1 | 135.4 |
| 1950........................ | 215.3 | 135.6 | 512.0 | 146.8 |
| Regions of United States | | | | |
| 1950: | | | | |
| Northeast................. | 110.9 | 97.6 | 179.2 | 119.1 |
| North Central............. | 212.2 | 137.3 | 397.4 | 222.8 |
| South..................... | 148.2 | 123.2 | 332.3 | 89.7* |
| West...................... | 702.9 | 225.2 | 1,889.3 | 449.7 |

* Croppers, 40.9 acres.

were often free in the past—explains much of the upward trend in the size of Western farms. During the war and postwar period the trend toward farm enlargement also has been favored by the increased opportunities farm workers have had to work in nonfarm jobs and the effect of this off-farm employment situation on the migration of farm people to cities.

*Table* 24. Classification of Farms by Size, United States, 1950

| Farm-size groups | Percentage distribution |
|---|---|
| Under 10 acres................. | 9.0 |
| 10–29 acres................. | 15.9 |
| 30–69 acres................. | 19.5 |
| 70–139 acres................. | 22.3 |
| 140–219 acres................. | 14.8 |
| 220–499 acres................. | 12.8 |
| 500–999 acres................. | 3.4 |
| 1,000 acres and over........... | 2.3 |
| Total...................... | 100.0 |

The data just reported give a somewhat misleading impression of the size of typical farms. As Table 24 indicates, one-fourth of the farms contained less than 30 acres, while two-thirds contained less than 140 acres. The over-all averages are brought up by the comparatively small proportionate number of large ranches, farms, and plantations found scattered throughout the country.

In the country as a whole and in the Northeast and North Central regions the 70–139-acre size group was the predominant size group for farms in 1950. The large number of sharecropper units (averaging 40.9 acres in size) in the South made the 30–69-acre group the predominant size group for that region. Approximately a tenth of the farm and ranch units in the West contained more than 1,000 acres. But because of the presence of large numbers of small irrigated farms and fruit groves, the 10–29-acre group was the predominant size group for the West.

Between 1920 and 1950 the number of small farms containing less than 10 acres almost doubled in number.[10] During the same period, the number of large operating units containing 1,000 acres or more almost doubled in number, while the total number of farms in the 20–259-acre size groups decreased by more than 1½ million. Evidence of this trend toward reduction of the number of farms in the medium-sized groups by parcellation into small farm holdings and by consolidation into larger holdings is found in all four of the regions. The increase in the number of farms containing less than 10 acres has not affected a very large acreage and does not indicate any special trend in farming. Many of these units have been acquired for rural-residence purposes by people who want more acreage than they can acquire in the cities. The areas added to the larger farms are mostly used for commercial farming.

So far as tenure status of operators is concerned, the data on size groups for all farms show that full owners and tenants tend to concentrate on the smaller farms, while part owners and managers are found mostly on the larger farm units. In 1945, slightly over half of the full owners and tenants had farms of less than 70 acres, and 75 per cent of the full owners and 61 per cent of the tenants were found on farms of less than 140 acres, while only 38 per cent of the part owners and 33 per cent of the managers were found on units of this size.[11]

*Farm Values and Equities.* Property values are always relative, and

[10] The comparison of census trend data on numbers of small farms is complicated by changing definitions as to what constitutes a farm. Between 1925 and 1945 a census farm was defined as an area of 3 acres or more on which there were agricultural operations, or if less than 3 acres, an area that produced agricultural products valued at $250 or more for home use or for sale. The 1920 definition was very similar except that it included farms of less than 3 acres with less than $250 production if they required the full-time services of one person. In 1950 the definition was changed to apply to areas of 3 acres or more on which the value of farm products in 1949, exclusive of home gardens, was $150 or more, and areas of less than 3 acres with farm-product sales of $150 or more in 1949. This change in definition has restricted the number of small units that qualify for classification as farms. Census Bureau personnel have estimated that around 200,000 additional small units would have been counted in 1950 had the 1945 definition of a farm applied.

[11] Data for 1950 not available.

when they are used for comparison purposes over time, they should be related to general price levels or other indicators of economic conditions. As Table 25 indicates, there was a tremendous increase between 1850 and 1950 in the average value of land and buildings, implements and machinery, and livestock per farm operating unit. The value of the average farmer's investment in each of these types of farm property tended to climb rather steadily until 1920. During the depression of the 1930's, property values declined somewhat, but they again started their upward climb during the 1940's. Comparison of the trend in real-estate values with the index of wholesale prices shows that farm-property values climbed at a faster rate between 1850 and the First World War than wholesale prices. Since the First World War this situation has no longer prevailed. Analyses of the farm real-estate market show that land values usually reflect price levels but that they ordinarily lag behind the upward and downward swings in farm price levels.[12]

*Table* 25. Average Value of Farm Property per Farm Operating Unit, United States, 1850 to 1950

| Year | Land and buildings | Implements and machinery | Livestock | Land and buildings per acre | Bureau of Labor Statistics index of general wholesale prices (1926 = 100) |
|---|---|---|---|---|---|
| 1850 | $ 2,258 | $ 105 | $ 376 | $11.14 | 62.3 |
| 1880 | 2,544 | 101 | 393 | 19.02 | 65.1 |
| 1900 | 2,896 | 131 | 496 | 19.81 | 56.1 |
| 1910 | 5,471 | 199 | 744 | 39.60 | 70.4 |
| 1920 | 10,284 | 557 | 1,235 | 69.38 | 154.4 |
| 1930 | 7,614 | 525 | 919 | 48.52 | 86.4 |
| 1940 | 5,518 | 502 | 742 | 31.71 | 78.6 |
| 1945 | 7,917 | 878 | 1,446 | 40.63 | 105.8 |
| 1950* | 13,911 | 2,651* | 2,450* | 66.75 | 161.5 |

* 1950 estimates calculated from data reported in *Agricultural Statistics*, 1951, Table 610, p. 532, U.S. Department of Agriculture. The other value data are based on census findings.

The national averages reported in Table 25 fail to show the wide range in average farm values between regions and states. In 1950, for example, the average value of land and buildings per farm ranged from $4,566 in Mississippi to $57,996 in Arizona, while the average value per acre ranged from $13.21 in arid and semiarid Wyoming to $292.84 per acre in New Jersey. The average value of the machinery and livestock found on farms also varies over a wide range. Many of the sharecropper units

[12] W. H. Scofield and R. D. Davidson, "The Farm Real Estate Situation, 1947–48 and 1948–49," U.S. Department of Agriculture Circular 823, pp. 29–31, 1949.

in the South have very small investments in equipment and livestock, while successful farmers or ranchers in other areas often have as much or more invested in their farming equipment or their livestock as they have invested in land and buildings.

Wide ranges in values also are observable within regions. But as Table 26 shows, there are greater differences between the average values of

*Table* 26. Average Value of Farm Real Estate by Tenure of Operators, United States and Major Regions, 1950

| Region | All farms | Full owners | Part owners | All tenants |
|---|---|---|---|---|
| United States............... | $13,911 | $10,716 | $25,133 | $12,943 |
| Northeast.................... | 11,662 | 10,124 | 18,965 | 13,558 |
| North Central............... | 18,328 | 10,729 | 26,795 | 24,087 |
| South....................... | 8,495 | 7,588 | 16,860 | 5,818* |
| West........................ | 28,807 | 19,352 | 53,080 | 31,969 |

* Croppers in the South, $3,333.

farm real estate held by members of the same tenure group in different regions than between the holdings of different tenure groups in the same region. The highest average property values for all tenure groups are found in the West and in the North Central regions, the same regions that have the farms of the largest average size.

Among the major tenure groups the part owners rank first after managers in every state and region in average value of land and buildings. In a third of the states the part owners operate properties valued at more than twice the value of those operated by the full owners. The average part-owner–operated farm in some of the Western states is worth almost four times as much as the average full-owner–operated unit.

In all except the Southern states and a few of the New England states the average tenant also operates a farm worth more than that operated by the average full owner. In so far as farm real-estate values are indicative of productive capacity, these data suggest that in all the regions except the South the average tenant operates a more productive farm unit than the average full owner but a less productive unit than the average part owner.

One of the problems that has grown steadily in importance with the increase in average farm property values is that of farm capital requirements. Whereas the young prospective owner was once able to start with a very limited supply of capital and his own labor on a government homestead, both owners and tenants in the commercial farming areas today must expect to start with a considerable investment in machinery and livestock. A measure of the general trend in farm capital requirements is provided by the figures in Table 27 which compare the capital invesments on typical Central Michigan farms in 1940 and 1951. This comparison is based upon farm account record data, and it should be pointed out that the size of the average record farm increased from 179 to 239 acres during this period. The total capital requirements in this area are somewhat higher than those that apply in most areas, but they are still below those that apply in many prosperous farming communities. Everywhere, however, the problem of increasing capital requirements has tended to complicate the capital-accumulation problem faced by would-be operators.

*Table 27*

| Investment item | 1940 | 1951 |
|---|---|---|
| Real estate.............. | $13,425 | $29,875 |
| Machinery.............. | 2,602 | 8,204 |
| Livestock............... | 3,101 | 9,836 |
| Feed and seed.......... | 1,430 | 3,976 |
| Total................ | $20,558 | $51,891 |

The great bulk of the investment and working capital used by American farmers comes from the following five sources: (1) farm earnings and savings from farm work, (2) the leasing of farms owned by others, (3) the use of farm credit, (4) gifts, inheritances, and family help, and (5) earnings from nonfarm employment. Farm earnings play an important part in helping the average farmer to get ahead. But very, very few farm workers become owners of productive family-sized farms today without the use of some combination of the other methods of capital accumulation.

Farm credit probably rates as the most important single source of farming capital used by landowners in the United States, but it is practically always used in combination with capital acquired or accumulated from other sources. Most farm-purchase arrangements involve some use of long-term credit. Liberal amounts of short-term credit are used for production purposes by owners and tenants alike.

The farm credit problem is not at all new in American history. Up until comparatively recently there was always a constant demand among the planters of the South and the pioneers on the Western frontier for an accessible supply of easy credit. Production credit in these areas often commanded interest rates in excess of 20 per cent per annum. The operation of several government farm-credit programs during the last 30 years has solved the more critical of these local credit problems. Adequate production credit is now available in most areas at rates varying from 4½ to 8 (mostly 5 or 6) per cent interest, while long-term real-estate credit is available at rates varying from 3 to 6 per cent interest.

The use of long-term credit for the financing of farm purchases and for other purposes has given rise to a farm-mortgage debt problem. According to official figures, total farm-mortgage debt in the United States reached its peak in 1923. Between then and 1946 this total debt was reduced to $4,682 million, or to less than half the 1923 figure. Most of this reduction represents farm-mortgage payments, particularly during the Second World War period. However, a large portion of the debt reduction during the early 1930's resulted from mortgage foreclosures and the scaling down of existing farm indebtedness. Since 1946 the total amount of new farm-mortgage indebtedness has exceeded the payments on outstanding debts.

The trend in farm-mortgage indebtedness since 1910 and its relationship to farm real-estate values is reported in Table 28. The percentage

*Table* 28. Value of Farm Property and Farm Debt, United States, 1910 to 1951

| Year | Value of farm real estate, millions | Real-estate mortgage debt, millions | Owner equity in real-estate value, per cent |
|------|------|------|------|
| 1910 | $34,801 | $3,208 | 90.8 |
| 1915 | 39,597 | 4,991 | 87.4 |
| 1920 | 66,316 | 8,449 | 87.3 |
| 1925 | 49,468 | 9,913 | 80.0 |
| 1930 | 47,880 | 9,631 | 79.9 |
| 1935 | 32,859 | 7,584 | 76.9 |
| 1940 | 33,642 | 6,586 | 80.4 |
| 1945 | 46,389 | 4,933 | 89.4 |
| 1946 | 52,114 | 4,682 | 91.0 |
| 1947 | 58,604 | 4,777 | 91.8 |
| 1948 | 62,813 | 4,882 | 92.2 |
| 1949 | 65,168 | 5,108 | 92.2 |
| 1950 | 63,527 | 5,407 | 91.5 |
| 1951 | 72,650 | 5,828 | 92.0 |

data reported on farmers' equities refer to the equities held by all owners, including those who have no outstanding mortgage debt. A more detailed examination of the situation shows that 27.5 per cent of the farms had mortgages in 1950, while 26.2 per cent of the land in farms was subject to mortgage. Mortgage debt accounted for 25.3 per cent of the value of the mortgaged farms in 1950 as compared with 41.5 per cent in 1940.

The mortgage situation in 1940 and 1945 for the farms owned or operated by the major operating tenure groups is reported in Table 29. From this tabulation it appears that there was a drop between 1940 and

*Table* 29. Number, Acreage, and Value of Farms Subject to Mortgage by Tenure Groups, United States, 1940 and 1950

(In per cent)

| Tenure groups | Number of farms mortgaged | | Farm acreage mortgaged | | Ratio of mortgage debt to value of mortgaged farms | |
|---|---|---|---|---|---|---|
| | 1940 | 1950 | 1940 | 1950 | 1940 | 1950 |
| Full owners.............. | 41.4 | 28.9 | 47.2 | 32.3 | 42.5 | 27.6 |
| Part owners (owned portion only)............. | 54.7 | 34.1 | 64.9 | 39.5 | 46.9 | 25.7 |
| Renters, managers (and rented portion of part-owner farms).......... | 31.2 | 20.8 | 34.3 | 15.3 | 37.8 | 20.7 |
| All tenure groups........ | 38.8 | 27.5 | 43.1 | 26.2 | 41.5 | 25.3 |

SOURCE: U.S. Departments of Commerce and Agriculture cooperative report on *Farm-mortgage Debt*, Tables 1 and 2, 1952.

1945 for every tenure operator group in the proportion of farms, acreage, and value subject to mortgage.

Comparison of the mortgage situation on the lands held by the three tenure groups shows that a larger proportion of the part-owner–operated farms and the owned portion of the acreage in these farms is subject to mortgage than is true of either the full-owner farms or the landlord-owned farms and acreage which is operated by tenants and managers. Much of this difference can be related to the age of the owners. Part owners on the average are slightly younger than full owners and thus have had a shorter period of time in which to pay off their mortgage indebtedness. They also own larger acreages and a larger percentage of farm real-estate value in proportion to their numbers than do the full owners. This larger investment together with their need for more production credit (and their often more commercial attitude toward the liberal use of credit) helps to explain the heavy reliance placed by part owners on the use of mortgage credit. At the same time, the high average value of the farms operated by part owners gives them more debt-paying capacity than other groups. They used this capacity to pay off a greater proportion of their debt between 1940 and 1950 than did either of the other two groups.

Landlords who had leased their lands or who had turned the management of their farms over to managers placed less reliance upon the use of mortgage credit than did either the full or the part owners. Most of these landlord-owners are somewhat older than the operating owners—their numbers being made up largely of relatively prosperous operating landlords, retired farmers or their widows or other heirs, or businessmen who have invested in farm property.

*Economic Classes of Farms.* Land tenure involves more than just the question of how land is held. It also involves consideration of the nature and extent of the resources held and used by various operators. This means that attention should be given to the size and productivity of farm business enterprises as well as to the size and value of the farm itself.

Reference has been made to the fact that the tenure-status classifications generally used in the past have not been as meaningful as they might be because they have provided little or no direct indication of the operator's efficiency, productivity, or contribution to national income. Experience shows that none of the three measures—tenure of operator, size of farm, or value of farm plant—provides a valid basis for comparing either the efficiency or productivity of farm operators.

Comparative efficiency is not always easy to determine and of necessity depends upon the criteria one uses in deciding whether efficiency should be measured in terms of output per operator, per acre, per dollar of investment, per man-work unit, or some other unit of input. Operator productivity, however, can be measured through the economic classification of farms according to value of agricultural production. An economic classification of this type is summarized in Table 30. It shows that the top 9 per cent of the farm units in 1950 accounted for over half of the total value of farm products sold in 1949 and that the top 22 per cent accounted for almost three-fourths of this total value. The bottom 31 per cent of the census farms accounted for only 1 per cent of total production, while the bottom 44 per cent accounted for only one-thirtieth of the total commercial production.[13]

The economic classification for 1950 reported in Table 30 divides the farm operating units reported by the census into two general groups: commercial farming units and other farming units. The part-time and residential units in the second group accounted for 30 per cent of the so-called farms in 1950. Actually, only a few of the 1.7 million units in these two classes can be considered as more than nominal farms. Because of their small size, their general lack of farm power (draft animals or

---

[13] The 1950 census was the first to classify farms by economic class. Some special tabulations involving different economic-class intervals have been reported, however, for the 1940 and 1945 censuses. Cf., for example, Louis J. Ducoff and Margaret J. Hagood, *Differentials in Productivity and in Farm Income of Agricultural Workers by Size of Enterprise and by Regions,* U.S. Bureau of Agricultural Economics, August, 1944 (mimeo.); John C. Ellickson and John M. Brewster, "Technological Advance and the Structure of American Agriculture," *Journal of Farm Economics,* Vol. 29, November, 1947; Sherman E. Johnson and Kenneth L. Bachman, "How Many Farms?" *The Agricultural Situation,* December, 1948; and K. L. Bachman and R. W. Jones, *Sizes of Farms in the United States,* U.S. Department of Agriculture Technical Bulletin 1019, July, 1950.

Table 30. Economic Classes of Farms in the United States, 1950

| Economic class | Num-ber of farms, thou-sands | Proportionate distribution, in per cent, by— | | | | |
| --- | --- | --- | --- | --- | --- | --- |
| | | Num-ber of farms | Farm acre-age | Crop-land har-vested | Value of land and build-ings | Value of farm prod-ucts sold (1949) |
| Commercial farms classified ac-cording to value of farm products reported sold in 1949................ | 3,706.4 | 68.9 | 88.1 | 94.9 | 87.7 | 99.0 |
| I. $25,000 or over......... | 103.2 | 1.9 | 21.6 | 11.8 | 15.2 | 26.4 |
| II. $10,000–$24,999......... | 381.2 | 7.1 | 18.6 | 22.1 | 21.1 | 25.2 |
| III.  5,000–  9,999......... | 721.2 | 13.4 | 18.5 | 26.6 | 22.1 | 23.1 |
| IV.  2,500–  4,999......... | 882.3 | 16.4 | 14.5 | 19.2 | 15.5 | 14.6 |
| V.  1,200–  2,499......... | 901.3 | 16.8 | 9.5 | 10.5 | 9.4 | 7.4 |
| VI.   250–  1,199......... | 717.2 | 13.3 | 5.2 | 4.7 | 4.4 | 2.3 |
| Other farms.................. | 1,672.8 | 31.1 | 11.9 | 5.1 | 12.3 | 1.0 |
| Part-time units*............. | 639.2 | 11.9 | 4.2 | 3.0 | 5.2 | 0.2 |
| Residential units†............ | 1,029.4 | 19.1 | 4.4 | 1.8 | 6.4 | 0.4 |
| Abnormal units‡............ | 4.2 | 0.07 | 3.3 | 0.3 | 0.7 | 0.4 |
| Total census farms........ | 5,379.2 | 100.0 | 100.0 | 100.0 | 100.0 | 100.0 |

* Part-time farms, as here defined, include those farms with a value of products sold of $250 to $1,999 and operators reporting 100 days or more of off-farm work or off-farm income exceeding the value of the agricultural products sold.

† Residential units include those that reported less than $250 value of products sold in 1949.

‡ Abnormal units include public and private institutional farms, community projects, and other similar types of enterprises.

tractors), and the fact that most of their operators make little or no pretense of being bona fide farmers, it is probably a mistake to consider these units as farms.

Regardless of whether the cases of nominal operators are separated from those of the more commercial farmers, it should be recognized that the nominal group has exerted an important effect on tenure statistics. As the data reported in Table 31 indicate, more than two-fifths of the full owners as compared with less than one-eighth of the part owners and slightly over one-fifth of the tenants were nominal operators. Among the tenant subgroups, high proportions of the cash and other and unspecified groups may be classed as nominal farmers. The retabulation of these same data in Table 32 indicates that the proportion of owner-operatorship among commercial operators is about 4 per cent lower than among

*Table* 31. Percentage Distribution of Tenure Groups by Economic Class, 1950

| Economic classes of farms | All tenure groups | Full owners | Part owners | Man-agers | Tenants | | | | | |
| | | | | | All | Cash | Cash-share | Share | Crop-per | Other and unspec-ified |
|---|---|---|---|---|---|---|---|---|---|---|
| Commercial farms..... | 68.9 | 58.7 | 88.4 | 83.7 | 79.2 | 62.6 | 98.4 | 84.9 | 81.7 | 53.3 |
| Class I...... | 1.9 | 1.2 | 4.9 | 28.1 | 1.3 | 1.9 | 1.9 | 1.8 | 0.1 | 0.7 |
| Class II..... | 7.1 | 4.6 | 14.9 | 23.9 | 7.6 | 6.5 | 19.3 | 9.5 | 0.6 | 3.4 |
| Class III.... | 13.4 | 10.2 | 22.7 | 20.7 | 14.8 | 12.2 | 35.4 | 17.7 | 3.8 | 7.5 |
| Class IV..... | 16.4 | 14.3 | 21.2 | 6.3 | 18.3 | 13.3 | 25.5 | 20.4 | 17.3 | 11.6 |
| Class V...... | 16.8 | 15.4 | 15.6 | 3.1 | 20.5 | 13.9 | 12.1 | 19.9 | 33.0 | 14.4 |
| Class VI..... | 13.3 | 13.0 | 9.1 | 1.6 | 16.7 | 14.8 | 4.2 | 15.6 | 26.9 | 15.7 |
| Other farms.... | 31.1 | 41.3 | 11.6 | 16.3 | 20.8 | 37.4 | 1.6 | 15.1 | 18.3 | 46.7 |
| Total........ | 100.0 | 100.0 | 100.0 | 100.0 | 100.0 | 100.0 | 100.0 | 100.0 | 100.0 | 100.0 |

SOURCE: Percentage data calculated from preliminary reports of 1950 Census of Agriculture.

*Table* 32. Percentage Distribution of Farms by Economic Class and Distribution of Total Value of Farm Products Sold in 1949 by Tenure Groups, 1950

| Tenure group | All census farms | Commercial-farm units | | | | | | | Other farms | Value of farm products sold in 1949 (commercial farms only) |
| | | All | Class I | Class II | Class III | Class IV | Class V | Class VI | | |
|---|---|---|---|---|---|---|---|---|---|---|
| Full owners....... | 57.4 | 48.9 | 36.4 | 37.7 | 43.5 | 50.0 | 52.9 | 55.8 | 76.2 | 40.4 |
| Part owners....... | 15.3 | 19.7 | 39.0 | 32.1 | 26.1 | 19.8 | 14.2 | 10.5 | 5.7 | 28.8 |
| Managers......... | 0.4 | 0.5 | 6.3 | 1.5 | 0.7 | 0.2 | 0.1 | 0.1 | 0.2 | 4.9 |
| All tenants........ | 26.9 | 30.9 | 18.3 | 28.7 | 29.7 | 30.0 | 32.8 | 33.6 | 17.9 | 25.9 |
| Cash.......... | 4.0 | 3.6 | 4.0 | 3.6 | 3.6 | 3.2 | 3.3 | 4.4 | 4.7 | 3.6 |
| Cash-share...... | 3.6 | 5.1 | 3.6 | 9.8 | 9.4 | 5.6 | 2.6 | 1.1 | 0.2 | 6.4 |
| Share.......... | 10.0 | 12.3 | 9.3 | 13.4 | 13.3 | 12.4 | 11.7 | 11.7 | 4.8 | 11.7 |
| Croppers....... | 6.4 | 7.6 | 0.4 | 0.5 | 1.8 | 6.8 | 12.7 | 13.0 | 3.8 | 2.7 |
| Others and un-specified.... | 2.9 | 2.3 | 1.0 | 1.4 | 1.6 | 2.0 | 2.5 | 3.4 | 4.4 | 1.5 |
| Total........ | 100.0 | 100.0 | 100.0 | 100.0 | 100.0 | 100.0 | 100.0 | 100.0 | 100.0 | 100.0 |

SOURCE: Percentage data calculated from preliminary reports of 1950 Census of Agriculture.

all census farm operators. The table also shows that the proportion of full owners is lowest in the class I economic group and that it tends to increase in each succeeding less productive group. Part owners and managers show their greatest proportionate strength on the class I and II farms, while tenants show their greatest numerical strength on the medium and less productive commercial units.

The high concentration of owner-operators on the nominal units and

on the smaller commercial enterprises suggests that farm owner-operatorship in and of itself should not be the primary objective in tenure
policy. An increasing proportion of owner-operatorship does not necessarily mean that farmers are better off. As a matter of fact, it seems
obvious that part of the increase in owner-operatorship reported since
1935 can be attributed to the suburbanization movement and its effect
in increasing the total number of rural residential units.

In addition to its contribution to a more realistic interpretation of farm-
land tenure statistics, the cross-classification of data on economic classes
of farms by tenure status affords a general measure of the relative efficiency and productivity of the several tenure groups. From the standpoint of their contributions to the gross value of farm products sold, the
full-owner group is most important. On an average per-operator basis,
however, the full owners rate as one of the least productive tenure
groups. Using the data for commercial farm units only, the various
tenure groups can be rated in the following order according to the ratio
between their contribution to the total value of farm products sold in
1949 and their number of commercial farm operators: managers 9.80,
part owners 1.46, share-cash tenants 1.25, share tenants 0.95, all tenants
0.84, full owners 0.83, other and unspecified 0.65, and croppers 0.36.

The high ratings assigned to the manager, part owner, and share-cash
tenant groups can be explained largely in terms of the nature of their
operations and by the fact that many of these operators, particularly
among the part owners, are in the most aggressive and accumulative
stage of their lifework cycle. The generally low rating assigned to the
full owners and to the other and unspecified tenant groups, on the other
hand, reflects the fact that these groups include numerous semiretired
and part-time operators who farm on a limited scale. The sharecroppers
also tend to fall into this least efficient productive group because they are
handicapped in the efficient use of their labor by their small farm acreages, their small investments in equipment, livestock and other operating
capital, and the general underemployment of much of their potential
labor force during a large part of the year.

Extreme care must be taken in judging the productivity of any farm
operator in terms of group averages. Actually, the operators in each
group are spread over the full range of economic classifications according
to value of gross commercial production (cf. Table 31). As a group, the
sharecroppers were least productive, but many sharecroppers produced
farm products of greater value in 1949 than the average share-cash tenant
or the average part owner. While numerous differences may appear on a
regional or local basis, the national data suggest that the average tenant
operating a commercial farm is as efficient and productive as the average
full owner. Both tenants and owners are found among the more efficient

producers. They also are found well intermixed among the ranks of the least producers.

## The Farm Tenancy Problem

Considerable has been written, particularly during the past two decades, concerning the farm tenancy problem. This problem probably came in for more public consideration and discussion during the late 1930's than at any other time. Much of the reason for spotlighting attention on tenancy at that time can be attributed to the high proportion of tenancy then reported in the country, to the general but crucial problem of poverty in agriculture which many people associated with tenancy, and to the publication of the report of the President's Special Committee on Farm Tenancy.[14]

Continued attention was given to the tenancy problem throughout the 1940's. But the complexion of the problem changed. With higher farm incomes, higher farm price levels, and increasing opportunities for non-farm employment, the tenancy problem became less acute. The magnitude of this change clearly indicates that much of the tenancy problem of the 1930's can be attributed directly to depressed business conditions and low farm income levels.

The problem of farm tenancy is essentially one of allocating the rights and responsibilities of farm operatorship between landlords and tenants. Since this allocation process involves the supplying and contribution of capital and labor as well as the sharing of income, it of necessity involves income and cost factors. But it also involves other details in leasing arrangements and landlord-tenant relations. Most studies of farm tenancy have been primarily concerned with inventories of situations and trends, policy recommendations, or the promotion of reforms. Less attention has been given to economic analyses of tenancy problems. Among the more promising tenancy problems that now suggest themselves for study are the relationships that exist between the use of varying types of leasing arrangements and operator efficiency and productivity, the operator's progress in climbing the ladder to ownership, his use of conservation practices, and his response to farm mechanization and other technological improvements.[15]

*The Place of Tenancy in the American Tenure System.* With the attention that has been given to the farm tenancy problem in recent years, there has been some tendency to condemn tenancy as bad. This line of reasoning runs counter to the usual concept of the place of farm tenancy in the American land-tenure system. Admittedly, many unfortunate

[14] *Farm Tenancy,* Report of the President's Committee, Washington, February, 1937.

[15] Max M. Tharp, "A Reappraisal of Farm Tenure Research," *Land Economics,* Vol. 24, p. 328, November, 1948.

tenancy conditions do exist, and programs involving varying amounts of public help or guidance may be needed to alleviate undesirable conditions and to promote farm and home ownership. At the same time, however, tenancy has a definite place in the tenure system.

Farm tenancy is often considered as a steppingstone to ownership. In this sense it represents one of the most important rungs on the agricultural ladder because it provides a means by which the young farmer can acquire operator experience and accumulate at least part of the fund of capital he needs to become an owner. Recent studies indicate that the agricultural ladder does not operate as generally as many people have assumed it should.[16] With the maturing of our economy there has been a distinct tendency for more and more would-be owner-operators to by-step the tenancy rung and to rely upon gifts, inheritance, father-son partnership arrangements or other forms of family assistance, or upon receipts from off-farm employment for the financial help they need to establish themselves as owners. But a substantial number of young farmers still use the tenancy rung in their climb to ownership.

The opportunity to rent farms or tracts of farm land provides a boon to owners as well as tenants. Many owners or part owners use this opportunity to increase the size of their farm operations to optimum size during the more productive years of their life cycle or during the period of the family cycle when they have an abundant supply of family labor. Prospective purchasers also employ the tenancy relationship to advantage at times by using it as a means for trying out the farm lands they might buy in the future.

Many of the would-be owners who start out to climb the agricultural ladder fail to achieve ownership or to hold it once it has been achieved. In those cases where the farmer cannot "make the grade" as an owner, he often can make more effective uses of his resources as a tenant than by working as a hired laborer. Experience shows that many farm operators actually do better as tenants than as owners. In many instances, the tenant himself concludes that he can operate more efficiently by renting good farm land and using his limited fund of capital for equipment, livestock, or supplies than by investing it in the type of farm he can afford. In other cases the tenant may operate better under landlord supervision than when he is left to make his own managerial decisions.

Tenancy also plays an important role in the tenure system by cushioning the retired owner's retreat down the ladder. Many farm owners never feel that they are ready or able to retire. But if and when they do retire, they usually have most, if not all, of their assets tied up in farm property. Many farm families treat their farms as their savings bank. The tenancy

[16] Raleigh Barlowe and John F. Timmons, "What Has Happened to the Agricultural Ladder?" *Journal of Farm Economics,* Vol. 32, pp. 30–47, February, 1950.

system, with its provision for the renting of landlord-held farms, makes it possible for many of these owners to retire and secure retirement incomes in the form of rents and at the same time keep their savings invested, at least for a time, in a business that they know something about.

The decreasing proportion of tenancy reported in the United States since 1940 together with the increasing emphasis given to various types of intrafamily farm-operating arrangements suggests that farm tenancy no longer occupies the important place it did a few years ago in the American farm tenure system. Whether this trend is permanent or will reverse itself once the favorable farm price and farm-acquisition conditions of the 1940's and early 1950's change remains to be seen.

In reckoning the over-all importance of tenancy in the American tenure system, one must remember that intrafamily profit-sharing and operating arrangements usually provide much the same function as tenancy. Like tenancy, they provide for a division of farming returns between operator and landlord, and they give the operator an opportunity to accumulate both capital and experience. So long as there are no basic changes in the American tenure system, it seems probable that tenancy and its alternative arrangements will remain important. In fact, their importance is such that one might reasonably assume that the normal operation of our tenure system calls for their use on between one-fourth and one-third of the farms of the country. Tenancy, as it has been generally recognized in the past, may become less important, but any trend in this direction will probably be associated with the increased use of tenancy and sharing arrangements that operate within the framework of the farm family.

*Landlord-Tenant Relations.* A substantial number of farm tenants in this country have never succeeded in improving their tenure status and have experienced only limited success in improving their socioeconomic status. The reasons for this are many. In some cases, low farm prices, crop failures, and personal or family problems are responsible. In other cases operators have made bad decisions or have failed to make effective use of the resources they have. Many times, however, the tenure system itself seems to be at fault. The tenant may suffer because he lacks security in his farming operations, because his landlord will not permit him to adjust his system of farming to include crop or livestock enterprises that would maximize his productivity, because he does not receive a fair division of the farm income, or because he lacks incentive for conserving and building up the productivity of his farm.

Most of these factors involve details in the landlord-tenant relationship. These relations vary over a considerable range. Some landlords work out detailed agreements with their tenants and may go out of their way to help their tenants, to give them a sense of security and importance, and even to sponsor them as owners. In other cases, however, the landlord, the tenant, or both may have only a vague notion of their rights or responsibilities and may attempt to maximize their own interests by exploiting the rightful interests of the other party. It is in these cases that misunderstandings develop, and it is cases of this sort that call for improved landlord-tenant arrangements.

Numerous problems in landlord-tenant relations exist. Among the more important of these are the problems of (1) vague rental agreements, (2) duration of leases, (3) farm maintenance and improvement, (4) distribution of farm income, (5) the landlord's lien against the tenant for rent, and (6) type of landlord and the nature of his interest in the farm.

1. *Vague rental agreements.* Only about one out of every five farm leases in this country are in writing, and many of these are vague on details or are especially designed to protect the landlord's property and assure his collection of the agreed amount of rent. Most lease agreements involve nothing more than a short oral discussion covering such items as when the tenant will move to the farm, the size of his labor force, the acres of principal crops that will be grown, what livestock will be kept, and how much rent will be paid. In some areas and with some groups, as with the sharecroppers in the South, actual discussion of the leasing arrangements may be limited to the first two of these items with all other details and decisions being left to custom or subsequent negotiation.

Many of the ills of the tenancy system can be traced to the use of oral agreements or one-sided written contracts. There is nothing wrong with an oral agreement so long as both parties clearly understand their rights and responsibilities. But the usual oral agreement, as well as many written agreements, are faulty and only provide a basis for future misunderstandings and poor-quality farming. Customary arrangements are recognized in many areas and serve to some extent as a substitute for more definite leasing terms. One solution to the problem of vague leases might lie in legislative recognition of a few basic leasing arrangements covering different farming situations that would apply in the absence of written agreements. The only real solution, however, lies in the more general use of written leases. Many of the model lease forms now provided cover all the major problems that are apt to arise.[17] One of their chief virtues lies in the fact that they call attention to many aspects of the leasing agreement that often are left to future negotiation and they clearly spell out the rights and responsibilities of both the landlord and the tenant.

2. *Duration of leases.* Uncertainty of occupancy is one of the chief

[17] Cf. Max M. Tharp, *Your Farm Lease,* U.S. Department of Agriculture Miscellaneous Publication 627, revised 1949. Model lease forms are also provided by many of the state land-grant colleges.

evils of tenancy. It is a major cause of tenant unrest, instability in farming operations, and the high mobility of tenants from farm to farm. A tenant may stay on one farm for a dozen years, but during this entire period he may never know from one year until the next whether he will be permitted to stay on or will be required to move on short notice.

The uncertainty of this arrangement discourages the tenant from building up the farm or making desirable improvements. Furthermore, it often prevents him from using his resources in an effective manner by engaging in livestock and other similar enterprises that call for long-term planning and operations. Yet despite this situation the vast majority of the farm leases cover periods of only 1 year and contain neither automatic renewal clauses nor requirements for adequate notice of termination.

Long-term leases have definite advantages, especially where the system of farming demands long-term planning.[18] If the tenant is a livestock farmer, for example, he often finds it difficult to find another farm with pastures, barns, and equipment that fit his needs. Similarly, the landlord whose farm is equipped for livestock farming may have trouble in locating a new tenant with the livestock, equipment, and managerial ability necessary for the optimum utilization of his farm. Long-term leases provide one means for granting the tenant more security of occupancy. But they have not been particularly popular with either landlords or tenants in cash-crop farming areas. In many cases, neither party wants to be bound by a lease for a long period. A better solution to the problem of uncertainty of occupancy in areas where long-term leases are not essential to efficient agriculture probably lies in the use of automatic renewal clauses and requirement of adequate notice of termination of the lease. The usual recommendation along this line provides that all farm leases shall continue automatically for the next year unless written notice of termination is given to the tenant or the landlord some 4 to 6 months before the end of the tenancy. It is usually assumed that the tenant needs more notice than the landlord, but both parties to the agreement deserve considerable advance notice of any plans for change.

Closely related to the problem of insecurity of occupancy is the problem of high tenant mobility. Frequent moving prevents the building up of livestock enterprises, leads to the exploitation of farm resources, and is costly to both landlords and tenants. In many cases, tenants actually improve their positions by moving. But all too often little or nothing is gained by moving, and the tenant may actually lose because of the high cost of moving, disruption of the continuity of his farming operations and his community contacts, and the adverse effect that moving may

[18] Marshall Harris, Max M. Tharp, and Howard A. Turner, *Better Farm Leases,* U.S. Department of Agriculture Farmers' Bulletin 1969, pp. 10–14, June, 1945.

have on his children's education. The shifting of tenants from farm to farm is frequently caused by inadequate farms, poor houses and buildings, and lack of adequate facilities. These factors in turn reflect the lack of security of occupancy that discourages the tenant from attempting to build up his farm or improve his housing conditions.

3. *Farm maintenance and improvement.* Very few farm leases contain provisions for compensating tenants for the unexhausted value of improvements they have made during their period of tenancy. In all fairness to the tenant, he cannot be expected to carry on a farm-improvement program unless he has some assurance that he will enjoy the benefits of his work and investment either through the continued use of his improvements or through compensation for their unexhausted value at the time he leaves the farm. This is one of the chief reasons why tenant-operated farms are more apt to be run-down or poorly maintained than owner-operated units.

The problems of maintaining farms in good operating condition, carrying on soil-building programs, modernizing farm houses, putting up fences and needed farm service buildings, installing running water or electric systems, laying drainage tile, and making other farm improvements are such that landlords and tenants can best work together. Very often the landlord feels that he cannot make improvements of this type alone, while the tenant hesitates to invest in any improvements that he cannot take with him when he leaves the farm. Numerous arrangements can be worked out whereby the landlord and tenant work together for the maintenance and improvement of the farm and its buildings.[19] For any of these plans to be truly workable, however, it is necessary that they contain some provisions for compensating the tenant for the unexhausted value of any improvements he makes with the consent of the landlord.

The operation of plans of this type can provide a real boon for farm tenants because, so long as their landlords are willing, it gives them definite incentive for improving their housing conditions and building up the productivity of their farms. From the standpoint of equity, the provision in farm leases for compensation of tenants for unexhausted improvements should be balanced by comparable provisions for compensating landlords for damage or dilapidation of farm property during the tenant's occupancy.

4. *Distribution of farm income.* In many parts of the United States, custom plays a dominant role in the determination of rental rates. The customary sharecropping and "third and fourth" share-tenancy arrangements of the South can be cited as vivid examples. But even where custom seems to be the all-important factor, the forces of supply and

[19] Marshall D. Harris, "A Suggested Adjustment in the Farm Tenancy System," *Journal of Farm Economics*, Vol. 19, pp. 895–896, November, 1937.

demand often operate to bring adjustments in rental rates. For example, when there is considerable competition between tenants and others who want to rent land, rental rates usually tend to increase. If the land is rented for cash, the rental rate is simply increased. If a sharing arrangement is used, there may be some adjustment in the sharing terms. But very often the principal crops will be shared according to custom, while additional bonuses are paid in cash or kind for special items such as pasture land or miscellaneous crops.

Considerable work remains to be done in determining what is and what is not "fair rent" and what effect varying rental arrangements have upon resource use. From the standpoint of theoretical use of resources, it can be demonstrated that the share tenant who provides all his nondurable factors of production will reach the point where his marginal costs equal his share of the marginal returns sooner than the average cash tenant or owner-operator. This type of analysis suggests that the share tenant can maximize his returns by farming his land less intensively than owner-operators or cash tenants.[20] In actual practice, however, this conclusion does not always seem to apply. Share-rented and cash-rented farms are operated with approximately the same degree of intensity. Among the reasons responsible for this situation one might list (1) the inability of the average tenant to recognize the exact point, or even the approximate point, at which his marginal cost equals his marginal return, (2) the fact that most landlords who rent on a share basis provide a share of the equipment, seed, fertilizer, and other production expenses, as well as the farm land and buildings, and (3) the fact that the landlord through his control over the terms of the lease and its prospects for renewal can insist that the tenant farm the land as intensively as if it were being owner-operated.

Farm-leasing arrangements are usually imperfect in that they seldom, if ever, "result in (1) the most efficient organization of resources on the farm relative to consumer demand as expressed in market prices and (2) an equitable division of the product among the owners of the various resources employed in production."[21] One of the hardest problems in determining equitable rental rates is that of devising arrangements that will compensate both the landlord and the tenant for their respective contributions to production. In theory, the landlord has a claim to the full economic rent of the land plus a return for his other inputs based on their marginal productivity. The problem with con-

---

[20] Cf. Rainer Schickele, "Effects of Tenure Systems on Agricultural Efficiency," *Journal of Farm Economics*, Vol. 23, pp. 185–198, February, 1941; Earl O. Heady, "Economics of Farm Leasing Systems," *Journal of Farm Economics*, Vol. 29, pp. 659–678, August, 1947; and D. Gale Johnson, "Resource Allocation under Share Contracts," *Journal of Political Economy*, Vol. 58, pp. 111–123, April, 1950.

[21] Heady, *op. cit.*, p. 660.

tract rent is that of determining in advance what this fair return should be and then translating it in terms of cash or share-rental arrangements.

Actually, there is no hard or fast rule for determining in advance what a "fair rent" is. Most rental rates are established in terms of past experience though various types of flexible arrangements are used to adjust the size of the actual rental payment to crop yields and changing price conditions. Landlords and tenants should work toward rental arrangements that call for the reasonable and equitable distribution of farm income. This is not hard to do in prosperous times. Serious problems can arise in low-income periods, however, when the need for income is such that both parties must press for personal advantage. So long as an acceptable sharing arrangement is used, share leases provide a basis for a reasonably fair division of farm income and expenses in both good and bad years. Much the same end can be achieved with cash leases when a sliding-scale arrangement is incorporated as an integral part of the cash leasing arrangement.

5. *Landlord's lien for rent.* Many aspects of landlord-tenant relationships are governed by law. Most of the legislation embodied in the usual landlord-tenant code is designed to spell out the rights and duties of landlords and tenants under varying conditions. Some of these laws enumerate the tenant's responsibilities to the landlord for maintenance of the property, payment of rent, etc. While the principle behind these measures is usually sound, their existence can at times complicate the tenant's problem in operating the farm.

An example of this is found in the usual lien that the landlord has against the tenant for rent. In many states this lien applies to the tenant's chattels as well as his crops and to the entire crop grown on the farm instead of just to the landlord's share of the crop. This situation complicates the tenant's problem in securing production credit because Federal credit agencies and most low-cost private credit agencies will not grant credit unless the tenant can get a waiver of his landlord's lien. Many landlords cooperate with the tenant so that he can secure the credit he needs for his operations. Where the landlord refuses to waive his statutory lien, the tenant usually is forced either to use the high-cost furnish credit provided by local merchants, landlords, and others or to operate with considerably less capital than he needs for the effective use of his other farming resources. This situation can probably best be remedied by limiting the landlord's lien so that tenants can secure production and operating credit from local banks and other credit agencies without obtaining a waiver of the landlord's lien.

6. *Type of landlord.* Considerable differences exist between landlords and the extent and nature of the interest they have in their farms and their tenants. Many landlords feel a close personal interest in maintain-

ing their farms and keeping a cordial relationship with their tenants. Another group, which includes large numbers of absentee and even some institutional owners, often has little interest in the farm or the tenant and is most interested in collecting all the rent it can. Still another group includes large numbers of widows and retired operators who have some interest in the farm but who are dependent upon their limited rental receipts for their living.[22]

Many of the most serious tenancy problems arise when the landlord is primarily interested in rent rather than in the farm itself. The tenant who rents from an absentee owner, for example, often finds that the landlord is unwilling to contribute anything for the maintenance or improvement of the farm or its buildings. Since the tenant has a very impersonal relationship with his landlord, he frequently is handicapped in his longer-term operations because of his uncertainty concerning his future status. Should he attempt to improve the farm at his own expense, his reward may come in form of a request for more rent or he may lose the farm to some other tenant who is willing to bid up the rent.

Similar situations arise when widows or retired owners are not inclined, or do not have the means, to maintain or develop their farm properties. Unless these landlords are especially interested in their heirs, they are likely to have little interest in long-time improvements. Their interests often call for maximization of current incomes even though this might lead to soil depletion and the exploitation and deterioration of their buildings and improvements.

No means have as yet been devised under our tenure system to control types of landlords or to prevent them from exploiting their tenants or farms. The development of better leasing arrangements can give the tenant some of the protection he needs in dealing with absentee as well as with other types of landlords. Other measures dealing with social-security benefits, transfer of farm ownership, and the maintenance and conservation of farm resources also can be used to deal with the problems that arise when personal interests in the maximization of current farm incomes conflict with the longer-run interests of society.

---

[22] The importance of this group is suggested by the 1946 survey of farm ownership in the Middle West, which shows that 25.5 per cent of the owners in that region could be classed as nonoperating landlords and that almost one-third of the owners in this group, as compared with only one-ninth in the total group, were women. Of the owners in the nonoperating landlord group, 37 per cent of the men and 56 per cent of the women were 65 years of age or over. Ninety-seven per cent of the women and 63 per cent of the men nonoperating owners over the age of 50 reported that they were dependent upon the rent from their farms for the major portion of their incomes. Cf. John F. Timmons and Raleigh Barlowe, *Farm Ownership in the Midwest*, North Central Regional Publication 4, Iowa Agricultural Experiment Station Research Bulletin 361, pp. 861, 866, 872, June, 1949.

*Family-farm Ownership*

Owner-operatorship of family-sized farms has long been regarded as one of the principal goals of American land and agricultural policy. There has often been disagreement over what constitutes a family-sized farm, and public programs at times have tended to work at cross-purposes with this goal. But the concept of the owner-operated family farm has always been popular, and public leaders and groups have frequently reemphasized its importance.[23]

The fostering and maintenance of family-farm ownership involves a number of problems related to the acquisition of ownership, the maintenance of ownership once it has been acquired, and the transfer of farms. In addition to these factors, family-farm ownership also is affected by concentration and parcellation of ownership holdings and by public land-ownership policies.

*Ownership-acquisition Problems.* The principal problem faced by most would-be farm owners in this country centers around their accumulation of the fund of investment capital they need to buy the farm they want. In some respects this problem has been made more serious by increasing land values and by higher capital requirements for livestock, equipment, and other production expenses. At the same time, however, the would-be owner of today often finds that he can earn and save more money as a tenant or as a farm or nonfarm laborer than was the case when farm capital requirements were lower. Also he can borrow money easier and on more liberal terms and he can look forward to a higher income as an owner than was often the case in the past.

All things considered, the young farmer of today probably faces a no more serious problem in acquiring and paying for his farm than did his father or his grandfather. He must pay much more for land than did the homesteaders who carved farms out of the frontier, but once he buys his land he has a going farm which is near established markets and which can be operated immediately on a commercial basis.

The question of whether or not the capital requirements for farming are too high can be answered only in terms of future production and income. If the farmer buys land on credit at the crest of the land-value cycle, he will probably find that he is called upon to pay a high price for his land out of a declining income from the farm. This problem was faced by many farmers who bought land in the early and late 1920's. On the other hand, if he buys when land prices are low, as during the late

[23] Cf. *Landownership Survey on Federal Reclamation Projects,* pp. 61–93, U.S. Bureau of Reclamation, 1946; Joseph Ackerman and Marshall Harris (eds.), *Family Farm Policy,* University of Chicago Press, Chicago, 1947; *Family Farm Policy Review,* U.S. Department of Agriculture, 1951 (mimeo.).

1930's and early 1940's, he may capitalize on the higher incomes that come with better times.

An indication of the principal methods of farm acquisition used by owners, as reported in the 1946 farm-ownership survey, is reported in Table 33. This tabulation shows that 26 per cent of the owners had ac-

*Table* 33. Methods of Farm-ownership Acquisition by Number of Owners, Acreage, and Value of Holdings, United States and Regions, 1946
(In per cent)

| Item and region | Method of farm acquisition | | | | |
| | No gift or inheritance | | | Some gift or inheritance | |
| | Pur-chase | Homesteading, part or all | Other | Gift or inherit-ance | Combinations with some gift or inheritance |
|---|---|---|---|---|---|
| Number of owners: | | | | | |
| United States......... | 68 | 2 | 4 | 11 | 15 |
| Northeast............. | 78 | 1 | 1 | 12 | 8 |
| North Central......... | 67 | 2 | 4 | 13 | 16 |
| South................ | 64 | 3 | 4 | 11 | 18 |
| West................. | 73 | 6 | 4 | 7 | 10 |
| Acreage: | | | | | |
| United States......... | 56 | 4 | 8 | 8 | 24 |
| Northeast............. | 72 | 1 | 2 | 14 | 11 |
| North Central......... | 58 | 4 | 5 | 10 | 23 |
| South................ | 54 | 1 | 9 | 9 | 27 |
| West................. | 50 | 12 | 15 | 4 | 19 |
| Value of farms: | | | | | |
| United States......... | 62 | 2 | 4 | 10 | 22 |
| Northeast............. | 78 | * | 2 | 12 | 8 |
| North Central......... | 60 | 1 | 4 | 12 | 23 |
| South................ | 59 | 2 | 5 | 9 | 25 |
| West................. | 66 | 5 | 6 | 6 | 17 |

* Less than 0.5 per cent.

SOURCE: Buis T. Inman and William H. Fippin, *Farm Land Ownership in the United States*, Tables 23 and 47, U.S. Department of Agriculture Miscellaneous Publication 699, 1949.

quired all or part of their holdings through gifts or inheritance and that these owners held 32 per cent of the farm acreage and value. The owners in the North Central region and in the South benefited to a greater extent from gifts and inheritance than did the owners in the Northeast and the West. Only fragmentary data are available concerning the trend in farm-acquisition methods, but these data generally indicate an increasing reliance on the use of gifts and inheritances in the farm-acquisition process.[24]

Approximately two-thirds of the present owners have purchased all of their land. As our economy becomes more mature, family assistance may become the major factor in farm acquisition. But even if this should occur, the public interest calls for programs that help to keep the door to ownership open to farmers who do not benefit from family assistance. These programs center around the provision of adequate low-cost long-term credit facilities. They might also involve farm training programs, the provision of public land-appraisal services, and emphasis on keeping farm capital requirements in line with the income productivity of farms.

*Maintaining Farm Ownership.* Many farmers have acquired ownership in the past only to lose it because the income they have received from their farms has not proved sufficient to support their families and still carry their credit and tax loads. This situation may result from low farm price levels, inadequate farms, overvaluation of farms for purchase or credit purposes, crop failures, family crises, and similar problems.

The programs needed to meet these problems are as diverse as the problems themselves. They may be limited to coverage of emergency situations or they may be designed to subsidize inefficient as well as worthy owners. Over the long run, it would be hard to justify any program designed to maintain all owners as owners because in farming as in other businesses the economy should allow for weeding out the less efficient operators. Experience suggests, however, that many of the owners who have lost their farms through mortgage foreclosure or tax reversion have been victims of circumstances. Various types of programs are needed to assist worthy farmers of this type by granting them greater security of occupancy and more security in their expectations.

In most cases farm price supports and other measures designed to maintain farm incomes can play an effective role in preventing mortgage foreclosures or tax reversion. At times, however, the owner's farm is too small or inadequate to meet his family needs. In such cases guidance or outright assistance may be needed to enlarge or improve the farm so that it might be considered an economic unit.

Buyers should be cautioned against buying farms on a "shoestring" during periods when prices seem high in relation to future income expectations. Loan agencies can often do the borrower a service by refusing to grant large loans, particularly in cases where the risk element is high, and by writing their loans to provide for amortized payments and to

[24] Cf. Timmons and Barlowe, *op. cit.*, pp. 888–889.

permit variable payments.[25] During depression or national emergency periods special mortgage-moratoria measures may be needed to protect owners against foreclosure proceedings. In all fairness to the mortgagee, however, standstill arrangements of this type should be used only so long as the borrower maintains the farm, operates it in an acceptable husbandly manner, and shows willingness to share his limited farm income with the lender.

Crop-insurance programs in natural hazard areas and personal life, health, and accident insurance programs also can be used to advantage as means of assuring the maintenance of farm ownership. Where farm property taxes are high, measures designed to reduce public services, to limit taxes, or to enlarge the tax base can help to reduce the dangers of tax delinquency and tax reversion.

*Transferring Farm Ownership.* The manner in which land is transferred from one owner to another and the cost of such transfers constitute a significant, but still often overlooked, aspect of land tenure. The examination and clearing of titles, preparation and maintenance of abstracts, and use of title insurance frequently result in high transfer costs and may occasion considerable delay in title transfers. Yet it is important for buyers to insist on clear titles to their farms because faulty titles may lead to insecurity of occupancy and the inefficient use of farm resources.

The problem of title transfers is much more serious in some areas than in others. In those areas where serious problems exist, the cost of title transfers often can be reduced through simplification of legal procedures and transfer practices by public guarantees of farm-land surveys, by establishing permanent boundary markers between properties, or by the adoption of the Torrens system or some similar system of land-title registration.

Another serious problem in the transferring of farm land sometimes arises in connection with ownership of fractional interests in mineral and oil rights.[26] When these rights are widely distributed among many individuals, the farmer who is primarily interested in occupying and using the surface may experience difficulty in planning his farming operations and in providing legal security for the credit he may need to finance these operations. These problems can usually be avoided where state legislation permits the separation of surface and subsurface ownership rights in land or where reservations of subsurface rights are limited to certain periods after which the land titles are automatically cleared.

---

[25] *Improving Land Credit Arrangements in the Midwest,* North Central Regional Publication 19, Purdue University Agricultural Experiment Station Bulletin 551, pp. 31–39, June, 1950.

[26] R. D. Davidson and L. A. Parcher, *The Influence of Mineral Rights on Transfers of Farm Real Estate in Oklahoma,* Oklahoma Agricultural Experiment Station Bulletin B-278, pp. 3–16, February, 1944.

Considerable interest has been focused during the past few years on the extensive waste, both economic and social, that is often associated with the transfer of farms from one generation to the next through the use of gifts, wills, and intestate transfers. Only about one out of every six farmers now has a will, and the fact that a high proportion of farm owners die without making satisfactory arrangements for the continued operation of their farms complicates the ownership picture. Unsettled estates may even lie idle because the heirs disagree over how they should be handled. Many farms are subdivided between several heirs, or the livestock and equipment are dispersed. In this process the farm usually loses much of its going-concern value, and, for a time at least, it usually becomes a less efficient production unit.

The final settlement of estates may be delayed for years after the owner's death. During this period plans for the eventual disposition of the property often remain vague, and the actual operator of the farm, whether he is an heir or an outsider, has no guarantee concerning his permanency of occupancy. Under these circumstances, farms frequently are allowed to deteriorate.

When an owner dies intestate—without leaving a will—his property is distributed according to the state laws of descent and distribution. Under the usual application of these laws all the children of a deceased owner share alike in his estate regardless of whether or not they stayed on the farm or made substantial contributions to the family livelihood or to the value of the farm enterprise. Unless the parent makes a will or other arrangements, the son or daughter who stays and looks after the parents receives only the legal equal share in the settlement of the estate. Heirs of this type often are willing to buy out the interests of other heirs, but they usually find it necessary to mortgage the farm. Even then, the sentimental feeling that the various heirs have for the home farm frequently makes it necessary for them to pay higher settlement prices than the long-time earning value of the farm will justify.

Farm owners can avoid many of the succession problems that arise on farms by making wills or other arrangements that clearly specify who is to get the farm. When one of the heirs has stayed on the farm and helped to support his parents, he probably should be favored in comparison with the other heirs. In cases of this type, owners should emphasize equitable rather than equal treatment of heirs.

Where suitable family and income arrangements can be worked out, it is often desirable to turn farms over to sons or other members of the family at the time the parent is ready to retire. Numerous intrafamily farm-transfer arrangements of this type have been worked out.[27] The chief ad-

[27] Several articles and bulletins have been written concerning the problem of succession on farms. One of the first is Kenneth H. Parsons and Eliot O. Waples,

vantages of these arrangements lie in the fact that they ensure continuity of operation of the farm going concern and they give the owner-in-prospect an opportunity to take over the full management of the farm at an earlier age than he would if he waited for settlement of the family estate. Arrangements of this type usually contain provisions guaranteeing a retirement income plus other perquisites to the retiring parents.

A number of other arrangements can be used to facilitate the settlement of estates and their continuous operation as productive farm units. Except in specified cases, it may be desirable to limit the period during which farm estates may be settled. Special property agreements can be used to protect the interests of children or other heirs who undertake the maintenance or improvement of the home farm during a period while an estate remains unsettled. Special sliding-scale settlement-price plans can be used to protect heirs during the period they are buying out estates against undue hazards from production failures or depression prices. Arrangements also can be made to prevent the undue deterioration of farms held as life estates.

*Concentration and Parcellation of Holdings.* Achievement of the family-farm-ownership goal in the United States is thwarted to some extent by the trend toward concentration and parcellation of ownership holdings. Concentration can be measured in numerous ways. The 1950 census indicates that 121,000 farms, slightly over 2 per cent of the farms in the nation, covered 1,000 acres or more. The data on economic classes of farms in 1950 (Table 30, p. 271) show that 2 per cent of the farms also had production valued at $25,000 or more and thus qualified for classification as large-scale farms. Both of these measures are indicative of the amount of concentration in ownership in this country, but both involve operating rather than ownership units and both include large numbers of farms that can properly be regarded as family-sized units.

Another measure of concentration is provided by the 1946 survey of farm ownership in the Middle West.[28] This study shows that 16 per cent of the owners had two farms (or farm tracts), 4.4 per cent had three farms, and 2.3 per cent had four or more farms per owner. The owners with four or more farms accounted for 8.4 per cent of the total number of farms, 9.4 per cent of the farm acreage, and 7.7 per cent of the farm value. The same study shows that the proportion of landlords with more than one farm increased from 12 per cent in 1900 and 13 per cent in 1920 to 21 per cent in 1926.

---

*Keeping the Farm in the Family,* Wisconsin Agricultural Experiment Station Research Bulletin 157, September, 1945. A more recent study based on research in several states is reported by Marshall Harris and Elton B. Hill, *Family Farm-Transfer Arrangements,* North Cental Regional Publication 18, Illinois Agicultural Experiment Station Circular 680, 1951.

[28] Timmons and Barlowe, *op. cit.,* pp. 912–915.

Unlike many parts of the world where concentration of ownership often is accompanied by inefficient use of much of the land, many of the large and concentrated holdings in this country are farmed rather intensively. In so far as the large-scale farms (Table 30) represent concentration of holdings, these farms represent the best-equipped and most productive units in the nation. The principal arguments against large holdings in this country center around the fact that they frequently are held by absentee or corporate owners who do little to promote community values and who are often in a position to outbid bona fide farmers who seek to buy farms of their own.

The case against large-scale farm ownership in the United States is far from clear-cut. Many people feel that ownership rights should be widely distributed and that concentration of ownership holdings savors of monopoly and represents a threat to the future of the family farm. Others argue that it would be a mistake to limit the size of farms at a time when technological advances make it both possible and desirable for the efficient operator to farm larger and larger areas. The experience of the Soviet Union with its huge state farms suggests that extremely large farms are uneconomic and that this factor alone can be expected to limit the size of operating units. It need not, however, affect the number of tenant or manager-operated units that can be held in one ownership.

Several methods can be used to prevent undue concentration of ownership in this country. During the 1930's a number of states enacted legislation limiting both the time mortgage-loan corporations could hold land and the areas they could hold. This type of legislation, though originally designed to deal with the holding of mortgage-foreclosed lands, can be adapted to prevent nonagricultural corporations from purchasing farm land, to limit the activities of farming corporations, or to prevent any large-scale farming. Modification of state and Federal income-tax regulations in order to prevent corporations or individuals from using farm-land investments as a means of avoiding taxes on earnings from other endeavors might also deter some prospective absentee owners from buying farm land.

The general property tax provides an effective tool for discouraging ownership concentration. It was used rather effectively by frontier settlers to discourage the holding of undeveloped farm land for speculation purposes. Its continued enforcement assures that the land will be used fairly intensively by most owners and that owners will not long continue to maintain holdings of uneconomic size. Graduated land taxes have been suggested as a means of taxing large farms at a higher property tax rate than small farms (cf. Chapter 13). This approach has been used in Australia and New Zealand but has not as yet been actively applied in this country.

Homestead tax exemptions also are designed to favor special types of property owners (veterans, widows, small owners) at the expense of others. Thirteen states now have homestead tax exemptions that exempt farm and home owners from all or part of the tax levies on as much as the first $5,000 of their assessed tax valuation. On the surface, these exemptions seem to favor small-owner operatorship at the expense of the landlord and the large owner. But the over-all effect of these exemptions on the achievement of the family-farm-ownership goal involves the impact that the tax programs used to secure replacement revenues in relation to the taxes lost through the exemptions on the incomes and savings of tenants and other prospective owners as well as owner-operators.[29] Where the tax load is shifted to landlords and the larger owners, the small owners benefit. When replacement revenues are secured through the use of regressive taxes such as a gross sales tax, however, small owners and prospective owners may actually suffer.

The problem of concentration of ownership in this country has not as yet developed to the point, as it has in many of the agrarian-reform nations of the world, where there is widespread popular support or clamor for public acquisition, subdivision, and distribution of large estates. This problem probably will not arise so long as the road to ownership remains open to the average would-be owner and so long as capital and labor, rather than land, are the really scarce factors in our farm-production pattern. Once land becomes the scarce and strategic item, as it is in many parts of the world, public policy may call for breaking large holdings up into smaller economic-sized units so that the land can be farmed more intensively.

In many parts of the world, parcellation of ownership and operatorship units is a problem that parallels ownership concentration in importance. This is particularly true in many parts of the Old World where farm tracts frequently have been subdivided so often as a result of inheritance that many peasants now have total holdings of little more than garden-plot size. Farm fields in these areas often are divided into numerous narrow ribbon strips, each owned by a different person in the village. Even the peasants with small holdings usually operate a considerable number of these small and sometimes widely scattered strips, and holdings involving 10 to 20 or more strips are not uncommon.[30]

The evils of parcellation and excessive subdivision in these countries

[29] Cf. R. Barlowe, "Homestead Tax Exemption: A Tenure Improvement Measure?" *Journal of Land and Public Utility Economics*, Vol. 23, pp. 360–370, November, 1947.

[30] An extreme example of parcellation is provided by the case of a German holding consolidated during the 1930's. The original holding of 23.9 hectares was divided into 438 separate plots (645 separate legally registered parcels). After consolidation the holding had 22.6 hectares in 14 plots. Cf. Robert Steuer, *Die Flurbereinigung*, Ernst Wilhelm Schultz Verlag, Minden, Westfalen, 1950.

are easily recognized in inefficient operations and the presence of numerous holdings of uneconomic size. Public programs have been undertaken in some areas to consolidate scattered holdings into more compact units. Some countries, such as Czechoslovakia, also have gone so far as to prohibit the subdivision of farm holdings when this results in the creation of new units of less than a specified minimum size.[31]

The problem of parcellation is by no means as important in the United States as in parts of Europe or Asia. But the processes of land purchase and inheritance have brought about the creation of many so-called farm units that are actually too small for economic operation as full-time farms. According to the 1950 census, 9 per cent of the farms contain less than 10 acres, while 25 per cent contain less than 30 acres. Many of these small farms are a direct outgrowth of the suburbanization movement which has brought a considerable increase in the number of small residential and part-time farming units around cities. So long as the owners of these units draw on nonfarm sources for much of their income these units may be all right. However, should their owners attempt to farm them on a full-time basis, they may soon become an integral part of the general problem of poverty in agriculture. When parcellation leads to uneconomic operations, the answer lies in either transferring the operators to more productive farms or in enlarging the small units to economic size.

*Public Ownership of Farm Land.* Approximately 29 per cent of the land area of the United States is held and administered by various Federal, state, and local governmental agencies. Well over half of this area is found in public forests, in special-use areas such as parks, wildlife refuges, military reservations, and highways, or can be designated as wasteland (cf. Table 19, p. 252). Of the remaining area in public ownership about 7 million acres are cropland, while 250 million acres can be classed as pasture or grazing land.

Few objections have been raised concerning the public ownership of cropland because the areas now held represent less than 2 per cent of the cropland in the country. These lands are used primarily for experimental purposes or are included in Indian and institutional holdings. More concern has been evidenced over the 36 per cent of the pasture and grazing lands of the nation that are in public ownership. Most of these holdings are located in the West. Included among them are 141 million acres administered under the Taylor Grazing Act together with large areas of grazed national forest lands, Indian lands, miscellaneous Federal lands, and state and county holdings. Some of these lands were purchased by the Federal government for grazing use, while others

---

[31] "Czechoslovakia's Law on Subdivision of Farm Holdings," *Land Economics*, Vol. 26, pp. 81–83, February, 1950.

were once privately owned but reverted to state or county ownership for nonpayment of taxes.

A high proportion of the public grazing lands are interspersed with railroad and other privately owned lands and have been used for public grazing purposes since the West was first opened for settlement. In a sense, many of these lands are residual areas because they were available for homesteading but never homesteaded, and at the same time they were not included in the government's reservations of forest, park, and mineral lands. In times past, stockmen often acquired title to base-camp and watering areas and relied on the surrounding public lands for grazing. During the last two decades, however, many of these lands have become subject to group-tenure arrangements as cooperative grazing associations have been organized to supervise the management of large areas of public and private grazing land.[32]

For the most part, public ownership of grazing land does not constitute a threat to the family-farm idea. But it does involve family-farm and ranch operations because practically all public grazing lands are leased to individuals or cooperative groups on a permit or fee basis and the continued use of these lands is essential to the successful operation of many farms and ranches.

There has been some agitation for the sale of public grazing lands to private owners. Generally speaking, there should be no objection to this procedure so long as the areas sold (1) can be divided into appropriate individual ownership units, (2) are economically capable of paying their own way in the future, (3) do not involve serious multiple-use conflicts, and (4) are not needed for other public purposes.[33] Very few of the lands, however, can meet these four criteria. Some of the lands already are included in national forests or other public reserves. Most of them involve mutiple-use administration for watershed, forestry, and recreational, as well as grazing, use and probably should remain subject to a considerable measure of public control. The fact that many of these lands are used under group tenure would make it difficult to carve out private grazing-land holdings of economic size without adversely affecting the interests of other users. Finally, the character of much of the public grazing land is such that private owners could ill afford to hold it and pay taxes on it during many years.

Under present conditions it seems probable that most of the public grazing lands of the West should and will remain in public ownership

---

[32] Cf. Chap. 14; also C. W. Loomer and V. Webster Johnson, *Group Tenure in the Administration of Public Lands*, U.S. Department of Agriculture Circular 829, December, 1949. By 1945, 65 grazing districts had been organized, covering 265 million acres.

[33] M. M. Kelso, "Current Issues in Federal Land Management in the Western United States," *Journal of Farm Economics*, Vol. 29, pp. 1295–1313, 1947.

subject to various types of group tenure. Consideration, however, should be given to the improvement of the leasing arrangements used on many state and Federally owned farm and ranch lands.

## Land-Tenure Policy

Because of general interest in land-tenure problems and trends, some attention should be given to tenure policy. This involves consideration of the goals of tenure policy together with an examination of the broad outlines of present policy as it applies to tenure conditions in this country and in other countries.

*Goals of Tenure Policy.* The United States has never had a clear or official statement of its land-tenure policy or its policy goals and objectives. Such policy pronouncements as have been issued have usually come piecemeal and have been incidental to the administration and disposal of the public domain or to the granting of farm credit. The concept of family-farm ownership and operatorship often has been regarded as an uppermost goal in American tenure policy; but like many popular and high-sounding slogans, this concept frequently has been ignored or forgotten when legislation regarding land use has been enacted.

During the past decade a number of people have given serious consideration to the problem of tenure goals, and several lists of goals have been prepared.[34] Generally, they agree that future tenure policy should attempt (1) to secure an equitable distribution of farm income among all tenure groups, (2) to foster greater efficiency in the farm production process, (3) to promote the conservation and development of the agricultural resources base, (4) to permit wide distribution of ownership control over land resources, but at the same time discourage the parcellation of farms into units of uneconomic size, (5) to promote the stability and welfare of rural institutions, (6) to provide individual farm operators with a feeling of security and dignity in their occupancy and possession of farm land, and (7) to leave the individual with considerable freedom of choice and with as much freedom for responsible personal action as is consistent with the general welfare.

Desirable as each of these objectives may be, it is recognized that they can and often do work at cross-purposes. Actually, they must all be treated together in the development of future tenure policy. In the final analysis

[34] Cf. Conrad Hammar, "The Land Tenure Ideal," *Journal of Land and Public Utility Economics*, Vol. 19, pp. 69–84, February, 1943; John F. Timmons, "Land Tenure Policy Goals," *Journal of Land and Public Utility Economics*, Vol. 19, pp. 165–179, May, 1943; Marshall Harris, "Objectives in Land Tenure Policy," *Caribbean Land Tenure Symposium*, pp. 30–48, Caribbean Commission, Trinidad, B.W.I., 1946; *Improving Farm Tenure in the Midwest*, North Central Regional Publication 2, Illinois Agricultural Experiment Station Bulletin 502, 1944; and Ackerman and Harris (eds.), *Family Farm Policy*, pp. 9–11, University of Chicago Press, Chicago, 1947.

they seem to call for three lines of action at the present time: (1) continued support of the family-farm owner-operatorship concept, (2) further development of means for helping young farmers to acquire efficient and productive farms of their own, and (3) general improvement of landlord-tenant and farm employer-employee relationships.

*Present Tenure Policy.* The present land-tenure policy of the United States is both broad in scope and vague as to details. Nowhere has it been codified in a simple and concise statement. Generally speaking, it accepts and endorses the policy goals outlined above, but there is considerable difference between policy objectives and policy accomplishments.

Much of the nation's tenure policy relates to land ownership and leasing arrangements and finds its roots anchored deep in the Anglo-Saxon concept of property rights, in Federal and state legal codes concerning property and contract relationships, and in the customs of farm people. Because of these situations and the natural reluctance of people to disturb the *status quo,* only limited progress has been made in improving many features of the tenure system—and most of the progress that has been made, particularly in recent years, has come indirectly as a result of higher farm incomes rather than through the direct acceptance of recommended reforms.

The most active aspect of farm-tenure policy in this country is that associated with the furtherance of family owner-operated farms. Several of the public land-disposition measures, such as the Preemption Act and the Homestead Act and more recently the 160-acre limitation on irrigated lands in reclamation projects, have been designed to promote this goal. Further expression of this objective in tenure policy is found in the public provision of farm credit facilities under the Federal Farm Loan Act and the tenant purchase program initiated by the Farm Security Administration and now administered by the Farmers Home Administration. Without doubt these programs have helped to promote owner-operatorship. But even so, one must agree with Salter that "they have not been sufficiently effective to assure a high degree of operator-ownership."[35]

So far as the policy goal of improving landlord-tenant relations is concerned one again finds with Salter that[36]

. . . it is difficult to find any significant evidence to indicate that this goal has actually been a part of public tenure policy. To be sure, for forty years now the farm economists have been making studies of farm tenancy conditions and have quite consistently recommended longer leases, written contracts, automatic renewals, compensation for unexhausted improvements, and the applica-

[35] Leonard A. Salter, Jr., "Tenure Policy Formulation in a Democracy," in *Family Farm Policy,* p. 124.

[36] *Ibid.,* p. 125. The quotation is from William J. Coleman and H. Alfred Hockley, *Legal Aspects of Landlord-Tenant Relationships in Oklahoma,* Oklahoma Agricultural Experiment Station Bulletin 241, p. 3, August, 1940.

tion of the Golden Rule. Yet it is possible to say of farm tenancy law, as Coleman and Hockley have said, that "hardly any other social field of comparable magnitude and importance has been so ignored by the various State Legislatures."

It is probably regrettable that much of the present land-tenure policy of this country involves more lip service than action in the direction of achieving the tenure ideal. This situation, however, has its favorable side because it indicates that despite some obvious weaknesses in the tenure system, the system itself is basically sound. Unlike many other areas in the world where there is strong sentiment in favor of agrarian reform, the American tenure system is characterized by a lack of any pressing demand for reform. True, the system in this country does have its weaknesses, and numerous adjustments and improvements might well be made, but the problems are far from insuperable. Problems that do exist for individual operators often may be solved by such simple expedients as a rise in farm prices, changing landlords, or using more land or capital in the production process.

# CHAPTER 12 *Institutional Arrangements*

The general manner in which man holds and uses land is determined to a considerable extent by a complex of physical, social, economic, and political factors. Implicit in the recognition of land problems and policies as a phase of our economy is the acknowledgment that various phases of these factors are not mutually exclusive, but rather are interrelated. One aspect of this interrelation that is particularly significant to land economists is the manner in which group behavior affects land use. Contemporary society is a complex of institutions that regulate the behavior of individuals. Institutions may take form as mere habits or customs, or formal organizations present in the production, distribution, and consumption of goods. They are a form of economic power and social control.

No economic system is static. The system is constantly changing, and the changes that occur often are manifest through institutional adjustments. For institutions to be effective they must possess enough stability to be a power in shaping the social process; but, also, to endure they must change.

Among the various types of institutional arrangements that are considered in this and the following chapter are rural zoning, grazing-district legislation, soil-conservation districts or other special districts, differential taxation, methods of handling tax-delinquent lands, credit policies, restrictive covenants on use of land, benefit payments, public purchase, and similar measures or acts that have legal, legislative, or administrative authorization and through which groups control, affect, or modify the use, occupancy, and tenure of land.

## Legal and Legislative Framework

Basic to this discussion is the concept of property and the over-all legal framework of land-regulatory measures. As earlier discussions have pointed out, property in land constitutes the legal rights one has to hold or use land. Private property in land may reside in one person or in several persons. The scope of the rights held is determined within a legal framework and may be changed by governments in the interest of a larger group—that is, the public. It is the legislatures and courts that resolve conflicts of interest and even change the scope of one's rights in landed property. During the past 20 to 30 years, for instance, new attitudes have evolved regarding the relationship between the paramount public interest in land and private property rights over land. When the use of private property in land conflicts with the public interest it must in some cases be converted into public property or be subjected to suitable restrictions, or steps must be taken through government action to improve existing land-use practices.

There are, however, constitutional and other legal limitations on government action. In part, these take the form of questions of jurisdictional authority, as between the Federal government and the state governments. In part, also, these limitations are inherent in the constitutional safeguards of individual rights in the Federal and state constitutions and, in part, in the character of private property in real estate as established by colonial, Federal, and state grants of public land to private individuals. The general subject is too complex and too diverse for comprehensive treatment outside a legal treatise. However, it may be helpful to indicate some of the more basic considerations.

It is also necessary to bear in mind that private ownership of land involves the exercise of exclusive rather than absolute rights over property. The private owner's rights are clearly limited as by public use of the police power, by the public right of taxation, and by the power of the Federal or state governments to take over the ownership of private property through exercise of the right of eminent domain. The police power, which resides in the states, in its broad aspects relates to the sovereign power of government to regulate persons and property and to restrict individual rights in the interest of public health, safety, morals, or the general welfare without compensation. Under the power of eminent domain the government can acquire property for a public use on the payment of just compensation. The power to tax is the right to levy taxes for a public purpose to defray costs of government.

Although no powers for regulation of private land use, tenure, or disposition are specifically granted to the Federal government under the Constitution, it has been found so elastic in other directions that one cannot always be certain of the unalterable character of present limitations on Federal action.

The general finance clause of the Constitution gives Congress authority to "lay and collect taxes, duties, imposts, and excises, to pay debts and provide for the common defense and general welfare of the United States;

but all duties, imposts, and excises shall be uniform throughout the United States" (Art. I, Sec. 8). Never was a comma so significant as the one following the word "excises" and preceding "to pay" (alleged to have been changed from a semicolon by the Reporter of the Constitutional Convention), for it has been the reason for a century-long dispute of most far-reaching importance.

The essential question has been with regard to the scope of the phrase "general welfare" and its relation to the finance power and the other enumerated powers. Legal opinion has been divided among three views. One view holds that the authority to promote the general welfare is co-ordinate with the other enumerated powers, as if the comma after excises were a semicolon, which would imply authority to promote it not only by raising and expending revenues but also by other means, such as regulation. An opposite view, known as the Madisonian theory, is that the phrase "to pay debts and provide . . . for the general welfare" restricts the power to raise and expend revenue, but is itself restricted by the other enumerated powers. This would mean that the general welfare, for which Congress can raise and expend revenue, can be promoted only by an exercise of the other specifically enumerated powers. An intermediate interpretation, known as the Hamiltonian theory, holds that the phrase mentioned is restrictive of the power to tax and spend, and therefore does not imply a general authority to promote the general welfare by any method thought to be desirable at the moment, *e.g.*, by direct regulations; but, on the other hand, the power to tax and spend in the interest of the general welfare is not limited by the other powers specifically enumerated in the Constitution. The latter view has been upheld by the Supreme Court on various occasions.

This question of interpretation was raised in the famous Hoosac Mills case—*United States v. Butler*, 297 U.S. 1 (1936)—in which the Supreme Court by a 5 to 4 decision invalidated a portion of the Agricultural Adjustment Act of 1933. The majority of the court questioned the existence of a Federal power to use subsidies to regulate agricultural production and land use when it was alleged that the right to regulate these activities was reserved to the states. In its decision the majority distinguished between the contracts the Federal government had made to pay individuals for complying with the acreage-reduction program and the long-established subvention to states for road building and education purposes. The objection was not to the use of Federal subsidies for the promotion of desirable land-use practices but to the use of the spending power to accomplish a form of regulation which in legal theory is reserved to the states.

It is to be noted that the Court did not undertake to decide whether control of agricultural production and land utilization is in the general welfare, even when accomplished through the finance powers, but did express objection to a policy of employing funds obtained from a processing tax to induce citizens to accept under contract a form of regulation by the Federal government not specifically authorized by the Constitution and alleged to be reserved to the states under the Tenth Amendment.[1]

This decision has left very much confused the question of the power of the Federal government to expend funds for the purpose of bringing about better land use on privately owned land. The particular issue, however, arose by reason of legal protest of taxpayers aggrieved by the processing tax levied for specific purposes of the Act. It is a fairly well-established principle, however, that the Court will not entertain a suit brought by taxpayers to restrain Federal expenditures from general revenues, for the Court has taken the position that where the expenditure is not derived exclusively and specifically from the revenues of a particular tax, it is impracticable to trace the injury of the particular plaintiff to its source among the extremely varied sources of Federal revenue.

For this reason the Soil Conservation and Domestic Allotment Act, which followed the Agricultural Adjustment Act and was aimed in part at similar objectives, was not supported by a specific processing tax. Thus far it has not been the subject of a decision by the Supreme Court. One might conclude, therefore, that the way has not yet been closed to the employment of Federal funds for the payment of subsidies to encourage uses of land in the interest of general welfare. The fact is that the Federal government is actually expending funds for a wide variety of purposes looking to improvement of land utilization on privately owned land.

The commerce clause, authorizing Congress to regulate trade and commerce among the several states and with foreign nations, may also provide a basis for Federal land policies. The power to control and regulate navigation on navigable streams might afford justification for various land-use measures involving Federal expenditure and even conceivably the regulation of private land use and tenure, provided it is demonstrated that changes therein affect the run-off of water in a manner beneficial to navigation. The extensive flood-control program of the Departments of Defense and Agriculture may rest partly on these grounds.

Air pollution is in a similar situation in which the Federal government might be able to control the contamination of air that moves across state boundaries, either under the commerce clause or the general-welfare provision. If so, the Federal government could, for instance, if deemed desirable, enact regulations applicable to the dust storms that arise in the Great Plains.

The question has been raised whether the commerce clause can be em-

---

[1] See the illuminating articles by Philip M. Glick, "The Soil and the Law," *Journal of Farm Economics*, Vol. 20, Nos. 2 and 3, May and August, 1938.

ployed to justify Federal regulation of the interstate sale of land, with a view to regulating land settlement. Apparently, the courts hold that a mere transfer of ownership in a commodity not physically moved from state to state does not constitute interstate commerce. However, under the finance clause, transaction taxes have been imposed on deeds, mortgage instruments, and other papers connected with land transfers. Conceivably, these might provide an indirect means of regulating land sales and possibly discouraging land speculation.

In fact, regulation through the indirect influence of taxation is a distinct possibility. The courts have refused to invalidate Federal revenue measures merely on the ground that they also indirectly accomplish important regulatory objectives. Protective tariffs have been upheld even when it was apparent that a less protective rate would yield a larger revenue, the courts holding that the exercise of judgment as to the effectiveness of the revenue measure is the function of Congress, provided it is clear that revenue is an objective. High taxes on intoxicating liquor, partly intended for curtailment of use, were similarly upheld. On the other hand, the Federal Child Labor Act was declared unconstitutional on the ground that the classification employed was virtually of no revenue significance, but obviously primarily for regulation.

*Some Restrictions on Federal or State Powers.* Such powers as the Federal government or the states possess with respect to land are subject to certain general constitutional restrictions mainly designed to safeguard rights of property and contract against undue governmental encroachment.

The more important are as follows:

1. The "due-process" clauses of the Fifth and Fourteenth Amendments of the Federal Constitution which provide that no person shall be deprived of liberty or property "without due process of law." Similar provisions are in state constitutions. This provision has been widely employed by the courts to restrict governmental actions that could be shown to impair unreasonably the value of property or infringe freedom of use or disposition. Hence, it has been a bulwark of the widespread conception of the absolutism of individual property rights in land and a potent obstacle to the exercise in the social interest of governmental regulatory powers. In this sense, it has been in more or less continual opposition to the police power. In fact, up to the present time it has served to restrict greatly the scope of the latter as thus far defined by the courts. There is reason to believe, as a result of the decision of the United States Supreme Court in the Nebbia milk-price case—*Nebbia v. New York,* 291 U.S. 502 (1934)—that the Court is more liberal in its interpretation of the scope of the police power than state courts have been hitherto. It was held in

that decision that the due-process clause of the Federal Constitution limits the regulatory power of the states only in the sense that the law shall not be unreasonable, arbitrary, or capricious, and the means selected shall have a substantial relation to the ends or objectives sought.[2]

Thus, the due-process clause serves to protect the individual in the exercise of his rights as a property owner, while the police power of the states tends to afford him protection as a member of the social group. The ever-growing emphasis on social interests is constantly widening the scope of the police power. We shall have occasion to consider the extent of the power in its application through particular land-use regulatory measures.

2. The principle that state expenditures must be confined to a clearly authorized public purpose. Specific limitations on the character or amount of expenditures occur also in many state constitutions.

3. A prohibition against legislative delegation of authority, derived by court interpretation from the theory of tripartite governmental organization with coordinate but discrete powers, and specifically included in some state constitutions. In general, the courts will permit the exercise of administrative discretion in the application of regulations provided the policies and principles are legislatively determined.

4. The provision of the Fourteenth Amendment of the Federal Constitution that a state may not deny to any person within its jurisdiction the equal protection of the laws. This is intended to prevent arbitrary and unreasonable discrimination but is held to permit differences of treatment based on reasonable classification provided uniformity of treatment is maintained within the class.

5. The Federal Constitutional requirement that interstate compacts must be subject to approval by the Federal government, as was true for the interstate compact that was made between several states for the apportioning of waters in the Colorado River Basin.

*Scope of Federal Authority with Respect to Federal Lands.* So far as lands in Federal ownership are concerned, the Federal government has rights at least as extensive as those of a private owner with a fee-simple title. As in the case of any private owner, those rights are subject to any easements or other estates that might have existed when the land was acquired or that might subsequently have been created by action of the Federal government itself. For the most part, comparatively few such estates existed with respect to the public domain at time of acquisition. Lands which have been acquired by the Federal government through purchase, however, are frequently subject to various easements and reservations. But, unlike lands in private ownership, the Supreme Court

[2] See Glick, *op. cit.*, No. 2, pp. 440*ff.*

has held that individuals cannot acquire a prescriptive right to use the public domain simply by habitual or customary use, although under certain conditions the public may acquire a right to use privately owned land in this way. Certain rights of the general public to the use of Federal or state land, when not reserved for some particular purpose, even when not based on a specific contract, are commonly recognized, such as the right to fish or to use navigable streams for navigation.

As to land owned by the Federal government, however, there is a zone of uncertainty concerning the extent to which limitations applicable to land in private ownership apply. It is certain that the states cannot tax Federally owned land without consent of the Federal government. It is not as yet clear, however, how far the states can go in the application of their police powers on Federal land without at least the tacit consent of the Federal government. The Constitution provides that Congress shall have power to dispose of and make all needful rules and regulations respecting the territory or other property belonging to the United States; and nothing in the Constitution shall be so construed as to prejudice any claims of the United States or of any particular state (Art. IV, Sec. 3). This means that Federal rules and regulations are paramount in so far as the use of Federal lands is concerned, although a state may, in some instances, regulate their use in case of failure of the Federal government to do so, but only subject to the consent—or tacit consent—of the latter.

In general, the states have the same civil and criminal jurisdiction in areas occupied by Federal lands that they have in areas privately owned, except in the District of Columbia and in areas occupied by forts, magazines, arsenals, dockyards, and needful public buildings, where the land was acquired by the Federal government with the consent of the state for exclusive governmental jurisdiction by the Federal government. The national parks are acquired under this arrangement, but much other land has been acquired by the Federal government without asking the states to grant exclusive jurisdiction. On such lands and on the public domain Federal laws for regulation of the use and disposition of the land itself apply concurrently with state laws. In case of conflict, the presumption is usually in favor of the former. For instance, local zoning regulations would not apply to the Federal government's lands, but it is possible that they might apply to the use of Federal lands by others, if the Federal government does not object. It is likewise doubtful that a state could acquire Federal land by an exercise of its right of eminent domain, although the exercise of the right of eminent domain by the Federal government in acquiring state-owned land has been upheld. There is some question, however, whether this Federal power would extend to state lands used for governmental purposes, such as the location of public buildings.

## Land Use and Rural Local Government

Land uses are significantly affected by the structure of local government in that the institutional structure may materially retard or stimulate particular types of land use. On the other hand, type of use largely determines the type of institutional structure, especially through the influence of land use on the population pattern and density and through the different requirements of various types of land use for public services.

In parts of the United States rural planning is confronted with maladjustments and incongruities attributable to the fact that the institutional and governmental structures and fiscal arrangements bear an illogical relationship to the prevailing land-use and associated population pattern, tending in turn to intensify maladjustments in land use and settlement. This was particularly true in the 1930's. In part, these maladjustments and incongruities are due to the tendency in state legislation to provide the same kind of institutional and fiscal arrangements for all parts of the state, irrespective of the great local differences in types of land use and population density.

This results in the extension into forest and range areas, with their relatively sparse populations, of types of governmental structures developed for areas of arable farming. Possibly one reason for the extension within and between states of uniform types of local government was the assumption, justified by the experience of many newly settled areas, that the forests or grazing economies found in new areas inevitably would be followed by arable farming, and that in turn by a diversified economy. But this has not occurred in all cases. Many cutover forest areas have not become fertile farming communities and as a result have suffered from the premature adoption of elaborate local governmental structures. Likewise, the depletion of soils, reduced carrying capacity of range lands, and the exhaustion of land resources have given rise in some areas to extensive farm abandonment, changes in the ownership patterns, and the aggravation of local governmental problems.

The urbanization movement and the extension of suburban conditions into regions hitherto rural also have necessitated some reappraisals of the structure and functions of local government, particularly to permit more comprehensive machinery and broader powers for planning and controlling the process of development. Far-reaching changes in transportation and communication also justify a reconsideration of the size of units of local government and their relation to one another.

*Consolidation of Units of Local Government.* Numerous proposals have been made for the consolidation of units of local government. Among the more significant are (1) the consolidation of school districts, (2) the elimination of school districts as units of administration and the transfer of their school-administration functions to townships or counties, (3) the consolidation of sparsely settled townships, and (4) the consolidation of small counties or counties in which a large proportion of the land is owned by the Federal or state government.

The economies that can be secured from consolidation, however, are generally somewhat less than expected because a large proportion of expenditures that occur are independent of the size of the units of administration. For instance, numbers of miles of roads and numbers of pupils in school may not be greatly changed merely by the act of consolidating. Consolidation has its most pronounced effect on expenditures for general administration, and these generally represent only a relatively small part of the total budget. Thus consolidation alone does not provide a conclusive remedy for the higher per-unit cost of government service in sparsely settled areas than in more densely settled areas.

Areas characterized by extensive types of land use, as forests or range grazing, are likely to have high per-unit costs of governmental services. Consolidation may lessen some of the expenses of overhead administration, but school and road requirements in such areas are likely to be so costly as to require (1) a lessening of the adequacy of governmental services, (2) an unduly high tax burden, or (3) a system of state aids. In many forested or range areas local units of government have been forced, even with the assistance of state aids, to an unduly high level of property taxation as compared with areas of denser population and greater wealth. The frequent result has been increased tax delinquency or farm abandonment, or otherwise retarded economic development.

There is a growing tendency to question the desirability of retaining the township form of local government in forested or other sparsely settled areas and even in predominantly agricultural territory. It has been pointed out that the old-fashioned town meeting has lost much of its vitality and democratic significance. With the increasing complexity of modern life there is a disposition for town meetings to become perfunctory, and it is felt that the need is not so much consolidation of townships as their abolition and the transfer of their functions to counties.

*Shifting of Functions among Existing Units of Government.* A noticeable tendency exists to reshuffle the functions of local government and assign them differently, with or without actually eliminating existing units. In part, this has involved assigning newly developed functions and, in part, the actual transfer of functions.

Among the new functions one of the most important has been relief. Even before the great expansion of the relief function during the 1930's, there was a tendency for the county to be employed as the unit of administration, with certain specialized institutions maintained on a state-wide basis. The work relief programs of the 1930's were obviously un-adapted to administration by units as small as townships. A great expansion of functions occurred with the distribution of specialized forms of relief, such as old-age pensions, mothers' pensions, aid for dependent children, pensions for the blind, and the administration of special provisions for hospitals, nurses, and other sanitary measures applicable to rural areas.

The development of roads, and particularly their improvement, has emphasized the inadequacy of township administration, partly because of the expensive equipment required for which the town is an uneconomic unit and partly because traffic requirements dictate the consideration of roads from a more comprehensive perspective than from a township. Traffic surveys have demonstrated that there are few highways, even unimproved highways, that are not used by more persons outside the locality than from the locality itself. In the other direction, there has been a tendency toward concentrating more authority in the state, first for state and Federal trunk highways, and even with respect to county trunk roads. The broad tendency is to center authority in the state for the formulation of the highway system, even the secondary, using counties as units of administration for construction and maintenance of the less important roads.

*Separation of State and Local Revenues and Equalization Policies.* During recent decades there has been a general and steady movement toward the separation of state and local revenues. The great expansion of governmental functions, particularly those maintained by the state, greatly intensified this movement and gave rise to a diversification of state sources of revenue, by development of taxes on public utilities, business-license taxes, automobile-license taxes, gasoline taxes, income and inheritance taxes, and, more recently, sales taxes. A number of states have completely withdrawn from the use of general property taxes as a source of state revenue.

A less extreme tendency than the concentration of administrative authority in the states has been the widespread development of the practice of granting subvention to local units of government. In the main, these subventions have been granted by states, although in some cases state legislation has provided for county subventions to subordinate units, as in Wisconsin, where counties and the state jointly grant aids to school districts. The Federal government also has entered the field by granting subventions for roads and relief, with a good deal of emphasis recently on Federal aid for education. As is well known, in the case of roads it has been the policy of the Federal government to grant aid to states to be distributed by them, largely in accordance with principles of distribution and technical requirements specified in the terms of the Federal grants.

Closely related to the policy of state aids has been the practice of sharing with counties, towns, or other local units the proceeds of certain taxes levied by the state. In its initial form this consisted in sharing of proceeds of property taxes and in some cases of sharing by the state and local units of the proceeds of the levies on property made for state uses. During the past two decades, however, the principal tax revenues shared have been automobile-license taxes, gasoline taxes, railway and public-utility taxes, income taxes, business taxes, and sales taxes. In general the practice of sharing taxes has represented a greater concession to localities than the policy of subventions, for the latter is more likely to be associated with legislation or administration controls over the character of service and mode of expenditure.

Closely related to subventions and tax-sharing measures are the various legislative provisions aimed at a greater equalization of tax burdens as between various units of local government. The earlier equalization provisions represented an attempt to counteract the tendency of townships or counties to escape the burden of state property taxes through the practice of underassessment. The aim was true equalization, not aids, and this form of equalization has gradually become less significant as a result of less dependence of state government on general property-tax revenue or complete independence of it; however, state equalization is still important because the allocation of certain state aids is based on it.

In general, the widespread resort to subventions and the closely related practices of tax-sharing and equalization measures represent an attempt to compromise between the forces making for greater concentration of administrative authority and fiscal responsibility, and the desire to preserve the traditional vitality of the smaller units of government. But subventions, tax-sharing, and equalization policies have had a significant relation to land-utilization policy and rural planning. Some of these relationships are:

1. There has resulted a reduction in the tax burden that would otherwise have had to rest on landed property, especially in sparsely populated areas of low productivity. This is important, especially in those areas where the property-tax burden was so heavy that it tended to destroy the local economy and its own base through extensive tax delinquency, farm abandonment, excessive soil mining, overgrazing, or the unduly rapid cutting of timber resources.

2. Subventions and tax-sharing policies have (*a*) tended to underwrite inefficient systems of governmental organization and services and

(*b*) helped to support illogical and maladjusted types of land utilization which without support would disappear or give way to more effective types of utilization. There is evidence that subventions have served to preserve school districts or towns which, because of sparse population or costliness and inefficiency of their functions, should be eliminated.

There also is evidence that families residing on submarginal land or maintaining an uneconomic type of utilization have continued in their present occupancy and mode of utilization through the partial assumption of the tax burden through state or Federal aids. In this type of case, the alternatives are simple. The present situation may continue; the government may discontinue its subventions, which may result in inadequate schools and other public services, with serious social consequences; or the subventions may be paid on an interim or provisional basis while attempts are made to alter the type of land utilization and pattern of occupancy through other policies such as public land purchase.

3. The existence of subventions coupled with laws requiring the provision of school facilities for every child has encouraged individuals and even real-estate interests to effect sporadic and remote settlement. Thus, school facilities or possibly roads have been provided for one, two, or at most, just a few families. In some instances the motive has been to increase the value and salability of real-estate holdings, or to provide employment for individuals in the community in road building or maintenance, driving school buses, or teaching school. Surveys in the northern Lake states, New England hill towns, and elsewhere during the 1930's revealed such tendencies.

Rural zoning and public land acquisition have been aimed at correcting in some measure high costs of local government in sparsely settled areas. But very little consideration has been given to the modification of subvention policies to discourage new settlement in unsuitable locations. This is due in part to the tendency to make such legislation state-wide in application without differentiating sufficiently between different types of land-use areas. Such differentiation necessarily awaits a more adequate classification of land than has been available in most states. A difficulty also is associated with the fact that land suitable for farming sometimes exists in small packets in the midst of extensive unsuitable areas, so that an uneconomical pattern of settlement would result from a classification of land in accordance with physical adaptability to utilization. This is another way of saying that land classification must be carried to the stage of social planning in such areas with due consideration of the relation of potential-population patterns to cost of government. Land that is physically suitable for intensive farming practices may not be economically suitable because of its isolated location.

*Land Taxation*

Fiscal problems in rural areas stem principally from reliance on real-estate taxes as a source of revenue and from the nature of local government. We have given some attention to steps taken to adjust local government to present problems, and now turn more specifically to the general property tax and policies in practice or advocated to relieve the property-tax burden.

*Burden of Taxation on Rural Real Estate.* Readjustments in the structure and functions of local government represent in part a striving for greater efficiency, but perhaps in greater measure are part and parcel of far-reaching fiscal readjustments made necessary by expansion in the number, character, and scope of governmental functions and the impossibility of providing for this expansion by the traditional method of taxes on real estate. Until about three decades ago there was a nation-wide tendency to load the increasing costs of state and local government on property, and especially on real estate. While this tendency was operative both in rural and urban areas, it has probably been most significant in its bearing on land use in rural areas.

Throughout the United States the burden of taxation on rural real estate became extremely heavy following the First World War. It exerted a potent influence on land utilization, land values, and tenure, and stimulated readjustments in these respects as well as in fiscal arrangements and the organization of local government.

Undoubtedly, in certain areas, particularly in portions of the western Great Plains, where a serious recession in prosperity was experienced during the 1920's and 1930's, taxes absorbed all the economic rent and virtually confiscated much of the value of improvements as well, thus going beyond the most extreme proposals of the single tax. Indeed, a number of facts indicate that by 1920 the weight of average farm real-estate taxes, taking the United States as a whole, was about as high as could readily be imposed and collected. In many areas extensive tax delinquency had already developed.

Taxes continued to increase during the 1920's and, likewise, tax delinquency. But from 1930 to 1934, inclusive, there was a sharp decline in taxes per acre on farm real estate, with a tendency during the next several years for average taxes to level off or increase slightly. However, the burden still remained relatively high because of depressed land values.

During the Second World War farm real-estate taxes increased significantly, but because of the shift to other types of taxes the increase was relatively less than during the First World War. Since 1945 farm real-estate taxes have increased materially and were in 1950 at an all-time high in terms of taxes per acre, but in relation to taxes per $100 of value the increase has been much less marked. Furthermore, as farm real-estate values are at a conservative level in relation to farm incomes, the tax per acre in terms of value is much less burdensome than during the 1920's. Table 34 shows the trend in farm real-estate taxes from 1910 to 1950.

*Table* 34. Tax Levies on Farm Real Estate, United States, 1910 to 1950

| Year | Taxes per acre | | Taxes per $100 of value† |
|---|---|---|---|
| | Amount | Index* (1909–1913 = 100) | |
| 1910 | $0.19 | 91 | $0.47 |
| 1915 | 0.26 | 128 | 0.57 |
| 1920 | 0.51 | 244 | 0.79 |
| 1925 | 0.56 | 270 | 1.07 |
| 1930 | 0.57 | 277 | 1.30 |
| 1935 | 0.37 | 180 | 1.15 |
| 1940 | 0.38 | 183 | 1.22 |
| 1945 | 0.41 | 199 | 0.90 |
| 1950 | 0.64 | 311 | 1.01 |

* Index number computed before rounding tax-per-acre data to nearest cent.

† Derived from tax-per-acre figures in the first column and value-per-acre figures based on census reports and farm real-estate-value index of the Bureau of Agricultural Economics.

The burden of taxation on rural realty and its serious repercussions in relation to land utilization are at times intensified by assessment policies that seemingly bear little relationship to either land values or modes of land utilization. There is especially a failure to adjust assessments to the use capabilities of land, present or potential. Rigid assessment levels frequently do not distinguish adequately between arable lands, range lands, and forest lands. The spread of land classification and land planning is gradually providing many tax jurisdictions with a factual basis for distinguishing in assessment between different major-use capabilities.

Inequitable assessments prove especially serious in areas where it is desirable to change relatively intensive to extensive types of use, especially where the assessment valuations assume intensive uses. Thus, in many parts of the Great Plains, where assessments reflected the assumption of a continuing small-grain economy, it was almost impossible during the 1930's for owners to shift to a grazing economy and still support a tax burden that could be justified only under arable farming conditions.

The burden of the general property tax in relation to land incomes resulted in large acreages of tax delinquency in substantial parts of the United States during the late 1920's and 1930's. This situation provided the principal reasons for the launching of the Federal land program of the 1930's, and in some of the states the land programs of the 1920's.

*Relation of Tax Delinquency to Land Tenure and Utilization.* Tax delinquency, especially when persistent, is likely to be closely interrelated with land tenure and utilization; and widespread delinquency gives rise to significant problems of land planning and policy. Technically, land becomes tax-delinquent when the taxes remain unpaid at the time payment is required by law. Virtually all tax jurisdictions, however, permit a period of grace during which the taxes may remain unpaid without other penalty than the payment of interest. After the expiration of this period, there is usually another period which may elapse before the land is put up for tax sale, subject to a fairly stiff penalty in the form of an addition to the face of the tax bill. On the expiration of this second period the property-tax certificates are supposed to be offered for sale, although in some tax jurisdictions administrative laxity may result in still further delay before this action is taken. The tax certificates give the buyer of the certificate the right to demand a tax deed to the property at the expiration of a redemption period during which the owner of the property may still eliminate the obligations against his property by paying accrued taxes, interests, and costs.

Thus several years may elapse before the owner loses title to his property or even before he is dispossessed of it. Moreover, in areas where land has been overassessed or where its market value has declined below the assessed value, there may be little demand for the purchase of tax certificates and, likewise, little inclination for the original owner to redeem before the expiration of the redemption period. In this case the county or state may be required to bid in the tax certificates. In such areas, if the governmental agency has no definite objective or facilities for public ownership and administration, it will naturally hesitate to take action, and may permit the former owners to continue in possession, although under an indeterminate form of tenure.

Tax delinquency may have greatly differing significance in various jurisdictions, depending on the legal and administrative policies in vogue, the stage or stages of delinquency of the different properties, and the economic circumstances responsible for it. In some tax jurisdictions a good deal of delinquency may represent merely a convenient means of obtaining credit, particularly when commercial interest rates are higher than those imposed by law for deferred tax payments. Thus, in 1932, Mississippi received a large amount of publicity because of the alleged fact that about one-fourth of the privately owned land of the state became tax-delinquent on April 1. This represented largely, however, voluntary delay in payment, not ultimate inability or lack of intention to pay taxes due. By August of that year unpaid taxes represented only 17 per cent of the total tax roll. The Commission expressed the view that by the time fixed by law for tax sale, not more than 5 per cent would be unpaid, and this largely on overvalued, cutover lands and speculative urban subdivisions.[3]

During the 1930's, however, tax delinquency was a serious problem in parts of Mississippi, as in the case of lands along the Mississippi River. Likewise, in the cutover areas of the United States and in the Great Plains tax delinquency became one of the major problems. The seriousness of tax delinquency varies widely as between states, and particularly between counties within states. At times during the 1930's over 100 million acres of land were tax-delinquent. It is recognized that in 1953 tax delinquency is not a pressing problem, but because of its scope in the past, attention should be given to tax-delinquent policies.

*Public Policies with Respect to Tax Delinquency.* Short-time tax delinquencies are of greater significance from a fiscal standpoint than from the standpoint of land problems and policies, except where extensive short-time delinquency is merely a stage on the way to long-time or chronic delinquency.

Much short-time delinquency is due to imperfections in the legal provisions for tax collection or laxity in administration. In the special *Report of the Committee on Tax Delinquency to the National Tax Association,* defects in fiscal procedure are outlined, and suggested remedies are proposed.[4] Since these are principally significant from a fiscal standpoint, it is not necessary to consider them in this connection. It is important, however, to eliminate those defects in existing provisions which tend to encourage the use of delinquency as a device for obtaining credit, avoiding the payment of taxes while awaiting an opportunity for speculative sale, and especially the arbitrary exercise of authority with respect to delinquency by local officials that is neither in the interest of sound administration nor good land policy.

Some short-term delinquencies may arise from time to time because of the impact of adverse price conditions on landowner incomes. But if the real estate itself is potentially capable over the immediate future of yielding a net return, this type of delinquency is not likely to result in extensive reversion. Even if the owner is unable to meet his tax obligations over a period of several years, creditors or new purchasers, including purchasers of tax certificates, are apt to take steps to protect the title.

[3] Fred R. Fairchild, Chairman, *Illustration from Preliminary Report of the Committee of the National Tax Association on Tax Delinquency,* presented at the Twenty-fifth National Tax Association Conference, Columbus, Ohio, Sept. 12 to 16, 1932.

[4] *Op. cit.,* tax report.

However, this type of delinquency may be serious from the standpoint of land policy through its effect in changing the character of land ownership and particularly as a factor making for instability of land tenure.

Chronic tax delinquency develops in areas where existing systems of land use hold out little promise of a net return sufficient to meet tax obligations and thus offer little inducement for continuing private ownership. This type of delinquency, therefore, is of special concern to the student of land problems because its prevalence is symptomatic of deep-seated maladjustments in land use or of an excessive tax burden and because the continuance of such tax delinquency calls for definite policies to free the land from its indeterminate tenure status and substitute a type of tenure that will permit it to be put to the use or uses for which it is economically adapted. Basic to this is legislation that will permit governmental agencies to obtain adequate title to the property, since by assumption its return to private use is impracticable because of unwillingness of private enterprise to retain it or acquire it. In a number of states the taxing agency is compelled to resort to a very expensive process of foreclosure to obtain title to the property, and even then there may remain liens which must either be satisfied by the governmental agency or left as a cloud on the title. In some cases the procedure of taking tax title is so complicated that the possibility of obtaining good title is extremely small.

Laws on taxation in most states were framed on the assumption that tax delinquency would be a temporary phenomenon and that lands that became tax-delinquent would be redeemed or could be sold to private individuals for the tax and penalties. County officials and state officials as well persistently cling to the hope that tax delinquency is a temporary phenomenon and that the larger part of the delinquent taxes will be paid. Thus the officials give the owners every opportunity to pay their taxes, with the hope that a turn for the better will arrive, and these taxes will be collected. The fact is that this has often happened, but for land to remain delinquent for several years or to remain in an unstable tenure situation for a major part of the time at the wishes of land exploiters is not a desirable public policy.

There are great variations among the various states as to the unit of government to which land reverts. In the New England states the town is the unit to which land reverts for taxes; in about three-eighths of the states the land reverts to the state and in about half the states it reverts to the counties. The details by which the land reverts to any of these governmental units vary in every state. In some of the states the laws by which the land reverts are indefinite, and no special procedure has been enacted for taking over the land by state or county. In several states there is no provision for handling the land after it has reverted. In addition to the wide variation in legislative provisions for reversion, the actual administrative practices are even more varied. In states where the land reverts to the county, the county officials determine what action is to be taken; in some states where the land reverts to the state, the local officials modify the procedure from county to county.

To deal with such a problem situation, the following suggestions for improvement in tax-delinquency procedure are offered:

1. In areas where delinquency is of the short-term distress type the use of tax moratoria may be justified, while they may be undesirable in areas of chronic delinquency since there they may merely intensify the fiscal difficulties of local units of government.

2. In areas of chronic delinquency it is desirable to appraise the entire situation from the point of view of the possibility of lessening the extent and persistence of delinquency through lightening the tax burden by the use of aids or a more equitable distribution of the tax burden. On the other hand, a more positive recognition of the advisability of the state or county taking title to reverted lands and providing for their administration is in many situations desirable because continued taxation and delinquency may serve only to perpetuate an uneconomical and uneconomic type of land utilization and an illogical structure of local government organization.

3. These considerations emphasize the desirability in such areas of legislative provisions that will not leave the question of reversion to be determined merely by the existing method of trying to dispose of tax certificates and hoping for sporadic sale. The effect of such a policy is to leave the actual taking over of the land by governmental agencies, not to consideration of public interest, but to the accidents of individual self-interest. The tracts actually taken over may be so scattered that they are incapable of economical administration. Moreover, under some conditions, individuals buy tax certificates as a means of culling out tracts so that they may acquire tracts, particularly along streams or lakes, that have significant value as recreational sites. This practice may only complicate the problem of administration of tax-reverted lands.

A tax-reversion procedure that is recognized as having real merit is the provision by law for a taxing district, county, or state to bring blanket foreclosure proceedings in rem against delinquent lands, after a reasonable time has elapsed or on failure of the owner to take reasonable steps to protect his interests. By bringing an action in rem rather than in personam it is unnecessary to notify by public summons all persons having an interest in the property, and thus costly title research and possible legal errors in notice are avoided. The provision for blanket foreclosure represents another savings in that it is not necessary to proceed against each tract of land. And as a public sale of the property is not required under this procedure, this is an additional economy.[5]

4. The question of what lands shall be taken over through reversion should be determined in accordance with a definite program of public acquisition and administration. This program would need to appraise with reasonable care (1) the possibilities of continuing private utilization, (2) the possibilities of eliminating public services through public acquisition and administration, (3) the prospect of eliminating obsolete or obsolescent units of local government through eliminating the possibility of private occupancy and utilization and thereby modifying materially the extension of subventions to such units, and (4) the fiscal effect on remaining governmental units of the elimination of the prospect of such revenues from taxes as might result from speeding up the process of reversion.

5. It is necessary to make provision for adequate machinery for the administration of reverted lands. In many states the absence of such machinery at present, particularly its nonavailability for the unit of government which by law is supposed to take title to reverted lands, now deters the taking of title even when delinquency is obviously chronic. Even where such administrative machinery exists it is frequently deterred because of the sporadic locations of the reverting lands. In some cases the unit of government supposed to take title to reverted lands may be deterred from taking title because it must continue to be responsible to other units of government for the nominal taxes. Such a situation obviously needs to be modified. The agency of government taking title, however, need not necessarily be the agency for land administration. When the county is the reversionary unit, provision may be made for technical aid by the state. In general, however, the system of reversion to the state seems preferable to reversion to and administration by lesser units of government.

6. It is important to supplement tax reversions and public land administration with public land-purchase programs designed to facilitate the blocking up of administrative areas.

*State and local policies relative to tax-delinquent lands in Michigan.*[6] The State of Michigan has had considerable experience in dealing with tax-delinquent lands and the policies developed relative to these lands are among the most advanced of any of the states. A review of Michigan's

---

[5] Henry Brandis, "Tax Sales and Foreclosures under the Model Tax Collection Law," *Law and Contemporary Problems*, Vol. III, pp. 406–415, Duke University, School of Law, June, 1936.

[6] Cf. R. Barlowe, *Administration of Tax-Reverted Lands in the Lake States*, Michigan Agricultural Experiment Station Technical Bulletin 225, 1951, for a more detailed discussion of this problem.

experience will give concreteness to the suggestions made for improvements in tax-delinquency policy.

The problem of tax delinquency was met rather early in Michigan. The year 1869

. . . saw the enactment of the first comprehensive Michigan law for the assessment of real property and the forfeiture of title in case of delinquency. This, however, proved to be an uncertain and, in many cases, an ineffective statute. It was repeatedly amended and revised over the years and not until 1893 was a sound, workable act passed which vested absolute title of tax delinquent descriptions in the state.[7]

This law with its provision for the reversion of unredeemed tax-delinquent properties to the state still provides the basis for the tax-reversion machinery used in Michigan. Considerable use was made of this law, particularly in the years following the depression of 1893, but most of the tax-reverted lands soon found their way back into private ownership through either tax homesteading or outright tax sales procedure. Between 1919 and 1930, the portion of the Michigan state and local general property-tax levy reported delinquent mounted from $3 million to over $60 million. By 1932, 17,600,000 acres of land, mostly in the northern counties, were reported as tax-delinquent. Tax moratoria and special tax-payment plans were used in an attempt to halt the tide of delinquency. But despite these measures, delinquencies continued, and by 1941 the state had come into possession of approximately 4.5 million acres of tax-reverted lands in the northern counties.

The administration of tax-reverted lands in Michigan is handled by the State Department of Conservation. Prior to 1937, tax-delinquent lands could not be certified as abandoned and be deeded to the state until they were delinquent for 5 or more years. This provision was changed significantly in 1937 when the time period for taking tax title was shortened to 3 years. As the law now stands, all parcels of property delinquent for taxes assessed in the third year (or any prior year) preceding the tax sales conducted by the county treasurer each May should be exposed for sale and be sold for total taxes, interest, and charges "to the person paying the full amount charged against such parcel, and accepting a conveyance of the smallest undivided fee simple interest therein." If the property remains unsold at the end of the treasurer's sale, it is bid off in the name of the state. The owners then have a 12-month period within which time they may redeem their property. If the tax-sale certificate to any parcel of property is not redeemed within this statutory period, its title is conveyed by deed to the state, and the land is placed under the control and jurisdiction of the Department of Conservation.

[7] Harold Titus, *The Land That Nobody Wanted*, Michigan State College Agricultural Experiment Station Special Bulletin 332, p. 8, 1945.

In an effort to safeguard the interests of delinquent owners, provision is made that if the previous owners of reverted lands apply for the purchase of these lands within 90 days after the title of such land vests in the state, the "land shall be offered for sale at public auction at not less than a price 25 per cent of the assessed valuation of such land as fixed and determined at the last assessment." This law also grants owners the special privilege of reacquiring a full and unrestricted title to their properties by matching the highest bids made on them within a 30-day period after their sale at public auction.

Until the repeal of the tax homestead law in 1935, tax-reverted lands, where examinations showed them to be suitable for farming purposes, were considered as available for homesteading. This arrangement resulted in the removal of several thousands of acres from the new public domain. Large acreage adjustments also resulted from the various exchanges of state holdings for Federal and private lands.

While most of the tax-reverted lands that come to the Conservation Department are primarily suited for forestry or game-area development, it is generally recognized that some of the lands are suited for agricultural, grazing, or other private uses. It has been the Department's policy to retain "in public ownership only those tax-reverted lands for which there is no private use or demand, or which appear to be needed by the general public for hunting, fishing and other conservation and recreational uses."[8] This policy has necessitated the classification of all the state lands to determine their best use. Classification has involved consideration of factors such as location, soil character, value for forest, game or recreational use, county zoning ordinances, and possible private use.

Following 1940, the Department received the active cooperation of the county land-use-planning committees in classifying state lands. These committees were made up of local people who were well acquainted with local conditions, and their recommendations "were constantly referred to in the administration and disposition of state lands."[9] In their recommendations these committees usually classified the lands into two major groups: (1) lands to be retained in state ownership for public use, and (2) lands to be made available for private use. Lands in the first class were further classified as suitable for Federal, state, county or local forests, game areas or parks, and for airports, dumping grounds, and other public uses. Lands in the second group were further classified into those considered best suited for farming, grazing, private forestry, private hunting and fishing, commercial resort, and other private uses.

As a result of this classification process almost all of the tax-reverted

[8] Michigan State Department of Conservation, *Twelfth Biennial Report, 1943–1944*, p. 55.
[9] *Ibid.*, p. 54.

lands have been reserved for public uses and have been administered as parts of rather well-defined conservation-project areas. Those lands not reserved for conservation uses and not applied for by their previous owners are subject to sale at public auction to the highest bidder at prices not less than the appraised values set by field examiners. These public sales are held several times each year at convenient locations after proper advertisement. Lands offered at public auction and not sold remain on the market subject to sale at any time at the appraisal price.

Under the law, a fee of 10 cents per acre on all tax-reverted lands and swamplands is paid annually out of the state general fund to the local units of government. These annual acreage payments are prorated between the townships and the school districts on an acreage basis in accordance with the ratio that their tax levies bear to each other.

The title of the state to and in tax-reverted lands is "deemed to be absolute and complete." However, at the tax sales the various parcels of delinquent property are bid for "in the name of the State for the State, county and township, in proportion to the taxes, interest and charges due each." This arrangement gives the local units of government a tax lien on any receipts that might result from the future sale of the land or its products. Provisions are made in the law for the liquidation of the tax equities that the local units hold in these lands through the payment of 25 cents per acre from the state general fund to the local county, township, and school districts having such lands.

In 1950, the Michigan Department of Conservation administered nearly 4.2 million acres of land. Not all of these land areas receive the same type of management and administration. The type and intensity of the management program carried out depend largely upon whether or not the land area is classified as forest, game area, park, or nonreserved. These areas are administered separately by the forestry, game, park, and lands divisions, and each division carries on an independent but, nevertheless, integrated program of land management.

*Single Tax.* Among the various proposals that have been made for improvements in land taxation and for the correction of maladjustments in land use and revenue, the single tax stands out as a proposal that has attracted considerable attention, at least in times past. Eloquently expounded by Henry George, the single-tax doctrine provides an attractive panacea for the various evils of land utilization and tenure, as well as other social ills. As such, it has appealed to many sincere people, who have believed that it would eliminate many of the evils that resulted from unrestricted private property in land.

Some of the basic ideas of Henry George's philosophy were set forth by John Locke in his exposition of the doctrine of natural rights and the idea that the right of property is justified only by personal labor; by the physiocrats, in their proposal for the *impôt unique* to appropriate a substantial part of the *produit net* of land; and by a number of pamphleteers during the latter part of the eighteenth century and the following century, among them Thomas Spence in a pamphlet in 1793 entitled *The Real Right of Man*, William Ogilvie in his *Essay on the Right of Property in Land*, Thomas Paine in *Agrarian Justice* in 1797, Patrick Dove in the *Theory of Human Progression* in 1850, and others, including some of the land reformers in this country during the period 1840 to 1860. It remained for Henry George, however, who was unacquainted with the work of these predecessors, to integrate the variety of ideas into a comprehensive social philosophy and to present it to the world with logical clarity and persuasiveness.

Henry George proposed that the government appropriate by taxation virtually all of the economic rent of land as distinguished from income attributable to improvements, operating equipment, and labor. He justified this proposal on the ground that economic rent and land values are "unearned," in the sense that they are held to be surpluses above necessary costs of production, and "do not enter into price"—a doctrine derived from the English classical school of economists. Thus, a tax on economic rent could not be shifted. Moreover, it was argued that economic rent and its derivative, land value, are due either to the natural qualities of the land, which the individual owner did not create by his own labor, or to social changes and improvements, such as the increase of population, public improvements, or the construction of railways.

It was argued, further, that such improvements merely tend to increase land rents and land values, thus giving "unearned increment" to the landowners. Progress, therefore, appeared to result in poverty for other than the landowning class. Building his philosophy on a literal acceptance of the Ricardian doctrine of functional distribution, Henry George argued that returns to labor and capital on superior lands and throughout the industrial structure are determined by returns to labor and capital on the poorest lands in use. Since the Ricardian doctrine assumed a progressive necessity to utilize poorer and poorer grades of land, the conclusion seemed to follow that progress would transfer an increasing proportion of the social income to landowners and, therefore, a decreasing share to the active contributors to production—labor and capital.

The single taxers hoped that the tax on rent of land alone would be sufficient to meet all governmental requirements for revenues, making it possible to exempt labor and capital and their products from taxation; hence the phrase "single tax." This, they expected, would greatly stimulate production and thereby reduce poverty. They proposed that land remain in private ownership and maintained that the absorption of the economic rent of land would eliminate speculation and remove reason for holding land out of use. They argued that this would give easy access to land to persons interested primarily in using it, without the necessity of investing capital in land values.

Since the time of Henry George the single-tax doctrine has undergone considerable modification, but from the standpoint of its inadequacy as a solution of serious land problems in the United States the following observations are offered.

1. Removal of the value from land by taxing away the economic rent while leaving land in private ownership would eliminate strong motives of self-interest for conserving the soil and other natural resources. People would hardly be inclined to employ labor and capital to conserve property that has no value to them. In so far as unimproved land could be had only by undertaking the obligation to pay the government tax, there would be a natural disposition to mine the fertility as rapidly as possible and then move on to another tract, if available. Such a lack of a permanent interest, moreover, would probably result in a tendency to make the flimsiest kinds of improvements. While it might be argued that the policy of fully appropriating the economic rent might cause landowners to permit their holdings to revert to the government, private ownership of the improvements would still be necessary unless these also were acquired by government; and this is not proposed in the single-tax program. To some extent, to be sure, private ownership would be substantial, but surely less than if there remained a substantial value in the land itself.

2. Closely related to ownership self-interest is the fact that the single tax would not solve the difficult problems arising from relationships between farm tenants and the owners of land. The uncertainty of landlord-tenant relationships, the resulting social and economic instability, and the tendency for tenants to lack interest in the conservation and improvement of natural resources would not be eliminated simply by a confiscatory tax on economic rent.

To be sure, it might be argued that the absorption of all economic rent would eliminate landlordism, since it would not appear worth while to be troubled with the responsibilities of land ownership except for the purpose of using or operating the land. The single tax, however, would leave the landowner in control of buildings, fences, and other improvements, and the improvements on the land would continue to be the occasion for the payment of rentals by those users who do not own it; and these rentals might include not only a return for use of the improvements and the economic rent of the land due the government, but also demands squeezed from hired labor or tenant labor through the leverage of the ownership of real estate. Experience has shown that land ownership may be employed, especially in a densely populated country, as an instrument of exploitation to compel farmers to operate for less than the current rates of return on labor and capital—that is, to pay to the landowner something above the economic rent.[10] The practice of rack-renting that prevailed in Ireland before the land-reform era illustrates this tendency.

3. It is difficult to see how the single tax would correct the serious maladjustments in the size of operating units in agriculture. Many units are far too small for efficient operation, while others are too large and unwieldy. On the other hand, the single taxers can point to the greater ease with which desirable readjustments in size of holdings could be achieved where it is unnecessary to invest capital in land values. To some extent this difficulty can be overcome now by renting land. Furthermore, difficulties in readjustment, such as existing improvements and institutional pattern and conflicting interests of those holding title with the interests of would-be users, would still be present under a single-tax policy.

4. The point just mentioned emphasizes the fact that the single-tax proposal, in spite of its extreme and drastic character as a system of taxation, is essentially a laissez-faire program. It leaves the forces of unrestricted capitalism and competition to work themselves out, irrespective of social objectives, under the naive assumption that the mere elimination of capital values and the appropriation of economic rent will free competition and the acquisitive forces of society to work out beneficent results.

For instance, it is not clear that the proposal would correct the evils growing out of the occupancy and use of "submarginal" lands or prevent the occupancy of such land. Although a rigid acceptance of the Ricardian rent theory would seem to obviate any continuing occupancy of land less productive than that at the margin, yet people, for one reason or another, do occupy for long periods land that will not yield a return sufficient to cover the costs of operation in a pecuniary economy.

5. One of the arguments for the single tax has been that it would prevent the holding of land out of use because of the fact that the entire future rent would be taken. In the first place, in the case of farm land it is doubtful that much land is held out of use that is capable of being profitably operated. And, furthermore, as long as there are capital values, farmers in a new country may occupy and develop land in anticipation of its increase in value; in other words, they push the margin lower than current price-cost relationships justify. It is true that extensive land speculation has at times prevented homesteaders from acquiring the ownership of good land; but if there is demand for the operation of the land speculatively held—in other words, if it is at or above the economic margin of utilization under the existing conditions—it would appear to be in the speculator's interest to make the land available to would-be users through renting or selling, on terms sufficiently favorable to induce its improve-

[10] Hassan A. Dawood, "Farm Land Acquisition Problems in Egypt," *Land Economics*, Vol. 26, p. 306, August, 1950.

ment and use, thereby avoiding existing taxes and other carrying charges. However, in the use of urban land it appears probable that the knowledge that any future economic rent would be appropriated would tend to prevent the holding of such land until it is "ripe" for a type of improvement not at present justified but likely to be desirable at a future period.

6. Finally, investment in land is often undistinguishable from other types of capital investment. And when investment in land has been made, it is not fair to tax away the income of land or rent while leaving untaxed the returns from buildings, factories, or other similar types of capital.

*Graduated Land Tax.* A graduated land tax represents a means of controlling the use and tenure in land. As the tax is regulatory in nature, the question as to whether or not it actually produces revenue is unimportant. The primary objective of graduated land taxes is to limit the amount of agricultural land owned or controlled by one person or one family. For this purpose, a tax is imposed at a progressive rate upon lands in excess of a certain arbitrary amount or value—that is, the rate itself increases with the increase of property. Such a tax is generally an additional one, not a substitute for the usual real-estate ad valorem tax.

Graduated land taxes have not been adopted in the United States, although legislation for such a measure has been introduced in several states. No court opinions have been rendered that really pass on the validity of this type of legislation.

Australia and New Zealand have both used the graduated land tax with some measure of success. At the time of the adoption of these laws both countries were still being settled, and the process of land development was complicated by the fact that extremely large plots of land had come under the control of a few people. New settlers found the good land taken up—in many cases for nonproductive purposes—and not available at prices they could afford. Also, as settlement increased and roads and other public facilities were extended, the value of land increased sharply. In an effort to tax away some of this unearned increment of land, to force the best land into more productive use, and to make more land available for newer settlers, the graduated land tax was adopted.

For the first few years, the administrative difficulties were extremely great because of evasion on every side. As administrative procedures developed, much of the evasion was eliminated by improving administrative practices and strengthening the law. The large estates in Australia and New Zealand were to a great extent either broken up in size or limited to the less productive lands. This process was also favored by the development of agriculture, continued immigration which enhanced land values and encouraged subdivision of large estates at a profit, and the government's policy of buying land and providing cheap, long-term credit to would-be purchasers.

In the United States some form of graduated land tax might provide relief from part of the burden of the real-estate tax for the owner-operator of a family-sized farm by drastically increasing the tax on large holdings and greatly reducing the tax on family farms. But it is argued that such relief, to the degree possible, can only be a temporary one, for if the tax is effective over a period of time, most of the larger holdings will be broken down, and the tax eventually will be distributed over all property. This result may be unimportant, however, because once the larger holdings are broken up, the principal objective sought in the use of the tax is attained. Not everyone will agree that there is a valid or economic case for breaking up large land holdings. In so far as society demands this end, however, graduated land taxes can be used for this purpose. Even though the rates may not be set very high, the possibility that they may be increased at any time may be an adequate measure for preventing large landholders from acquiring more and, to some extent, from retaining all the lands they have.

In the drafting of a graduated tax there are several important considerations. In the interest of equitability of taxation, a plan has been suggested whereby the tax would be based on the labor requirements of the average family-sized farm. Under this plan the acreage needed for a well-managed farm using that amount of labor would be computed for the various types of farming, and then this amount of land would be exempt from taxation. The rate would be graduated upward, slowly or steeply, for each additional acre-labor unit. Such a plan, while presenting many administrative difficulties, probably has considerable merit from a fairness viewpoint in its operation as a measure of control. It makes for equitable taxation of both the tobacco farmer, with a small but high-priced acreage, and the cattleman, with a great deal of lower-priced land. At the same time, however, consideration should be given to the highest and best land-use potentialities of the area.

All plans for a graduated land tax should call for central administration. The state cannot hope for success if it allows every county assessor to make the assessment upon which the tax is based. Nothing is more important or difficult of achievement in connection with this tax than that the assessments be fair and uniform. Any plans, also, should provide adequate machinery for appeal. The agency which administers the tax would need an adequate well-trained force to make investigations, since there will be many attempts to transfer property, to register it in various names, and to use other means of tax evasion.

*Special Property-Tax Arrangements.* As has been pointed out, general property taxes are often a heavy burden on land. One proposal or method to remedy such a situation is the adjustment of the payment of property taxes to the nature of the crop grown or to the productivity of the land. This involves a classification of land for tax purposes.

The classification movement for the purpose of taxation is not a new movement. It persisted for decades after the Revolutionary War until the administrative difficulties and the sentiment of Jeffersonian democracy led to the uniformity rule. However, since the turn of the century the movement for classification has gained momentum, particularly in areas where agricultural land accounts for a large part of total real-estate values. Recently, several states have taken steps for a reassessment of land and other real property. For instance, in Montana a number of counties have reclassified all farm and ranch land by four major land-use classes: tillable irrigated land, nonirrigated farm land, wild hay land, and grazing land. The land in each of these classes is then graded according to its productivity.[11]

When land classification involves the grouping of land by classes according to the productive use capabilities of the land, the classes established become the basis for different assessed valuations. The net effect of such a procedure is to shift taxes from poorer to better lands, assuming no change in the cost of local government. For instance, the tax burden for specific landowners may be increased or decreased, depending on the class of land owned and varying in proportion to the amount of land that may be owned in the different land classes. If taxes are equitably distributed, this should in itself be an inducement to adjust land uses to the use capabilities of the land. However, as taxes are originally a small part of the total costs of production, the tax relief generally experienced would not likely be too effective in shifting land use or keeping land in a particularly desirable use. The merit of the classification may thus reside more in equity in taxation than in reform in land use.

One of the main purposes of classification of land for tax purposes is to bring about a more equitable distribution of the tax burden. Tax burdens on property are a result of two factors: assessed valuation and rate of levy. The more nearly the assessed value of all property approaches true values, the less discriminatory is any particular underassessment, in that the rates are a less significant factor when property is assessed at full value, assuming, of course, the costs of government remain the same. Another factor that should be borne in mind in the assessment of operating units by classes of property is that such a procedure may result in assessing property not at its going-concern value, but rather on the total value of its component parts, which may be greater or less than going-

[11] For a more detailed discussion of this subject, see Samuel L. Crockett, "Status of Land Classification for Tax Purposes," *Agricultural Economics Research,* Bureau of Agricultural Economics, Vol. 11, No. 1, January, 1950.

concern value but seldom equal to it. The point is that the assessment of property by classes calls for competent appraisals if the results are to be most satisfactory. Adjusted property taxes are often only a poor substitute for good assessments.

If land is near the margin for a particular use or submarginal, then a reduction of taxes may be significant as an inducement to shift from a present undesirable use to a desirable use, or to continue a desirable use if the present use is desirable. But it is also true that in some situations land is of such a low productivity that it may not be possible to adjust taxes to its income-yielding capacity in that it is not administratively feasible to push taxes near a zero levy. This would be necessary if certain lands were to remain continually in private ownership or if individuals were able to assume ownership of most of the public-domain lands. The use of such lands in a manner best calculated to sustain their productive capacity, or to build them up, requires a well-directed public land-management program. Rather than try to adjust taxes on lands of very low productivity, it might be preferable to bring such lands under public ownership, or if they are in public ownership, to be sure that they remain there under a program of conservational use.

*Yield taxes.* Yield taxes represent a type of differential taxation, and about one-third of the states have some type of yield-tax legislation for forest lands. Generally, the land is assessed at a low annual level, but main emphasis is on a yield tax at the time of harvesting the timber. The arguments in favor of special taxation of forest land run in terms of the particular nature of the forest crop; that is, the long period required for maturity. Because of this fact special methods of taxation for forests have been developed in the interest of conservation and reforestation. However, the evidence does not reveal that such taxes have been particularly significant in encouraging sustained cutting, very likely because of the economic advantage of clean cutting at times of high prices, risks of leaving trees exposed to fire hazards, and the uncertainties of the future.

Reforestation, for similar reasons, is not particularly suited to private enterprise; however, it is felt that adjustments have a significant place as a part of an enlarged program for private forest production and for the encouragement of more forest production on forest lands that are a part of farm operating units. The mere fact that yield taxes have not been too effective to date does not mean that they may not become a desirable measure for encouraging sustained forest production on forest lands. A forward-looking law to this end was recently passed in the state of New Hampshire, providing for a tax of 10 per cent on the returns from forest products harvested, with a rebate of 3 per cent to owners handling forest land under practices approved by the state.

CHAPTER 13 *Institutional Arrangements (Continued)*

*Police-Power Measures*

Rural people and professional workers are interested in land-use regulatory measures that affect the use and occupancy of land and are carried on through counties or other units of local government. Before enacting such controls usually state legislatures must pass enabling statutes conferring the necessary authority. Under state enabling legislation local units of government may then establish land-use regulatory measures. As previously indicated, the constitutional basis for such regulations is the police power. In this connection it may be well to restate that the police power is the general power of government to regulate human conduct and the use of property, without compensation or inducement, in the paramount interests of public health, safety, morals, or the general welfare.[1]

*General Scope.* In considering those land-use regulations that have their bases in the exercise of the police power, zoning ordinances that have been widely adopted in cities and in a number of counties immediately come to mind. However, there are many other types of control measures that have been or can be enacted under the police power. For example, weed laws, enacted as early as 1847, are now in force generally throughout the states. Such laws requiring the destruction of noxious weeds are upheld by the courts. Various plant quarantine laws and regulations are of particular interest because they prohibit the planting or even compel the destruction of certain plants. These laws date back at least to 1869. Among them are laws affecting cedar trees. In the Plains region cedar trees are used as windbreaks around farmsteads. Laws that require the destruction of these cedar trees obviously limit the use of land, and the landowners suffer economic losses when the trees are destroyed—losses for which they are not compensated. In a case arising under a Nebraska law requiring the destruction of cedar trees within

[1] Herman Walker, Jr., "Police Power for Counties," *Journal of Land and Public Utility Economics*, August, 1941.

two miles of an orchard of 1,000 trees, the late Judge Kenyon, in holding this law valid, said: "As the defendants point out, we have in the instant case something in the nature of rural zoning."[2] This is believed to be the first reference to rural zoning ever made by a court.

It has long been accepted that laws can compel landowners to drain their land as a part of a system of drainage; or that livestock owners can be required to fence their livestock in or otherwise protect crops from livestock damages. Even more interesting illustrations of the police power are found in the laws of some range states affecting the grazing of cattle and sheep. In 1875, the Idaho Territory enacted a law prohibiting the grazing of sheep within two miles of a dwelling. This law applied at first to two counties, later to others, and finally to the entire state.

The purpose of this law was to protect the settler and encourage settlement by reserving the use of the public domain for cattle grazing around the settler's home. The Federal Supreme Court upheld this law as a valid use of the state police power, even though it was attacked as a violation of the Fourteenth Amendment and of federal statutes affecting the disposition of the public domain. The Court held that the encouragement given to settlers by this law was a use of the police power for the general welfare.[3]

In some instances, the conservation movement that began around the turn of the century resulted in land-use regulations providing for the removal of brush and slash, restrictions on culling of trees, and prohibitions on the disposal of waste water, gas, and oil. In an advisory opinion to the state legislature in Maine, the state supreme court said about a proposed conservation bill to restrict and regulate the culling of trees:[4]

. . . we do not think the proposed legislation would operate to "take" private property within the inhibition of the constitution. While it might restrict the owner of wild and uncultivated lands in his use of them, might delay his taking some of the product, might defer his anticipated profits, and even thereby might cause him some loss of profit, it would nevertheless leave him his lands, their product, and increase untouched, and without diminution of title, estate, or quantity. He would still have large measure of control and large opportunity to realize in values. He might suffer delay, but not deprivation.

Previous reference has been made to the Nebbia case. In this case the Supreme Court clearly stated that the police power of the state extends to the regulation of property for all paramount public interests. In the words of Justice Roberts:[5]

[2] *Upton v. Felton,* 4 Fed. Supp. 585, 589 (1932).
[3] C. I. Hendrickson, "Rural Zoning: Controlling Land Utilization and the Police Power," *Journal of Farm Economics,* Vol. 18, No. 3, p. 480, August, 1936.
[4] *Opinion of the Justices,* 103 Me. 506, 69 Atl. 627, 629, 19 L.R.A. (N.S.) 442, (1908).
[5] *Nebbia v. New York,* 291 U.S. 502, 525, 527, 1934.

The owner's rights may be subordinated to the needs of other private owners whose pursuits are vital to the paramount interests of the community. The state may control the use of property in various ways; may prohibit advertising billboards except of a prescribed size and location, or their use for certain kinds of advertising; may in certain circumstances authorize encroachments by party walls in cities; may fix the height of buildings, the character of materials, and methods of construction, the adjoining area which must be left open, and may exclude from residential sections offensive trades, industries and structures likely injuriously to affect the public health or safety; or may establish zones within which certain types of buildings or businesses are permitted and others excluded. And although the Fourteenth Amendment extends protection to aliens as well as citizens, a state may for adequate reasons of policy exclude aliens altogether from the use and occupancy of land.

. . . The Constitution does not guarantee the unrestricted privilege to engage in a business or to conduct it as one pleases. Certain kinds of business may be prohibited; and the right to conduct a business, or to pursue a calling, may be conditioned. Regulation of a business to prevent waste of the state's resources may be justified. And statutes prescribing the terms upon which those conducting certain businesses may contract, or imposing terms if they do enter into agreements, are within the state's competency.

There is no question but that the state can regulate the use and occupancy of land if in doing so it acts in the public interest. However, for the protection of individuals, regulations enacted must be reasonable, and the measures used must have a reasonable relation to the objective sought, and proper legal procedure must be followed in the adoption of a control measure.

*Rural Zoning.* One of the most important applications of the police power to the direction and control of private land-use practices in the interest of public health, safety, morals, and general welfare occurs in the use of zoning ordinances. The zoning power has been used most extensively in urban areas. It is just as applicable, however, to rural lands.

Rural zoning began in Wisconsin when the legislature amended a strictly urban-zoning enabling law in 1929 by providing that county boards may by ordinance "regulate, restrict, and determine the areas within which agriculture, forestry, and recreation may be conducted." Thus, there was born a means by which local groups of people may exercise reasonable control over the use of land and structures in rural areas. Regulations are applied by districts, and within each district they must be uniform; but in different districts, different regulations may be applied.

It may be well at this point to clarify the distinction between the power to zone and the power to suppress nuisances. Two differences are important: (1) Zoning is a legal technique for guiding future orderly growth of a community, county, or area, by regulating and restricting the use of land, buildings, and structures for trade, industry, residence, or other purposes. The power to suppress nuisances is concerned with the abatement or prohibition of what is offensive, disorderly, or unsanitary. (2) If the objectionable use is an existing nonconforming use and not a nuisance, usually it is not affected by the zoning ordinance, but new nonconforming uses are prohibited.

Furthermore, zoning should not be confused with planning. Broadly speaking, planning involves the systematic development of an area with particular reference to the location, character, and extent of its prospective land-use areas (agricultural, industrial, commercial, residential, recreational, etc.) and of its transport, communications, and utility systems. Zoning, on the other hand, as has been indicated, relates to the regulation and restriction of the height, size, and use of buildings and structures, the use of land, and the density of population.

Zoning ordinances must find their justification in some aspect of the police power. This being true, they must always contain some mention of "public health, safety, morals, or general welfare." And these general-welfare provisions are expressed as the following specific purposes in rural-zoning enabling laws: to prevent wasteful scattering of population; to reduce the waste of excessive miles of roads; to facilitate adequate but economic public improvements; to prevent tax delinquency; to conserve soil fertility; to facilitate water flowage, water supply, and drainage; to secure safety from floods or windstorms; to conserve scenery; to direct building development; to restrict unsightly development; to prevent overcrowding of land; to guide development of nonurban areas; to encourage formation of community units; to promote desirable living conditions; and to conserve and develop natural resources.

As the scope of these purposes suggests, there are several types of zoning in rural areas. The type first adopted in northern Wisconsin, although generally referred to as "rural zoning," might more correctly be termed open-country use zoning. Under this type of zoning, the use of land for recreation, agriculture, and forestry is controlled. In contrast to this type of zoning is suburban zoning, which is rather common around large cities. It is concerned with the adaptation of ordinances to intensive land-use areas for regulating and restricting the use of buildings, structures, and land for trade, industry, residence, or similar uses. The primary objective of suburban zoning is to protect the urban and urbanizing territory outside of cities and to preserve additional territory for future urban expansion. The ordinances are concerned with eliminating those conditions that make for unattractive approaches to cities, degrading types of development, and obstacles to orderly development.

Two other types of zoning in rural areas that should be mentioned are roadside zoning and flood-plain zoning. The former involves, for instance, the setback of buildings and the regulation of billboards, while the latter involves primarily restrictions in areas subject to frequent floods. There is a growing interest in roadside zoning, particularly with regard to controlling development along main traveled highways outside of cities.

Flood-plain zoning may take the form of total exclusion of occupancy from the flood plain, of exclusion of buildings designed for specific purposes, or of regulation of building construction. An example of flood-control zoning is the regulation adopted in Duval County, Fla., which provides that "no building intended for residential purposes shall be moved into or constructed on land subject to periodic or frequent flooding, nor shall any existing building so located be enlarged, repaired, or altered." In connection with planning along streams in or near cities, flood-plain zoning is one measure that can be used not only to prevent loss in lives and property but to help convert what are often unsightly scenes into attractive river-road drives and parks.

Mention should also be made of comprehensive zoning, a term often used to refer to zoning throughout a county, and including open-country, suburban, and roadside zoning encompassed in a single zoning ordinance.

*Adoption of rural zoning.* By 1951, 38 states had enacted laws empowering any or designated classes of counties, towns, or townships to enact rural-zoning ordinances. Enabling laws applicable to certain counties were adopted in 31 states, and in 12 states, town or township zoning laws were passed. In 5 states—Michigan, Minnesota, Ohio, Pennsylvania, and Wisconsin—enabling laws grant zoning power to counties and also to towns or townships. The states remaining without some type of rural-zoning enabling legislation in 1951 were Arkansas, Delaware, Mississippi, Montana, New Mexico, North Dakota, Texas, Vermont, West Virginia, and Wyoming.[6]

Rural zoning ordinances have been adopted by 173 counties in 23 states. Wisconsin heads the nation in number of counties having zoning ordinances, with more than half of its counties zoned. In Wisconsin as well as in Minnesota and Michigan, rural or open-country use zoning has definitely been established.

In California, 26 of the 58 counties have adopted zoning ordinances. The California ordinances include dimension and site-area regulations, regulations pertaining to the use of buildings, structures, and land in suburban areas, and roadside zoning. A few counties in some states have created forest zoning districts, and general agricultural zones have been established in most states. In a number of states the zoning ordinances

[6] Cf. Erling D. Solberg, *Rural Zoning in the United States,* U.S. Department of Agriculture Agriculture Information Bulletin 59, January, 1952; also see his "Rural Zoning, Present and Future," *Journal of Farm Economics,* Vol. 33, pp. 756–767, November, 1951.

adopted are mainly suburban in character—highway zoning and restrictions on use of land for business establishments.

Obviously, zoning ordinances vary greatly between the strictly rural or open-country type with emphasis on restricting agricultural land use, as found in the cutover area of the Lake states, and the suburban, highway, residential, commercial, and other types of zoning found adjacent to cities or army camps. The latter group of ordinances at times appear almost as an extension of urban zoning regulations to the surrounding rural areas.

While in Wisconsin the rural zoning enabling legislation embodied the idea of planned land use based on the natural characteristics of the areas concerned, much of the support the legislation received came from those who believed that it would prevent increasing public costs attributable to scattered settlement. The problem of scattered settlement was aggravated by numerous instances of settlement on poor land and the presence of much undeveloped land likely to be settled. Since the character of large areas of land was such as to make the prospects of even a fair standard of family living extremely improbable, the likelihood of further settlement carried with it the threat of mounting public costs. Taxes were high and tax delinquency was a real problem, and some restrictions on settlement seemed desirable. The Wisconsin zoning effort was thus primarily directed at preventing future increases in public costs by limiting the type of settlement which produced such increases.

Zoning alone could not be expected to result in an immediate reduction in public expenditures; but it could prevent the increase in expenditures that would be necessitated by additional scattered settlement. Many of the Wisconsin counties that enacted rural zoning ordinances escaped considerable expenditures that would have been necessary to provide roads and school facilities to prospective scattered settlers. Settlers have been kept out of isolated areas and directed to partially developed areas already provided with public facilities. Thus rural zoning not only provides a means for controlling increases in costs of governmental services to isolated settlers; it also makes it possible for areas to avoid economic and social conditions usually found associated with isolated settlement by (1) preventing such rural poverty as would logically result from bringing of unsuitable land into agricultural use, (2) protecting and preserving the recreational resources of the area, and (3) encouraging the development of forestry, recreation, and wildlife on lands best suited for these purposes.

*Zoning and other measures.* As rural zoning does not provide for the discontinuance of established uses, other measures are needed to accomplish this purpose. The removal of established settlers in zoned areas will result in direct savings in governmental costs, hasten the blocking up and administration of the areas for more economic uses, and provide an opportunity for families to adjust to more suitable circumstances. Among the measures necessary to accomplish these ends are (1) public purchase of land in a nonconforming use, (2) exchange of publicly owned land in developed areas for the holdings of settlers in zoned districts, (3) discretion in the provision of credit and expenditures for roads and schools in areas where settlement is restricted, (4) reversion of tax-delinquent land and demolition of buildings on tax-deed tracts acquired in restricted districts, and (5) adjustment of the tax system and state-aid policies to encourage the desirable uses of land in zoned districts.

In regard to encouragement of desirable uses, for instance, if the use of land in a district is restricted to forestry, the tax upon that land should be such that it is feasible to carry on forestry on all land deemed suitable for private ownership. And incentive should be provided for the development of forests on all publicly owned land. For example, under the Wisconsin Forest Crop Law, 10 cents an acre is contributed by the state to local units of government for all lands placed in county forests. Privately owned forest croplands are taxed at 10 cents an acre. The state is reimbursed for funds granted to the local units of government or for concessions made on private forest croplands by a yield tax on the timber at time of harvest.

All public policies that affect the use of land should be administered in such a way that the designated permissible uses are encouraged and the restricted uses are discouraged. In many cases, the steps necessary are administrative, as the enforcement of zoning regulations and other supplementary measures. In other cases, changes in legislation are necessary for an integrated and effective program. Furthermore, zoning and supplementary measures should make the need for changes in the organization and functions of local government so obvious as to stimulate some action in this direction. For instance, the consolidation or reorganization of schools, townships, etc., and the transfer of governmental functions among units should be encouraged and might, in certain instances, be absolutely necessary, *e.g.*, after the evacuation of established residences in minor political subdivisions. This would be particularly true if zoning is followed by measures to encourage the discontinuance of nonconforming uses and by adjustments in taxation in line with the designated legal uses of land.

In areas such as parts of the Great Plains, where the problems are quite different from those found in cutover areas, rural zoning can be used to help bring about land-use adjustments. Some of the uses of zoning might be (1) the prevention of further scattered year-round settlement, and (2) the prevention of cash-crop production on land unsuited for this use.

Zoning might be used effectively to strengthen grazing-district associations through prevention of plowing or replowing of grazing lands, thereby enabling such associations to obtain longer leases for grazing purposes. And likewise, soil-conservation districts might be strengthened by zoning through enactment of regulations for control of settlement.

Through some type of zoning it should be possible to provide for continuous use of grazing land in a more desirable manner and thus give a degree of stability to range improvements and conservation measures that might not be possible otherwise. For instance, without some type of restriction on land use, the conservation benefits obtained from restoration programs might prove to be only transitory; for if there were no safeguards, a few years of adequate rainfall might encourage landowners to plow up grazing land for wheat production, even though this action was not in the social interest and might even be contrary to the long-range interest of the individual.

In the case of rural zoning a significant problem is to determine the operational effectiveness of enabling acts, ordinances, and regulations. By studying the contrast between land-use law in action and the same law as found in the statutes much can be learned. Sufficient information about present legislation in actual operation is not available for a full understanding of its limitations, the existing administrative difficulties, and the integration of zoning with other land-use measures.

Studies of legislative enactments that are now in operation would contribute valuable information in appraising present zoning programs. Factors that need to be studied include (1) the administrative and local interpretations of laws and local attitudes regarding them, (2) procedures for the enactment and enforcement of regulations, (3) procedures for administrative exceptions, (4) the consideration of certain legal rights of individuals conferred by these laws, and (5) the presence or absence of integration with other laws, regulations, programs or policies, whether Federal, state, or local.

*Covenants and Interests Limiting Use of Land.*[7] In some respects restrictive covenants and deed restrictions are similar to zoning in that they provide a possible means for controlling land use. However, unlike zoning, which is a control by a unit of local government through the exercise of police power, deed restrictions and restrictive covenants result from the action or agreements of individual landowners or groups of landowners.

In considering the possible use of restrictive covenants to control land use, attention should first be given to the nature of easements. Although it is very difficult to distinguish clearly between covenants and easements, since a covenant may sometimes create an easement, it is possi-

---

[7] The authors are indebted to Erling D. Solberg for his assistance in the preparation of this section.

ble to indicate broadly certain of their main characteristics. Normally, an easement is a privilege to use the land of another, or certain portions thereof, for a particular purpose, or the right one may possess against another to refrain from certain acts. For example, there is the privilege created by an easement to pass over the land of another, or to install and maintain gas mains or power lines, or to discharge floodwater in spillways over another's land. These are in the nature of affirmative easements. A right to prevent a person from removing lateral support to land or shutting out light to a building is a negative easement, that is, it is a right to prevent the withdrawal of a privilege.

In the case of restrictive covenants, they normally involve agreements that accompany the transfer of title to land and restrict the use, condition of use, and occupancy of land. The restrictive provisions may be in the deed of transfer and thus may run with the land, or through actual knowledge or constructive notice of such provisions they may become effective.

Restrictive covenants are rather common in urban areas. Some of the well-known examples are (1) limiting the use of land to dwelling-house purposes, including a restriction as to minimum cost or minimum floor space; (2) restrictions requiring buildings to be set back certain distances from the street or from the front-, side-, and back-lot lines; (3) restrictions regulating the depth of cellars; (4) restrictions prohibiting the use of land for trade or business such as use for a tavern; and (5) restrictions against ownership or occupancy by certain races. Of course, all restrictions to which parties may agree may not be constitutional. It is necessary that they conform to constitutional safeguards. For instance, the Supreme Court has held that covenants excluding Negroes from living in certain residential sections are nonenforceable, in that they violate the Fourteenth Amendment to the Constitution, which provides that there shall be no discrimination because of color.

The same legal techniques that are presently used to control land use in urban areas could be adapted to fit analogous situations in rural areas. For example, instead of, as in an urban subdivision, restricting land use to residential purposes only, the restriction in some rural areas might properly limit land use to grazing purposes or, in other rural areas, to forestry. Restrictive covenants in rural areas might possibly be adapted also to prevent parcellation of holdings.

For lands acquired by the Federal government, as in the case of lands purchased under the Submarginal Land Program or military lands that may later be disposed of, deed restrictions could limit future uses in their disposition. When acquired by the government, a large percentage of these lands were in maladjusted uses. This was the main justification of the Submarginal Land Purchase Program. Some of the military lands acquired were also being cropped, but were better adapted to grazing or forestry, and operating units were frequently too small. The Federal government could, on disposing of military lands as surplus, restrict their future uses by limitations in the deeds. Such deed restrictions would prevent these lands from again drifting back into maladjusted uses by providing that after classification lands best suited to forestry or grazing be restricted to that use. Similarly, future parcellation might also be prevented.

County and state governments annually obtain title to tax-forfeited rural lands, and during the 1930's millions of acres were acquired. Part of these lands, because they are in maladjusted use, are subject to repeated reversion, particularly lands on the forest-farming fringe and on the grazing–dry-farming fringe on the Great Plains. When such lands have reverted, before their return to private ownership they might well be classified according to their best prospective uses. The tax deeds on resale could then contain limitations restricting the use of such lands in accordance with the objectives sought.

The state of Minnesota has a statute, for example, that authorizes county boards to attach to sale of tax-forfeited lands conditions limiting their use. The act provides that all lands forfeited to the state for taxes shall be classified by the county boards as "conservation" or "nonconservation" lands. Lands classified as conservation shall be held by the county or sold to the state and shall be devoted to the purposes of forestry, water conservation, flood control, parks, game refuges, controlled game-management areas, public shooting grounds, or other recreational or conservation uses. Lands classified as nonconservation shall be sold by the county at public or private sale at not less than appraised value.[8] The laws[9] provide that:

There may be attached to the sale of any parcel of forfeited land, if in the judgment of the county board it seems advisable, conditions limiting the use of the parcel so sold or limiting the public expenditures that shall be made for the benefit of the parcel or otherwise safeguarding against the sale and occupancy of these parcels unduly burdening the public treasury.

Restrictive covenants also may be used as an alternative for land purchase. For instance, the Federal government or the state might through the use of suitable covenants obtain from present owners, for a cash or service consideration, the right to restrict future uses of the land. Thus, in certain land-use areas where the proper corrective is changing the type of land use as contrasted to changing the intensity of present utiliza-

[8] Minn. Statutes 1941, Secs. 282.01 *et seq. Mason's Minnesota Statutes,* 1927, Secs. 2137–15 *et seq.*
[9] Minn. Statutes 1941, Sec. 282.03. *Mason's Minnesota Statutes,* 1927, Sec. 2137–17. *Session Laws,* 1935, Chap. 386, Sec. 3.

tion, control by use of restrictive covenants may offer an alternative to adjustment in use by governmental purchase and ownership, as occurred during the 1920's. If the purpose of a land-purchase project is to change land use in a maladjusted area from cropping to grazing or forestry, the state or Federal government, instead of acquiring fee-simple titles, might buy only the right to restrict the use of the land. However, the restrictive covenants probably could go farther and also control the intensity of use. Such covenants might provide that grazing or forestry practices on the lands sold should conform to regulations of a grazing or forest-management agency.

Correction of maladjusted land use by means of restrictive covenants in contrast to governmental purchase would not remove the land from the tax rolls. If a state or Federal agency acquires only the right to restrict the use of the land, the land remains in private ownership. If tax-forfeited land is involved, the state or county resells the land in the usual manner, but the tax deed contains a limitation on future uses. Of course, land that reverts for taxes should be equitably assessed for tax purposes at its true value after resale under a restricted deed.

That there would be real problems in the administration of such lands is well recognized, for it would be difficult to control use through the ownership of only a part of the rights in land. However, if restrictive covenants were used as an integral part of a total land program, they might, in certain situations, prove to be a desirable complement, less costly than government purchase, and a basis for more effective cooperative land management between Federal, state, and local governments.

*Coordination of Police-Power Measures.* The devices or social tools that have been dealt with in this section, as well as others, have their basis, as earlier indicated, in the police power of state and local governments. In view of the multiplicity of political subdivisions overlying one another on the local level, the question naturally arises: If administrative authority were better integrated, could not the police power be more wisely and efficiently exercised through appropriate measures in the interest of bringing about improved relationship of people to the land? This again brings up the whole problem of the organization and functions of local government. The problem centers in whether or not effective local government may be had without far more unification or integration of functions than exists at the present time. Successful integration of administration is closely related to the unification of the local "legislative power."[10]

---

[10] For further consideration of this subject, see V. Webster Johnson and Herman Walker, Jr., "Centralization and Coordination of Police Power for Land Control Measures," *Journal of Land and Public Utility Economics*, February, 1941.

## Special Districts

Numerous special districts and *ad hoc* units of government have been established at various times as a means of bringing about adjustments in land utilization. Zoning districts represent a type of special district, but not in the sense of possessing powers in themselves for specific purposes.

The major purpose of special districts is the provision of a means by which conflicting interests with respect to land use and control can be dealt with in a democratic manner. Through group action, individuals living within an area can do things in the interest of their total well-being, and generally to the advantage of each individual, that cannot be done by the same individuals acting separately. Soil-conservation districts and grazing districts are familiar examples of special districts for effectuating, directing, or controlling land uses. Irrigation and drainage districts are other examples.

*Soil-Conservation Districts.* All of the states have enacted soil-conservation-district enabling legislation. The Standard Soil Conservation District Act, drafted during the early 1930's in the Department of Agriculture, served as a model for the states in the enactment of soil-conservation-district legislation. Under the procedure of the standard act, soil-conservation districts may be organized in order (1) to establish and administer erosion-control demonstration projects, on which conservatory agricultural and engineering practices are secured on private lands through understandings and agreements, (2) to carry on soil-conservation work, and (3) to prescribe reasonable land-use regulations for the prevention and control of erosion, in the interest of the general welfare.

The Act states that when organized,

. . . each District will have power to do research in erosion control; to conduct demonstrational projects; to carry out preventive and control measures; to enter into contracts with farmers and give them financial and other assistance; to buy lands for retirement or for project purposes; to make loans and gifts of equipment, machinery, seeds, etc., to farmers; to take over and operate State and Federal erosion-control projects, and to recommend land use plans for soil conservation. These powers can be carried out upon private lands only with the consent of the owner.

In addition to the above listed powers, the supervisors of each District may formulate an ordinance prescribing land use regulations for soil conservation. Such regulations cannot go into effect, however, until after they have been submitted to a referendum of the land occupiers and have been approved in such referendum by a majority of the votes cast. The regulations may be amended or repealed, but only after such amendment or repeal has again been submitted to a referendum. These regulations may include provisions requiring engineering operations such as construction of terraces, checkdams, etc.; requirements for particular methods of cultivation, such as contour cultivating, lister furrowing, strip cropping, planting of trees and grasses, etc.; specifications of cropping programs and tillage practices, including rotations; and requirement that steep or otherwise highly erosive land be retired from cultivation.[11]

One of the objectives of the standard act was to bring all the land and land users in an area under one organization if it were decided to initiate a soil-conservation program, and to enable the majority of the farmers in such an area, if deemed desirable, to enforce regulations on uncooperative individuals. Thus the aim was to create an organization for the cooperative working together of farmers that would still be large enough to operate effectively as an educational unit. At the same time the districts provide a mechanism for controlling recalcitrant individuals when such action is necessary for the achievement of the conservation measures considered desirable. In some cases it is argued that this objective can best be secured by including all the land within a watershed or a substantial water-erosion area within one jurisdiction, regardless of existing political boundaries. It can be contended, however, that regulations arise from human relationships and that community of interests within counties may be as significant in certain instances as natural physical boundaries in obtaining an effective educational program and in bringing about the adoption of desired land-use regulations.

A wide diversity in organizational arrangements and administrative relationships has arisen in the adoption of soil-conservation legislation by the several states. This situation is advantageous for study of the effectiveness of different administrative forms and procedures as they are being utilized in similar or dissimilar circumstances. For instance, in 1950 the legislation in 15 states did not provide for land-use control measures.[12] Also, state enabling acts have created variations in the powers given the districts, in standards for determining district boundaries, in organizational arrangements and operating procedures within the districts, and in administrative relationships with higher levels of the soil-conservation program. Within the states, the districts themselves have further varied their administrative mechanisms within the framework of their enabling acts.[13]

[11] P. M. Glick, *State Legislation for Erosion Control*, Resettlement Administration Land Policy Circular, p. 21, July, 1937.

[12] The 15 states were Arizona, Connecticut, Delaware, Idaho, Indiana, Iowa, Maine, Massachusetts, Michigan, Missouri, New Hampshire, New York, Ohio, Pennsylvania, and Rhode Island.

[13] For instance, certain states now require districts to be organized on a county basis. Only California and Colorado have authorized their districts to tax. In California, district governing bodies are required by state law to meet once a month. Among the states there are wide variations in requirements for adoption of land-use regulations, as that the vote must represent a stipulated percentage of the district's acreage, that a certain precentage of those eligible must vote, etc. For a good discus-

Beginning in 1933, soil-conservation work of the Federal government was centered on a series of demonstration projects. Farmers entered into a 5-year cooperative contract with the Soil Conservation Service. A soil-conservation plan was developed for each farm within the watershed covered by the agreement. Through the aid of technicians of the Soil Conservation Service and with the help of Civilian Conservation Corps camps, the Federal soil-conservation program was launched.

Since then, the method of operating has changed materially. The rapid spread of soil-conservation districts during the latter part of the 1930's has provided a means for the Federal and state governments to provide technical help to locally organized groups of farmers who cooperatively are engaged in dealing with soil-conservation problems. Soil-conserving practices have been put into operation on thousands of the nation's farms through the medium of soil-conservation districts. The districts have encouraged and promoted through the Soil Conservation Service an analysis of soils; studied slope, the extent and degree of erosion, and land uses; made determinations of the use capabilities of land or kind and intensity of use; appraised treatment of land needed to reach desired land-use practices; and provided for trained conservationists to assist farmers with land problems on their farms.

In addition to this type of work, which was carried on in more than 2,100 districts in 1950, some districts engaged in the management of lands, to be discussed in the next section dealing with grazing districts; and in about a dozen districts, principally in Colorado, and one district in South Dakota and another in Oregon, police-power regulations have been adopted in soil-conservation districts. The type of regulation that has been set up deals essentially with situations in regard to the use of land for grazing, and particularly the control of trespass.

Land-use ordinances that have been adopted by the Colorado soil-conservation districts fall into three groups as to purpose: (1) regulation of grazing on open-range lands, (2) prohibition against plowing out sod land and other types of land, unless special permission is granted by the district board of supervisors, and (3) requirements for specified practices to prevent wind erosion. Ordinances regulating the use of open grazing land were in operation only a short time and were directed primarily at nonresident stockmen and never effectively enforced. "Sod land" ordinances also appear to have encountered a great deal of opposition and have had little effectiveness, if any, in preventing the breaking of land for wheat production. The wind or "blow-land" ordinances seem to have been most successful, but recent years have been particularly

---

sion of the diversity in organizational arrangements and administrative relationships cf. Robert W. Parks, *Soil Conservation Districts in Action*, Iowa State College Press, Ames, Iowa, 1953.

favorable to them. The test of their effectiveness will come during a period of prolonged drought.

Although the regulations adopted by soil-conservation districts must necessarily be related to the prevention and control of soil erosion, it is possible that significant portions of a program of land-use adjustment may be effected through district regulations. If the cultivation of land can be prevented in certain areas in order to control erosion, a large part of the incentive for settling in such areas is removed. However, if it is desirable to prevent future settlement in areas of substantial size having a considerable percentage of land which is not subject to erosion, it may be necessary to include the nonerosive land in "zones," which might not be legally permissible within the purpose of soil-conservation districts. This might be accomplished, however, by rural zoning.

The prevention of soil erosion is intimately tied in with land-use practices on particular farms. In areas where the chief maladjustment in land use consists of planting slopes which are too steep for cultivation, in plowing up lands which are subject to severe blowing, or in following other practices conducive to severe erosion—sheet, gully, or wind—soil-conservation district agreements and regulations should be able to contribute toward the correction of such maladjustments. Reasonable provisions for the degree of control deemed necessary may be provided in agreements governing land-use practices on single-ownership units, or such ownership units may be subjected to enacted regulations covering an area of which they are a part. The fact that progress in enacting regulations has been slow to date should not be overly discouraging. Control measures are looked upon as a drastic form of regulation, foreign to the experiences of rural people and undoubtedly will require a long period of education and understanding before adoption. Progress has been made by agreements with farmers, and this is a necessary step in the adoption of any type of police-power controls.

Soil-conservation districts have spread rapidly as a means for dealing with the soil-conservation programs. And the states are showing more and more a disposition to increase their contributions to the districts. All in all, it appears that soil-conservation districts are here to stay. And in view of the fact that soil conservation, and conservation in its broader aspect, will probably become an increasingly significant problem, it is not unreasonable to conclude that the district set-up will in some form become much stronger and a potent factor in a comprehensive land-use program. As districts are in effect governmental subdivisions of the state, they may well, in time, become the instruments for carrying out a number of measures for the control of land-use practices, *e.g.*, forest-control practices and cutting. Although soil-conservation laws relate essentially to erosion-control programs, it is possible that local administrative units may be given the power to carry out complementary or supplementary measures, as for instance rural zoning or other special programs, through soil-conservation districts.

*Grazing Districts and Associations.*[14] In the administration of public grazing land, an important role is played by Taylor grazing districts, forestry districts, state grazing districts and associations, and soil-conservation districts, in determining the carrying capacity of the range, in issuing permits, in making rules governing land-use allotments, and in specifying practices for improvements in range conditions. The purpose of grazing districts and associations from the viewpoint of the organizing agency is to establish a mechanism through which group consideration, understanding, and action can be brought to bear on problems of range management. On the other hand, from the position of the land users, districts and associations provide a means for security and stability of ranch operations.

A glance at the nature and scope of Western range problems will indicate the setting in which grazing districts and associations function. In the eleven Western states of California, Oregon, Washington, New Mexico, Arizona, Idaho, Utah, Montana, Wyoming, Colorado, and Nevada, one of the principal uses of the land is the production of livestock through grazing. Only about 5 per cent of the more than three-fourths of a billion acres is in crops; the remainder is largely used for grazing purposes.

The physical condition of the land varies widely; more than 50 per cent is in Federal ownership; and a proportion of the area is subject to multiple-use practices. The type and intensity of uses are, of course, determined to a large degree by the physical characteristics of the land, location, elevation, and the general level of economic activity. Much of the grazing land is at high elevation, it is dry or arid in character, and parts of it are subject to extreme variations in rainfall. A large part of this land is used in connection with private farms and ranching units which often have valley or irrigated lands that supply a large part of the winter feed.

The complexity of the use and ownership pattern can be illustrated by the holdings of the Forest Service. Forest lands are used not only for grazing and timber production, but for recreation, production of wildlife, and watershed protection. When lands have several uses, the multiple-use pattern often gives rise to conflicting use, and this in turn to conflicts of interests between land users and public land-management agencies. Thus, in the case of forest lands, conflicts arise between grazing

---

[14] For a fuller discussion of grazing districts and associations, see C. W. Loomer and V. Webster Johnson, *Group Tenure in the Administration of Public Lands*, U.S. Department of Agriculture Circular 829, December, 1949.

and watershed values. For much of the land in the upper altitudes the best and most strategic use is for watershed purposes. Its great value lies in providing a water supply for millions of acres of irrigated land and for domestic uses; therefore it is vital to protect watershed values and to improve deteriorating watersheds. Overgrazing practices are definitely in conflict with this paramount objective.

In view of the different multiple-use interests, wide differences in carrying-capacity of land, intermingling of public and private ownership, interspersing of large and small holdings, and extent of the area over which livestock graze, it should be apparent that there are problems in securing adequate and efficient operating units. In addition to possessing ample grazing land, livestock men are particularly interested in security and stability, both of which are related to the future degree of control that they will be able to exercise over grazing lands.

In a number of the Western states, cooperative grazing districts have been organized. Montana (in 1933) was the first state to enact special legislation for the incorporation of cooperative grazing associations. The significant feature of the Montana districts is the cooperation by a group of stockmen to form a nonprofit business organization for the leasing or ownership, management, and apportionment of rights on an area of grazing land. Rules and regulations governing procedure are formulated by a state grazing commission.

Two principal objectives led to the formation of cooperative grazing associations in Montana: (1) to secure control of "open" lands, principally public domain and abandoned homesteads that were uneconomically utilized, and (2) to obtain more effective control over lands that were leased in small units by individuals on a short-term basis under competitive conditions. These were situations that had made for insecurity in operations and were leading to impoverishment rather than improvement and rehabilitation of range resources. A considerable portion of the land in the range areas had a checkerboard type of ownership pattern, composed of lands held by private resident owners, mortgage and investment companies, nonresident private owners, counties (through tax delinquency), the state, and the Federal government. Thus, in order to gain control of his range, a stockman had to deal with many parties. He also was confronted with the problem of securing adequate water for his stock. Tracts with water rights were generally leased, while tracts without water often were used without any legal right, unless the owner lived in the vicinity or had them under fence. Competitive bidding for leases on the more desirable parcels often resulted in rental rates far in excess of the land's actual grazing value.

The Montana law empowers grazing associations to acquire grazing land by purchase, lease, or otherwise, from private owners or from state, county, or Federal agencies; to control and manage range use by means of preferences, permits, and allotments; to acquire or construct fences, water facilities, and other range improvements; to specify the breed, quality, and numbers of male animals turned into common grazing areas; to fix the amount of grazing fees and assessments on range users, and to hire range riders and other employees; to purchase or market livestock, livestock products, equipment, and supplies; to undertake reseeding and other range-improvement practices; and, generally, to conduct the fiscal and management practices necessary for grazing-district operation. Following the experience of Montana, a number of states have passed special laws for grazing associations.

Simultaneously with the cooperative grazing association movement, interest developed in the use of soil-conservation districts for the same purpose, as soil-conservation districts possess ample power to secure control of and manage grazing lands. Their use became particularly prevalent in areas where large acreages had been purchased under the Submarginal Land Program.

Since the passage of the Taylor Grazing Act, which was designed " . . . to stop injury to the public grazing lands by preventing overgrazing and soil deterioration, to provide for their orderly use, improvement, and development, and to stabilize the livestock industry dependent upon the public range,"[15] a large number of Taylor grazing districts have been established in the Western states. In these districts there are advisory boards which in general are local boards elected to represent range users and to consult with representatives of the Bureau of Land Management in the administration of Taylor grazing land. In a similar manner, it has been the policy of the Forest Service to provide for recognition of and cooperation with local organizations of livestock operators in the administration of forest lands. Advisory boards, in contrast to grazing associations, have no proprietary rights in land. Cooperative grazing associations control land by lease, permit, or deed, but an advisory board may only advise or recommend.

Cooperative grazing associations or grazing districts as organized under state law vary significantly in type and scope and are adjustable to local conditions and needs. Another advantage that they possess is that stockmen actively participate in the management process and in formulating rules of operation. The powers possessed by a district or association can be adequately prescribed by the state and standards of conduct set forth. In other words, there are no major problems from the standpoint of setting up an effective mechanism for operation. The weaknesses of such associations lie more in the inherent instability of any

<hr>

[15] Approved June 28, 1934 (48 Stat. 1269), as amended June 26, 1936 (49 Stat. 1976) and July 14, 1930 (53 Stat. 1002).

local group to deal effectively with problems that transcend local interests; that is, to have the interest in or the means to deal effectively with problems with which a larger public is significantly concerned.

It is also true that any local organization may find it hard to continue on a going-concern basis because of inability adequately to control the resource base, difficulties due to violent fluctuations in the weather cycle, and adverse economic conditions. For example, variable weather conditions and high prices have recently tested the grazing associations in the northern Great Plains. Variable weather and high prices have a weakening influence because intensified competition for grazing land moves large acreages of state and county land into private ownership. The result is that the need for cooperation among stockmen to control and regulate tenure disappears.

Advisory boards appear best suited to situations in which (1) multiple use is present and desirable, and (2) public lands constitute a high percentage of the total area under the jurisdiction of a single government agency. National forests are included in the first category, while in the second category may be included some of the areas now administered by the Taylor grazing districts. The multiple use of land means that the interest of no one group, as that of the livestock interests, should be determining where another interest or combination of interests may be of paramount social significance. In localities in which public land is under the jurisdiction of a single agency, as the Bureau of Land Management, the interests of local groups should generally be adequately protected by advisory boards. On the other hand, a major shortcoming of the advisory system is that it does not provide an opportunity to centralize the management of land held in various kinds of ownership. It also may be not too successful in securing the confidence of land users in that they do not actively participate in the administration and thus are not likely at times to feel that their contributions are fully considered.

In the management of public lands, some group composed of representatives of government, as in the case of advisory boards or elected representatives of a local cooperative grazing association, determines the regulations or going rules. The relationship between land users and the group or organization possessing the controlling interests is one of apportioning benefits and burdens by a unit of government or its equivalent. Over any considerable period of time, obviously, the regulations and working rules established must necessarily be reasonable in light of the relationships between land users and those holding the controlling interests; otherwise, the organizational set-up will not function smoothly as a going concern. The problem is to develop a democratic mechanism that will apportion the benefits and burdens arising in the allocation of grazing privileges or rights to the satisfaction of all concerned. The stockmen are interested in the uses of the range at the proper time of the season and at a price that will yield them a profit. On the other hand, although the government is very much interested in the well-being of the livestock industry, it must be concerned that the range produce—now and in the future—to its maximum capacity.

This is basically a different problem from the transferring of rights to private land between landowners and tenants through a lease. In the case of public lands the apportioning of rights and burdens is in the nature of a rationing transaction, while with private landlords and tenants the relationship is one of a bargaining transaction between persons assumed equal in the eyes of the law.

The distinction has a direct relation to the public interest involved in the management of grazing lands. The resolving of conflicts between individual land users who necessarily possess motives in terms of their own interest and some rationing group that is organized to deal with broader social interests is the crux of the problem of public land management. The resolving of conflicts and determination of the going rules are in the nature of a governmental function.

A few individuals feel that the way to deal with problems that arise between government and land users in the management of public lands is to eliminate the problem situations, that is, abolish public land management by placing the land in private ownership. In view of the physical characteristics of most of the existing public grazing lands and the institutional framework within which public lands are found, such a proposal is not tenable. Most students of public land-management problems, however, do feel that improvements can be made for more effective administration and that this in turn will lead to the improvement and development of grazing resources. Although much has been accomplished to this end, further study might well be given to (1) provisions for renewal of annual use permits; (2) provisions for advance notice of changes in allotments, fees, and other conditions in the permits; (3) provisions for collecting damages from users for misuse of resources, such as overstocking and overgrazing; (4) payments or adjustments to users for the value of unexhausted improvements (such as reseeding, fencing, and land improvement) in case the permit is terminated or cancelled; and (5) more effective provisions or organizational arrangements for equitable raising or lowering of rental rates and for dealing with disagreements that may arise over rental terms and use of public lands. Some students of public range problems feel that much more attention should be given to new arrangements and institutional devices for dealing with conflicts that arise in the use of public grazing lands.[16] This is recognition

[16] See Maurice M. Kelso, "Current Issues in Federal Land Management in the Western United States," *Journal of Farm Economics*, November, 1947.

of the fact that the core of the problem of public land management is the formulation and improvement of means for the apportionment of benefits and responsibilities among land users.

*Irrigation and Drainage Districts.* Some type of organization is necessary to handle the development, financing, and operation of irrigation and drainage enterprises, except in those cases in which individuals have control over their own water resources. In most instances, such situations would be mainly confined to the pumping of ground water by individual farmers and to individual farm drainage systems.

In areas such as the Mississippi Delta, the lower part of Florida, and along the Atlantic Seacoast, hundreds of drainage districts have been organized for the construction, operation, and maintenance of drainage facilities. In the 17 Western states in 1950 more than one-third of all crop production was from irrigated land, and most of this land was under some type of irrigation organization.

As a whole, most drainage organizations are inadequate to deal effectively with present problems. Many of them need to be rehabilitated financially, organizationally, and functionally. But to do this effectively it may be necessary to provide more centralized supervision of drainage-district operation, to help with the development of coordinated drainage programs for watersheds, and to assist with the coordination of improvements between drainage districts. The maintenance of ditches and other improvements has at times been woefully neglected. Water is a "good" the movement of which ignores legally established district lines, and it should be obvious that in a system of drainage, as in the Mississippi Delta, it is highly important that the formation and operation of districts be so organized as to permit the development of a coordinated water–land-use program.

Another distinctive characteristic of water that might well be mentioned is that in irrigation one of the main differences between "land" and water rests in the meaning of "water rights." And around water rights arise many significant problems and needs. A water right is a right to the use of water, and not to the body of the water itself.

There are two fundamental doctrines of water rights that separately or in varying combinations govern the right to use water. The riparian doctrine, which is the common-law doctrine, recognizes the right of the owner of land bordering upon a watercourse to make reasonable use of the water. The water used must be used on bordering or riparian lands. However, the doctrine has been modified in some states, as, for instance, to permit use of water on adjoining lands. Another significant characteristic is that rights under the riparian doctrine are not lost by failure to use the water.

In contrast, the appropriation doctrine rests on priority of use, coupled with actual and beneficial use of the water. Beneficial use of water is the basis, measure, and limit of the appropriative right. Priority of use is recognized; a right to use water is lost through failure to use available water; and water rights are not limited to land riparian to a watercourse.

The field of water rights is exceedingly complex. In the apportionment of water rights and in the recognition of them there has been much litigation in resolving conflicts of interests. In controlling and apportioning the use of water, district organizations have arisen as a necessary means for the management of water and establishment of group controls over the use of water.

The principal types of irrigation-enterprise organizations, other than Federal agencies, are (1) districts, (2) cooperatives or mutual companies, and (3) commercial irrigation companies.

Beginning with the adoption of the Wright Act by California in 1887, all of the 17 Western states have enacted irrigation-district laws.

The organization of a district under these laws, and the construction or acquisition of its irrigation works and their operation and maintenance, are not dependent upon the consent and agreement of all landowners within the boundaries of the district area to be served by the works; but a substantial proportion must consent. Through taxing authority, districts can levy assessments against all lands within their boundaries that benefit from the works of the district, thus making it possible to spread the cost of the district operations over the entire benefited area, whether or not a minority of the landowners favor the irrigation development. Thus the district is a public cooperative undertaking in which the majority cooperate voluntarily and an unwilling minority may be forced to cooperate.[17]

Cooperative or mutual irrigation companies are private, nonprofit associations, either incorporated or unincorporated, organized to supply water to their stockholders or members at cost. In the private mutual company the cooperation is wholly voluntary. In 1950 about one-third of the irrigated area of the West was served by this type of organization.

Commercial irrigation companies are private organizations that supply water to farmers for a price and operate for a profit. They include (1) development companies, such as those organized, for instance, in connection with the Carey Act, that sold water rights or land with water rights to individuals with an agreement that the irrigation system would be transferred to the users when the purchase price was liquidated; (2) private contract companies that agree to supply water indefinitely; and (3) public utility companies that supply water to land users at rates that are subject to state regulation.

As irrigation districts are in the nature of units of local government,

---

[17] *Irrigation Agriculture in the West,* U.S. Department of Agriculture Miscellaneous Publication 670, p. 6, November, 1948.

they have the advantages that accompany a unit of government in borrowing money, in raising funds by taxation, and in benefiting from state supervision. If properly administered, the district organization offers the best promise, on the whole, of satisfactorily serving land users and of protecting the interest of the public in the undertaking of irrigation development. However, basic to the successful functioning of district organization is a well-developed system of government control over the use and apportionment of rights in water. And in the interest of the best use of land and water resources, in some cases, much can be said for the state retaining sole ownership of the water and making it available to users by long-term lease arrangements.

## Credit

The lending programs of Federal, Federally supervised, and private credit agencies can have important influence on land use and the ownership of land. The influences may be either positive or negative.

If the physical and economic conditions that exist within an area are such that further settlement should be discouraged, considerable pressure to this end could be exerted by the refusal of government agencies or those supervised by government to make loans to persons who settle in areas contrary to public policy. This alone, of course, would not deter all persons or all agencies from undertaking settlement in such areas, but it would exert considerable influence. Credit control as a means of preventing unwise settlement can be particularly effective in marginal areas because such areas are generally capital-deficit areas and those who undertake operations there are likely to need borrowed funds.

On the positive side, there are several methods of encouraging particular types of land use through use of loan funds, differential interest rates, favorable methods of repayment, and new legislation to deal with special situations. And it is particularly important that credit policies adopted be integrated and coordinated with the broader aspects of comprehensive land-use planning. This will increase the effectiveness of credit policies in that the total accomplishments will be much greater as each measure will contribute to the effectiveness of each other measure. John D. Black has pointed out the importance of credit for farm enlargement, land improvement, and farm ownership. Some of the things that he has to say are very pertinent to our discussion.[18]

The most serious gap in our present agricultural credit system is loans to enable farmers to get enough land to make an economic unit. You may say that farmers who already have farms have no difficulty in borrowing on a mortgage in order to buy additional land. This is true of those who do not

[18] John D. Black, "Agricultural Credit Policy in the United States, 1945," *Journal of Farm Economics,* August, 1945, pp. 596–604.

need more land very much. The ones who really need it are those who already have mortgages on small farms and are having difficulty carrying even the mortgage which they have because their farms yield such small returns; or they are not mortgaged but their earning power is so low on their present farms that lending agencies do not consider them safe risks. Farmers in either of these situations are in a vicious circle. They are not able to borrow because they have so little resources; and only with great difficulty can they increase their resources without borrowing in order to get command of more resources.

Some way needs to be found of breaking into this vicious circle, and credit can be an instrument to this end. But it must be used as such an instrument with much care. A large fraction of the farmers in these difficult circumstances are too far along in years to safely reach out and buy more land. Others of them are poor farmers, or at least can be made into successful farmers only with great pains. Others are unthrifty and improvident farmers. But in the midst of all these in an ordinary state are many thousands of relatively young men who need only to be given a chance in order to increase their earning power. . . . If these can be helped, in twenty years we will have improved the earning power and increased the income of several hundred thousands of our good young men.

Black then goes on to state that the productivity of much land that is now in farms could be increased materially by drainage, pump irrigation, land clearing, pasture improvement, and woodland improvement. Credit would aid to this end.

Proposals have been made to set up a credit system for woodland improvement or forest restoration on farms. For instance, the establishment of a forest credit division within the Farm Credit Administration has been proposed to supervise farm-woodland credit and to coordinate this function with those of the Federal land banks.

Millions of acres of forest lands are in farms that could be developed for forestry purposes and pasture improvement. The benefits that would flow from the development of these lands not only would mean increased farm income but also a reduction in flood hazards, maintenance of the level of ground water, control of soil erosion, increased food and cover for wildlife, and improved outdoor recreation. Some public subsidies, in the form probably of very low interest rates, would appear to be justified by the public benefits that would accrue. However, to protect the public investment, some type of regulations would seem to be necessary, as, for instance, measures to control the cutting of timber. And loans should be restricted to properties that are managed in accordance with sound principles of conservation, including good forestry practices.

It is true that both the Farm Credit Administration and the Farmers Home Administration are concerned with soil conservation and through their programs are working for improvements in conservation practices. The Farm Credit Administration, through its loan policy, the adjustment of farm debts during the 1930's, and other similar actions, has contributed to the conservation of farm resources by discouraging exploitation. At least one land bank has developed a soil-improvement loan for which a complete farm plan is required as a condition to the granting of a loan. Production credit association may also provide credit for soil-improvement practices. All the Federal land banks make loans for soil-improvement and farm-improvement practices, but as yet, because of the risks involved, they do not meet the situation outlined in the previous paragraphs.

In the case of the credit extended by the FHA, approval of credit is based in part on the soundness of the farm as an economic unit and in part on the ability of the borrower to carry out good conservation practices and sound farm management. In the farm-ownership program, the agency maintains some degree of supervision during the life of the loan, and the contract contains a clause that the borrower will maintain and improve the farm and prevent wastage of resources. Both in the older 100 per cent direct-loan program and in the recently inaugurated mortgage-insurance program, the land is appraised on the basis of its productivity, and the loan is serviced and supervised in the interest of good farming and land-use practices.

For the purpose at hand, it is hardly appropriate to go into a discussion of the organization and functions of the principal agricultural credit institutions in the United States. It is, however, well to stress the point that within the functions of existing agencies one of the most significant problems is the expansion of credit for farm and land improvements. Needs vary greatly within a given area and between different parts of the country; and although the major part of farm and land improvements will be borne by landowners, it will also involve substantial public investments. The task is to make credit a more useful tool of benefit to the individual and the nation in a fuller use of our land resources and for sustained increased production.

### Selection of Measures

In considering the place of institutional adjustments in the solution of land-use problems, a first step is a clear understanding of the nature of existing problems and a knowledge of the advantages and limitations of different measures. Ordinarily this will require: (1) A determination of the land-use maladjustments that need correction and the formulation of general remedial objectives. At this stage underlying land policies are formulated. (2) The selection of the types of measures or methods by which, separately or in combination, solutions to problems are possible. (3) The formulation of detailed methods for effecting institutional changes in a particular jurisdiction. This process involves development of specific legislative or administrative measures in the light of the legal and administrative structure and the cultural practices of a people. (4) Finally, the effective administration of the specific measure or measures adopted.

If the land-use measures adopted are to be sound and supported by the landowners and operators of the areas affected, they must be preceded and accompanied at every step by a program of education, the aim of which is to familiarize all landowners and operators with the various types of measures which may be used for effecting the transition, their responsibilities in connection with the different measures, and the results which may be expected to follow their adoption. One danger to be guarded against is a tendency to overemphasize the importance of some one specific measure and the possible tendency to accept individual measures as cure-alls or complete adjustment programs. It is well to understand that different measures are most effective in accomplishing different objectives; and in order to attain adjustments involving a number of different changes in land use, a combination of measures will be most effective. But although the desirability of a many-sided approach is recognized, it is also true that it may not be desirable to urge the adoption of too bewildering a program at any one time.

It is also recognized that at the present time interest in directional measures in the states has substantially subsided; nevertheless, a knowledge of various types of controls and their uses and possibilities is important.

*The Rise of Planning*

The word "plan" has come to have an extraordinary significance in the thinking of the American people. It is not a new word, but rather an old one that has acquired special connotations.

Planning goes back to the cave man, who devised careful stratagems for catching wild game and for circumventing his foes. In the evolution of economic society, the family early became an important unit of planning. Over time it has retained many of its planning functions, particularly those associated with family well-being and the distribution of family income. But it has lost some of its group-planning responsibilities, first to clans and tribes and later to cities, states, nations, and in some cases international bodies. Also with progress in the division of labor and with the rise of industrialism, the individual, rather than the family, often has become the principal agency for planning.

Individual planning has probably reached its highest point under the capitalistic free-enterprise system. Individual success under this system is dependent largely upon the individual's ability (1) to plan and organize his economic activities, and (2) to adjust his plans and actions both to his natural environment and to the competitive and collective forces generated by other persons in society.

The early proponents of capitalism stressed the importance of a free enterprise laissez-faire doctrine under which an "unseen guiding hand" would direct the sum total of individual planning and economic effort toward attainment of the best interests of society. Under this doctrine competition was to play a dominant role in weeding out the inefficient and unproductive enterprises and workers in society. But it was assumed that sufficient competition would always be present to prevent the rise and exercise of monopolistic powers. In practice, the capitalistic system has seldom, if ever, operated completely free from public or private controls. Some producers, because of their superior organizing powers, financial backing, or other factors, have been able to use various monopolistic or semimonopolistic devices to control markets or production and thus maximize their own interests by avoiding many of the problems of free competition. Labor also has tended to organize so as to enhance its bargaining position and its ability to demand social legislation. Because of these tendencies toward group planning and action and because of the increasing complexity of modern economic life, the government also has extended controls over the economic order in an attempt to prevent maladjustments and to promote the attainment of socially desirable goals.

In spite of the fact that the free-enterprise system of this county has always been subject to varying amounts of public and private control, it has been enormously productive. It has fostered and nurtured many of our ideas regarding personal freedom and democracy. It has cultivated a profound respect for individual rights and opportunities together with general resentment against individual, corporate, or public abuse of power. Because of this situation, it has been possible to enact social legislation and to take group action for the alleviation of economic and social distress without greatly limiting the average individual's freedom of action.

A trend toward increasing public and social control over the economic system has been experienced by many nations during recent decades. Not all nations, however, have been able to deal with their rising problems of economic inequities and social unrest in the same peaceful and democratic manner as the United States. The need for group action and national planning in many countries has given rise to totalitarianism and police states.

With all its advantages of unity of aim and effort, policy planning in the totalitarian state usually fails to reflect the varied and varying ideals, interests, and desires of the people. In the police state planning is or may easily become a problem in techniques of control, whereas in a democracy planning is or should be a problem in values. Police states use planning to maintain or enhance the power of the *Fuehrer*, the party, and the nation. In so doing, they use planning techniques to cultivate and control the hearts and minds of men and at the same time to repress freedom of thought and action, to stifle criticism and opposition, and in many cases to degrade humanity by seeking to make man little more than a cog in the slave-state economy. Planning in a democracy, on the other hand, involves consideration of the ends and means involved in the attainment of socially desirable goals. The planning process is implemented by a desire to maximize social welfare, to enhance the dignity and well-being of the nation's citizens, and to preserve individual liberties to the fullest extent possible.

*Planning under Democracy*

The noun "plan" has been defined as primarily "a methodical arrangement of the various means or successive steps believed to be necessary or conducive to the attainment of some objective"; secondarily, "a drawing showing the parts in their proportion as well as their relation."[1] The second part of the definition relates to form rather than substance. Drawings or maps are convenient means for indicating plans in their spatial relationships. Sometimes spatial relationships are the most important elements in the plan, as in planning the layout of a city. But back of the merely spatial relationships, there are likely to lie—especially in rural planning—objectives, and the formulation of policies aimed at modifying economic, social, or institutional relationships. In society these relationships are legion, and their interrelationships and interaction are intricate.

The two broad aims of government planning are (1) to do for groups that which they cannot do themselves and which is socially desirable, and (2) to coordinate and subject to the test of general welfare those phases of economic activity that fall within the sphere of private initiative. Thus planning in a democracy must involve a method of determining what is socially desirable.

Planning is essential to the survival of democracy because it is needed to mitigate the many conflicts of interest that arise from individualistic competition and the no less serious evils of unrestricted monopoly, and to effectively combat totalitarian forces. But the process of planning must be made and kept democratic. As M. L. Wilson has observed:[2]

> The policies upon which planning is based must of necessity be approved by a substantial majority of citizens. In a democracy, we still have much to learn in the way of devising new institutions and new mechanisms for making planning a product of the democratic process. There must be an extended and broadened educational system that will improve the ability of the citizenry to take part in the process of policy-making.

This statement is as true now as it was during the interwar period. In some respects it may be more true today in that the forces of social evolution, and especially the economic and political policies of totalitarian nations, are compelling democracies to put added effort into planning.

Some persons, however, feel that democratic planning is incompatible with democracy. The fear is associated, not with the need to look ahead, but with the belief that government interference with the free choices

[1] Standard Dictionary.
[2] M. L. Wilson, *Economic Agriculture and the Rural and General Social Welfare,* Proceedings, Fifth International Conference of Agricultural Economists, 1938.

of individuals must ultimately lead to some sort of totalitarian society. Thus, according to Hayek,[3] planning means

. . . a central direction of all economic activity according to a single plan, laying down how the resources of society should be "consciously directed" to serve particular ends in a definite way.

A somewhat similar fear was expressed by Howard S. Ellis in his presidential address at the 1949 meeting of the American Economic Association:[4]

Some planning is, and some is not, compatible with the maximizing of the field of individual free choice. Some planning signifies the formation of institutions such as the International Monetary Fund, which was designed—at least in some notable respects—to restore free-market processes. Planning in another sense, such as the agricultural price-parity program, is well calculated to undermine market processes and make the economy subject solely to political forces. All too often planning of this variety is defended as "welfare economics," although it negates economics and ignores the loss of welfare imposed upon the economy as a whole by the gain of a special segment. It is impossible to oppose "planning" if it simply means forethought, consistency, and rational provision for contingencies in public policy; but very often the term simply covers the growth of political decision at the expense of the economic calculus.

A totalitarian state, or a society dominated by power-blocs of labor, agriculture, and industry cannot give expression to the economic calculus. Economics is necessarily a matter fundamentally of individual choice and it is thus necessarily also libertarian and individualistic. Authoritarian societies will gladly bid farewell to the economic way of thinking. But not only will personal liberty have taken leave, but also the processes by which the individual secures from his limited resources the best satisfaction of his individual wants. It would not be the century of the common man.

According to this conception, economics does not deal with problems involving "group action in restraint, liberation and expansion of individual action" as held by John R. Commons. Ellis would seem to say that for such a purpose "economics does not exist." For instance, he asserts that the agricultural price-parity program is not economic planning simply for the reason that politics also enters into the decision-making process.

It is true that economics deals with choices, but must it be confined to individual choices in a time of group conflict and group action? The group aspects of the present farm price-support program, for example, do not exclude it from the realm of economics. Furthermore, our corporate structure is essentially a way of organizing group activity. Present-day

[3] Friedrich A. Hayek, *The Road to Serfdom,* p. 35, Chicago University Press, Chicago, 1944.

[4] Howard S. Ellis, "The Economic Way of Thinking," *The American Economic Review,* Vol. 40, No. 1, p. 12, March, 1950.

problems of economics must deal with price control, farm subsidies, labor relations, competition and monopoly, and full employment, and in a setting where social, economic, and political forces are operating.

## The Concept of Social Planning

In this chapter we are concerned primarily with planning as it relates to land resources, and then not to all aspects. In discussing a subject as broad as land-resource planning, it is obviously necessary to select some phases of the field for consideration. Many aspects of land planning have already been covered, particularly in Chapter 4.

As planning is not a new experience, it has for a long time had its individual and public aspects. Rural people have long been engaged in planning without any direct public assistance. It is not with this phase of planning that we are here concerned, but rather with land-resources planning from a public viewpoint, with particular reference to some activities of the Federal government and to those of the states.

Land planning is a segment of social planning aimed at the broad objectives of bringing about the utilization of the land resources of a given area in ways conducive to the general welfare, both present and future. "Planning for the wise use of land resources is simply organized social intelligence striving toward determined objectives through a designed course of public action."[5]

Various considerations of conditions and policies at the broad national, or even international, level constitute a very necessary basis for the orientation of land planning. These include some of the important conditions discussed in earlier chapters, such as the outlook for land requirements and broad national objectives in balancing available resources against requirements. In addition, consideration must be given to trade policies as they influence the demand for and prices of the products of various types of land use; to monetary and credit policies as they affect trends in general price levels; to population policies as they affect the general ratio of population to natural resources and its distribution throughout the nation; and to industrial policies in their influence on the geographic distribution of population, particularly as between rural and urban employments, and in their influence on the levels of return to labor in rural occupations.

*Objectives of Planning.* Among the over-all objectives of planning in the national economy, the following are generally accepted: (1) enlargement of the national income, (2) wider distribution of the national income, (3) maintenance of freedom of enterprise, (4) greater economic

[5] John F. Timmons and William G. Murray (eds.), *Land Problems and Policies*, Iowa State College Press, Ames, Iowa, 1950. See chapter on "Planning the Use of Land Resources" by V. Webster Johnson.

security of the people, (5) broader economic opportunities for individuals, (6) efficiency and conservation in resource use, and (7) maintenance and improvement of national standing and prestige throughout the world.

These objectives are similar to the general objectives of national policy briefly considered in Chapter 1. Few would quarrel with such general objectives, and we can readily recall instances of common action taken for their achievement. It is with specific programs of action that differences of opinion arise between individuals.

In the United States there has been for several decades a considerable amount of governmental planning, mainly for the application of specialized policies, in ever-widening spheres of activity, conceded as falling within the proper scope of governmental functions. For instance, the underlying philosophy of legislation in behalf of the agriculture price-support programs is that it is in the public interest for farmers to obtain a reasonable level of farm income and that without effective group action this is not possible. To obtain effective action Federal support is necessary, for market prices or freely competitive equilibrium prices in the absence of government assistance may result in widespread serious economic and social distress. Government price policy is an attempt to make a phase of our economy more effective in the productive and distributive processes. If what is done at any given time is not sound, of course the consequences are bad and should be corrected. The test of what is in the public interest is what the people in the long run want and will support.

Government planning for further improvement in the agricultural industry is based upon characteristics peculiar to agriculture. Not only does agriculture vitally concern all the people; it likewise differs from most industries in several significant ways.

These differences affect, and to some extent determine, the organization of agricultural production and, as a consequence, the life and well-being of farm people. The characteristics peculiar to agriculture [in the United States] which should be considered when developing a long-range agricultural policy and program include:

1. The production required to fill the primary needs of every urban and rural family for food and clothing originates principally on the Nation's farms.

2. As a consequence, the entire population benefits directly from technical progress that assures an abundant supply of farm products at a reduced cost of production.

3. Abundant production of food and fiber, however, is dependent largely upon maintenance of the high productivity of the soil which is readily exhaustible.

4. Conservation, restoration, and development of the soil for future production, therefore, contribute directly to the welfare of all the people.

5. Even under the best conditions, however, agricultural production cannot

be controlled completely, or even within narrow bounds. It varies widely from year to year because of variable weather, pests, and diseases.

6. Moreover, farm production cannot be started and stopped at will to meet changing conditions of demand, for farm-production processes are continuous and controlled mainly by the seasonal growth of crops and the natural life cycle of animals.

7. Since many farm products are perishable in character and are produced seasonally, they must be sold when ready for market, regardless of the demand and price situation at that particular time.

8. The problems growing out of these characteristics are intensified by the fact that the large number of small independent farmers are at a distinct disadvantage in dealing with the relatively small number of large, well-organized commercial establishments, in both the sale of products and the purchase of supplies.

9. The many independent farm operators are unable as individuals to conduct the research and experimentation necessary to maintain technical progress comparable to that attained by large industrial corporations.

10. Similarly, because of the scattered location of farms, most rural people are unable to provide, without assistance, many of the services that are readily available to most city dwellers.

11. On the other hand, the high birth rate among rural people makes possible the large farm-to-city migration of manpower which is necessary to continue the growth of urban centers.

A long-range policy for agriculture should take into account these peculiar characteristics of farming and rural life. The public interest in agricultural policy arises from the present and future benefits to all the people of a sound, well-defined, and fully coordinated long-range program for agriculture.[6]

Some of these characteristics are not peculiar to agriculture alone. Nevertheless, few will contend that as a whole they do not show that agriculture is possessed of characteristics that call for public planning and action. This is accepted public policy.

In rural areas, a sound land program is a basic part of agricultural policy. This is because the use and control of land are essential to sustained production of our food needs. More specifically, land-resource planning has as its objectives: (1) to produce the needed quantity and quality of agricultural products, (2) to extend soil conservation throughout all its needed aspects, (3) to develop and restore many lands for agriculture, forestry, grazing, recreation, and other principal uses, (4) to give more stability to desirable land uses, (5) to improve effective tenure arrangements on both public and private land and thus improve their condition of use, and (6) to maintain a fair income to land users through shifts in land uses and an improved pattern of production.

[6] *Long-Range Agricultural Policy and Program*, Report of the Committee on Agriculture and Forestry, U.S. Senate, pursuant to S. Res. 147, 80th Cong., 2d Sess., S. Rep. 885, pp. 14–15, 1948.

These objectives have received considerable attention and discussion in preceding chapters. Plans and programs to these ends have to some extent been explored, and some observations have been made as to past achievements and the nature and scope of the task ahead. Therefore we need not again review specific land programs.

As has been pointed out, in carrying out these objectives a number of courses of action are involved, and in a democratic society the programs developed at any given time very likely have conflicting purposes; but this is a part of the democratic process in the rationalization of conflicts. If planning succeeds in moving forward in some organized and systematic manner toward certain objectives, it achieves its purpose.

Essential to the accomplishment of planning objectives is the presence of a social philosophy that will support their attainment. For example, to set up policies for encouragement of family-owner-operated farms requires a belief in the family-farm ideal and coordination of a family-farm policy with other programs. At times, social action has proceeded toward objectives without duly considering the relationship of the various objectives to one another, or even the extent to which the goals are consistent. This has been true in the case of the family farm, but as indicated, we must recognize that a certain amount of muddling along is a part of the democratic process and that true social planning must constantly be engaged in correcting its own weaknesses and limitations.

Land planning must continually change in scope and character as points of view and policies change. It is therefore dynamic, not static. It is the process of intelligently adjusting the uses of land to the gradually changing conceptions of social well-being rather than the making of a pattern good for all time. Furthermore, it extends beyond the mere determination of the use for which land should be employed. It must, of course, involve consideration of intensity of land use and the measures necessary to give effect to the ends sought. For instance, the contributions of land, capital, and labor must be studied, and regulatory measures required or institutional adjustments necessary explored.

Furthermore, plans and programs need to be integrated. For instance, an adequate program of public forests is an essential phase of a well-rounded national land plan, and the selection of specific areas for public forests should be made with due reference to their relative social utility for other uses, such as watershed protection or grazing, as well as with reference to other factors, such as the pattern of local government and the local revenue system. If the selection of lands for public forests is made merely with a view to the cheapness of the land, the character of the cover, and the adaptability to forest growth, other essential considerations in a symmetrical land-use plan may be sacrificed.

Many opponents of the idea of planning have wrongly assumed that it involves an attempt to formulate a blueprint of action good for all time. Recognizing the numerous imponderable and unpredictable elements, such as foreign wars, violent price changes, technical changes and inventions, radical modifications in tastes and fashions, and cataclysms of nature, as, for instance, protracted periods of deficient moisture supply, they have superficially concluded that planning is a futile undertaking. This line of argument, however, loses its conclusiveness when planning is regarded as a continuing process with  provisions for considering the impact of new and unforeseen factors and determining from the standpoint of the public welfare the requisite adjustments.

## Levels in Planning

Every type of planning must have a focus or center of interest about which are grouped certain conditions and relationships, some close and some remote from the center of interest or point of view from which the planning procedure is undertaken. The various conditions and relationships that are of significance to a particular focus may be regarded as within the horizon which bounds that sphere of interest. Thus industrial planning and employer-labor relations, monetary planning, planning for transportation and communication, foreign-trade planning, fiscal planning, and planning for the integration and greater economy and efficiency of governmental structure, land planning, and social planning, each in the narrower sense may be regarded as falling within a broad planning horizon. And these and other types of planning involve different levels of government.

There are many who would lay special stress on local planning, especially in the conduct of land planning—and rightly so, for land planning is particularly concerned with location factors and spatial considerations and relationships. But much local planning is merely the local application of national policies. A good example of this is the work of the agricultural adjustment committees of the Production and Marketing Administration, which must adjust themselves to changes in national policies, while at the same time helping, in collaboration with numerous localities, to define policies at the national level.

During the county planning movement, which is briefly reviewed later in this chapter, it was soon discovered that many problems could not possibly be solved merely at local, or even state, levels. For instance, hundreds of counties discovered that they had a redundant rural population in relation to available land resources, especially when the resources were employed primarily for commercial production. If these resources had been used most efficiently from that standpoint, the surplus population would have had to be provided for in some other way. The only answer the counties had to this problem was to let the surplus population move "somewhere else."[7]

Merely because local planning groups encounter problems that arise from conditions outside of the locality and are dependent for their solution on policies that must be formulated at the national level, we need not assume that the resulting sense of frustration may not be wholesome. When thousands of local planning committees become aware of a common problem and fully acquainted with its causes and character, we shall be well on the way to solving it; for the educated public opinion thus generated will demand and, perhaps, point the way to a solution. Thus, local planning will not become merely a device for registering a narrow provincialism of outlook and for dealing with problems that can be solved solely by local action, but will serve also as an "instrument for popular clarification of the real nature of agricultural problems, and for the indigenous development of national policies."[8]

Just as there needs to be clarity as to the particular goal with which one is concerned in a planning undertaking, the area of planning is an important consideration. There has been a good deal of general discussion among persons interested in rural or land planning as to the relative merits of employing various types of geographic units, and various kinds of units have been used in planning undertakings.

The most prevalent unit of planning hitherto has been the city; and there has been far greater progress in the development of technical procedures, legal sanctions, and administrative machinery in this sphere of planning than in any other. The rapid extension of city boundaries, the necessity of regulating the processes of subdivision and integrating the plans of cities and towns lying in the same vicinity, and, particularly, the need for making provision for recreational areas, water supply, cemeteries, landing fields, and boulevards in outlying areas have in recent years resulted in provisions for metropolitan planning. For some of the larger cities, the type of planning may affect areas many miles from the urban center.

Regional planning, as the term is commonly used, is concerned with the economic and social development of a geographic region composed of contiguous states that possess some degree of similarity in historical background and in types of economic and social problems. Such geographic units of planning, for example, are the Pacific Northwest or the New England states.

It is evident, however, that neither of these areas has physiographic

[7] Paul H. Johnstone, "Somewhere Else," *Land Policy Review*, November–December, 1939.
[8] *Ibid.*

unity. New England has a considerable variety of geology, soil, and climatic conditions, not to mention the great economic and social differences between northern and southern New England. The topographic range in the Pacific Northwest is extreme, varying from coastal plain to rugged mountains. The range of precipitation extends from the wettest portions of the United States along the Pacific to areas of extreme aridity east of the Cascades. Temperature contrasts in different parts of the region are almost as extreme. Such great differences in physiographic conditions are bound to result in a considerable lack of economic and social homogeneity.

It is to be expected that when such large areas as New England and the Pacific Northwest are selected, a high degree of homogeneity is unlikely. But such areas may have a good deal in common in the contiguity of the various states, their historical background, and their general location within the nation. Moreover, in the process of planning it is possible to subdivide them into more nearly homogeneous subunits of planning. In the case of rural or land planning this is a necessary element.

Sometimes the geographic unit of planning may be a distinctive physiographic area, such as the southern Appalachians or the Georgia piedmont. Even such units, however, are much too large to make possible throughout the area a great degree of homogeneity in topography, soil, climate, and economic and social conditions.

When the interest is principally in the supply, flow, use, or conservation of water, a logical unit of planning is a watershed; but a watershed may be as large as the Mississippi Valley or it may be as small as one of its minor tributaries, for example, the Kickapoo River in Wisconsin. One of the largest units of this type that has become a going concern of intensive planning is the Tennessee River. Many bills have been introduced in Congress for the establishment of "authorities," after the fashion of that set up for the Tennessee; but it is also recognized that in some watersheds the problems of interfluvial areas may be more important than the problems of river flow and that these interfluvial problems may be neglected if the focus is too definitely on water and its flow. Moreover, watersheds frequently cut across physiographic and natural land-use areas and may be essentially lacking in cultural unity.

Necessarily, flood-control, irrigation, drainage, stream-pollution, and power projects must be addressed to a consideration of the stream as a whole. In fact, there has been an enormous waste, particularly in irrigation and drainage projects, by reason of the earlier tendency to plan them on an essentially local and piecemeal basis, instead of with reference to the relationship of conservation and control of water in the watershed as a whole. The consideration of interfluvial conditions implies an adequate coordination of various plans and not necessarily the selection of watersheds as the universal and exclusive units of rural planning.

In a number of river basins, as the Missouri, Columbia, and Colorado, comprehensive planning for a geographic area is under way. Its primary aim is the integrating of activities of a number of agencies and departments of the Federal government and agencies of the states involved into a unified program to develop, utilize, and conserve the resources of the basins. Current emphasis on planning in some river basins has arisen from the sharp conflicts between governmental agencies, each with a "plan," and each more or less narrowly confining its interests to its particular plan.

A special area, such as a national or state forest or park, Indian reservation, or similar area, is sometimes the unit of planning. This is essentially an administrative type of planning for a specific objective, but it can be one phase of geographic planning.

## Development of Planning in the United States

*Early Urban Developments.* The development of planning activity and planning agencies at the various political levels in this country proceeded with considerable rapidity during the advent of the New Deal. During the past decade progress has been less marked, particularly in reference to land resources. A brief review of some of the major developments in planning in the United States should be helpful in providing an impression of the significance of planning in our national life.

In the early colonial period there was some planning in regard to the use and settlement of land; social planning was involved in the establishment of the New England town system. In urban planning we are familiar with the layout for Washington, D.C., devised by Major L'Enfant, and formal landscaping is, of course, an old art, as is manifested in the elaborate layout for Versailles which was instituted by Louis XIV. Systematic city planning, however, is in the main a development of the twentieth century.

About the beginning of the century there was organized at Louisville, Ky., the American Park and Outdoor Art Association, which 7 years later combined with the American League for Civic Improvement to form the American Civic Association. J. Horace McFarland, its president for many years, used the organization to awaken hundreds of cities to the ugliness and inefficiencies resulting from lack of planning. For more than a decade the association has been a potent agency for promoting interest in planning, gradually broadening its scope through collaboration with the National Conference on City Planning, organized in 1909, the American City Planning Institute, and other organizations interested in promoting national and state parks, the planning of highways and other public works, and rural land-use planning.

A landmark in the progress of city planning was the adoption of the

New York zoning ordinance in 1916. For, with the advent of zoning, there became available a body of sanctions for the enforcement of plans; and at the same time, potential regulations were provided to deal with situations in need of effective planning programs. At the present time most of the larger towns and cities have some type of planning or zoning, together with planning boards for making necessary adjustments in zoning ordinances and for developing major thoroughfare plans, proposals for playgrounds and parks, and programs for providing more adequate housing conditions.

A most significant development of city planning during the past decade has been the establishment of planning authorities, procedures, and various sanctions for the planning of the outer fringe of cities. This has been particularly important for integrating the planning of the extension of neighboring cities and towns and coordinating the provisions for their water supply, connecting boulevards, and recreational areas. A number of states have authorized the establishment of metropolitan district-planning boards, in some cases with regulatory powers. In this connection there has been a reconsideration of boundary lines and an extension of control over suburban platting of subdivisions. The result at times is a tendency to formulate county-wide plans and to develop county planning and zoning authorities in urban or suburban areas where the county appeared to provide a logical unit for the more comprehensive planning and control of areas on the fringes of cities. As early as 1932 and 1933, New York extended its regional planning act to authorize county planning. The trend toward county planning of this type, as in southern California, is to be distinguished from county planning for strictly rural areas.

*National Resources Planning Board.* One of the first of the Federal agencies established to stimulate public planning and to provide a focus for activities was the National Resources Planning Board, which was given legislative authorization as the planning arm of the President by the Reorganization Act of 1939. Its predecessor agencies, the National Resources Board and the National Resources Committee, were maintained for a time by emergency funds and performed useful work of initial exploration and organizational development. These successive agencies encouraged the development of parallel and closely related, though not subordinate, planning boards and committees in 42 states, of which 37 were authorized by specific state legislation, and in Alaska, Puerto Rico, and Hawaii.

The National Resources Planning Board itself was composed largely of heads of a number of departments and independent agencies; its activities were largely administered by an advisory committee, mainly through the chairman and executive secretary of that body with the aid of a small technical staff. Under the Reorganization Act of 1939 the character of the Board was changed. It then became more than an ex-offiicio cabinet committee and was composed of five members appointed by the President.

The Board and its predecessor agencies laid special emphasis on land planning, planning for water utilization and conservation, and the coordination of mineral utilization and conservation. They sponsored a number of special nationwide reports on population trends, industrial organization, and land requirements, resources, and policies. Without possessing specific authority for interdepartmental coordination they were instrumental in encouraging collaboration.

Lacking nationwide machinery for local planning, the National Resources Planning Board worked largely through state and regional planning organizations and through the local planning machinery of the Federal departments, such as the local planning organizations of the Resettlement Administration and the Department of Agriculture. The Board increased its own facilities for contacts at the local level with Federal, state, and local agencies by establishing regional offices. In its report for 1939 it points to "a continuous movement in the direction of regional planning, by the establishment of regional planning commissions, by interstate compacts and by the decentralization of Federal administrative agencies." Regional boards, with more or less associated planning machinery, supplementing that of the states included, were developed for New England, the northern Lake states, the northern Great Plains, the Pacific Northwest, and for a number of watersheds of regional scope under interstate compacts, such as interstate commissions on the Delaware, Potomac, and Ohio Rivers and joint Federal-state investigations on the Pecos and the Rio Grande Rivers.

The National Resources Planning Board was one of the major, if not the foremost, planning organizations at the executive level concerned with the development, integration, and coordination of plans. One of its principal activities under the general leadership of a land committee was to study and issue reports on land and water resources. The reports issued, however, were not plans in the sense that they provided the basis for administrative operation. They dealt rather with fundamentals that related directly to public needs and set forth broad recommendations for obtaining these needs.[9] Even so, Congress came to look with disfavor upon the Board, and the later years of its existence were due largely to the fight that President Roosevelt made for its continuance. Finally, however, Roosevelt was not able to save the Board and it passed out of existence on Jan. 1, 1944. Congress was opposed to the type of planning done by the Board and felt that if there was to be an administrative agency to deal with planning, its powers and duties should be carefully defined and

[9] John D. Millett, *The Process and Organization of Government Planning*, pp. 18–19, Columbia University Press, New York, 1947.

the members approved by the Senate. In brief, many members of Congress felt that the Board was exercising power over a subject that should be under Congressional supervision. Several members of Congress were also not in general sympathy with the recommendations of the Board.

The nation's experience with such movements as the National Resources Planning Board has not been too encouraging. However, such agencies have served as effective planning organizations. The fact stands out that vested interests feared their presence because they dealt with the over-all integration and coordination of planning. Agencies, organizations, and legislative bodies cherish their established prerogatives.

## Planning in the U.S. Department of Agriculture

*Early Developments.* The early efforts in land planning by the Department of Agriculture, alone and in cooperation with state agricultural colleges, and by the colleges themselves, emphasized land classification and land utilization. Soil surveys, a type of land classification, were rapidly expanded, and economic and social stress in many rural areas gave rise to many land-utilization studies. As a result questions were raised as to the economic productivity of different classes of lands. Thus we find that during the latter part of the 1920's and during the 1930's economic land classification was stressed in the planning process.

As has been pointed out, economic land classification is a phase of land planning and is concerned with determining what use, or uses, of each type of land is desirable, not merely from the standpoint of benefits to the individual operator but also in view of considerations of general public welfare. The recommendations made as to best use not only indicated the most desirable major use, such as arable farming, range grazing, forestry, recreation, or wildlife refuges, but also specified the subtype of the particular major use recommended. Thus, if arable farming was the major use, there was also involved the type of farming considered desirable. This was important not merely to make the process of planning more specific, but because the determination of the major use as compared with other possible major uses depended on the advantages and disadvantages of the various subtypes, some of which were wholly undesirable.

The concept of systematic planning for the surface uses of land in rural areas was given an initial impetus in the formation of the National Land Use Planning Committee, established as a result of the National Conference on Land Utilization, held in Chicago in November, 1931. The work of this committee was mainly educational and promotive but also served to pave the way for the more definite planning programs. With the exception of administrative agencies, such as the Forest Service and National Park Service, most of the development of planning machinery for rural areas in the United States has occurred since 1930.

The variety of agencies in the U.S. Department of Agriculture that were engaged in planning led to an attempt to employ area planning at local levels to effect coordination and integration. A first step was the establishment in the Office of the Secretary of an office of Land Use Coordination, charged with the function of effecting coordination of administrative policies and procedures at the national level, including coordination with other Federal departments and agencies, largely through the National Resources Committee. A second step was designation of the Bureau of Agricultural Economics as the focus of cooperation by the various bureaus in the integration of their policies and procedures at national, state, and county levels.

*County Agricultural Planning Committees.* At local levels, beginning in 1938, county agricultural planning committees in most of the states were composed of officials of the state agricultural college, state representatives of several bureaus of the U.S. Department of Agriculture, and a number of leading farmers. County land-use planning committees were formed in approximately two-thirds of the agricultural counties, dovetailed as to membership with the committees of the "Triple A." In many of the counties, township or community committees were formed, integrating their plans through the county committees.

The work of these county land-use planning committees was to proceed by three successive stages: (1) preliminary or preparatory work, (2) intensive planning, and (3) an attempt in selected counties to develop a unified and closely integrated program of action on the part of the various Federal agencies operating in the county whose activities affect land use. The first phase consisted of subdividing the county into a number of land-use areas—each relatively homogeneous in physical characteristics, present land use, types of land-use problems—and then assembling data descriptive of the characteristics of each such distinctive area.

The second phase consisted of determining the use or uses to which each of the characteristic areas was best adapted. Central in this phase of the undertaking was the determination of areas adapted to farming, as distinguished from those not so adapted, a decision of major importance in the application of the various programs. It was also helpful in the planning of rural roads and in the application of various policies of state and county governments.

The third phase consisted of determining what shifts in land use and changes in type of farming were indicated by the economic land classifications of the intensive phase, and what measures should be taken to bring about the changes proposed. It was in this phase that the development of a unified program through collaboration with the county committees of the representatives of various Federal and state administrative agencies was contemplated.

Provision was made for keeping the procedure sufficiently elastic to adapt it to the widely varying conditions of various parts of the United States, but also for sufficient uniformity and standardization to assure comparability of results and their usefulness at the national level.

The county planning program spread to all states except Pennsylvania. Although originally designed to unify land-use-planning activities, it came to include many other objectives of rural well-being and, in effect, to encompass the whole field of social and economic agricultural planning. Thus, during the latter part of its existence, its objectives were stated as (1) to coordinate interrelated phases of the agricultural program, (2) to coordinate local, state, and Federal land-use activities, (3) to develop an improved working relationship between the Department of Agriculture and the state agricultural colleges, and (4) to provide for democratic farmer participation in the development of farm policies and programs.[10]

The county planning movement was of relatively short duration, lasting less than 4 years. In 1941, Congress withheld the appropriation of funds to the Bureau of Agricultural Economics for state and county planning. In view of the Bureau's central position in the movement, the program as formally organized came to an end.

While the county planning program was new and somewhat experimental, it was highly significant because of the widespread recognition it gave to the importance of land and community planning and because of its essentially democratic character. It constitutes a notable advance in the direction of democratizing bureaucracy by introducing popular participation in the planning and application, and even the formulation, of policies. The effectiveness of the program was greatly curtailed, however, by conflicting interests that developed between agencies within Departments, and between Departments and other organizations, and because a fear that county planning was invading vested-interest fields. But the fact that county planning, particularly as it applies to land use, is still a going concern in a number of states speaks highly for its effectiveness as a program.

*Rural Public Works.* A tremendous boost for both urban and metropolitan planning on the one hand and rural planning on the other was provided by the decision to alleviate unemployment through work relief rather than through doles. During the Hoover Administration the idea was developed of smoothing the fluctuations of the business cycle by governmental spending for public works, an idea then supported by eminent economists who advocated expansion of public works in times of depression, and contraction during periods of expansion. The initial idea was limited to the normal governmental expenditures for public works, such as the regular program for construction of roads and public buildings and river and harbor improvements. It was proposed that the government

[10] *Report of the Secretary of Agriculture*, p. 174, Washington, 1942.

develop architectural and engineering blueprints and specifications well in advance of construction, so that with the advent of depression the plans could be quickly put into operation as a means of checking the process of deflation. In accordance with this idea Congress passed in 1931 the Employment Stabilization Act, providing for a 6-year program of Federal public works to be revised annually. To fulfill this purpose a Federal Employment Stabilization Board was established to stimulate advance blueprinting on the part of the various Federal departments concerned with public works. The acute depression of the early 1930's soon forced the expansion of the relatively normal Federal expenditures on the program to extraordinary expenditures as a means both of relieving unemployment and stimulating recovery.

The enormous volume of construction inaugurated by both the Public Works Administration and the Works Progress Administration revealed strikingly the lack of well-developed plans. Not only were architectural and engineering blueprints lacking, but most serious of all was the lack of fundamental machinery and procedures for the selection of projects in accordance with master plans under which the individual plans would be interrelated and coordinated. The need for the latter type of planning became obvious when it became necessary to rate projects not merely on their individual merits but on their relative merits and to establish priorities in a comprehensive program of development. However, in spite of such deficiencies, the achievements brought about in rural areas were marked, and a definite basis was laid for the use of public works as a force in maintaining a stable national economy through the sponsorship of useful public-improvement projects.

Shortly after 1940, a number of postwar planning committees were set up within the Department of Agriculture. One of these committees was charged with the responsibility for outlining a shelf of rural public works projects in the agricultural field. The work of this committee was related to an over-all request submitted by the President in 1943 to the different departments and agencies of government to develop a program of public works as an integral part of the budget process. It was generally felt at the time that the war would be followed by a slump in employment and that a shelf of public-works projects should be planned in advance as one means that could be used in coping with a business recession.

Many of the regular activities of the Department of Agriculture fall particularly within the scope of possible rural public works programs. The work in forestry, soil conservation, rural electrification, river-basin development, and flood control, for instance, lend themselves readily to work programs.

Public works as applied to land resources offer possibilities on both public and private lands. On public lands the big needs are on forest and grazing lands and in recreational areas. The job is that of improving and sustaining the production of forest products and of using forest lands so as to contribute to the broad aspects of land conservation and desirable land use. A similar task is present in the case of grazing lands. Our recreational areas are also far from adequately developed, and we have too few of them. Recreational areas and facilities need to be adequate from a physical standpoint, and developed, in regard to types, in a manner that meets man's recreational needs while still preserving the natural advantages of wildlife areas. Public works can contribute significantly to the fulfillment of such essential functions of public land use.

The need for public works planned in the public interest is also substantial on private agricultural lands. For instance, many types of land-conservation projects are definitely in the public interest, and public expenditures are necessary to provide the needed conservation measures. In part, individuals need guidance and financial assistance if the degree of conservation socially desirable is to be achieved; and help received should serve as an inducement for a fuller contribution toward conservation on the part of the individual.

There are also numerous cases in which substantial benefits to private lands result from public works developments on adjacent public lands. And in some types of improvements large areas of private land, some of which may be quite a distance from the actual physical works, may be substantially benefited. In such cases, it would seem equitable to require contributions related in some way to the private benefits received.

Experiences with public works during the past 10 years as well as consideration of future public works clearly indicate that some of the most worth-while work opportunities are located upon private land. The prohibition against public works on private lands inflicts a limitation on future public works activities which not only handicaps the function of public works programs as a "balance wheel" in the economy but also impairs the worthwhileness of projects which may be undertaken. But experiences . . . indicate that . . . caution should be exercised that private individuals and groups do not use public funds for selfish advancement and gain.

As a protection against selfish gains and windfall profits accruing to private landowners, projects on private lands should not be undertaken until (1) a substantial public interest is demonstrated; (2) arrangements are made to share costs in relation to benefits received, qualified by ability to pay; (3) landowners demonstrate that they have the will to do what the project seeks to attain; (4) landowners back up their good faith with agreements to make material contributions to the project; and (5) responsible assurance is guaranteed as to completion and maintenance of the project.[11]

[11] V. Webster Johnson and John F. Timmons, "Public Works on Private Land," *Journal of Farm Economics*, Vol. 26, No. 4, p. 684, November, 1944.

The implementation, protection, and maintenance of public works on private land may call for public acquisition or exercise of rights over land through easement controls, the public use of the police power, or by limitation of holdings or taxation to prevent excessive benefits accruing to private owners as a direct benefit from public expenditures. The point to bear in mind is that some of the most worth-while projects as measured in terms of the public interest are to be found on private lands. This is because private lands have many serious soil-conservation problems and land-resource-development needs, the nature and scope of which require some public assistance. Thus a large area of public interest is present, and the task is how best to protect this interest through initial assistance and safeguards, and at the same time prevent unjustifiable private gains at public expense.

*River-Basin Development.* One of the most recent significant movements in land-resources planning in the Department of Agriculture and, in fact, in some respects a landmark in agricultural planning is the work taking place in major river basins. Attention is primarily focused on the Missouri, Columbia, Colorado, Arkansas, Red, White, and Rio Grande River Basins, with particular emphasis on the Missouri Basin. In addition to programs in river basins as a major part of over-all development, there are also many watershed and flood-control programs under way for conservation and development of land resources that are carried out under the flood-control acts.

The work that is being done in the Missouri Basin represents an effort to bring about integrated planning through the cooperation of a number of agencies in the Department of Agriculture, the Bureau of Reclamation of the Department of the Interior, the Corps of Engineers of the Department of the Army, the Federal Power Commission of the Department of Commerce, and the agricultural water and forestry agencies of 10 states. Representatives of these Federal and state agencies compose the Missouri Inter-Agency Committee which is charged with the responsibility of developing an integrated plan.

The Department's part in this task is to complement the vast mainstream engineering developments and to supplement the planning work of an agricultural nature being done by the Bureau of Reclamation in the development of the resources of the basin. The agricultural plan calls for a comprehensive integrated program of development during a 30-year period.[12]

[12] The *Missouri River Basin Agricultural Program*, 81 Cong., 1st Sess., H. Doc. 373, is the first report submitted to Congress by the Department of Agriculture to set forth a broad program specifically designed "to conserve and improve the soil for sustained productive use, protect and enhance the forest resource, abate flood and sediment damages, provide for more efficient land use through irrigation and

The type of committee organization set up in the Missouri Valley to integrate the work is a new experience in planning. It has all the weaknesses of any loosely organized federation in dealing with problems that demand administrative action and, on the other hand, all the advantages of keeping intact the specialized tasks or functions of functional-line agencies. Undoubtedly, the success of the venture will depend to no small extent upon how successful the committee is in its effort to integrate the contributions of the different agencies. In integrated planning it is essential that certain responsibilities of functional agencies be adjusted to the aims of the program as a whole. This involves a sharing of functions and responsibilities among agencies, a recognition that certain agencies are better equipped to do certain jobs; and not, as has been said, a setup based partially on a fear that something must be done to stave off a possible Missouri Valley Authority.

Since the committee cannot be a decision-making body, it is possible that the integrated aspects of the program may accordingly suffer—not because of any lack of cooperation on the part of agencies, but simply because the mechanism does not provide for the type of decision making that is necessary in an 8- to 10-billion-dollar program.

## Aspects of Planning in the U.S. Department of the Interior

Brief mention should be made of the land-planning activities of the Department of the Interior of the Federal government. Lands under its jurisdiction vary widely in physical characteristics and use, ranging from grazing areas to dense forest, and from barren deserts to some of the world's most scenic areas. They consist of lands in grazing districts and unreserved public grazing lands, commercial forests, national parks, wildlife refuges and game ranges, Indian reservations, mineral lands, and lands that may be reclaimed for agricultural use by irrigation.

In the Department of the Interior, planning is very much a part of the job of administering different types of land. Planning is thus a function of management. The coordination and integration of the land-use and land-management activities are carried out in the Office of the Secretary. The primary aim is the conservation and development of land resources under its jurisdiction for the benefit of the people of the United States. This means the practice of sound land-use policies on those lands directly under the Department's management; where lands are under lease, the

---

drainage, protect the water resources, and in many other ways contribute to the full and efficient development, utilization and conservation of a region." Obviously the work proposed overlaps the work under way and proposed by the Bureau of Reclamation, and problems of interpretation and coordination are present between the Department of Agriculture and the Department of the Interior.

full protection of public interests; and for some lands which because of location and physical characteristics might best be in private ownership, a careful appraisal and classification before disposal.

At present, one of the major planning activities the Department of the Interior is concerned with is the irrigation of arid lands, both public and private, under the provisions of the Reclamation Act of 1902 and supplementary legislation. This phase of the Department's planning work has been covered, at least in a general manner, in previous discussions, particularly in relation to river-basin development programs and land settlement and development activities. Because of the multiplicity of land uses present in river basins, the task involves not only integration and coordination between bureaus of the Department of the Interior, but also between Departments of the Federal government and between Federal Departments and state agencies.

## Integration of Plans

Public planning is a process that must be carried on at different levels of government—Federal, state, and local. In truly democratic planning, all of these units should actively participate in planning and programing and should not operate so as to guard narrow selfish interests. It is, of course, the interests of the people most immediately affected that will generally be most zealously guarded, but even this aim should not overshadow the major objectives.

The purpose of coordinated and integrated planning is to provide the maximum benefits to the largest number of people for the longest possible time. This involves concern for future benefits and the conservation of such benefits in the interest of the people. Thus, if the aim of planning is to maximize benefits, and it is recognized that all units of government must and should have a significant part in planning and policy making, and the government planning is useful and essential, it should follow that effective means or mechanisms must be provided for planning.

All units of government have important interests in the conservation, development, and efficient use of resources under sustained production. Because of the position of the Federal government and the degree to which effective action needs to be taken at this level, there is need for a strong planning organization in the Federal government in order to view land-use plans in the interests of the largest possible group of people. If this is not done, the interests of strong groups or agencies outside of government can use state and local units of government in support of sectional interests which may possibly negate national interests. This is not to suggest a highly centralized planning system nor in any way infringement on the power and responsibilities of state and local governments, but simply to say that there are certain responsibilities that must be met at the Federal level in the interest of planning for the welfare of the nation as a whole. It is not possible completely to delegate or parcel out national interests to lower units of government and expect that such interests will be duly protected.

Many of the social, economic, and political decisions bearing on land utilization must be made by the Federal government or materially influenced by it. Thus it seems imperative that some sort of over-all Federal planning agency should exist to appraise public needs and to serve as a mechanism for the integration and coordination of different plans. Unless some such organization exists, we can only hope that the divergent interests of different groups will be ironed out through the bargaining process of the groups and that the results reached will be in the national interest. No one would wish to underestimate the importance of this process, but one can question the advisability of relying on this means as the main basis for the sound planning of our land resources. Our experiences in this field should enable us to move forward on an enlightened and integrated basis for effective planning on the part of local, state, and Federal units of government.

CHAPTER 15  *Land Reform*

Since the Second World War, land reform has mushroomed as a problem of considerable importance in many parts of the world. Actually, it is not a new problem. History is replete with accounts of peasant uprisings and other attempts to ameliorate the harsh land-tenure conditions developed under feudalism. Only during the past two or three centuries, however, has much progress been made in actually securing reforms that have led to freer tenure conditions or to a wider distribution of ownership rights. The demand for land reform often has played a significant role in the struggle of the common people for greater economic and political freedom. It is not without reason then that the French Revolution of 1789, the popular uprisings of 1848, and the armistice of 1918, all were followed by land-reform programs that affected various parts of Europe.

Like many other land-reform movements, the present movement has been touched off by political change, growing nationalism, and the demand of rural people for greater recognition. The present movement is notable primarily in that it has made itself felt in Asia, and to a lesser extent in Latin America and Africa, as well as in Europe. But, it is also important because of its association with the burning political issues of the day and with the world goal of peace and prosperity.

Both the democratic nations and the Communist powers recognize the importance of land reform as a political issue throughout much of the world today. The Communists use promises of land reform as bait to secure the adherence and cooperation of large masses of the rural population in their effort to seize political and economic power. They are taking advantage of social unrest on the land. Peasants, throughout large parts of the world, are seeking a greater stake in the land. In some cases, they have moved on to the lands of landlords and have taken over the control of the land. Many landlords—in parts of Southeast Asia—do not feel safe on their land, and some have not visited their holdings in several years. Such situations are fertile conditions for the spread of communism, provided the democratic nations do not help tenant farmers secure a greater interest in the land they cultivate.

Police action on the part of governments does not solve basic problems of social unrest. At best, it merely staves off problems of human adjustment demanding solution. Democratic nations are interested in land reform because the people are demanding it, and the breaking down and wiping out of the vestiges of landlord feudalism are essential to the growth of democratic institutions and the improved welfare of rural people.

One of the chief planks in the grand strategy for world peace must necessarily center around the provision of greater food production, higher living standards, and greater opportunities for development for the less advantaged peoples of the world. Land reform, for many areas, provides the necessary step toward the fulfillment of these ends.[1] It must be recognized, however, that land reform does not provide a panacea for the world's problems. It represents only a portion, although a highly significant portion, of the over-all program that must be carried out if the peoples of the world are to benefit from the fruits of economic development.

## Meaning of Land Reform

The field of land reform is

concerned with improvement of agricultural economic institutions, *i.e.*, agricultural land ownership and tenancy, land rents, taxation of agricultural land or income from land, and also agricultural credit and producer marketing. Agricultural technology, physical problems of land utilization and development, conservation of resources, methods and levels of productivity, and problems of rural industries will be included insofar as they are relevant to the institutional problems enumerated above.[2]

So considered, land reform deals, to a large extent, with the improvement of land-tenure systems and other related institutions. It is thus concerned with the various arrangements by which farmers or others hold or control land. Control over land is exercised through ownership

[1] The importance of land reform as a world issue has recently been recognized by the United Nations General Assembly (1950), the Inter-American Conference on Agriculture (1950), the Food and Agriculture Organization of the United Nations (1951), and the Economic and Social Council of the United Nations (1951). The relationship between land reform and world peace was well expressed by Charles F. Brannan, Secretary of Agriculture, when he said: "Evidently a little bit of land, a little bit of opportunity, can do for world peace something that great armies cannot possibly accomplish. It is something that happens inside a person. It is something that cannot be shot or chained." (From address to Association of Land-Grant Colleges and Universities, November, 1950.)

[2] From a statement prepared by the Inter-Agency Committee on Land Reform Problems, composed of representatives from agencies in the United States government, 1951.

and contractual relationships and through a position of superior bargaining power. In addition to rights in land possessed by tenants and owners, others may modify or control these rights by established institutional arrangements, as through credit and marketing methods.

A practical working concept of land reform must involve land ownership, landlord-tenant relationships, size of operating units, and various institutions that affect the stability, security of expectations, and efficient use of land resources as brought about through property rights in land and by economic and legal controls over land. Land reform seeks that pattern of land distribution among individual producers which, conforming to regional cultures, ensures a wide distribution of land as property or as rights in land among producers, security of their tenure, and a fair share to them of the agricultural product. In view of the nature of the field, obviously, this chapter will necessarily have to be rather general or sketchy in scope.

## Significance of Land Reform

Land reform has a place in the growth and development of democratic institutions. Economic and political unrest arise from and are encouraged by instability and insecurity on the land and particularly in the presence of depressing and even deplorable living conditions. In the underdeveloped countries of the world around 60 to 80 per cent of the people are engaged in agriculture. A high proportion of the agricultural population in these areas lives very poorly and the production per man is low because of primitive or inadequate methods of production and because of the nature of their land tenure, credit and marketing facilities, and other undemocratic institutional arrangements.

In the United States—a nation rich in natural resources and with a strong belief in the individual ownership of property—conditions have been relatively favorable to the development of democratic institutions. Here, the abundance of resources in relation to population has given impetus to individualism and the resolving of economic conflicts by free competition.

Jefferson was one of the architects of the evolving American democracy. He firmly believed that a wide dispersion of private property was essential to the establishment of democracy and the safest assurance that it would endure. To him "small landholders were the most precious part of the State." In speaking of settlers in New England, Daniel Webster expressed Jefferson's thoughts when he said:

Their situation demanded a parceling out and division of the land, and it may fairly be said that this necessary act fixed the future frame and form of their government. The character of their political institutions was determined by the fundamentals respecting property. The consequence of all these causes has been a great subdivision of the soil and a great equality of condition, the true basis, most certainly, of popular government.

Property in land is a source of control, power, and liberty; and in a democracy a wide diffusion of rights in land or an opportunity to acquire such rights is believed an essential force making for individual freedom and creative individualism.

*Land Reform and Economic Development.* The growth and development of democratic institutions are related to the amount of income within a nation and its distribution. In underdeveloped countries income from land is the chief source of wealth, and ownership of land the prevailing standard of income distribution; thus, there often is a need for introducing changes in land tenure and related institutions when over-all programs of social reorganization are contemplated.

The experience of Mexico, first in agrarian reform and later in an all-around policy of economic development, illustrates the case. During the last four decades, Mexico has experienced the most extraordinary change in its social, political and economic structure. The student of contemporary Mexico— whether sociologist, economist, artist, or political scientist—finds such an overwhelming display of new facts, trends and institutions in such a rapid process of change as to almost defy analysis. The catalyst which set in motion this process of economic development was land reform.[3]

This statement is open to various degrees of agreement, primarily because it involves a whole field itself. Yet, most people, it is believed, will contend that land reform is one of the economic organizational changes needed in many situations that must come before a more productive economy can be built. And within the field of land reform, its various phases are of varying significance in different situations. For instance, in some countries agricultural credit is of first importance, while in other places the need for land redistribution is most strategic. Acquisition of land ownership through land redistribution or other means may mean little if ownership is not associated with rights and privileges because of excessive indebtedness or certain kinds of external controls. Interest should center in various measures that supplement or complement one another in the development of a well-rounded program for rural improvement, of which a wide diffusion of land ownership is but one of several objectives. Furthermore, the order of general economic development depends very much on the agricultural situation within a country and the availability of resources for development.[4]

[3] Edmundo Flores, paper read before the Conference on World Land Tenure Problems at the University of Wisconsin, Madison, Wis., Oct. 23, 1951.

[4] For an excellent discussion of this whole problem see, *Measures for the Economic Development of Under-developed Countries,* Report by a Group of Experts Appointed by the Secretary-General of the United Nations, New York, May, 1951.

Importance attaches not only to measures considered desirable, but to the method and techniques of getting jobs done. In the carrying out of land-reform programs, political considerations, matters of economic powers, and established customs are most likely to be crucial factors.

## Population and Land Reform

Population and its growth and impact upon land resources are interrelated factors of vital importance in a study of land problems and the relative degree of achievement possible through technological advances and institutional adjustments. As was pointed out earlier, ratios of population to land, if they are to be meaningful, must be considered in connection with the degree of industrialization and with the character of the available natural resources.

Land problems arise from maladjustments between people and land resources. The supply of land resources is limited by physical and economic factors. The physical supply is fixed; the economic supply is variable in relation to population, price, and technological improvements; and population is a changing factor.

The present world-population situation calls for an increase in total food supply of around 2 to 3 per cent a year. To meet this need, production must increase on existing farms, and land suitable for farming must be developed under desirable institutional arrangements. In new land areas and wherever land improvement is a substantial undertaking—largely by public assistance—it is essential that a good tenure system be required as a part of a development program. The attainment of such socially desirable objectives is part of the justification for the use of public funds that benefit individual landholders.

Considerable progress has been made in increased yields through technological developments—use of improved seed varieties, insecticide control, optimum application of fertilizers, and introduction of new types of tools and machines. Yet, progress is often stymied in that the landowner is an absentee owner, and his interests, activities, and aims are elsewhere. Landless tenants, sharecroppers, and laborers that suffer from a destructive system of tenure are not good producers, nor do they possess much expansive power as tillers of the soil.

The excessive pressure of population on land resources in parts of the world must be reckoned as a hard fact. Unless there is a decline in the rate of population growth in many densely populated agricultural areas, the road to achieving more desirable levels of production, nutrition, and economic development will be barred by serious impediments. Facts must be faced and not clothed in fantasy. Furthermore, a solution to the problem rests "upon the gradual development of non-agricultural resources and the orderly transfer of people from agricultural to non-agricultural pursuits. Only in this way can a more efficient balance be obtained between land resources and the agricultural population."[5] But industrialization will need to progress slowly, not only because of the level of development within countries, but also because under existing human conditions rapid industrialization could readily lead to more exploitation of the masses.

One might add that population is a human problem, but as a human problem we have not faced up to it. We rather shied away from it for reasons that are well known—among them being the fact that the developed areas of the world have often experienced food surpluses. But the world is now interrelated as never before; nations are concerned with the needs of other nations. They can no longer vest their foreign interest largely in market information and demand outlets and let the consequences be what they may. Nations must think in terms of levels of living and food requirements of peoples throughout the world.

Population has increased most rapidly in Asia and Southeast Asia. Between 1936 and 1947 half of the reported increase in world population occurred in this area. A disturbing fact is that in those parts of the world where the population increase has been most rapid, the people have a diet of only around 2,000 calories per day. It also seems that an inadequate diet is associated with the fecundity of man. The fact that those that till the land own very little land may well be a retarding factor in raising their standard of living through control of the size of the family.

In this situation, however,

. . . land reform is not a solution to the population problem of densely settled agrarian areas. It is conceivable that solutions to population problems could be achieved without land reform. Nonetheless, the two are intimately related as continuing cause and effect. Land reforms taken in disregard of the population situation may involve no solutions to that problem but only a continuing race to move slowly or to stay in the same place. Land reform taken in full realization of the problems of population growth and as part of a comprehensive national attack on the problem may act as a powerful catalyst to stimulate the altered cultural values and the changing individual motivations that lead to family limitation. If land reform helps to establish this altered physical and cultural environment, the problem for the society, and particularly for the public health people, becomes that of the discovery and the diffusion of the means of control that are acceptable to the people of the society and consistent with their historic values.[6]

[5] D. A. Fitzgerald, "Land Tenure and Economic Development," *Land Economics*, November, 1951, p. 385.

[6] Irene Taeuber, *The Population of Southeast Asia*, paper delivered at the Conference on World Tenure Problems, Madison, Wis., October, 1951.

## Land-Tenure Arrangements

For a long time a struggle has been going on to improve the position of the man on the land. Under feudalism, the land was the natural habitat of authoritarianism. Landlords ruled through a position of superior power. Throughout most of the world, at times, there have been landlords and serfs. The serfs were the tillers of the soil and keepers of the flocks. At the dawn of the modern era in Western society, the serfs received but a bare subsistence, but the man that tilled the soil was filled with the deepest hunger to be the lord of the soil he tilled. This passion worked itself out in different ways in western Europe; and in America, the great abundance of land was a "safety valve" to oppression by a land aristocracy.

The French Revolution, it may be recalled, was really a struggle between the businessman and bourgeois of the middle class and the landed aristocracy. The businessmen and the middle classes needed the help of the masses of peasants. They therefore promised the peasants ownership rights over their tracts in return for support in the struggle against the landlords. This pattern has been repeated in other areas, as in czarist Russia where the revolution of 1917 succeeded largely because the leaders were able to enlist peasant support by promising them land and the fruits of the soil that they tilled.

*Land Redistribution.* As a part of the evolution of democratic government there has been a growth in land ownership by farm people. In this section, it is only possible to discuss some examples of the acquisition of freeholds by individuals, under different conditions and at different times in history. In the main, land has been acquired by farmers or peasants through land settlement, legislative and credit programs, or by outright government confiscation of large holdings.

In the United States, the abundance of land in relation to population made for a relatively satisfactory land-ownership pattern. It is recognized, however, that while we do have a growing concentration of land ownerships, unnecessarily large farms, and migratory labor problems, the United States, as a whole, is still predominantly a nation of owner-operated family farms. Living standards are generally high, and tenants are in a position to move up the agricultural ladder, although the large initial investment necessary to get started in farming is making this increasingly difficult.

One of the most consistent phases of our land policy has been the establishment and improvement of family farms. The cash and credit land-sales methods, the free-land movement of the homestead era, rural credit programs, extension programs, and experimental work on crop and livestock production have all encouraged the establishment or improvement of family-farm operations. And it has been found that for most types of farming, the family farm is a highly efficient and productive type of organization, both from an individual and social viewpoint, particularly when owner-operated or operated under favorable lease arrangements.

Before discussing experiences of countries with land redistribution, mention should be made of some tasks basic to a democratic redistribution of land. One of the problems is the amount of land to be retained by landlords. This involves the establishment of retention acreages by different classes of land. It is necessary to know with respect to each landlord the amount of land owned, its location and character. A land-productivity classification and a land-ownership classification are steps in the establishment of fair retention acreages and in fixing fair purchase and sale prices of lands expropriated. It is apparent that the taking of land by governments should be just to the landlords and that the resale of the land to tenant purchasers should be at a fair price—that is, reasonable in relation to the productive capacity of the land, on just terms, and at a price that leaves to tenant purchasers a return above their carrying costs sufficient to provide for improved living and a better life.

*Western and southern Europe.* In western Europe, land-redistribution programs of Ireland and Denmark serve as good examples of early experiences in this field, while in Italy, land redistribution is presently an active program. In these three countries, democratic procedures have been followed, and land has been made available primarily through government purchase, resale, or extension of agricultural credit, and a combination of these methods.

Improvements of land tenure in Ireland began during the latter part of the last half of the nineteenth century, first through the regulation of relations between landlords and tenants and then by assisting tenants to become landowners. During the first part of the nineteenth century, landlords were in a particularly favorable position because of the pressure of population on the land resources. Because of their bargaining power, they were able to collect excessive rentals and evict tenants at will. A number of measures were proposed in favor of tenant rights, but the agitation for reform was so strongly opposed by the landlords' interests that no legislation was enacted.

In 1870, however, through the leadership of Gladstone, the British government passed the Landlord and Tenant Act. This measure was a step in giving security of tenure to the tenant through compensation for improvement in case he had to move and also provisions for the purchase of land by the tenants. But there were many exceptions and legal loopholes in the legislation, and the purchasing tenants were required to pay down at least one-fourth of the purchase price of the land.

Fifteen years later, the Purchase Land Act of 1885 was enacted. Under it tenants could purchase the land that they were operating by means of government loans repayable over 49 years at 4 per cent interest. Under this Act and subsequent legislation, marked progress was made in land-purchase operations during the next 40 years.

Whereas in 1870 tenants constituted 97 per cent of the farm occupiers, in 1906 they formed only 70.8 per cent, and in 1916 only 36.1 per cent. In the Irish Free State in 1929 only 2.6 per cent of the agricultural area was in the hands of tenants. Meanwhile, hopeless tenants by the hundreds and thousands had been transformed into owners holding to their farms, full payment for which was to be made through annuities much lower than their former rents.[7]

Denmark is another country of western Europe that through government action has made remarkable progress in the transformation of tenants to owner-operators. As in Ireland, land-ownership reform occurred over a period of years, but it began much earlier in Denmark and extended over a longer period of time. For instance, before 1800 all leases were required by law to extend throughout the life of the tenant and his wife. The rights and obligations of tenants and landlords were defined by law, and credit was made available at a low interest rate for peasants to purchase land.

By 1835 nearly 65 per cent of the peasants were owners of their lands, and by the turn of the century tenancy had practically disappeared in Denmark. The land reform that occurred was the result primarily of a determined effort on the part of the Danish government to improve the welfare of the tenants through the establishment of equitable rights for them, the provision of a liberal credit system patterned to fit their needs, and the development of farmers' cooperatives to assist peasants to meet competition in the marketing of their products.

One of the most recent developments in Europe is the large-scale land-redistribution program under way in Italy. This program embodies not only expropriation and reallotment of large, underdeveloped estates, but also land reclamation and development. The maximum development of usable agricultural land in Italy is precluded so long as large estates exist in areas where owners are unwilling or unable to undertake land improvement and development. This is particularly true in southern Italy.

In 1950, two laws were enacted authorizing the expropriation and redistribution of land in this area and other depressed areas of Italy. By January, 1953, slightly more than 310,000 acres of land had been distributed to approximately 32,000 families. The land is being allotted to landless farm workers who are to repay the expropriation price, which is based on taxable assessed value, plus part of the development costs over

[7] Elizabeth R. Hooker, *Readjustments of Agriculture Tenure in Ireland*, p. 120, University of North Carolina Press, Chapel Hill, N.C., 1938. This book is an excellent discussion of land-tenure reform in Ireland.

a 30-year period. Landlords are reimbursed in special government bonds, a part of which can be immediately redeemed in cash if the funds are used for the development of their remaining lands. The size of farm units is largely determined on the basis of ratio of landless peasants to available land and of size of family, which could readily result in the laying out of farm units that are too small in view of the large number of families seeking land in relation to available land.

Following the expropriation of the land, reclamation and development works are carried out, including plowing, erosion and flood control, irrigation dams and ditches, new roads, and farm buildings. Badly eroded hillsides are being terraced, and olive, fruit, and forest trees planted. In 1950 and 1951, under the Marshall Plan, the equivalent of about $110 million in counterpart funds was approved for agricultural development in the southern half of Italy, a substantial part of which was used for development and reclamation work on expropriated lands. Counterpart funds that arise under the Marshall Plan are local currency receipts from the sale of United States aid program goods in the markets of foreign countries. The expenditure of these funds is regulated by agreement with the United States.

The Italian land-reform program is off to a good start. It has given spirit, aggressiveness, and hope to the people. But much work needs to be done, and farm credit, cooperative marketing and processing, and health and educational programs are vital to give strength to the movement. The allotment of land is but one step, and one which imposes on the government many other responsibilities in carrying through the establishment of going-concern family farms or even the establishment of part-time farms. Important responsibilities must be met, and intelligent guidance is required in the development of stable and profitable family farms.

In connection with land redistribution in Europe, it should be mentioned that programs are under way, as in Sweden, that are aimed at the systematic enlarging of uneconomically small farms. The right to take over properties by payment of just compensation has been authorized, and the policy is often supported by state grants and loans in the establishment of economic units. This points out the need of avoiding in land redistribution, where it is carried on, the creation of small uneconomic farm units. Land should not be made to serve as a basis for "poor relief farms."

*Japan.* The land-reform program of Japan is the most dramatic of recent years. It was pushed in order to multiply the number of freeholders and to prevent the Communists from making political capital by posing as advocates of peasants' interests. The program has as its objectives (1) the transfer of land ownership to tenants, (2) the improvement of landlord-tenancy practices, and (3) the development of lands for new settlers by reclamation. In addition, other agricultural-resource programs of Japan are directed to the development of agricultural land and its efficient use at a high level of sustained production; also to the restoration and development of forest, fuel, and grasslands, and to placing these lands under management practices that make for increased production and decreased resource exploitation. In general, the uplands in Japan, which comprise the forest, fuel, and grasslands, are used extensively and wastefully and are characterized by underuse. The productivity of these lands can be improved very substantially.

In Japan, the average farm holding is about 2 acres, with about 40 per cent less than 1 acre. Previous to the land-reform program, inaugurated in 1945, about 46 per cent of the total cultivated land was tenant-operated and about two-thirds of the Japanese farmers rented all or part of the land they cultivated. Rents were high, ranging from 50 to 70 per cent of the harvest, and tenants occupied the land solely at the will of the landlords.

From October, 1946, to 1951, about one-third of the cultivated land of Japan, or nearly 4,400,000 acres, were purchased for sale to tenant purchasers; and of the 3.5 million acres of uncultivated land acquired for reclamation, approximately 1.5 million have been resold to tenants. For the land remaining in tenancy there are provisions for "written leases, rental ceilings, cash rentals, restrictions on land transfer, and safeguards against arbitrary changes in rental contracts."[8]

During the purchase and transfer of the land to tenant purchasers, considerable general inflation occurred, which worked to the advantage of the tenants and to the disadvantage of the landlords. Tenant purchasers were able often to pay for their land in 1 or 2 years. Thus land indebtedness is low in Japan. "According to the 1950 census, the composition of rural dwellers has completely changed. The owner farmers now comprise 67 per cent; owner farmers who also rent land represent 26 per cent; tenant farmers who also own some land, 7 per cent; and pure tenant farmers represent only 5 per cent of all farm households in Japan."[9]

A redistribution of land ownership has been carried out in Japan. It should prove of increasing benefit to farmers and add meaning to democracy and freedom; it encompasses programs that should make for hope and individual agressiveness and guard against agressive imperialism. The true answers, of course, lie in the future. But whatever may be the

[8] For an excellent discussion of land programs in Japan see *Agricultural Programs in Japan, 1945–51*, Supreme Command of the Allied Powers, Natural Resources Section, Report 148, Tokyo, 1951.

[9] Keike Owada, *Land Reform in Japan*, paper delivered at the Conference on World Land Tenure Problems, University of Wisconsin, Madison, Wis., Oct. 8 to Nov. 20, 1951.

ultimate influence of the land program the benefits would certainly seem to be substantial in a world of rapid social change.

*Mexico.* Mexico enjoys a distinctive place among Latin American countries because of the constructive steps it has taken to redistribute land to peasants and workers and because of its irrigation and land-development programs. Throughout the early history of Mexico, the agrarian structure rested on the exploitation of agricultural laborers, and the presence of a land monopoly tended to perpetuate antiquated methods of farming rather than foster or encourage the introduction of the newer arts of production.

The changes in the Constitution of 1917 that defined the nature of private property and set forth who may or may not hold private property were basic to the land-reform movement in Mexico. The nation was declared to be the original owner of land and water resources and was granted the power of determining the rights of individuals to land. Individual property rights were made subject to limitations imposed in the public interest. Four basic steps were taken to establish this position: "(1) the restoration of land to villages; (2) the outright grant of lands to villages in cases where they are needed even though previous ownership cannot be proved; (3) the recovery of public lands and waters that were previously alienated illegally in opposition to the public welfare; and (4) the destruction of the large landed estate by limiting legally the size of private holdings."[10]

In the early settlement of Mexico, land was allotted to villages or towns under a system of land distribution called *ejidos*. These community lands gradually became concentrated in large agricultural holdings or haciendas. The class of large landholders wielded immense economic and political power, and agricultural conditions were maintained in a deplorable backward state.

Land reform in Mexico reestablished the government's rights in *ejido* land. In the reallotment of these lands, they are operated either individually or collectively, and the holders of individual plots have permanent tenure except that they cannot sell or mortgage the land. Individual operation predominates for cropland, except in the case of certain irrigated lands, while collective use is most prevalent for pasture and forest lands. During the period from 1917 to 1946 more than 75 million acres were redistributed to peasants and workers.

Another aspect of the land-reform program of Mexico involves the reclamation of potentially cultivatable lands. A large irrigation and power-development program is now under way. During the past 20 years more than 2½ million acres have been developed through irrigation, and

[10] Nathan L. Whetten, "Mexican Land Reform," *Foreign Agriculture*, Vol. 15, No. 9, p. 197, September, 1951.

this program is being pushed to take full advantage of the land-resource potentials to provide a better life for the growing population.

The redistribution of land in underdeveloped countries in owner-operated family-sized farms and its improvement are often key steps in the establishment of going-concern farm units. But of equal importance, and often supplementary thereto, is the consolidation of scattered parcels, provision of credit on reasonable terms, an effective extension program, an efficient marketing system, and price-support programs.

*Land Consolidation.* Land consolidation and reallocation programs usually involve the regrouping of scattered ownership parcels. The need to consolidate land-ownership parcels is one of the most pressing land problems in some countries. In most countries of Europe, and in India, Southeast Asia, and Egypt, land consolidation, or the making of owner-ship units more compact, is of great significance in developing economic farm units and strengthening the rural economy. In land consolidation the number of ownership units generally remains the same or sub-stantially the same, but the number of parcels of land in an ownership unit after consolidation is from one-fourth to one-half of the former num-ber. Programs of land consolidation are actively under way in several countries, as in France, Netherlands, Germany, Austria, and Japan. A number of benefits arise from land consolidation.

Through the consolidation of scattered parcels, it is possible to increase agricultural production substantially and at the same time to reduce farm-operating costs. Official estimates of production increases range from 20 to 30 per cent, and cost decreases from 10 to 15 per cent. Of equal significance is the fact that the land-tenure patterns that follow land reallocation provide a basis for improved land-use and conservation practices and an impetus for more effective agricultural planning and programing. It is not possible to take reasonable advantage of mechanized production operation where land ownerships are composed of many ownership parcels, or to carry on over-all programs for agricultural credit, land improvement, and other rural activities. Land consolidation in the Netherlands is a good example of the accrual of such benefits. Previous to the land-consolidation movement, land some distance from farmsteads was to a large extent underutilized, improperly drained, and not subject to good crop-rotation practices. Land consolidation has often involved replanning the drainage and road systems and accordingly has facilitated the more effective utilization of outlying lands and in many instances the creation of new farmsteads.

*France and the Netherlands.* In France, there are about 25 million acres that suffer from excessive fragmentation or parcellization. These 25 million acres represent about one-third of the cultivated area and one-half of the arable land of France. In some instances, there are as many as 250 to 300 parcels for each 25 acres of land. In extreme cases, holdings consist of a few square meters, a grapevine, or a single olive tree.[11]

Fragmentation of holdings in France has been caused by medieval rotation practices, inheritance laws requiring equal division among heirs, land hunger, and the lag between technological improvements and institutional adjustments. Another reason is that the nature of the land market has contributed to the purchase of scattered holdings. In the sale of large estates it has been more profitable to cut them up into small lots for sale rather than sell the estates as a whole. Land has been a savings bank for the peasant, and as savings are accumulated he has figuratively deposited his savings in scattered parcels of land.

The work that has been going on in France in consolidation of land holdings has been carried on principally in wheat and sugar beet areas, or areas that are somewhat advanced in technological development. As a whole, the program has been retarded because of insufficient personnel to carry on the work and a lack of an adequate education program to fully explore with the people the benefits that arise from land consolidation. Opposition to consolidation comes from the very small landholders, on whose holdings benefits will not likely arise, as is true in the case of small garden plots. The consolidation movement also is retarded by the indifference, if not hostility, of the many owners who fear that they will receive land of lower productive capacity than they now hold.

Attempts to deal with fragmentation are of long standing. A number of the early laws permitted and encouraged consolidation; however, there was no legal basis for successfully attacking the problem in France until the law of 1941. Former laws functioned largely upon the energies and enthusiasm of a few interested persons and were concerned exclusively with the combining of parcels in order to make larger parcels. Under such circumstances, consolidation proceeded at a slow rate, and fragmentation occurred faster than land consolidation. The present law is concerned not only with enlarging holdings, but with the location of parcels, roads, drainage, and land planning and development. Briefly, it encompasses area planning.

In the Netherlands where land consolidation is an active and most forward-looking program, it has been found that good land-consolidation procedure depends upon an organizational set-up that provides substantially for these steps:

1. Application by majority of landowners or some percentage of landowners of major part of area.

---

[11] Cf. Frederic O. Sargent, "Fragmentation of French Farm Land, Its Nature, Extent and Causes," *Land Economics*, vol. 28, pp. 218–229, August, 1952; also Jean Roche, *Important Aspects of Land Consolidation in France,* paper delivered at Conference on World Land Tenure Problems at Madison, Wis., Oct. 26, 1951.

2. Approval of application by local and central bodies. Authorization for necessary hearings, protests, etc.

3. Execution of land consolidation.

   *a.* Survey of land-ownership tracts—exact size of area and boundaries necessary.

   *b.* Abstract of titles.

   *c.* Land appraisal—relative value of different ownership tracts must be known for an equitable reallotment of land and to compensate for fractional additions or subtractions from land ownerships.

   *d.* Public inspection of valuations established; provision for appeals, and settlement of appeals by due process of law.

   *e.* Reallotment of land in proportion to value; provisions for public inspection of scheme, hearings, etc.

   *f.* Development of road system; water courses; and area-development plans.

   *g.* Land-consolidation plan submitted for public review, settlement of objections and final adoption of plan.

   *h.* Drawing up new land deeds, exchange of properties, and undertaking necessary public and private land improvements.

From these steps it is apparent that land consolidation generally involves considerable time. On an average, 2 or 3 years are required to complete a program in an area, and then, at best, only a partial consolidation of parcels is carried out in that it is not politically possible in one effort to reallot land so that each farmer has all his land in one ownership unit. This would involve too great a shift for public acceptance. Furthermore, many times the hazards of production and types of farming make it desirable that there be some scattering of ownership parcels.

Where land consolidation is a significant problem, it is desirable to have legislation prohibiting further subdivision of farm units below a reasonable minimum size and to bar a resubdivision of land that has been consolidated. Unless legislation of this kind exists, subdivision of lands may readily proceed too fast or nullify the benefits of land consolidation; and as some public subsidy is incurred in consolidations, public investments should not be permitted to be readily dissipated.

Another way of dealing with production problems on small farms in parts of the world has been by cooperative land management. For instance, in Israel there are cooperative farms that are managed as a group, and profits shared, at times, in terms of family needs; in other cases, farms are managed on a private basis, but take advantage of cooperative enterprise in farm production. In recent years, India and Pakistan have also experimented with cooperative management. In general, small land holdings in certain cases have been consolidated into a cooperative farm and returns from the farm apportioned in relation to value of land and farm inventory brought in and work performed.

*Landlord-Tenant Relations.* In some parts of the world land tenancy is the prevalent form of tenure. This is true, for instance, in much of Southeast Asia, the countries of the Middle East, and several South American countries. Tenancy, in itself, obviously is not bad. Where the rentals are not exorbitant and where the tenant enjoys a reasonable degree of security and stability and has an opportunity to acquire land ownership, tenancy may be regarded as a desirable institution. However, in many situations this is not the case. Where rentals take the major part of the income from land and land is held as a closed investment, tenants have little, if any, economic incentive to increase agricultural production and thus improve their own well-being. The security of tenants on the land may be little better than that of a laborer. In fact, so-called tenants often have only the status of laborers.

In some cases, however, as in England, tenants possess substantial rights and security of tenure. Some persons contend that their share of the bundle of the rights in landed property is in effect greater than that of the landlords. Whatever the situation, it is not material to this discussion; the point is that tenants can possess rights granting security and stability of tenure or there can be within the tenant class a wide diffusion of substantial property rights in land.

Major problems in land tenancy arise from amount and form of rental payments, oral lease arrangements, insecurity of tenure, inability to acquire capital, depletion of land resources, and the lack of demonstrational and educational programs for improvement of tenant operations and relationships between landlords and tenants. Tenants often occupy the land at the will of landlords; landlords live in cities or villages and look to the income from land as their principal source of income; and the relationship between landlords and tenants, and between both and the land, is often that of exploitation.

Measures that have been taken to improve the position of tenants and make for better landlord-tenant relationships include regulations that:

1. Stipulate the maximum rents payable by tenants. For instance, in Taiwan (Formosa) land rents shall not exceed 37.5 per cent of the total yield of the main crop.

2. Require all contracts to be in written form and on file.

3. Protect tenure rights through establishing a period of duration of the lease; provisions in regard to termination of the lease; and conditions under which the tenant possesses right of renewal or purchase of land leased.

4. Require payment of rent in cash rather than in kind, and if in kind,

regulations governing such payment so as to prevent taking undue advantage of the tenant.

5. Establish a system of penalties against landlords for failure to abide by regulations, and rights of tenants to come into court to protect their interests.

Tenure improvement in Taiwan, mentioned above, is a part of a land-reform program that was launched in 1949. The program consists of three steps. The first step was to reduce the rent to 37.5 per cent of the main crop and to secure the tenure of land by written contract. Previously, rents had ranged from 50 to 80 per cent of the crop production. The rent-reduction phase of the program has been carried out. The second step set limits to size of holdings—a landowner being allowed to own only a certain amount of land as prescribed by law. In early 1953, the Taiwan government began the purchase of private lands to be expropriated, some 430,000 acres, and to resell these lands to tenant purchasers at an equitable price, payable in installments over a number of years.

In India, a significant step in tenure improvement was taken when the zamindari system was abolished. This system, which involved numerous share-collecting intermediaries between the state and the cultivators, was partially responsible for the low state of agriculture in India. The main economic benefit from the abolition of zamindari and other like systems should be the simplification of the land-tenure system, greater security of tenure for the tenants, and increased returns to tenants. Where achieved, it should be easier to revise rents or to introduce agrarian reforms. The tenant who acquires new rights will have greater incentive to improve his land. However, in the states of India where the zamindari system has been abolished, sufficient time has not elapsed since the introduction of this reform to make for any substantial accrual of benefits to tenant farmers.

The fear which is sometimes expressed that the credit and supervision previously supplied by the landlords will not be available to the tenants is hardly justified because the abolition of intermediaries will increase the credit-worthiness of the tenants themselves and lay a basis for a more effective rural credit system. Supervision can be better rendered by an effectively organized and serviced training program. It is the release of "log jams" such as the elimination of layers of unnecessary intermediaries that can set in motion a whole series of land planning and development activities.

Of interest in dealing with tenancy problems where large-scale operations are necessary is the type of tenure arrangement developed in Puerto Rico, where about 10 per cent of the total sugar cane land is operated under a system of profit-sharing farms. This system attempts to combine the most efficient production and large-scale operation with best land use. Profit-sharing farms are under the control of a land authority, which employs farm managers and hires laborers, who share the profits at the end of each fiscal year. A weakness of the system is that the men who work the land do not have property rights in the land. They are in effect laborers with bonus rights. However, this problem could be overcome through establishment of some system of rights in the land through issuance of membership certificates. A plan might be developed that would go as far as to give each man ownership to a specific tract of land, but reserve to the government the degree of management necessary for large-scale efficient production.

## Agricultural Credit

In many countries the lack of an adequate supply of agricultural credit at reasonable terms constitutes a major impediment to agricultural development and the improved well-being of rural people. In some cases, the provision of more and better credit facilities must come before much progress can be expected, agricultural credit being a strategic factor to getting under way a program for the improvement and development of rural agricultural institutions.

A good agricultural credit program enables farm people to take better advantage of their capabilities and opportunities to improve themselves by their own efforts. This is very important in underdeveloped countries in making for economic progress and in developing individual initiative and local leadership. Credit institutions, and particularly cooperatives, are also an organizational arrangement for conducting effective educational programs.

Agricultural credit problems in many countries of the world center largely around methods of raising loan funds or capital; the types of agricultural credit systems that will extend credit to small farmers, directly or through cooperative organizations; the lending practices and policies of granting credit at reasonable rates and terms; and the place of training, supervision, and research in an agricultural credit program.

Agricultural production increases and improved rural living must be achieved largely through increasing yields per acre, production per animal unit, and the number of acres and animal units handled per person. It is also necessary to find economic means of increasing the area devoted to agricultural production. Furthermore, improved marketing methods and facilities must accompany the expanded output of goods.

The achievement of these objectives means increased use of farm working capital. Usually this calls for increased use of credit. The effectiveness of the farmers' efforts can be so greatly increased through proper use of capital that it is a real key to enlarging both the volume and efficiency of production, and to improving rural living conditions.

In the use of credit, it must be recognized that credit systems and procedures must be adapted to the conditions, customs, and culture present in a country and that progress at best may be slow in the development of an effective agricultural credit system but, nevertheless, will be substantial if the system is well formulated to the needs of the country.

One characteristic of agricultural loans in underdeveloped countries is the absence of a clear distinction between production and consumption loans. These two types of loans are often combined in the same credit transaction. In this regard, many farmers go from one year to the next receiving the credit they need, producing crops, and at harvest turning over to creditors all their produce except what they need for their own use. These conditions provide no incentive for improved farm practices, nor do they make possible much agricultural progress. A barter or semi-barter economy is not conducive to economic development.

In underdeveloped areas agricultural credit too often is supplied from one of three sources: "(1) the village shopkeeper who gives credit on day-to-day purchases at rates of one hundred per cent to two hundred and fifty per cent per annum; (2) . . . the landlord who himself borrows from government agencies or moneylenders to lend to tenant cultivators against the security of the crop; (3) and the . . . middleman or moneylender."[12] The moneylenders are generally highly organized, have monopoly control over credit needs, and are in a position to charge excessive rates of interest. For loans advanced to farmers the degree of harshness and avarice displayed by a moneylender depends upon the volume of credit available, risk, and volume of business done by farmers. When tenants must pay 25, 100, or even 400 per cent for credit advances, it is impossible to reinvest much of what is produced in further production. Little is left for productive enterprise.

Credit to farmers often is associated with a right to purchase the crop at harvesttime. In these cases, the moneylender, because of his favorable bargaining position, is generally able to purchase the crop below market price. Moneylenders occupy a pivotal position in credit channels and in the distribution network of rural areas in the underdeveloped countries. Loans are extended informally on a person-to-person basis, are flexible to the needs of the borrower, and the funds loaned are savings of moneylenders for the benefit of farmers. Thus, the moneylenders do render a service, but, nevertheless, one that should be replaced over a period of time with a system of credit less exploitative of the farmers' productive capacity. Furthermore, high money charges are a potent type of economic

---

[12] *Land Reform: Defects in Agrarian Structure as Obstacles to Economic Development*, p. 38, United Nations, New York, 1951.

control that often results in unsatisfactory forms of land tenure and, at times, in a concentration of landholdings in the hands of large landowners and moneylenders.

As an illustration of progress being made to meet some of these problems, in 1952 the Philippine government enacted two pieces of agricultural credit legislation. One of the acts provides for the establishment of rural banks that can be of particular service to the small farmers who have land or other resources in amounts that make them acceptable risks for financing by private banks. The other act provides for an agricultural credit and cooperative-financing system for small farmers and cooperatives that have limited resources and are not able to secure funds in the private market. Under this act, emphasis will be placed on development of farmers' marketing cooperatives; extension of production loans to small farmers; and the establishment of a supervised credit program, the overall service costs of supervision to be provided by the government.

A major problem in some countries is the nonexistence of well-organized capital markets in which bonds or debentures can be sold. Thus loan funds must come from savings of farmers or from other sources, such as merchants or governments. Savings of farmers are often very small or non-existent; merchants charge excessive rates of interest; and governments have been unable to supply needed credit because of inadequate funds or fear of inflation through issue of credit obligations. This brings up the need of exploring various ways of mobilizing loan funds.

In underdeveloped countries, the task of mobilizing savings is particularly difficult even where there is economic and political stability and confidence in the solvency of the government and in the local currency. In varying degrees, low levels of production and income, dense and rapid growth of population, and rigidities in an existing social structure materially limit savings and investment. The basic economy in these countries is agricultural, with small-scale industries and trade. Therefore, a principal source of capital accumulation must be agriculture itself, and the amount of such savings can be increased by expanding agricultural production. This fact—that agriculture is one of the main sources of capital accumulation—is often overlooked. Its productive capacity accordingly should reserve for agriculture a larger share of the wealth produced on farms, rather than permitting it to be drained off by excessive exploitation. Thus, some type of forced savings at the farm level should have a place in the formulation of capital in underdeveloped countries and should be an important consideration in mobilizing capital for an agricultural credit system. One way of accomplishing this objective is by reserving a part of the interest charge for capital accumulation.

The shortage of credit may also arise from the fact that the rural credit institutions are not adapted to the needs of the farmers. In other situations, in addition to a lack of credit facilities and loanable funds, people are impoverished and are farming under conditions that are not conducive to the extension of credit at reasonable rates and terms. When individuals are operating land under deplorable tenure conditions and in the presence of an archaic marketing system, the fundamental basis for a sound credit system is lacking. More drastic land-reform action may then be necessary.

In other situations, farmers are operating on a secure and stable basis and the credit facilities are adequate, but methods of making loans are altogether too restrictive for credit to play the part it can and should play for improved farm practices and land use and for better rural living. Such a situation exists in parts of Western Europe. It is rather common practice for those who borrow from agricultural credit institutions to be jointly and fully liable for the total outstanding indebtedness. Moreover, a mortgage on real estate is generally required for short-term or production loans. Thus, many farmers cannot provide the required security.

It should also be pointed out that agricultural credit to small farmers is often costly. The making of small loans involves considerable time and costs of collection. In addition, there is a need for supervision or training as a part of the loan process. Thus, if a farmer must bear all these costs the rate of interest is likely to be very high. As loans should be made at reasonable rates and on a sound basis to both the lender and borrower, it follows that in the making of small loans to farmers at interest rates comparable to acceptable commercial rates the government must bear a part of the over-all costs. But these costs should be clearly separated from the individual loan transaction; that is, they should not result in the making of unsound loans that would undermine the stability of a credit system.

It may be pointed out that supervision of farmers who have borrowed in accordance with an agreed plan of operation is actually an effective form of extension work. Thus, for the government to bear this cost as a phase of a credit program may well be a most effective way of extending public assistance to farmers.

To the extent that corrective measures have been initiated in underdeveloped countries to meet the credit needs of small farmers, considerable reliance has been placed on the use of cooperative credit institutions. These have been sponsored and financed by government funds through the pooling of financial resources of farmers or through a combination of government funds and private capital. These credit agencies have only partially succeeded in meeting the needs of farmers. They have been hampered by lack of adequate funds, organizational difficulties, inexperience, inability to service loans, and the chronic insufficiency of farmers' incomes. Much of this difficulty may be associated with a lack of comprehensive over-all planning that treats credit as but one aspect of a well-rounded agricultural program.

A somewhat different but, nevertheless, very important aspect of rural credit arises in the breaking up of large estates. In the implementation of a land-redistribution program, a difficult and often strategic problem concerns the transference of funds in land to other types of investment. This is essentially a credit problem. One of the characteristics of underdeveloped countries is that the wealth generally is held or controlled by a relatively few people; and land is the main source of capital investment. Returns from land are generally high, but capital accumulation is low. Landlords indulge rather heavily in consumption goods. Thus the forces operating for general economic development are weak. Both agricultural development and industrial growth, where possible and feasible, are essential for the over-all economic progress of underdeveloped countries. In a land-reform program, one of the problems, as indicated, is a need for breaking up large landholdings into owner-operated family farms. Another problem of equal importance is the need for industrial development. It is recognized that many of the large holdings are efficiently operated and engaged in a type of production that lends itself well to large-scale operations. And in some countries, there are very limited opportunities for industrial development. However, in many of the underdeveloped countries there are substantial opportunities for economic development, both within agriculture and within industry.

In the public acquisition of large holdings for resale as family-size farms to tenants, the general procedure in many countries has been for the government to pay for the lands with nonnegotiable interest-bearing bonds.[13] These are payable in a number of equal annual installments that roughly equals the number of years over which the tenant purchasers amortize their debt. In these cases, the payments made by tenants are used to pay off the bonds issued to acquire the land. Under such a plan, total costs measured by a fixed price of the land plus interest charges are liquidated by annual collections from tenants. Thus the debt is paid off and the inflationary effects are neutralized in that payments to landlords tend to equal collections from tenant purchasers. Of course, in actual practice, it may be necessary to make payments partly in cash to landlords as a matter of equity and also to relieve undue distress that may

[13] While this is the prevailing practice in many democratic countries today, it is by no means the only method that has been used. In Eastern Europe, following the First World War, and in most of the countries now behind the Iron Curtain, large areas have been acquired by outright confiscation or partial payment at preinflation prices. It is also possible to give lands or sell them to tenants at prices far above or below the costs of public acquisition.

arise in the settlement of estates. In any event, it is particularly important that payments for land do not result in an inflationary situation that undermines the stability of an entire economy.

It should also be noted that if liquidation of land bonds occurs during general economic inflation—as has occurred in recent years—a proportional burden is placed on landlords receiving payments for land over a period of years. One way to adjust to such a burden is to make payment in relation to an index of major farm-commodity prices or in kind rather than in cash. The administration of such credit payments, however, would be most difficult in underdeveloped countries and, furthermore, over a period of years could result in seriously impairing the carrying through of a land-redistribution program.

To return to the inflationary effects of rapid redemption of land bonds or the issuance of negotiable bonds, in view of the need for alternative types of investment, it would be well, in so far as feasible, to meet these problems by bringing about the development of new industrial plants, dams, power resources, and agricultural processing and fertilizer facilities at the same time that a land-redistribution program is carried on within the country. For this purpose, a special government agency could be designed or established to select and purchase large landholdings at fair compensation for redistribution and sale to tenant farmers. As a part of the plan, a central bank might be set up for financing land redistribution and industrial development, a bank with broad powers of planning and supervising various types of privately established new industries. Funds received from the sale of land could be invested in such developments, or land bonds could be given as security for industrial securities. This would provide an alternative investment opportunity for landlords and should result in economic growth. Such a type of financial arrangement and economic planning might well be an effective tool for economic development.

Approval of the convertibility or exchange of land bonds would be essential in order to direct, as far as possible, the flow of investment into productive enterprises and to limit the inflationary effects of industrial expansion. And by providing landlords with an alternative type of investment—which should appeal to many of them—governments would also be putting to productive use the training and entrepreneurial talents of the landlord class, human resources badly needed in underdeveloped countries in fostering economic development in an atmosphere favorable to economic progress.[14]

As a conclusion to this brief discussion of agricultural credit and closely

[14] For a fuller discussion of this subject see V. Webster Johnson and John E. Metcalf "Land Redistribution and Industrial Development," *Land Economics*, Vol. 29, No. 2, pp. 154–160, May, 1953.

associated problems, agricultural credit as a phase of land reform can be said to offer definite contributions to: (1) make possible greater use of fertilizers, improved seeds, more modern farm tools and machines, and better livestock production; (2) bring about improvements in land-tenure situations; (3) establish and improve conditions on family farms; (4) develop and settle new land; and (5) help farmers' cooperative organizations market agricultural products effectively. Finally, an adequate agricultural credit service is a means of capitalizing most fully on all technological advances in agriculture and is a factor in the industrial growth of a country.

*Taxation*

Taxes on land and its products have been and can be used to effect changes in land use and ownership as well as to raise revenue. In regard to taxes on land or rural real estate as a source of revenue, it can be said that such taxes contribute a disproportionately low share of the tax burden in underdeveloped countries. Land is the main source of income, but it makes a small contribution to the support of schools, roads, and public services. Much of the land is not even on the tax rolls. An essential step to improvement is an accurate tax-record roll, that is, the recording of tracts of land by location and ownership. Title clearance is also important. This is necessary for the accurate assessment of land for taxes and to take such action as may be desirable if taxes levied are not paid. It also is basic to the purchase and sale of lands by individuals, or by governments as a phase of a land-reform program. And what has been said applies particularly to countries where large estates predominate.

Land taxes have been used at times in an endeavor to break up large estates and to discourage concentration. However, their use for this purpose has not been particularly fruitful for several reasons. In countries like the United States, legal doctrines such as the "uniformity clause" have discouraged the use of graduated and progressive tax rates gauged to size or value of holdings. As a net result, the taxes on large farms have not been higher in proportion to assessed values than those on smaller holdings. Administrative difficulties and the exercise of political power by large landowners in keeping land taxes low have prevented their successful use as a counterconcentration force. However, higher or graduated land taxes can be used effectively for breaking up large estates and forcing underdeveloped lands into more intensive use. Inheritance and estate taxes also can be used effectively for breaking up large estates. The "death duties" of England provide an excellent example of what can be done in this regard, if desired.

Price-control measures also may have somewhat the same effect upon farmers as direct taxes upon land and its products. Following the Second

World War, Czechoslovakia used a three-level government-controlled price system that favored the operators of small farms and discriminated against the owners and operators of large farms. Continuation of policies of this type over extended periods would favor the break-up of the larger farm holdings. Even when uniform price controls are applied, the farmer may feel that he is taxed or discriminated against in the interests of the general economy. In Taiwan and Thailand, for example, the price of rice has been fixed considerably below its price in the world market, the purpose being to hold down the cost of living and control inflation, and also to provide a very substantial part of government revenues. Rice is the principal crop produced, and it accounts for around 40 per cent of the consumer expenditures in these countries. A rise in rice prices would necessitate a general rise of wages and wholesale prices. The control of rice prices, however, helps to prevent an inflationary spiral that obviously would undermine the stability of the economy.

Taxes on small landowners may be reduced through an elimination of numerous types of levies on commodities and through a reduction of land taxes on small producers. Land taxes might be made progressive in relation to the size of the holding and the use capabilities of the land. Wider use could also be made of the income tax. The difficulty of equitably administering an income tax on farmers is well recognized, but there are opportunities for amelioration in this field through progressive income taxation, with minimum tax exemptions and personal allowances. At best, the income tax is not one of the easier taxes to administer, but, in this regard, in the rather well developed countries the difficulties should not be significantly different from those in the United States.

## Research and Training

Long-time improvements in rural institutions come with the intellectual growth and understanding of people. As has been pointed out, progress calls for changes in the land-ownership pattern, improved landlord-tenant relations, innovations in rural credit and marketing facilities, and other changes in agrarian structures. Bringing about these improvements by the democratic process is admittedly often slow and difficult. However, an enlightened public in a democracy can move fast when hasty action is needed. Two essential requirements for speedy action are (1) a framework within which to move and the will to take action, and (2) basic information for intelligent understanding and action.

Basic information is needed to understand fully the situation and conditions that hinder the opportunities of farmers and the extent to which agricultural maladjustments are due to defective institutional arrangements. It is necessary to know the impacts of farm problems on farm people. It also is important to have an understanding of various alternative courses of action—needed legislation, facilities, measures, etc., that should be considered in the solving or alleviation of problems. There is no substitute for objective penetrating investigations that go to the very roots of difficulties and then come forward with a proposed course of action.

The nature of the problem, the degree to which the problem is known, factual data available, and the urgency for action in a given situation should determine the intensity of study. Valuable information and understanding will come from the investigation of specific problems—from the grass roots to the top—and the application of measures to the solution or alleviation of these problem situations.

The information assembled and understanding acquired through studies are basic to the adoption of effective land programs. Along with the development of new programs must go educational programs that bring to farmers improved techniques of production and the understanding necessary to make programs effective and that plant ideas for the development of additional programs. Planning in underdeveloped countries is a very substantial undertaking. It requires an inventory of existing resources, fundamental changes in the social and economic structure of a country, a large effort of mass education, and intelligent use of resources. At the farm and community level, a program of agricultural education and training should also be vigorously pushed. In the process of research and training, farm people and educational leaders must move forward together.

It is well known that a number of agencies of the Federal government are helping foreign governments help themselves through technical-assistance programs and economic aids. International agencies are likewise playing an effective part. In the field of agriculture, emphasis has been on assistance to increase food production through replacement of obsolete and inadequate farm machinery with steel plows, cultivators, and tractors; the introduction of better seeds, such as hybrid corn, and improved varieties; and through technical-training programs in the technological aspects of farm production.[15]

Some assistance has been extended in bringing about improvements in rural institutions or land-reform activities. However, cooperative assist-

---

[15] For example, the end of the war found Western Europe's agricultural plant badly shattered. Land was impoverished. By 1952, total output climbed to 12 per cent above prewar. This represented a net gain of more than 30 per cent since the beginning of the Marshall Plan in April, 1948. It would be of interest also to note progress in other areas, as in India, where the United States has a technical-assistance program. Moreover, in India, the Ford Foundation has under way a substantial community educational program.

ance in this field has barely scratched the surface of present-day problems. The cooperative job that lies ahead is big, difficult, and tough, and will require courage, tact, and determined effort on the part of the free nations. The spread of communism is often just a cancerous growth nourished by a changing social order. Present-day land problems call for social changes and the development of economic institutions that make for the growth of democratic goals.

# Bibliography

CHAPTER 1

Carver, Thomas N.: *Essays in Social Justice*, Chap. 20, Harvard University Press, Cambridge, Mass., 1915.

Gray, Lewis C.: "The Field of Research in Land Economics," *American Economic Review*, Vol. 18, Supplement, 1928.

Hibbard, Benjamin H.: "Objectives in Our National Agricultural Policy," *Journal of Farm Economics*, Vol. 20, February, 1938.

Johnson, V. Webster: "Land Economics Research," *Land Economics*, Vol. 25, May, 1949.

———: "Twenty-five Years of Progress: Division of Land Economics," *Journal of Land and Public Utility Economics*, Vol. 21, February, 1945.

Ratcliff, Richard U.: *Urban Land Economics*, McGraw-Hill Book Company, Inc., New York, 1949.

Renne, Roland R.: *Land Economics*, Preface and Chap. 1, Harper & Brothers, New York, 1947.

Salter, Leonard A.: *A Critical Review of Research in Land Economics*, University of Minnesota Press, Minneapolis, Minn., 1948.

———: "The Content of Land Economics and Research Methods Adapted to Its Needs," *Journal of Farm Economics*, Vol. 24, February, 1942.

Turner, Frederick Jackson: *The Frontier in American History*, especially the first essay entitled "The Significance of the Frontier in American History," Henry Holt and Company, New York, 1920.


CHAPTER 2

Akagi, Hidemachi: *The Town Proprietors of the New England Colonies: A Study of Their Development, Organization, Activities and Controversies, 1620–1770*, Chaps. 1, 4, 6, and 7, University of Pennsylvania Press, Philadelphia, 1924.

Ashley, Sir William J.: *An Introduction to English Economic History and Theory*, Book I, Chap. 1, and Book II, Chap. 4, Longmans, Green and Company, London, 1892.

Bennett, H. S.: *Life on the English Manor: A Study of Peasant Conditions: 1150–1400*, The University Press, Cambridge, England, 1937.

Bond, Beverley W.: "The Quit Rent System in the American Colonies," *American Historical Review*, Vol. 17, April, 1912; also published with an introduction by Charles M. Andrews by the Yale University Press, New Haven, Conn., 1919.

Christman, Henry: *Tin Horns and Calico*, Henry Holt and Company, Inc., New York, 1945.

Cunow, Heinrich: "Land Tenure in Western Europe, British Empire, and the United States," *Encyclopedia of the Social Sciences,* Vol. 9, The Macmillan Company, New York, 1944.

Egleston, Melville: *The Land System of the New England Colonies,* Johns Hopkins University Studies in History and Political Science, Vol. 4, No. 11–12, N. Murray Company, 1886.

Ford, Amelia C.: *Colonial Precedents of Our National Land System As It Existed in 1800,* University of Wisconsin Bulletin 352, History Series, Vol. 2, No. 2, 1910.

Holdsworth, William S.: *An Historical Introduction to the Land Law,* Oxford University Press, New York, 1927.

Orwin, C. S.: *The Open Fields,* Oxford University Press, New York, 1938.

Osgood, Herbert L.: *The American Colonies in the Seventeenth Century,* Vol. I, Chap. 11, and Vol II, Chap. 2, The Macmillan Company, New York, 1904–1907.

Pollock, Frederick, and Frederic W. Maitland: *History of English Law,* Cambridge University Press, Cambridge, Mass., 1923.

Taylor, Henry C.: *The Decline of Landowning Farmers in England,* University of Wisconsin Bulletin 96, Chaps. 4 and 5, 1904.

## CHAPTER 3

Davidson, R. D.: *Federal and State Rural Lands, 1950,* U.S. Department of Agriculture Circular 909, 1952.

Edwards, Everett E.: "American Agriculture: The First 300 Years," *Farmers in a Changing World, Yearbook of Agriculture,* 1940, U.S. Department of Agriculture, 1940.

Gray, Lewis C.: *History of Agriculture in the Southern United States,* Vol. 2, Chap. 27, Carnegie Institution of Washington, Washington, 1933.

Hibbard, Benjamin H.: *A History of the Public Land Policies,* The Macmillan Company, New York, 1924.

McKitrick, Reuben: *The Public Land System of Texas, 1823–1910,* University of Wisconsin Bulletin 905, 1918.

Paxson, Frederic L.: *History of the American Frontier, 1763–1893,* Houghton Mifflin Company, Boston, 1924.

Peffer, E. Louise: *The Closing of the Public Domain,* Stanford University Press, Stanford, Calif., 1951.

Powell, John Wesley: *Report on the Lands of the Arid Regions of the United States,* Government Printing Office, Washington, 1879.

Robbins, Roy M.: *Our Landed Heritage,* Princeton University Press, Princeton, N.J., 1942.

Treat, Payson Jackson: *The National Land System, 1785–1820,* E. B. Treat and Company, Boston, 1910.

## CHAPTER 4

Brink, Wellington, *Big Hugh,* The Macmillan Company, New York, 1950.

Clawson, Marion: *Uncle Sam's Acres,* Dodd, Mead & Company, Inc., New York, 1951.

*The Future of the Great Plains,* Report of the President's Great Plains Committee, Washington, 1936.

Gray, Lewis C.: "Federal Purchase and Administration of Submarginal Land in the Great Plains," *Journal of Farm Economics,* Vol. 21, February, 1939.

―――: "The Social and Economic Implications of the National Land Program," *Journal of Farm Economics,* Vol. 18, May, 1936.

―――: *Land Planning,* Public Policy Pamphlet 19, University of Chicago Press, Chicago, 1936. (Reproduced in slightly modified form in *Planned Society, Yesterday, Today and Tomorrow,* Findlay Mackenzie (ed.), Prentice-Hall, Inc., New York, 1939.

Jesness, O. B. (ed.): *Readings on Agricultural Policy,* Part IV, The Blakiston Company, Philadelphia, 1949.

National Land-Use Planning Committee: *The Problems of Submarginal Areas and Desirable Adjustments with Particular Reference to Public Acquisition of Land,* U.S. Department of Agriculture Miscellaneous Publication 6, April, 1933.

Pinchot, Gifford: "How Conservation Began in the United States," *Agricultural History,* Vol. 11, October, 1937.

Robbins, Roy M.: *Our Landed Heritage,* Part IV, Princeton University Press, Princeton, N.J., 1942.

Salter, Leonard A.: *A Critical Review of Research in Land Economics,* University of Minnesota Press, Minneapolis, Minn., 1948.

Sparhawk, William N.: "The History of Forestry in America," *Trees,* Yearbook of Agriculture, 1949, U.S. Department of Agriculture, 1949.

*Supplementary Report of the Land Planning Committee,* National Resources Board, Washington, 1935.

Timmons, John F., and W. G. Murray (ed.): *Land Problems and Policies,* Iowa State College Press, Ames, Iowa, 1950.

Tolley, Howard R.: "Some Essentials of a Good Agricultural Policy," *Farmers in a Changing World, Yearbook of Agriculture,* 1940, U.S. Department of Agriculture, 1940.

Van Hise, C. H., and L. C. Havemeyer: *Conservation of Our National Resources,* The Macmillan Company, New York, 1930.


CHAPTER 5

Barnes, Carleton P.: *Land Classification: Objectives and Requirements,* Resettlement Administration, Land Use Planning Publication 1, Washington, 1936 (processed).

―――: *The Value of Economic Studies in Determining the Use Capabilities of Land Classes,* Proceedings, Soil Science Society of America, Vol. 1, 1936.

Black, John D.: *Research in Agricultural Land Utilization: Scope and Method,* Social Science Research Council Bulletin 2, June, 1931.

―――: *An Introduction to Production Economics,* Chaps. 11 and 12, Henry Holt and Company, Inc., New York, 1926.

Conklin, Howard, and Sherwood O. Berg: *A Preliminary Report on Developments in Land Classification Methods,* Cornell University Agricultural Experiment Station, Agricultural Economics Report 688, December, 1948.

Ely, Richard T., and George S. Wehrwein: *Land Economics,* Chap. 5, The Macmillan Company, New York, 1940.

Harrison, Robert W., and Paul L. Searfoss: *Classification of Agricultural Area, Frederick County, Maryland,* Maryland Agricultural Experiment Station Bulletin 440, April, 1941.

Hibbard, Benjamin H.: *Agricultural Economics,* Chaps. 9 and 10, McGraw-Hill Book Company, Inc., New York, 1949.

Hoover, Edgar M.: *The Location of Economic Activity,* Chap. 4, McGraw-Hill Book Company, Inc., New York, 1948.

Kellogg, Charles E., and J. Kenneth Albleiter: *A Method of Rural Land Classification,* U.S. Department of Agriculture Technical Bulletin 469, February, 1935.

*Land Classification in the United States,* Report of the Land Classification Sub-Committee of the Land Committee, National Resources Planning Board, Washington, March, 1941.

Peterson, George M.: *Diminishing Returns and Planned Economy,* The Ronald Press Company, New York, 1937.

*Proceedings of the First National Conference on the Classification of Land,* Missouri Agricultural Experiment Station Bulletin 421, December, 1940.

Renne, Roland R.: *Land Economics,* Chap. 5, Harper & Brothers, New York, 1947.

Spillman, W. J., and Emil Lang: *The Law of Diminishing Returns,* World Book Company, Yonkers, N.Y., 1924.

Taylor, Carl C., *et al.: Rural Life in the United States,* Parts III and IV, Alfred A. Knopf, Inc., New York, 1949.

Taylor, Henry C.: *Outlines of Agricultural Economics,* The Macmillan Company, New York, 1925.

Timmons, John F., and William G. Murray (ed.): *Land Problems and Policies,* Chap. 5, Iowa State College Press, Ames, Iowa, 1950.

## CHAPTER 6

Clark, John M.: *Economics of Planning Public Works,* Government Printing Office, Washington, 1935.

Federal Inter-Agency River Basin Committee: *Proposed Practices for Economic Analysis of River Basin Projects,* Prepared for the Sub-Committee on Benefits and Costs, Washington, May, 1950.

Frank, Bernard: "Some Aspects of the Evaluation of Watershed Flood Control Projects," *Journal of Land and Public Utility Economics,* Vol. 18, November, 1942.

*Missouri River Basin Agricultural Program,* 81st Cong., 1st Sess., H. Doc. 373, 1949.

Murray, William G.: *Farm Appraisal,* Iowa State College Press, Ames, Iowa, 1940.

Regan, M. M., and Fred A. Clarenbach: "Emergency Control in the Farm Real Estate Market," *Journal of Farm Economics,* Vol. 24, No. 4, November, 1942.

―――― and A. R. Johnson: *The Farm Real Estate Situation, 1945–46,* U.S. Department of Agriculture Circular 754, 1946.

―――― and E. C. Weitzell: "Economic Evaluation of Soil and Water Conservation Measures and Programs," *Journal of Farm Economics,* Vol. XXIX, November, 1947.

Rensmeier, J. S.: *The Tennessee Valley Authority,* Vanderbilt University Press, Nashville, Tenn., 1942.

Scofield, W. H., and R. D. Davidson: *The Farm Real Estate Situation, 1947–48 and 1948–49,* U.S. Department of Agriculture Circular 823, 1950.

Teele, R. P.: *The Economics of Land Reclamation in the United States,* Chap. 8, McGraw-Hill Book Company, Inc., New York, 1927.

White, Gilbert F.: "The Limit of Economic Justification for Flood Control," *Journal of Land and Public Utility Economics,* Vol. 12, May, 1936.


CHAPTER 7

Bennett, Hugh H.: *Elements of Soil Conservation,* McGraw-Hill Book Company, Inc., New York, 1947.

Bunce, Arthur C.: *The Economics of Soil Conservation,* Iowa State College Press, Ames, Iowa, 1942.

Ciriacy-Wantrup, S. V.: *Resource Conservation, Economics and Policies,* University of California Press, Berkeley, Calif., 1952.

Gray, Lewis C.: "Economic Possibilities of Conservation," *Quarterly Journal of Economics,* Vol. 27, May, 1913.

Hambidge, Gove: "Soils and Men: A Summary," *Yearbook of Agriculture,* 1938, U.S. Department of Agriculture, 1938.

Hammar, Conrad H.: "Society and Conservation," *Journal of Farm Economics,* Vol. 24, February, 1942.

————: "Economic Aspects of Conservation," *Journal of Land and Public Utility Economics,* Vol. 7, August, 1931.

Havemeyer, Loomis: *Conservation of Our National Resources,* based on Van Hise's *The Conservation of Natural Resources in the United States,* The Macmillan Company, New York, 1936.

Heady, Earl O., and O. J. Scoville: *Principles of Conservation Economics and Policy,* Iowa Agricultural Experiment Station Research Bulletin 382, 1951.

Hotelling, Harold: "The Economics of Exhaustible Resources," *The Journal of Political Economy,* Vol. 39, April, 1931.

Jacks, G. V., and R. O. Whyte: *Vanishing Lands: A World Survey of Soil Erosion,* Doubleday & Company, Inc., New York, 1939.

Lee, Alvin T. M., and John E. Mason: *Land Use and Soil Conservation in Haywood County, North Carolina,* North Carolina State College Agricultural Economics Information Series 17, 1948.

Parkins, A. E., and J. R. Whitaker: *Our National Resources and Their Conservation,* Chaps. 4, 6, 8, and 13, John Wiley & Sons, Inc., New York, 1936.

*Proceedings of the Inter-American Conference on Conservation of Renewable Natural Resources,* Denver, Colorado, Sept. 7 to 20, 1948, U.S. Department of State, 1949.

*Proceedings of the United Nations Scientific Conference on the Conservation and Utilization of Resources,* Aug. 17 to Sept. 6, 1949, Vols. I, IV, V, and VI, Lake Success, New York.

Sears, Paul B.: *Deserts on the March,* University of Oklahoma Press, Norman, Okla., 1935.

Timmons, John F.: "Institutional Obstacles to Land Improvements," *Journal of Land and Public Utility Economics,* Vol. 22, May, 1946.

CHAPTER 8

Baker, O. E.: *Population Prospect in Relation to the World's Agricultural Resources,* University of Maryland, College Park, Md., 1947.

Barlowe, Raleigh: "Population Pressure and Food Production Potentialities," *Land Economics,* Vol. 25, August, 1949.

Castro, Josue de: *Geography of Hunger,* Little, Brown & Company, Boston, 1952.

Davis, Joseph S.: "Our Changed Population Outlook," *American Economic Review,* Vol. 42, June, 1952.

————: "Our Amazing Population Upsurge," *Journal of Farm Economics,* Part 2, Vol. 31, November, 1949; *The Population Upsurge in the United States,* Stanford University Land Research Institute, Stanford, Calif., 1949.

Davis, Kingsley: *The Population of India and Pakistan,* Princeton University Press, Princeton, N. J., 1951.

*Demographic Yearbooks of the United Nations,* 1949–1950, 1951.

East, Edward M.: *Mankind at the Crossroads,* Charles Scribner's Sons, New York, 1923.

*Illustrative Projections of the Population of the United States, 1950–1960,* U.S. Bureau of the Census, Series P-25, No. 43, 1950.

Murkerjee, Radhakamal: *Races, Lands and Food,* The Dryden Press, Inc., New York, 1946.

Notestein, Frank W.: "Population: The Long View," *Food for the World,* University of Chicago Press, Chicago, 1945.

Osborn, Fairfield: "Crowded Off the Earth," *Atlantic Monthly, March,* 1948; "The Country That Can Feed the World," *Atlantic Monthly,* April, 1948.

Ross, Edward A.: *Standing Room Only,* Appleton-Century-Crofts, Inc., New York, 1928.

Taeuber, Conrad and Irene: "World Population Trends," *Journal of Farm Economics,* Part 2, Vol. 31, February, 1949.

Timmons, John F., and William G. Murray (eds.): *Land Problems and Policies,* Chap. 3, Iowa State College Press, Ames, Iowa, 1950.

Whelpton, P. K.: *Forecasts of the Population of the United States, 1945–75,* U.S. Bureau of the Census, 1947.


CHAPTER 9

*Agricultural Programs of the United States, Current and Prospective,* U.S. Department of Agriculture, November, 1952.

Allin, Bushrod W., *et al.: What Peace Can Mean to the American Farmer— Postwar Agriculture and Employment,* U.S. Department of Agriculture Miscellaneous Publication 562, 1945.

Alsberg, Carl: "The Food Supply in the Migration Process," in Limits of Land Settlement, Council on Foreign Relations, Inc., New York, 1937.

Black, John D., and Maxine E. Kiefer: *Future Food and Agriculture Policy,* McGraw-Hill Book Company, Inc., New York, 1948.

Cavin, J. P., Marguerite C. Burk, *et al.: Consumption of Food in the United States, 1909–48,* U.S. Department of Agriculture Miscellaneous Publication 691, 1949.

Christensen, Raymond P.: *Efficient Use of Food Resources in the United States,* U.S. Department of Agriculture Research Bulletin 963, October, 1948.

*Forests and National Prosperity,* U.S. Forest Service Publication 668, 1948.

Gray, L. C., O. E. Baker, *et. al.:* "The Use of Our Land for Crops, Pasture and Forest," *Yearbook of Agriculture,* 1923, U.S. Department of Agriculture, 1923.

Johnson, Sherman E.: *Changes in American Farming,* U.S. Department of Agriculture Miscellaneous Publication 707, 1949.

Kellogg, Charles E.: "Food Production Potentialities and Problems," *Journal of Farm Economics,* Part 2, Vol. 31, February, 1949.

*Long Range Agricultural Policy,* A Study of Selected Trends and Factors Relating to the Long Range Prospect for American Agriculture for the Committee on Agriculture, 80th Cong., 2d Sess., 1948.

Osborn, Fairfield: *Our Plundered Planet,* Little, Brown & Company, Boston, 1948.

Pearson, Frank A., and Floyd A. Harper: *The World's Hunger,* Cornell University Press, Ithaca, N.Y., 1945.

Renner, George T., *et al.: Global Geography,* Part 1, The Thomas Y. Crowell Company, New York, 1945.

Reuss, L. A., H. H. Wooten, and F. J. Marschner: *Inventory of Major Land Uses, United States,* U.S. Department of Agriculture Miscellaneous Publication 663, 1945.

*Resources for Freedom,* Government Printing Office, Washington, July, 1952.

Salter, Robert M.: "World Soil and Fertilizer Resources in Relation to Food Needs," *Science Magazine,* Vol. 105, No. 2734, May 23, 1947.

Smith, J. Russell: *Industrial and Commercial Geography,* Part I, Henry Holt and Company, Inc., New York, 1939.

Timmons, J. F., and W. G. Murray (eds.): *Land Problems and Policies,* Chap. 4, Iowa State College Press, Ames, Iowa, 1950.

Vogt, William: *Road to Survival,* William Sloane Associates, New York, 1948.

## CHAPTER 10

Binns, Sir Bernard O.: *Land Settlement for Agriculture,* Food and Agriculture Organization of the United Nations, Rome, 1951.

Black, John D., and Lewis C. Gray: *Land Settlement and Colonization in the Great Lakes States,* U.S. Department of Agriculture Bulletin 1295, 1925.

———— and W. A. Hartman: *Economic Aspects of Land Settlement in the Cutover Region of the Great Lakes States,* U.S. Department of Agriculture Circular 160, 1931.

*Farm Opportunities in the United States* prepared by a land settlement work group, U.S. Department of Agriculture, July, 1945.

Goodrich, Carter, *et al.: Migration and Economic Opportunity,* Chaps. 6 and 8, University of Pennsylvania Press, Philadelphia, 1936.

Harrison, Robert W.: "Research in Land Development in the Alluvial Valley of the Lower Mississippi River," *Journal of Farm Economics,* Vol. 34, February, 1952.

———— and George F. Jenks: *Methods and Cost of Clearing Land in Northeast Arkansas,* Arkansas Agricultural Experiment Station Bulletin 495, 1950.

Hartman, W. A.: *State Land-Settlement Problems and Policies in the United States,* U.S. Department of Agriculture Bulletin 357, 1933.

Jones, Phillip E., John E. Mason, and Joseph T. Elvove: *New Settlement Problems in the Northeastern Louisiana Delta,* Louisiana Agricultural Experiment Station Bulletin 335, 1942.

Lee, Alvin T. M.: *Land Utilization in New Jersey: A Land Development Scheme in the New Jersey Pine Area,* New Jersey Agricultural Experiment Station Bulletin 665, 1939.

*Migration and Settlement on the Pacific Coast,* Idaho Agricultural Experiment Station Report 5, 1941.

*National Irrigation Policy: Its Development and Significance,* 76th Cong., 1st Sess., S. Doc. 36, 1939.

Purcell, Margaret R., and H. H. Wooten: *Farm Land Development: Present and Future,* U.S. Department of Agriculture Circular 825, 1949.

Wooten, Hugh H.: "Farming Opportunities for Veterans," *Journal of Land and Public Utility Economics,* Vol. 21, August, 1945.

## CHAPTER 11

Ackerman, Joseph, and Marshall Harris (eds.): *Family Farm Policy,* University of Chicago Press, Chicago, 1947.

Bachman, Kenneth L., and Ronald W. Jones: *Sizes of Farms in the United States,* U.S. Department of Agriculture Technical Bulletin 1010, 1950.

Barlowe, Raleigh, and John F. Timmons: "What Has Happened to the Agricultural Ladder?" *Journal of Farm Economics,* Vol. 32, February, 1950.

Clapp, E. H., *et. al.:* "The Remedies: Policies for Public Lands and Policies for Private Lands," *Soils and Men, Yearbook of Agriculture,* 1938, U.S. Department of Agriculture.

Ely, Richard T., and G. S. Wehrwein: *Land Economics,* The Macmillan Company, New York, 1940.

*Farm Tenancy,* President's Special Committee on Farm Tenancy, Washington, February, 1937.

*Farm Tenure Improvement in the United States,* U.S. Department of Agriculture, 1945.

Gibson, W. L., Jr., and F. D. Hansing: "Father-Son Farm Agreements in Virginia," *Agricultural Economics Research,* Vol. 1, July, 1949.

*Graphic Summary of Farm Tenure in the United States,* U.S. Department of Agriculture and Commerce, 1953.

Gray, Lewis C., *et al.:* "The Causes: Traditional Attitudes and Institutions," *Soils and Men, Yearbook of Agriculture,* 1938, U.S. Department of Agriculture.

Griswold, A. Whitney: *Farming and Democracy,* Harcourt, Brace and Company, Inc., New York, 1948.

Harris, Marshall: "A New Agricultural Ladder," *Land Economics,* Vol. 24, August, 1950.

———: "Legal Aspects of Land Tenure," *Journal of Farm Economics,* Vol. 23, February, 1941.

——— and Elton B. Hill: *Family Farm-transfer Arrangements,* Illinois Agricultural Extension Service Circular 680, 1951.

Hoffsommer, Harold, *et al.:* *The Social and Economic Significance of Land Tenure in the Southwestern States,* University of North Carolina Press, Chapel Hill, N.C., 1950.

*Improving Farm Tenure in the Midwest,* Illinois Agricultural Experiment Station Bulletin 502, 1944.

Kelso, M. M.: "Needed Research in Farm Tenancy," *Journal of Farm Economics,* Vol. 23, February, 1941.

Maddox, J. G.: "Land Tenure Research in a National Land Policy," *Journal of Farm Economics,* Vol. 19, February, 1937.

Maris, Paul V.: *The Land Is Mine: From Tenancy to Family Farm Ownership,* U.S. Department of Agriculture, 1950.

Parsons, K. H., and Eliot O. Waples: *Keeping the Farm in the Family,* Wisconsin Agricultural Experiment Station Bulletin 157, 1945.

Renne, Roland R.: *Land Economics,* Harper & Brothers, New York, 1947.

Salter, Leonard A.: *A Critical Review of Research in Land Economics,* University of Minnesota Press, Minneapolis, Minn., 1948.

———: *Land Tenure in Process,* Wisconsin Agricultural Experiment Station Bulletin 146, 1943.

Schickele, Rainer: "Theories Concerning Land Tenure," *Journal of Farm Economics,* Vol. 34, December, 1952.

———: "Effects of Tenure Systems on Agricultural Efficiency," *Journal of Farm Economics,* Vol. 23, February, 1941.

Taylor, C. C., *et. al.: Trends in Tenure Status of Farm Workers in the United States since 1880,* U.S. Department of Agriculture Bulletin, July, 1948.

Tharp, Max M.: *Farm Land Ownership in the Southeast,* South Carolina Agricultural Experiment Station Bulletin 378, 1949.

———: "A Reappraisal of Farm Tenure Research," *Land Economics,* Vol. 24, November, 1948.

Timmons, John F.: "Farm Ownership in the United States: An Appraisal of the Present Situation and Emerging Problems," *Journal of Farm Economics,* Vol. 30, February, 1948.

——— and Raleigh Barlowe: *Farm Ownership in the Midwest,* North Central Regional Publication 4, Iowa Agricultural Experiment Station Research Bulletin 361, 1949.

Wehrwein, George S.: "Place of Tenancy in a System of Land Tenure," *Journal of Land and Public Utility Economics,* Vol. 1, January, 1925.


CHAPTERS 12 AND 13

Barlowe, Raleigh: *Administration of Tax-reverted Lands in the Lake States,* Michigan Agricultural Experiment Station Technical Bulletin 225, 1951.

Clawson, Marion: *The Western Range Livestock Industry,* McGraw-Hill Book Company, Inc., New York, 1950.

———: "Determination of Sales and Lease Values of Private and Public Range Lands," *Journal of Farm Economics,* Vol. 20, August, 1938.

Ely, Richard T., and George S. Wehrwein: *Land Economics,* Chap. 11, The Macmillan Company, New York, 1940.

Frank, Bernard: "Some Aspects of the Evaluation of Watershed Flood Control Projects," *Journal of Land and Public Utility Economics,* Vol. 18, November, 1942.

——— and Clifford A. Betts: *Water and Our Forests,* U.S. Department of Agriculture Miscellaneous Publication 600, 1946.

Glick, Philip M.: "The Soil and the Law," *Journal of Farm Economics,* Vol. 20, Nos. 2 and 3, May and August, 1938.

Greenshields, Elco L., and Stanley W. Voelker: *Integration of Irrigated and Dry-Land Farming in the North Platte Valley in 1946,* U.S. Department of Agriculture, 1947 (processed).

Harding, S. T.: *Water Rights for Irrigation,* Stanford University Press, Stanford, Calif., 1936.

Hendrickson, C. I.: *Rural Zoning,* U.S. Department of Agriculture, 1935.

Hutchins, Wells A.: *Problems in the Law of Water Rights in the West,* U.S. Department of Agriculture Miscellaneous Publication 418, 1942.

*Irrigation Agriculture in the West,* U.S. Department of Agriculture Miscellaneous Publication 670, 1948.

Loomer, C. W., and Glenn H. Craig: *Collective Tenure on Grazing Land in Montana,* Montana Experiment Station Bulletin 406, 1943.

―――― and V. W. Johnson: *Group Tenure in the Administration of Public Lands,* U.S. Department of Agriculture Circular 829, December, 1949.

Mead, Elwood: *Irrigation Institutions,* Chaps. 4, 13, and 14, The Macmillan Company, New York, 1903.

*Proceedings of the United Nations Scientific Conference on the Conservation and Utilization of Resources,* August 17 to Sept. 6, 1949, Lake Success, New York.

Report of the President's Great Plains Committee, *The Future of the Great Plains,* Washington, 1936.

Rowlands, Walter, Fred Trenk, and Raymond Penn: *Rural Zoning in Wisconsin,* Wisconsin Agricultural Experiment Station Bulletin 479, November, 1948.

Solberg, Erling: *Rural Zoning in the United States,* U.S. Department of Agriculture Agriculture Information Bulletin 59, January, 1952.

*State Legislation for Better Land Use,* A Special Report by an Interbureau Committee of the U.S. Department of Agriculture, 1941.

Teele, R. P.: *The Economics of Land Reclamation in the United States,* McGraw-Hill Book Company, Inc., New York, 1927.

Walker, Herman, Jr.: *Problems and Suggestions in the Drafting of Rural Zoning Enabling Legislation,* Resettlement Administration, Land Use Planning Publication 10, Washington, 1936.

―――― : *Some Considerations in Support of the Constitutionality of Rural Zoning as a Police Power Measure,* Resettlement Administration, Land-Use Planning Publication 11, Washington, 1936.

Webb, Walter Prescott: *The Great Plains,* Ginn & Company, Boston, 1931.

Wertheimer, Ralph B.: *Flood-Plain Zoning,* California State Planning Board, 1942.

―――― : "Constitutionality of Rural Zoning," *California Law Review,* Vol. 26, No. 2, 1938.

*The Western Range,* 74th Cong., 2d Sess., S. Doc. 199, 1936.

*Zoning and Civic Development,* U.S. Chamber of Commerce, 1950.

CHAPTER 14

Banfield, Edward C.: "Organization for Policy Planning in the U.S. Department of Agriculture," *Journal of Farm Economics,* Vol. 34, February, 1952.

Clark, John M.: *Economics of Planning Public Works,* Government Printing Office, Washington, 1935.

Clark, W. C.: "Proposed Valley Authority Legislation," *American Political Science Review,* Vol. 40, February, 1946.

*Columbia River Basin,* U.S. Department of the Interior, 1946 (processed).

Galbraith, J. K.: *The Economic Effects of the Federal Public Works Expenditures, 1933–38,* National Resources Planning Board, Washington, 1940.

Hansen, Alvin H., and Harvey Perloff: *State and Local Finance in the National Economy,* W. W. Norton & Company, New York, 1944.

Hart, H. C.: "Valley Development and Valley Administration in the Missouri Basin," *Public Administration Review,* Vol. 8, Winter, 1948.

Johnson, V. Webster: "Planning the Use of Land Resources," Chap. 14 in *Land Problems and Policies* by J. F. Timmons and W. B. Murray (eds.), Iowa State College Press, Ames, Iowa, 1950.

———, John F. Timmons, and E. J. Howenstine: "Rural Public Works," *Journal of Land and Public Utility Economics,* Vol. 23, February and May, 1947.

Mackenzie, Findlay (ed.): *Planned Society, Yesterday, Today, and Tomorrow,* chapter on "Land Planning" by Lewis C. Gray, Prentice-Hall, Inc., New York, 1937.

Miller, L. A.: "Battle That Squanders Billions," *Saturday Evening Post,* May 14, 1949.

Millett, John D.: *The Process and Organization of Government Planning,* Columbia University Press, New York, 1947.

*Missouri River Basin Agricultural Program,* 81st Cong., 1st Sess., H. Doc. 373, 1949.

*Public Works and Rural Land Use,* National Resources Planning Board, Washington, 1942.

*Regional Factors in National Planning and Development,* U.S. National Resources Committee, 1935.

Renne, R. R.: *Land Economics,* Chaps. 18 and 19, Harper & Brothers, New York, 1947.

*Report of Missouri Basin Survey Commission,* Government Printing Office, Washington, March, 1953.

Tolley, Howard R.: *The Farmer Citizen at War,* The Macmillan Company, New York, 1943.

Wooten, Hugh H.: "The Agricultural Flood Control Program," *Journal of Land and Public Utility Economics,* Vol. 22, No. 1, February, 1946.

CHAPTER 15

Ackerman, Joseph, and Marshall Harris (eds.): *Family Farm Policy,* University of Chicago Press, Chicago, 1947.

Binns, Bernard O.: *The Consolidation of Fragmented Agricultural Holdings,* Food and Agriculture Organization Agricultural Studies 11, Washington, 1950.

*Conference on World Land Tenure Problems,* Proceedings, University of Wisconsin, Madison, Wis., 1951.

Hayes, Carleton J. H.: *A Political and Cultural History of Modern Europe,* Chap. 21, The Macmillan Company, New York, 1933.

Hewes, Laurence I.: *Japanese Land Reform Program,* Natural Resources Section, Supreme Commander for the Allied Powers, Report No. 127, Tokyo, 1950.

*Land Reform: A World Challenge,* U.S. Department of State Publication 4445, Economic Cooperation Series 29, 1952.

*Land Reform—Defects in Agrarian Structures as Obstacles to Economic Development,* United Nations, New York, 1951.

*Land Reform in Italy,* Ministry of Agriculture and Forestry, Rome, 1953.

*Measures for the Economic Development of Under-Developed Countries,* Report by a Group of Experts of the United Nations, New York, 1951.

Mitchell, C. Clyde: *Land Reform in Asia; A Case Study,* National Planning Association Pamphlet 78, Washington, 1952.

*Proceedings of International Conference on Agricultural and Cooperative Credit,* Aug. 4 to Oct. 2, 1952, Vols. 1 and 2, University of California, Berkeley, Calif.

*World Land Reform,* A Selective Bibliography, U.S. Department of Agriculture Library List 55, 1951.

# Index